# A SYSTEM

OF

# CHRISTIAN DOCTRINE.

BY

## DR. I. A. DORNER,

OBERCONSISTORIALRATH AND PROFESSOR OF THEOLOGY, BERLIN.

TRANSLATED BY

REV. ALFRED CAVE, B.A.,
PRINCIPAL AND PROFESSOR OF THEOLOGY, HACKNEY COLLEGE, LONDON;

AND

REV. J. S. BANKS,
PROFESSOR OF THEOLOGY, WESLEYAN COLLEGE, LEEDS.

VOL. III.

## NOTE.

This volume has been translated by Principal Cave, with the exception of pp. 374–429, which is the work of Professor Banks. The Proofs of this, as of the other three volumes, have been revised by both Translators.

Wipf and Stock Publishers
199 W 8th Ave, Suite 3
Eugene, OR 97401

A System of Christian Doctrine, 4 Volumes
By Dorner, J. A.
ISBN: 978-1-4982-9443-0
Publication date 5/24/2005
Previously published by T. & T. Clark, 1885

Four volume set ISBN: 978-1-59752-216-8

# CONTENTS.

## PART II.

### SPECIFIC CHRISTIAN DOCTRINE—*Continued.*

FIRST PART: THE DOCTRINE OF SIN—*Continued.*

*Second Head: Of the Origin of Empirical Evil.*

| SECT. | | PAGE |
|---|---|---|
| 79. | Biblical and Ecclesiastical Doctrine, | 9 |
| 80. | Theories on the Origin of Evil, | 18 |
| 81. | The Origin of Evil generally, | 39 |
| 82. | Explanation of the Empirical Universality of Sin, | 42 |
| 83. | Union of the Claims of the Generic and Personal Life, | 54 |
| 84. | Transition to the Third Head: The State of Sin in the World in its Harmony with the Christian Idea of God and with the Divine Government, | 78 |

*Appendix: The Doctrine of the Devil.*

| 85. | Biblical and Ecclesiastical Doctrine, | 85 |
|---|---|---|
| 86. | Dogmatic Investigation, | 97 |

*Third Head: Evil in relation to the Divine Government.*

*First Point: The Doctrine of Death.*

| 87. | Biblical Doctrine, | 114 |
|---|---|---|
| 87b. | Ecclesiastical Doctrine, | 119 |
| 88. | Dogmatic Investigation, | 120 |

*Second Point.*

| 89. | Transition from Ponerology to Christology, | 133 |

# SECOND PART.

## THE CHRISTIAN SALVATION.

### FIRST MAIN DIVISION.

#### THE DOCTRINE OF CHRIST.

*Biblical Doctrine of Christ in general.*

| SECT. | | PAGE |
|---|---|---|
| 90. Old Testament Doctrine, | . . . . . | 145 |
| 91. New Testament Doctrine, | . . . . . | 155 |

*Ecclesiastical Formation of Christology.*

| | | |
|---|---|---|
| 92. First Period, to A.D. 381, | . . . . . | 199 |
| 93–97. Second Period, A.D. 381–1800, | . . . . | 210 |
| 93. I. To the Reformation, | . . . . . | 210 |
| 94–96. II. Time of the Reformation—Lutheran Christology (Luther, Melanchthon, Brenz, Chemnitz, *Formula Concordiæ*), and the Reformed Christology till about A.D. 1700, | . . . | 223 |
| 94. Time of the Reformation, | . . . . . | 223 |
| 95. Time of the Reformation—*continuation*, | . . . | 233 |
| 96. The Reformed Christology, | . . . . . | 238 |
| 97. III. From A.D. 1700–1800, | . . . . . | 243 |
| 98. Third Period, from A.D. 1800 to the Present, | . . . | 252 |

*Dogmatic Exposition.*

| | | |
|---|---|---|
| 99. Survey, | . . . . . . . | 279 |

#### FIRST SUBDIVISION.

| | | |
|---|---|---|
| 100. Christ's Pre-existence, | . . . . . | 283 |

#### SECOND SUBDIVISION.

##### CHRIST'S TEMPORAL PRESENCE ON EARTH.

| | | |
|---|---|---|
| 101. Relation of the Ideas of Conservation and Creation to that of Incarnation, | . . . . . . | 300 |
| 102. The Unity of the God-human Personality, | . . . | 308 |
| 103. The Uniqueness of the God-man, | . . . . | 319 |
| 104. Growth as the Essential Form of the Realization of the God-man, | . | 328 |

## CONTENTS.

### First Head: *Christ's Natural God-Humanity.*

| SECT. | | PAGE |
|---|---|---|
| 105. | The Act of Incarnation; the Birth of a Virgin, | 340 |
| 106. | The Essential Godmanhood, | 349 |

### Second Head: *Christ's Ethical God-Humanity.*

| 107. | Christ's Ethical Godmanhood, | 359 |
|---|---|---|
| 108. | Transition to the Official Godmanhood, | 374 |

### Third Head: *The Official God-Humanity of Christ on Earth.*

| 109. | Justification of the Doctrine of the Threefold Office, | 381 |
|---|---|---|
| 110. | First Point: The Kingly Office, | 392 |
| 111. | Second Point: The Prophetic Office, | 397 |

#### THIRD POINT: THE HIGH-PRIESTLY OFFICE.

##### A.—*Biblical Doctrine.*

| 112. | Old Testament Conception, | 401 |
|---|---|---|
| 113. | New Testament Teaching, | 411 |

# PART II.—(*Continued.*)

## THE SPECIFIC DOCTRINE.—(*Continued.*)
## THE DOCTRINE OF EVIL.—(*Continued.*)

### SECOND HEAD.

#### ON THE ORIGIN OF EMPIRICAL EVIL.

§ 79.

IT is the teaching of the Bible as well as the dominant teaching of the Church, that neither in a positive nor a negative sense is God the cause of the realization of evil, but the creature. Thus, primary evil was not an evil state, but an evil act which became inherent and also affected the cohesion of the race in good things. The historical commencement of sin in our race is found both by the Scriptures and the Church in our first parents, without excluding thereby the succeeding generations from the guilt of sin and its common production.

LITERATURE.—On the DOCTRINES OF THE ANCIENTS: Märker, *Das Princip des Bösen nach den Begriffen der Griechen*, 1842. Ackermann, *Ueber das Christliche in der Platon. Philos.* 1835. Nägelsbach, *Die homerische Theologie; Religionsglaube der Griechen*. Zeller, *Die Philosophie der Griechen*, vols. ii. and iii.

(especially *Plato, Stoa, Epikur*). Baur, *Das manichäische Religionssystem*, 1831; *Das Christliche des Platonismus oder Sokrates und Christus*, 1837. PHILOSOPHERS: Spinoza, *Ethik*. Leibnitz, *Theodicée*. King, *De origine mali*. Kant, *Religion innerhalb der Grenzen der blossen Vernunft; Kritik der praktischen Vernunft*. Fichte, *Sittenlehre*, 1798 and 1812. Schelling, *Philosophie und Religion; Freiheitslehre*, 1808; *Philosophie der Offenbarung*, 2 vols. Voight, *Ueber Freiheit und Nothwendigkeit*, 1828. Bockshammer, *Die Freiheit des menschlichen Willens*, 1821. Daub, *Judas Ischarioth oder das Böse im Verhältniss zum Guten*, 1816-1818, 2 vols. Herbart, *Gespräch über das Böse*, 1817. Schleiermacher, *Abhandlung über die Erwählung*, 1819, and see his *Glaubenslehre*. The following are related to Schleiermacher: Heinr. Ritter, *Ueber das Böse* in Pelts *Mitarbeiten*, 1839, pp. 41–117, and *Ueber das Böse und seine Folgen*, 1869; also Peter Romang, *Willensfreiheit und Determinismus*, 1836. Parow, *Aphorismen*, 1839, pp. 111, etc. (he gives a criticism of the hypotheses upon the origin of evil). Steffens, *Christlichc Religions-philosophie*, 1839, vol. ii. pp. 1–100. Sigwart, *Das Problem von der Freiheit und Unfreiheit des menschlichen Willens*, in the *Tübingen Zeitschrift*, 1839. Hegel, *Phänomenologie* and *Rechts-philosophie*. Vatke, *Die menschliche Freiheit in ihrem Verhältniss zur Sünde und zur göttlichen Gnade*, 1841. Marheinecke, *Dogmatik*, 1847, pp. 196–240 (who treats of the Doctrine of Evil as the third part of the Doctrine of Creation). A mean position between Schleiermacher and Hegel is taken by Ulrich Wirth, *System der speculativen Ethik*, vol. i. 1841, pp. 41–50, 117–155. In the more ANCIENT THEOLOGICAL LITERATURE, consult: Augustine, *Contra Faustum Manichæum*, book iv.; *Enchiridion ad Laurentium*, cap. xi. de libero arbitrio; *De Diversis Quæstionibus* (and compare thereupon Wiggers, *Geschichte des Augustinismus und Pelagianismus;* Jacobi, *Ueber Pelagius;* Wörter, *Pelagianismus, ut supra;* Bindemann and Dorner, *ut supra*, upon Augustine). Laurentius Valla. Thomas Aquinas, *Summa Theologiæ*. Duns Scotus, *Reportata, Opus Oxoniense*, bk. ii. Erasmus, *De libero arbitrio*. Luther, *De servo arbitrio*, 1525. Melanchthon, *Loci*, 1521. Calvin, *Institutio Religionis Christianæ*, bks. i. ii. iii., and see his *Tractate on Predestination*. Jonathan Edwards, *The Freedom of the Will and Original Sin*. Of the more RECENT THEOLOGY the following works deserve special mention: Sartorius, *Die lutherische Lehre vom Unvermögen des freien Willens zur höheren Sittlichkeit*, 1821, and his *Lehre von der heiligen Liebe*, vol. i. 1841. Tholuck, *Von der Sünde und dem Versöhner*, edit. 8, 1862. Chr. Fr. Schmid, *De peccato partic.* i.–iii.; *Christliche Sittenlehre*, edited by

Heller, 1861. Martensen, *Die christl. Dogmatik,* § 93. Krabbe, *Die Lehre von der Sünde und vom Tod,* etc., 1836. Against his views, Mau, *Vom Tod und dessen Aufhebung durch Christi Auferstehung, Pelts Mitarbeiten,* 1839. Against the views of both, Reich, *Die Auferstehung des Herrn als Heilsthatsache,* 1845. Kern, *Ueber die Sünde,* Tüb. Ztschrift, 1832. Stirm, *Anthropologische Untersuchungen,* Tüb. Ztschrift, 1835. Ernesti, *Die Theorie vom Ursprung der Sünde aus der Sinnlichkeit im Licht des Paulinischen Lehrgehalts,* 2 vols. 1855, etc. Julius Müller, *Lehre von der Sünde,* 2 vols. 1838, edit. 3. 1849, edit. 4. 1858 (criticized by Vatke, *Hallische Jahrb.* 1840, and by Heinrich Ritter in *Pelts Mitarbeiten;* and the 2d edition by me in *Reuters Repertorium,* 1845). Rothe, *Theologische Ethik,* vol. i. §§ 28, 31, 44, 98, 121–123, vol. ii. pp. 170–251 (he gives a criticism of Julius Müller's work, whilst Müller in his 3d edit. gives a criticism of Rothe's). Philippi, *Kirchliche Glaubenslehre,* vol. iii. 1859. Thomasius, *Dogmatik,* vol. i. 1853, 2d edit. 1856 (who likewise criticizes Julius Müller). Chr. E. Luthardt, *Die Lehre vom freien Willen,* etc., 1863. Frank, *System d. christl. Wahrheit,* vol. i. 1878, p. 400.

*Observation.*—Having investigated in the First Head[1] the *idea* or the *nature* of evil, and that according to its main forms, we now more definitely pass to the sphere of reality, where we find evil to be a fact in our race, universally distributed, which calls for explanation. This universality of actual sin is the immediate presupposition of Christianity as the religion of the redemption of humanity, and verifies its claim to be necessary for all, even without previous demonstration as to whence this universality arises. The recognition of this fact does not depend upon a definite theory of the origin of evil and its universal spread, but it is already certain empirically. For sin is not something which one sometimes hears of as we hear of an occasional phenomenon in remote countries, but it is very near us; and the fact that the question where sin is recoils upon the questioner to his shame, is the loudest testimony to the universality of sin. Every one of any experience, in observation of himself and of others, starts from the unavoidable presupposition that all men are sinners; every one has something to forgive his neighbour, and knows that he himself stands in need of forgiveness from men and from God.[2] And because this fact is already certain experimentally, theories which would explain it, have not so much a religious as a scientific importance, and consequently only an importance which is secondary

[1] Comp. § 73.   [2] Matt. vi. 12; 1 John i. 8; Jas. iii. 2.

and dogmatic. From the religious point of view this only is to be required, that the fact itself should not be affected by the theories concerning it, nor be brought into dispute. For this fact is no less testified by the Christian consciousness than by universal experience, a consciousness which in all Christians has reference to an unredeemed state in which sin ruled prior to the state of grace. Seeing, then, that in the manner in which the Church recurs to Adam and to the original sin which was initiated by him, there is only contained a theory as to the *basis* of the universality of sin, which is also certain experimentally quite independently of this theory, and cannot be itself affected by any theory, it was by a correct tact that Luther[1] placed the doctrine of inherited sin in the third series of articles, *i.e.* under those which have for heading: *De sequentibus agere poterimus cum doctis et prudentibus viris vel etiam inter nos ipsos.* Still science cannot rest content with the empirical universal reality of evil. Its province is to inquire after the origin of the same, partly in order to exclude false points of view by which other doctrines are violated, and partly in order to apprehend its nature (as if to make it a proof of the doctrine of the idea of evil) in such perfection that its universality may also be apprehended to be necessary from its nature or idea, when once it has become an actual fact in a race like ours. Only thus will the doctrine of the origin of evil become the keystone in the apprehension of the actual nature of evil.

A.—*The Biblical Doctrine.*

The Holy Scriptures do not derive universal human sinfulness, already contained in the O. T.,[2] from the actual sin of every individual, depravity as the evil device of the human heart rather dating from youth and from birth. Even the Rabbis have spoken of a יְצִירָה רָעָה. In the N. T. the passage of the Epistle to the Ephesians,[3] often quoted as of classic value, utters in reference to the question of the origin of evil a less definite sound than is frequently assumed: for the words τέκνα ὀργῆς coalesce and are to be taken in a similar manner to our German phrase *Ein Kind des Todes* ["a dead man," literally a child of death]; the reference is

---

[1] Art. Smalc. 317.   [2] Gen. viii. 21; Job iv. 17, xiv. 1; Ps. l. 5.
[3] Eph. ii. 3: ἥμεν φύσει τέκνα ὀργῆς.

not to childhood; and the expression φύσει relates to the state of the natural man generally, and does not specially relate to the state commencing at birth. That natural state is the antithesis to the grace revealed in history. On the other hand, the words of Jesus in John [1] apply to a fleshly nature from birth, that is, to a nature opposed to the Holy Spirit of God, which of itself excludes from the kingdom of God, and makes a new birth from above necessary.

On the other hand, the Scriptures teach that the sinfulness now innate in us is not innate in humanity as such, is not imprinted at creation therefore, but that this state is to be originally derived from the fact of human sin. To speak with the utmost precision, the Cosmogony is distinguished in the Genesis from the Ponerogony.[2] It is only subsequently [3] to the creation that the rise of evil in the world (not merely of death) by the disobedience of our first parents and the entrance of death by sin is described. According to the narrative, the *possibility* of sin lies in the fact that man is not initially perfect in knowledge nor established in the unity of his will with the conscious Divine will, but that his will can be seduced from good, if an external allurement blind him, and his psychical egoity exclusively gains the upper hand. The *reality* of sin is derived from the concurrence of sensuous desire and a false love of freedom, which questions the Divine law and love, and, distrustful of God, seeks equality with God in a freedom which, being extra-Divine, is a semblance of freedom. The representation is symbolical, and would be so understood;[4] but it is no mere representation of the Fall as it comes to pass in every individual at all times and in all places; the passage has to do with the first human pair and their historical fall, so that in the narrative there is accordingly given actual history, although in a husk of symbolism. The historical kernel is, that the first human beings *became* sinners by disobedience, and died by sin; they were not already sinful by nature.[5]

---

[1] iii. 6 : τὸ γεγεννημένον ἐκ σαρκὸς σάρξ ἐστιν.
[2] Gen. i. 31 : And God saw everything He had made, and behold it was very good.
[3] Gen. iii.   [4] Gen. iii. 1.
[5] Rothe would merely see in Gen. iii. a Thanatogony; he thinks that the O. T., and especially the Elohist, teaches nothing about an original sin. Only

In the N. T. John viii. 44 does not refer to the murder of Cain,[1] but the devil is the murderer of humanity from the beginning, having brought death upon the first human beings, when by falsehood he induced them to sin. It is true that in Gen. iii. there is no express mention of the devil; the serpent is treated as an animal; but the insight of later times cannot regard the devil as unconcerned in the origin of evil in humanity.[2] When Paul speaks of Eve as weaker from the beginning, and calls Adam as compared with Christ χοϊκός and ψυχικός,[3] he does not mean to teach thereby either sin in Eve or a fall before the Fall, nor is ψυχικός identical with sinful, carnal, but refers to the imperfection of the initial stage in which creation is not yet perfected. Even prior to the Fall, in the state of obedience, the first Adam was nevertheless not as yet the second who is from heaven, and from whom pneumatical humanity dates. That the causality of evil is not supposed, according to the passage in the Epistle to the Corinthians, to lie in the original constitution of human nature,[4] is clear from another leading passage.[5] Paul does not say that with Adam, that is, with his creation, sin, that is, sinfulness, has come into the world; his statement is that through one man, that is, through his causality, ἁμαρτία has become a cosmical potentiality, through his *deed* has become a *state*. Previously sin did not exist even as such a potentiality and as a state; consequently Adam's deed is regarded as a causality. That this is the meaning of διά the following words show, where the expressions παράπτωμα,

a natural and moral corruption of humanity is, he thinks, taught as an undoubted fact in Ps. ciii. 10–14, lxxviii. 38. Certainly the O. T. refers little to this narrative (and upon this fact Rothe relies); only the Book of Wisdom, ii. 24, expressly gives a developed doctrine formed on the model of Gen. iii. ; still Rothe must also concede that Hos. vi. 7 and Isa. xliii. 27 can be referred to Adam. It is also to be considered that the universality of sin in humanity comes less into consciousness in the O. T., because from the days of Abraham the glance is concentrated pre-eminently upon the chosen people and its sin. It is in prophecy that Israel first unites itself again with the heathen in looking forwards in hope and backwards in remembrance of their common origin; in the time of the Law, on the contrary, the contents of Gen. i.–iii. were a treasure placed in no prominence, and the significance of which was almost unrecognized.

[1] 1 John iii. 12 shows this well.    [2] Wisd. ii. 24; comp. Rev. xii. 9, xx. 2.
[3] 1 Cor. xv. 45–47.    [4] As Rothe thinks, *Dogmatik*, p. 312.
[5] Rom. v. 12, etc.

παράβασις, παρακοή are employed, all of which relate to sinful act.[1] The meaning therefore is: not through Adam's existence, but through him as an agent, through his deed, has sin become a potentiality in the world.—The fruit of sin is in the first place death,[2] but sinfulness was also a consequence of the sinful act, and from Adam has imparted itself to his race. This conclusion, indeed, is not to be safely drawn from the ἐφ' ᾧ, but from the whole course of thought in the parallel between the first Adam and the second. The second is doubtless described as the actual cause of righteousness and eternal life, and it is just the realization passing from one individual upon a great circle of life, although in an opposite manner, which forms the point of comparison. The context consequently requires the first Adam also to be thought of as a cause, namely, of the opposite of righteousness, *i.e.* of sinfulness and death, in the race.[3] The result, therefore, of the Biblical teaching is that all men, from the days of Adam on, stand in need of redemption, and that a Divine judgment of reprobation rests upon them as sinners,[4] from which Christ alone can set them free.[5] A more intimate explanation of the way and manner in which Adam became a cause of the sinfulness of his posterity, is given neither by Paul nor John. But Paul also thinks freedom not absolutely extinguished, but thinks the causality of posterity to be concerned in their sin.[6]

B.—*The Doctrine of the Evangelical Churches.*

Both the Evangelical Confessions teach that God is not the cause of evil. On the Lutheran side the *Confessio Augustana*[7] says indeed: "The cause of evil is to be found in the will

---

[1] Rom. v. 14–19.      [2] Rom. v. 52, vi. 23 ; Jas. i. 15.
[3] This is also expressly stated in v. 19 : διὰ τῆς παρακοῆς τοῦ ἑνὸς ἁμαρτωλοὶ κατεστάθησαν οἱ πολλοί, which does not mean :—A symbolical representation was made in Adam that all are sinners ; otherwise causality would also have to be denied in the antithesis, Christ, and we must say that in Christ a symbolical representation only was made that all are righteous.
[4] Rom. v. 18 : κατάκριμα ; comp. iii. 19.
[5] Rom. viii. 1.      [6] This is also found in Rom. v. 12.
[7] C. A. xix., in the German text of the older Wittenberg edition.

of the devil and of the godless who, immediately they are abandoned by God, turn from God to the Wicked One." This German text favours the interpretation, that not because of a positive act of God, but in consequence of the withdrawal of His hand (the withholding of the *donum perseverantiæ*), is the will of the creature turned from God to the Wicked One, in which case God would remain the negative cause of evil. For this rendering of the *Invariata* the contemporary state of the predestination question may answer.¹ The *Variata* omitted this *Passus*, inasmuch as Melanchthon subsequently found therein an unadvisable expression. The words of the German text of the *Invariata*² might also be understood, it is true, in such a way that the will of the creature is already presupposed to be evil when God withdraws His hand, this abandonment thus being not the cause but already the punishment of sin. In this case the following words—that the will immediately turns to the Wicked One (after the withdrawal of the Divine hand) —could not refer to the Fall, but must rather signify the state and dominion of sin, into which men fall when themselves abandoned. But this would be forced, and in the article which bears the heading "*De causa peccati*" mention would not be made of the origin of sin, but of the cause of its increment and dominion merely.—The withdrawal of the Divine hand might simply mean, although again the meaning would be forced, that God withdrew that overwhelming activity of His Spirit for good when the temptation came, in order that man might freely decide, and he immediately (freely) fell into disobedience; and the Latin text is quite compatible with this rendering.³ But whatever be the state of the question, the *Variata* has omitted the equivocal passage on good grounds,

---

¹ For in a contemporaneous letter of Melanchthon's to Brenz (*Corpus Reformatorum*, ii. p. 547), Melanchthon accepts a predestination in general. Of course he has not intended to make an express declaration upon this point according to this letter, undoubtedly having a sense of uncertainty which later on led him to pursue other paths.

² [For the benefit of those who are unfamiliar with the several texts of the Augsburg Confession, we may state that Melanchthon's first edition, whether in Latin or German, is commonly called *Invariata*, and his three subsequent editions of 1531, 1535–1540, 1541–1542, are called *Variatæ*. See *Corpus Reformatorum* for the several texts critically revised, vol. xxvi.—TRANSL.]

³ But it says no more of Adam's sin. The passage runs: De causa peccati docent, quod, tametsi Deus creat et conservat naturam, tamen causa peccati est

and the Lutheran Church undoubtedly has always rejected every form of the Divine origination of evil, and has only accepted the Augsburg Confession in this sense. The *Formula Concordiæ*, as well as the *Variata*, shows this most clearly. It says,[1] that sin comes from the devil and the evil will of man. There is no more mention made of a withdrawal of grace (that phrase which is not seldom met with in Reformation times, or the refusal of the *donum perseverantiæ*). On the contrary, it is expressly said [2] that the Divine prescience embraces everything, but not as cause; it is neither the cause of sin nor of evil and damnation. The sin (or the evil will) of our first parents is at the same time regarded as the cause and historic medium of the sinful constitution of the race (in the language of Dogmatics, as *peccatum originans*).[3] The Divine relation to the *peccatum originale*, or the primary sin, is said to be this, that He is not even now the creator and producer of evil, but that simultaneously with the essentially good nature which God still creates and sustains, evil becomes propagated, since it transmits itself in a physical manner.[4] As far as the *Reformed Doctrine* is concerned, a few Reformed confessions [5] of course deny all contingency in opposition to the Divine *ordinatio*, and therefore the freedom of the will; but they still explain that God is not the originator of evil,[6] although partly in the form that evil is evil not *respectu Dei sed Satanæ*. They do not indeed state how evil, which is notwithstanding not a mere subjective phenomenon in their view, can be kept aloof from the Divine causality. Yet if God ordains absolutely everything, the willing of evil as evil seems to be embraced by His ordaining will. The narrow Calvinistic creeds thus leave at this point a hiatus,—a riddle,—a scientific defect. But

voluntas malorum, videlicet Diaboli et impiorum, *quæ non adjuvante Deo avertit se a Deo*. The words *non adjuvante Deo* are not to be understood *because God does not give aid (to the good)*, but *without God affording aid to evil*. The *Variata* puts: *impiorum hominum, quæ avertit se a Deo ad alias res contra mandata Dei*. Similarly J. Müller, edit. 2, vol. i. pp. 358, etc.
[1] 639 b, §§ 7-9. [2] 818, 79.
[3] 639 b, § 7. *Corruptio naturæ per carnalem conceptionem propagatur.*
[4] *Ibid.*: *ex semine per peccatum corrupto, per carnalem conceptionem.*
[5] At least the Heidelberg Catechism, the Anglican Articles, and especially the *Confessio Marchica*, I.
[6] Comp. *Helv.* 1566, cap. viii.; *Mülhus*, 2; *Gall.* vii. 8; *Belg.* xiii.; *Heidelb. Cat.* Fr. 7; March. 14; Can. Dordr. c. I. art. 5.

seeing that their religious tact praiseworthily speaks out so definitely against making God the cause of evil, although without squaring themselves with the Divine omnipotence, it is not allowable to attribute to them as their doctrine a consequence which may be apparently drawn, but which is expressly repudiated by the Reformed doctrine. Rather is the doctrinal position of the Reformed Churches that *Deus non est autor, causa, reus peccati*, although they cleave with more energy than the Lutheran Churches to the thought that all-governing prescience must also in some way embrace evil. They refer back to Adam as the mediating causality of the universality of sin in spite of the Creationism dominant amongst them, but with the difference that part, the minority indeed, holds a supralapsarian doctrine, *i.e.* that Adam's fall is not thought of as a free act, but as somehow necessary, though without making God the cause of evil as such, whilst the majority regard Adam's fall as his free sinful act, and consequently hold an infralapsarian doctrine.

*Observation.*—A few Reformed theologians emphasize the *donum perseverantiæ* as a necessary Divine gift if evil is not to gain the mastery, and assume that God did not give that gift to Adam; and thus, they say, sin has been given, although not brought about by a positive Divine act. This reminds one of Bellarmin's doctrine of the original state, inasmuch as it refers to an original Dualism in man, although it contains on the other hand the roughest contradiction to a bestowal of the *donum perseverantiæ* as the golden bridle of the natural appetite.

C.—*Theories of the Origin of Evil.*

§ 80.

All attempts to conceive the realization of evil as a thing originally necessary are wrecked upon the fact that, even if they do not afford a mere definition or description of evil instead of its derivation, they end in a Dualism, which on its side, when consistently carried out, affects the idea of God and transfers the origination of evil to the Deity. But it can only apparently and not truly be that evil comes from God. Therefore the desire to conceive of evil generally as a necessary thing always logically ends in the transformation of the same into a mere semblance, into the denial of its reality. But this is not to solve the problem, it is to deny its subject-matter. If evil, therefore, is neither to be referred to God nor to be regarded as semblance merely, no other course remains than so to seek its origin in a *creaturely* principle that the reality of evil is based upon this alone. The necessity of the possibility of evil is capable of philosophical construction, and so is the impossibility that its realization *must* follow. The latter is only historically cognizable.

*Observation.*—When the text asserts the impossibility of the philosophical construction (*Nichtconstruirbarkeit*) of a necessary arising of evil, the meaning is not that the problem is too difficult for the utterance of a definite opinion thereupon, or that evil weighs upon us as a riddle merely: the assertion is, that the question as to a necessary origin of the reality of evil is demonstrably a *sideroxylon*, because it is impossible to inquire into the origin of a thing which is denied again by the very institution of the inquiry. We would not maintain the opinion of the inconceivability of evil in its origin; on the contrary, we maintain—
(1) A knowledge of the impossibility of a necessary realization of the same;
(2) A knowledge of its necessary possibility; and
(3) A knowledge of the sufficient cause of its realization.
The paragraph further implies that all attempts at the construction of the reality of evil generally as a necessity fall into three main classes, the *first* of which hypotheses somehow sees in human *finitude* the necessary basis of evil, and consistently advances to the *second* or *Dualistic* class, just as this necessarily advances to the *third* class, which seeks to derive evil from God.

*First Class.—The Derivation from Finitude.*

We shall have here to presuppose the idea of evil to be already found. We shall therefore regard no theories which, instead of touching upon the derivation of evil, merely give definitions or descriptions of it, and which were rejected by us previously (§ 76, etc.). To the category before us those theories belong which suppose evil to be given in our finite existence, be it that they identify evil with finiteness generally, or be it that they identify it with a precise finite constitution regarded as essential and permanent, for example, essential weakness of the spiritual faculties, or essential disharmony between the faculties of body and spirit. Of higher standing and value as theories are the points of view which do not assert the universal and eternal necessity of evil, but merely *assert it to be a particular stadium.* These theories hold not to being but *becoming.* Evil is to them the necessary stepping-stone to good; the ethico-religious problem of humanity has and retains, they say, its value and is soluble. But development, which is nevertheless the road to perfection traced out for man, cannot, it is thought, be imagined without a passage through evil. Not that development as such and of itself is bad; imperfection of itself is of course not as yet abnormity; but development is impossible for man by a homogeneous, ever harmonious and single advance, but only by the evolving of an opposite, which may become an *opposition.* An attempt may be made to prove this view from corporeality, or from the spiritual side, or by a combination of both methods.

In the first place: The faculties of the sensuous life, although innocent in themselves, according to the ordained order of the development of the spiritual faculties, precede and are already strong before the spirit awakes, which finds itself, it is said, in its relation to the senses too weak at the very outset for resistance. So says Schleiermacher casually, in which statement he does not assert (as is often thought) that the sinful development was necessary for the sake of progress generally, but only that the disharmonious opposition in question was once the form of growth ordained for us, but Christ, although a true man, was not subject thereto. But since, in Schleiermacher's view, there is no necessary opposition between flesh and spirit, an ever richer Divine communication coming to man from the first, he must find the ground of the antagonism between spirit and flesh in the refusal of this communication, and therefore in God, and this view passes over into the Divine derivation of evil. Schleiermacher cannot and does not wish to show the precedence of the flesh to be an universal and essentially necessary law of true human nature. Therefore it is not humanity as such, but a Divine ordinance, by means of which the opposition between the flesh and the spirit is posited as a modification of universal human nature, according to Schleiermacher. Rothe goes to work with more profundity. He says that an inward spiritual communication which is a match for the strengthened natural life *cannot* happen at the beginning, because the spirit, the rational soul, is not innate, but can only enter after the place for it has been prepared by the advanced development of the physical life, after the condition of its actual existence has been given. But if the impulses of the corporeal and psychical life are of themselves good, and all natural faculties have their appropriate order,[1] a necessary opposition cannot arise upon the subsequent entrance of the spirit. If in his view the natural organism is created for the spirit, it is not evident why it should necessarily and inimically oppose the personality, and the less since even the requirements of personality are not inimical to the normal bodily and psychical life and its demands. And the fact bears another aspect, inasmuch as Rothe adds to it his doctrine of matter and of the natural incorrectness of individuality, which inevitably leads to the dualistic hypothesis. Besides, seeing that Rothe affirms a correct individuality in Christ, retained in purity by the Divine communication afforded Him, and that, too, without supposing the truth of his humanity to suffer thereby, he has not maintained the necessity of evil for human nature as such, but we are referred finally in this respect, as in the case of Schleiermacher, to God as the negative or mediate cause of evil.

That we may evade physical dualism, it is possible, instead of recurring to corporeality, to seek to derive the necessity of evil from the laws of *spiritual* growth, whether of the will or

---

[1] Which, according to Rothe, is certainly not the case (outside of Christ), since he confesses openly to allowing a dualistic element to enter here. His hypothesis of the later origin of the human soul, which without a Divine act remains inexplicable as a mere act of nature, must moreover assume a constitution in the elementary human existence essentially distinct from all physical being.

the intelligence. From the side of the *will* this may be done as follows. " Man," it may be said, " is endowed with development only on the supposition of a new living form which is different, distinct, and opposed to the initial natural form; but this is not effected without opposition from the natural form, which will assert itself against the novel form, and thus an opposition and struggle arises between the flesh and the spirit, that is, there arises a sinful development." Similarly it is said on the side of *consciousness*, that " in order for man to be self-conscious, he must apprehend and fix himself in his independent existence, and in order to centralize himself he must exclude or repel everything which is not himself; but seeing that he, to attain himself, excludes or suppresses the consciousness of the species and of God, he stands at the outset in necessary contrast to love."—Of course a development is not possible without an externalization of the moments of self-consciousness and of the consciousness of God and the race,—without a separation between the natural and the free, and in such dissolution lies the possibility of evil. But its necessary realization is not given in such a fact, since the gradual character of development generally is not regarded as sin, and thus an already controverted definition of evil is adduced instead of its derivation. The advent of *free agency* and the supposition of a new form of life cannot be in itself actual evil, any more than the earlier form of life, since as arising from the Divine hand it was created good. Even the combination of the two, the addition of a form essentially new, cannot generate opposition, seeing that the earlier form was adjusted to the new, and thus brings a willing plasticity to meet it. The self-assertiveness of the innocent natural form of life merely constitutes an attraction to the spirit to take up a position freely in relation to the same. But the necessity for this attraction to determine and dominate the spirit with overwhelming force is neither given by the nature of the spirit nor by that of the natural side. And it is a similar case with *consciousness.* Self-consciousness does not arise by mere negation of the consciousness of another, or by not thinking of the same, but conversely by the self-distinguishing of the Ego from the non-Ego, from the world and God, which are therefore supposed simultaneously in the thought of the Ego, namely as the non-Ego, and from which the Ego knows how to distinguish itself. But since distinction is by no means identical with opposition, it follows that self-consciousness does not stand in any way in a necessary or even momentary opposition to the consciousness of God and the world. Schleiermacher has shown excellently in his *Glaubenslehre* how self-consciousness arises by the exclusion of the consciousness of God to so small a degree, that it rather attains its perfection for the first time with the consciousness of its absolute dependence, or with the fact that it itself frames the distinction between God and itself, which distinction is also in turn the essential relation of both to each other.

The Hegelian school, finally, either unites the cognitive and volitional sides,[1] or combines with both the natural side. But although the combination of three non-probative moments does not compensate for the force of demonstration they lack, specifically the following are objections to Hegel's exposition. The nobility of man, he rightly says, consists not merely in remaining a natural being, but in self-constitution and in becoming what he (essentially) is by means of freedom and reason. But he continues: "Immediately or in his natural state man resembles the animals in barbarism, in sensuousness and selfishness."—But the necessity of a natural state which causes evil, of an egoistic barbarism, is not proved with the immediateness of origin, but is only asserted. Why should any but a good material be requisite for free self-assertion, for an ethically formative faculty? In fact, Hegel himself again denies the evil character of this initial natural state. In the animal life, with which he compares it, he finds innocence and not evil, indeed he believes evil proper only to be reached in the further development and by means of the spiritual factor, in which particularity reflects itself without producing indeed the necessity for the spirit of this egoistic will. For the attempt to prove that the development from natural to spiritual life must pass through disruption and freedom, must first enter as undisciplined sensuous caprice, cannot possibly be successful. The universal good, he further thinks, in order to be willed, being this and not its opposite, must become conscious and be distinct as willing from its opposite. The decided affirmation of the good is only, he says, the negation of the negation or of

[1] So Reiff in his treatise, *Ueber das Wesen der Religion*, Tüb. Zeitschrift.

the opposite of good; but the opposite of good to be negatived, the egoistic, must likewise be real, otherwise the profoundest negation of evil could not accrue. But a conscious exclusion of evil is possible, even apart from something which may be the internal or external reality of the same. Conscious free decision only depends on a double possibility being presented to the will by the instrumentality of the intellect, *i.e.* by the instrumentality of the knowledge of the morally good which has relation to freedom; but it can never be proved that the reality of evil, be it even as a point of transition, is requisite for the ethical process. Moreover, although the thought of evil as a possibility is necessary to conscious right decision, the thought of evil is not an evil thought; it does not even necessarily presuppose actual evil in experience, whether personal or foreign evil, as Vatke thinks,[1] but is given with the definite thought of moral good as such, or of law. Since, that is to say, an act cannot possibly be evil in the strict sense, to which the consciousness of good and evil and therefore the thought of evil is still wanting, if we are supposed capable of obtaining this thought only from the experience of evil, the evil act must have already taken place that it might be able to take place. As opposed to all these attempts, two things are to be remembered:—

First: it cannot be demonstrated that he who remains sinless in his development must cease to be man. There is an internal contradiction also in wishing to prove the universal necessity of evil merely as a point of transition. For, on the contrary, one of our forms of life can only be called evil because it contradicts the idea of our being, that is, the ideal norm which would embrace and control not merely the stage of perfection, but all the stages of life, each according to its fashion. So long as a form of life is still recognized as evil and would be derived as evil, it is asserted with the evil being of the same, that in opposition thereto the good form of life is in itself possible and not chimerical, and thus the necessity of evil must not be asserted. It is thus conceded that every stage of life can really become its own ideal in the sphere of humanity, as has happened in Christ according to the Christian faith. If this ideal were altogether something impossible, it would

[1] *Die menschliche Freiheit*, 1841, pp. 262, etc.

not be a mere ideal, but only the apparent norm of what was worthy, and evil would only be apparent evil. If, therefore, there still remains thinkable a kind of necessity of evil within the course of the world, it cannot be an original necessity, but only one that is occasioned, additional, or fundamentally accidental, as is clear from the fact that the consciousness of the same is combined with the consciousness of contingency in reference to the idea of man, in spite of his evil empirical constitution.

Secondly: all these theories, inasmuch as they still concede the existence of evil, fall by consequence into Dualism. For should evil merely be generally necessary as the point of transition for the rational creature, so that a pure life ceases to be a truly human being, evil would belong to the idea of man or to its development, and in the same man absolutely desired good would be opposed to absolutely compulsory evil. And even God could not of Himself have ordained the necessary transition through evil which He absolutely hates, but only as constrained by a power foreign to Himself. We are thus conducted to the

*Second Class.—The Dualistic Hypotheses*

Certainly Dualism cannot proceed from the interests of speculation; it militates severely against the unity which the reason desires; it consequently has an empirical origin. It seeks to comprehend the contrasts of the physical and spiritual life, which it sees to intersect in experience, under two ultimate and opposite principles or generic ideas at any rate, renouncing the attainability of an ultimate unity. If the eyes are averted from its lowest forms, which merely concern the contrast of the salutary or pernicious, of the beautiful or hateful, and which are therefore simply æsthetic, Dualism is distinguished itself by a profound impression of the reality and far-reaching power of evil, and will not conceive of evil as mere appearance, a theory towards which the theories of finitude incline. The still unwritten history of its manifold forms is conditioned partly by the increasing consciousness of the moral, partly by the tendency of the reason to an ultimate unity, allowing no rest to Dualism in any of its forms.

Its MILDEST form speaks of a μὴ ὄν as a *limit* to God in all His action, and accords with the theory of finitude. The limit is as an adverse law above God, whereby all His products are limited and thereby affected with evil. We have spoken of this theory as a false definition of evil (§ 76. 1). The STRONGER form condenses this limitation into eternal *matter*, which stands opposed to the creative activity of God. If now matter is supposed to be the cause of evil, it cannot be regarded as that which is absolutely without form and attributes (ἄμορφον, ἄποιον), but it must be supposed to have a resisting nature opposed to the good working of God. This ungovernable feature, if it is to explain anything, must belong to the primary idea of matter, and by virtue thereof the work of God never succeeds but partially. After every creative Divine act there remains an indomitable phlegm, after every sublimation there is a precipitation, a dark remainder, an ἔκτωμα, a real opposition to omnipotence which is unable to get the better thereof. Further, the contra-divine would in this case be in the last resort something neuter and impersonal. These two first forms are forms of physical or cosmological Dualism.

THIRDLY. But since evil is not merely neuter and thing-like, but only rational natures can be evil, spirit and will or persons, cosmological Dualism must pass over into personifying Dualism. To this category belongs Ahriman in later Parseeism, and Satan in the sects of the Middle Ages. Side by side with the primary personal good principle, they assume that sin exists as the eternal evil principle. But such eternal duality infringing the unity of reason, the human spirit did not tolerate this pure Dualism, but sought to reconcile duality with unity in some way, either eschatological, in which case a future conquest of the evil principle by the good is assumed, and the duality of principle and the necessity of evil are therefore merely temporary, or a more consistent way, in which that which must succumb in the end cannot have been Divine at the outset in the same sense as the victorious principle, that is to say, that it cannot be Divine in such a manner as to be referred to a common primary origin, out of whose womb the opposite principles were born. This womb, being the mother of what is absolutely opposed, must be indifference between good and evil. But in this way Dualism already passes into the third class, which would apprehend necessity of evil as somehow arising from the ultimate unity.

*Observation* 1. A modern form of Dualism is that of Schopenhauer and that of Von Hartmann, who regard Will and Presentation, or the volitional and the logical, as two mutually opposing powers in the Absolute. Even if Presentation (which only comprehends the phenomenal) may also be derived from Will, they as little afford a reconciliation of their duality with their primary origin or in themselves as show an actual derivation.

*Observation* 2. The doctrine of Satan, although Jacob Böhme and Schelling apply it in the interests of the necessity of evil, in the interests of a kind of Dualism in God Himself, is unadapted according to the Biblical form to this end, because according to the Scriptures Satan is indeed spiritual wickedness, but as a creature is without creative power. It is also implied that, so far from explaining the origin of evil, he also himself belongs to the empire of evil to be explained.

*Third Class.—The Derivation of Evil from the Supreme Unity.*

If the origin of evil is sought in God Himself, it may result either from the inner Divine *Essence* itself, or from the Divine attributes as they are mirrored in the Divine idea of the world, and in the world as realized.

Schelling—in his middle period related in this matter to Jacob Böhme—and Hegel regard evil as grounded in the inner Divine life (thus identifying the life of the world and the life of God).[1] At this point it was impossible for them to remain,—that the supreme unity is a mere indifference of opposites; for how are the latter to be derived from the former, if they are merely negatived therein, and what would

---

[1] J. Böhme assumed in God a dark, fiery principle side by side with a light principle; similarly Schelling also in his *Freiheitslehre*. By means of a struggle the light principle breaks, he says, like lightning through the fire spirit, which remains as ever vanquished the basis in the inner Divine life. The self-working of the first principle would thus be the cause of sin (the working according to the ground, egoity or particular volition). The heart in theories of this kind is the thought, which Hegel also shares, that life does not exist without opposites, which become contradictions. Comp. Vatke, pp. 262, etc., 312, etc.

that unity itself be but a Zervane Akerene, the dead ground on which, we know not how, such opposite life moves and a decline from unity takes place? In his natural philosophy period Schelling had long thought the supreme unity to be indifference or zero, starting from which the decline, the world and its opposites, was only to be derived by an inexplicable chance. But he was always endeavouring, as was Hegel, to think, according to his own method, the supreme unity living. The supreme unity, no mere non-existence of opposites, is to them but an interpenetration of opposites which constitute perfect Divine life. There is further this difference between Schelling's doctrine of freedom and Hegel's, that the former regards the whole from the view-point of will, the latter from that of thought. Both think that an opposite is necessary to life; according to Schelling the opposite of egoity or of the particular and universal will, according to Hegel the opposite of inseity and aseity. Only by an opposite, consequently, is God perfect, namely by His supreme control, God being according to Schelling an *actu* existent God, Spirit and absolute Personality, as the absolute animation of the particular will or of the will of the basis by means of the universal will, God being according to Hegel a self-existent Spirit. According to both, this process of diremption and unification is at the same time a world process, since human history is also supposed to be the history of God, and this process is a gradually progressive one. God takes, they say, the fate of development upon Himself; Theogony, Cosmogony, Ponerogony in this case coalesce into one problem.—Upon this idea of God we do not further speak in this place; we simply say a word upon the fundamental thought, that *there is requisite for life, even for Divine life, an opposite advancing to antagonism*. Not merely is this not proved, the opposite is provable. How could the Divine life be thought to be perfect, and therefore absolute, if it must cherish conflicts within itself, or if the inner life of God be subject to a succession of developments and do not bear within itself its absolute unification as eternally as it bears the diremption of moments? But even generally, were life to live by contradiction, it would itself be an eternal contradiction; were evil itself to belong somehow to the Divine process of life, this would be an eternal contradiction to the idea of God itself. Consequently, in the endeavour to apprehend the necessity of evil, the inner process of the Divine life will at all events have to remain beyond consideration. In His inner being God is eternally perfect.

But does one or the other of the Divine *attributes*, which seek and find in the world the spheres of their revelation, and thus realize the Divine idea of the world, bring in its train the unavoidable origination of evil in the world? As a matter of fact, sagacity has endeavoured to find such a derivation in all the leading Divine attributes. Thus a derivation has been found in the Divine OMNIPOTENCE. In order that the whole creative power of God may be revealed, thinks Thomas Aquinas, all possible stages of existence of the ladder of being must be filled up. Therefore the world is only completely what it is meant to be, a revelation of the Divine omnipotence and wisdom, inasmuch as it does not lack the most profound stages.[1] Only thus is it the complete expression of the creative power. The demonstration of omnipotence, the production of everything at all possible or thinkable, would accordingly be an absolute necessity for God. God's ability and volition would absolutely coincide. But God being the rather perfect as absolute love, His ability or His power cannot be the law of His working; His love determines what His ability shall effect. Love is the power over His omnipotence. According to this derivation, too, evil would merely be thought *a lower stage of Good*, quantitatively distinct therefrom, and as a smaller quantum of being and a part of being would in the interests of the world-whole remain condemned to be ever evil. Besides, it is not perceptible how far imperfection is supposed to be requisite to the revelation of the Divine power. It may be rather said that, inasmuch as variety also belongs to the perfection of the world, the co-existence of the more perfect and the more imperfect is necessarily requisite to the good of the world. This leads to the æsthetic attempt at derivation.

[1] *Summa*, I. quæst. 47, art. 2. *Non-perfectum esset universum, si tantum unus gradus bonitatis inveniretur in rebus.* But the grades of being, in comparison with God, are a *defectus, corruptio*. Comp. Landerer, Art. on Thomas Aquinas in Herzog's *Real-Encycl.*, vol. xvi. p. 64.

Many have wished to derive the necessity in the fact of evil from the idea of BEAUTY; so many dualistic systems.[1] Evil, it is then said, is in the complete picture of the world what contrast is in painting, offensive to him who is wholly occupied with detail, necessary and good to the contemplation which regards the whole. Indeed, evil is the dark contrast to good, and without shadow, it is said, there would only remain a monotonous uniformity. As in music dissonances do not annul but enrich harmony, as in the highest form of poetry which embraces the other forms not pure heroes of good enter, but the noble man only first rightly raises himself to the category of good man in opposition to evil characters, *so* is evil said to be necessary in the world, and to serve to make it various and beautiful.[2] This conception may also be associated with that previously mentioned, that life only arises by conflict, that good and evil are the two poles which always exist side by side in human life, only that in this case everything is made subservient to the æsthetic idea. It cannot be denied that there is much apparent truth in this theory. Accustomed to this world and the power of evil in it, it is difficult for us not to attribute the same to a world which is full of life. Christianity affords the ground for this: " It doth not yet appear what we shall be." The power, the inner dominion, and the manifoldness of good are only revealed imperfectly to start with. The victory of the spirit in the world of phenomena will only be the last thing in the drama of the world. Now it is the turn of faith, not sight, and that in the moral interest. Still we already know enough now not to confound manifoldness with the necessity of conflict between good and evil. Good is by no means mere abstract identity, unity, or monotony, but a principle of diversified life. Certainly evil is inimical to diversity, for it is disorganizing; it simply borrows an appearance of variety from good and the empire of its powers. Evil of itself everywhere hastes to one and the same thing, to death and its vain uniformity. But

[1] Comp. Baur, *Das manichäische Religionssystem*, p. 41 ; but even Plotinus (*Enneaden*, lib. viii. cap. 7 and 5), Augustine (especially in his earlier writings), Scotus Erigena, and Leibnitz belong to this category.
[2] Comp. Blasche, *Das Böse im Einklang mit der göttlichen Weltorduung*, 1827.

## THEORIES OF THE ORIGIN. 31

good strengthens and develops the manifoldness destined for its realm. And granting even that this theory possesses more ability of proof in reference to the true source of manifoldness, the deduction of the necessity of evil for the sake of beauty would include the insufferable thought that the moral sphere must itself submit to moral evil in order to be the more beautiful. But this is to commingle a foreign principle with the highest sphere which must lay claim to universal dominion. How shall we demand of the highest sphere, the laws of which alone produce what is required by universal and absolute validity, that it allow evil to be good, because it agrees with the æsthetic interest? How can it be rational to think that the ethical must submit to deliver up or relinquish to æsthetic forms, whilst the æsthetic is notwithstanding not the highest sphere, but internally dependent upon and conditioned by the ethical, as is shown in the fact that in tragedy itself, where good appears to submit to evil, an actual and no mere apparent victory of evil is unbeautiful, being an unresolved and shrieking dissonance, and stands in contradiction to itself, because in contradiction to the ethical? Still the root error again lies in the illusive demand that we are to turn away from particulars, we are to learn to behold the whole in which the particular supplements itself to perfection. In this the physical mode of thought again crops up, to which the idea of personality and moral good is wanting. Individuality and finitude constitute no opposition to the ethical and its totality; for the good in general can be willed by the individual personality, and the individual good act is ennobled by the whole of a good disposition; in the individual personal spirit, love has space for the whole good, for good generally, although in individual manner. Personality may assimilate the intensively infinite, indeed it is the appropriate sphere thereof, and the ethical idea of the same does not allow that particulars should be compelled to fall a sacrifice to beauty, and be destined to become a mere means for the whole.

From the category of INTELLIGENCE evil may in the first place be so derived that God cannot realize Himself, His absolute Self-consciousness, without thinking, and thinking of forming His opposite. As neuter and impersonal this opposite would be matter, of which we have spoken previously (p. 26).

But if the *thought* and creation of His real opposite necessarily belongs to the absolute self-consciousness of God, it must also be consistently asserted at any rate, that God cannot know Himself to be ethical, without thinking and framing His *ethical* opposite, *evil*. But even Rothe has not advanced to such a statement. In his later writings he has not for a moment acknowledged the supposition of matter as opposed to the Divine to be necessary for the Divine self-consciousness. Were it otherwise, there would still be the eternal necessity of assuming a personal evil in order that God might know Himself as personal good.—Therefore the turn of thought would have more probability that God as the *wise* God desires to communicate His wisdom. But the apprehension of an object is always conditioned by the apprehension of its opposite. Therefore, in order to impart true knowledge of good, God must also posit evil. But if good were generally only cognizable by its *real* opposite, it must also be said that God Himself can only know the eternal good He is by means of an evil as real and eternal, a view which, if it does not conduct to the priority of evil to good, conducts the more surely to that law of the antithesis in the spiritual life of God itself, of which we have previously spoken. It is true that even Lactantius has said : *Malum interpretamentum boni*. But, as shown above, we must rather say : *Bonum interpretamentum boni malique*, just as light manifests both itself and its opposite. All definite knowledge of an object of course includes the knowledge of its opposite ; but as regards good, which, according to what has been said earlier in our discussion, must logically be first, this knowledge comes from itself, namely the knowledge of evil as a *possible* opposite. It is to be conceded that the consequences of evil appear more clearly if it does not remain merely possible ; but the nature of evil—and this is still the main thing—will make itself at the first sensible to the purest mind as its opposite, whilst the man who is really spotted by evil also receives his share of the beclouding falsehood of evil. If it can always be said that the way through sin might become the most thorough development; and that a more living conception of the same is afforded by the reality of evil, still that does not prove that sin generates purer knowledge ; rather is it true that good can effect this solely by the destruction of the falsehood of sin and its mystifications. Thus it is not the positing of evil by God which is shown to be necessary; only the place is shown which evil, if it really exists without Divine aid, takes in relation to God, and why evil can be tolerated by Him as a means of elevation. God remains conscious of the power to make evil somehow serviceable to the realm of good.

The derivation from the Divine RIGHTEOUSNESS. The supralapsarian mode of thought taught that men exist as means for the Divine honour, which is the exclusive end. But the Divine honour consists in the revelation of His attributes. Righteousness is also an absolute Divine attribute, and must therefore find its full revelation in the world. But the side of the Divine *gloria* which constitutes His righteousness cannot be revealed, if His mercy alone is manifested. Therefore it must be the eternal counsel of God that His righteousness should become manifest in one definite number, and His mercy in another number; and hence some individuals are willed from eternity as those upon whom He may show His mercy, and others as *vasa irœ*, or as such as may be passed over by mercy, in order that God may reveal in them His hatred of evil, and His righteousness as opposed to their *culpa*. For they are willingly in evil.[1] — For the sake of the final double aim all are in this case brought into the necessity of trespass, a fact which does not coincide with what is taught at the same time, viz. that God created men sinless, in order that He might not be guilty of evil. For if He afterwards withdraws His good Spirit, or denies that Divine communication which is necessary to the preservation of innocence, the guilt of evil is not so much laid upon men as upon God. Righteousness does not consist either with supposing that God originated what is punishable or with His not changing it if He alone could change it. Such a revelation of righteousness would immediately be its violation; for righteousness does not aim at being the mere revelation of the worth of a being, but at recompensing the worth also. Add to this that the elect have no more worth in themselves than the *reprobi,* unless there is assumed in them from the

---

[1] So in the main Theodore Beza in the *Colloquium Moempelgardense,* pp. 523-535, following the indications made by Calvin himself; *e.g. Institut.* lib. iii. cap. xxiii. 7, 8.

beginning (with Capito) a seed of *reprobatio*, which would be Manichæan, and would annul the equality as to the need of salvation and capacity of salvation. A touch of Manichæanism lies at the basis of Supralapsarianism generally. For from the first the *Electi* and the *Reprobi* are willed and created by God for absolutely opposite ends of existence.[1] And if the *idea of God* is regarded, there is wanting the purely ethical character in the view that all men are thought to be *means* for the glorification of God not impartially (which contradicts His love), and that the physical category of omnipotence preponderates over the ethical. The omnipotent will of God is thought to be alone decisive, and although it is assumed that this will is good in itself, inasmuch as God does not proceed arbitrarily but according to law in revealing the Divine attributes for the glory of God, still no advantage is thus gained; a dualism is rather introduced into God, since He is supposed to be necessitated to do what is absolutely opposed, making one good and blessed, and adjudging another the opposite, justice and mercy being considered as mutually exclusive, and their revelation revealed therefore in different subjects. For only the power of God is revealed in both classes of men, whilst every man participates in the revelation merely of one or the other of the two attributes. But justice and love, indivisibly united in God and possessed of power over omnipotence, seeks after a combined presentation in the world, so that justice may even reveal itself in the *electi*, and so that, on the other hand, God cannot be the cause of some becoming and remaining objects of justice merely.

The derivation from LOVE. Schleiermacher will not have all men, no, nor even a part of men, to be thought to be mere means, but would have all thought to be ends; indeed, according to him, all attain the goal at last, although by passage through initial sin.[2] He does not teach (as he is often supposed to) the necessity of evil for human development generally. The descriptive, non-constructive character of his system is opposed thereto. Omnipotence of course assumes with him a quite overwhelming position, and he assumes the absoluteness of the *decretum* of Calvin. But there

[1] So Calvin expressly teaches, although the enjoining will is of value to all.
[2] Comp. his treatise on *Erwählung*.

was in his view no necessity for omnipotence to establish a sinful development. And he not merely denies a positive Divine act as constituting evil, but even denies that evil as such was ordained by God; *so far as evil is evil*, he says, *it is certainly unrelated to God, and so far as it is related to God, it is not evil*, but in connection with redemption it is regarded as the incomplete, which beheld together with Christ forms a perfect whole. It is ordained, he says, together with the loving deed of redemption, and precedes it as its presupposition, in order that this demonstration of love may reveal itself the more gloriously, and find ready prepared a receptivity for itself. Above all, God has granted, he thinks, to men, prior to Christ, such a grade of consciousness of Himself, from which already some good may result; for example, knowledge of the duty, with which evil was also given, because the communication of the Spirit was not a match for the handicapped sensuousness of the flesh. If such original powerlessness of the God-consciousness contradicts the idea of God, the supposition of a mutable being also conflicts, he thinks, with that idea; He would be able to institute no development, but only what was absolutely perfect.[1] It is only the same thing differently expressed, when in his treatise on Calvin's doctrine of election he adopts the famous distinction between *voluntas* and *præceptum*, to which Luther was also led in his *De Servo Arbitrio*. The legislative and efficient omnipotent will may part in the interests of that revelation of love; God may communicate the knowledge of the *præceptum* before he imparts the power to solve the problem. Knowledge may thus haste on before the ability to divinely control. Through the disproportion between the knowledge of the law communicated and the communication of power, actual evil and its consciousness is, he thinks, brought about. He thus seeks to escape the *conception of evil as a mere defect*. The reverse of this defect indeed is, according to him, the positive original power of sense or flesh. In fact, seeing that not evil, but the God-consciousness must be thought to be the first, in the entire absence of which evil cannot be spoken of, that self-assertive preponderance of the

[1] *Der Christliche Glaube*, § 80, 81. Here also the distinction is insufficiently estimated between imperfection and abnormity.

sensuousness which becomes sin because of the God-consciousness is to be regarded as a disturbance and perversion, namely, in comparison with the idea of man which is placed by the God-consciousness before his eyes as the great problem.[1] Disturbance, so far as man attains his idea, is to be thought analogous with that idea, just as the courses of the planets may undergo perturbations which resolve themselves again on the whole into harmony. This solution might suffice, if we were able to sever sinful man into two separate wholes, into a purely animal being, which may be called innocent, inasmuch as guilt equally with virtue is absolutely transcendent thereto, and into an Ego who is conscious of law, the knowledge of which indeed is alone to be called good. But we should thus lose the idea of man altogether, which rather consists in a living unity of the rational and sensuous, and unconditionally requires a harmonious relation between the two spheres rendered effectual by the will. The consciousness of God and of the creaturely inheres in one and the same man, and both are present at the same time to the will, together with the consciousness as to which of the two he is to subordinate to the other, God or the world. He is only actually man, when he has the consciousness of his unconditioned obligation to good, with which the volition of evil forms a dissonance which absolutely should not be. Therefore a distinction cannot be made on the Divine side between this unconditioned law (*præceptum*) and the *voluntas* in such a way as not to introduce disharmony into God, if He at the same time directs by means of conscience the unconditioned and earnest demand for good in man, and on the other hand withholds that which is indispensable to the fulfilment of that requirement; or if He establishes a preponderance of sense, and has not increased the power of the God-consciousness, whilst at the same time and in the same human and living unity He allows this preponder-

[1] His meaning is: if we thought of men purely as sensuous beings without any God-consciousness, their sensuousness would be innocent, and nothing unworthy of God would be supposed by it. But it cannot be thought unworthy of God that He should implant in man something further, namely a knowledge of the law, of the goal (to be reached more securely in Christ), and therewith the desire thereafter; on the contrary, a necessity to give forthwith an ability to do together with this knowledge, cannot be asserted in reference to God.

ance by means of conscience to be condemned by the *præceptum* as sinful. Evil does not consist in man's not yet being initially what he will one day become; for then evil must be called normal, and only be esteemed exceptionable by an error. Evil is something different from mere development. Man has to turn round to regain the right starting-point, and has not to go forward simply. Evil is the discord of man with his idea, as and so far as that idea should be realized at the given moment. It is true (and this is the truth in the distinction between *præceptum* and *voluntas*) that the will which enjoins good and the will which brings forth good are not able to coalesce immediately, but rather, that an ethical process may be necessary, must a knowledge of the good precede a volition of it. But the necessity of sin notwithstanding is not thus given. Sin is not being imperfect at all, but the contravention of what ought to be at a given moment, and of what can lay claim to unconditioned value. The moral law, itself ordaining a development, does not make the same demand of every stage of human life. If man wills what he ought at the given moment, to which it of course pertains that his desire should turn to God and His assistance, the productive will of God does not remain in repose, but supplies what man needs. The opposite would be contrary to His ethical being. God therefore cannot be even the negative cause of evil; and where His productive will of love does not work, a lack of receptivity for His action, arising not from Him but from the creature, can alone bear the blame.

*Observation.*—It is noteworthy that Calvin and Schleiermacher, like Determinism generally, allow on the one hand the Divine prescience to become immediately an absolute predestination, and teach a coincidence of the Divine thought and action, and that on the other hand they affirm in evil a separation between the law-giving thought of the ethical intelligence directed upon the will and the *voluntas* or the Divine constitution. This is a strong proof that Determinism, or the denial of the principle of a mutable independent causality in the creature, cannot be carried through homogeneously and consistently, unless either the law-giving will is denied, and the *præceptum* by which evil is condemned is reduced to semblance, or conversely the origin of evil slides back to the productive will, and God is made the cause of evil; that is to say, either evil or the law becomes mere appearance, which comes to the same thing.[1] If man is not to regard evil as appearance merely, and is nevertheless not to seek its ground in the creature, nothing remains but to fall back into Dualism, which happens inasmuch as a contradiction is transferred to the action of God Himself, though it be but a contradiction between *voluntas* and *præceptum*. But such contradiction in the Divine action must also affect His inner being, and this is the case in all the theories now considered. The acceptance of a self-consciousness in God, which only grows to be absolute, would form a manifest contradiction to the Divine absoluteness, as would the acceptance of a necessary antithesis in God. But the derivations from the Divine attributes come into a conflict of the Divine omnipotence or beauty or wisdom or justice with the ethical being of God, whilst finally in Schleiermacher the conflict remains between the law-giving justice and the presupposition which is regarded necessary for the introduction of redemption, and therefore for the revelation of the Divine love. But God must be thought to be the harmonious being in Himself as well as in His action; whatever must be referred to a conflict in Him, can only seem to have existence; evil would therefore become mere false semblance if it is either positively or negatively grounded in God. Relatively to the Divine standpoint it could not be evil; and seeing that we know this, it could only remain phenomenal even relatively to us, because measured by the absolute standard it must not be contradivine, but divinely willed. And the outlet being thus cut off that God does not will evil, but He is bound by an eternal opponent power, only the issue remains possible that the cause of actual evil is absolutely not to be found in the Divine sphere, and that a necessity of evil to be thence derived is impossible. Consequently it must have the last principle of its reality in the causality of the creature somehow, whilst the possibility of evil is of course constituted by God for the sake of good.

[1] The latter is the case with Schleiermacher, since he says that the combination of man in a state of development with mature moral consciousness communicates to man a premature knowledge, so to speak, of the entire moral problem, which anticipates the stage he has reached and excels his powers; for, regarding such things as he is unable to do as obligatory, the consciousness of falling behind his duty or sin is thus augmented. Such a consciousness would be wrong; and such a dereliction of what is not truly duty would only be apparent sin.

D.—*Dogmatic Doctrine of the Origin and Universality of Sin.*

§ 81.

The origin of evil in general has its adequate ground in creaturely freedom. Only the possibility of evil can therefore coincide with the creation, and God cannot be called the author of its reality.

1. The reality of evil generally according to its origin.

If evil had no adequate cause, it would be apparent merely. But it is no semblance unhappily, as conscience and experience show, and all derivations of it which transform it into mere appearance, contradict conscience, and are a new victory of evil albeit in the form of error or appearance. But all derivations of evil which refer it to God must transmute it into appearance. Consequently the causality of evil is to be sought outside of God. The theories of finitude and of the dualism of two primary principles seek indeed to prove this. But not merely is it true, as has been shown, that they can only be inferred, if they themselves relegate the origin of evil to the Divine sphere itself; but generally it is to be said that every theory of the *necessary* origin of evil whatever must cause that origin to be referred to God, God being the supreme principle of all necessity. It thus follows,—not to make evil appearance merely by conceiving it as necessity,—that the non-necessity of its origin is to be taught; otherwise the ethical necessity of *good*, its absolute obligatoriness and its unconditioned duty would be excluded by virtue of an opposing physical necessity of evil, which would dominate reality.

2. But the necessary denial of the physical necessity of evil altogether is only the negative side to the *positive* statement as to the place where the causality of evil lies. The following consideration forms the transition to the positive cause. It is not merely the physical necessity of *evil* which is an impossibilty, but also equally the physical necessity of *good*. Freedom, that is, the power of the personal ethical self-determination of the rational creature, was necessary to the ethical. Without the possibility of choice we should be self-

less, mere physical beings, moved by unconquerable impulses which would be implanted within us from without or from within, moral automata, and not responsible persons, whose love to God, being free, is a worthy gift even for God Himself. Freedom, imprinted upon man at creation, is therefore to be straightway demanded to the end and in the interests that space be made for the possibility of an ethical existence and process, and not as a mere shift for the explanation of evil.[1] If then freedom is supposed, as is necessary if God would have a moral world, there is at the same time given the necessary possibility of evil, the necessary existence of a mutable, mobile, creaturely principle endowed with the ability of being an adequate cause of actual evil, but not with the necessity of being such, and therein lies therefore the positive complement to the denial of the necessity of actual evil. Recourse to creaturely freedom for the elucidation of evil is therefore not arbitrary, but necessary; but as recourse to the caprice of the creature, recourse to possible irrationality. If therefore the origin of actual sin in the race generally is placed before the eye, the question is not to be raised, why man has determined for evil and not otherwise? Evil cannot be referred to any further basis than free will, which will be, and would concentrate in itself, unfettered freedom, and absolutely determines how it wills. Not merely as if we might not know a wider base, but because there is no other, and this is sufficient. If we substituted a necessitating base for the actually extant evil act of will, instead of stopping at the will which proved itself arbitrariness as it need not be but as it was capable of being, we should deny freedom, and with it also the personally ethical in the strict sense, and be compelled to have recourse somehow to one of the theories recognised to be untenable.

3. When we are referred to creaturely freedom for the explanation of evil, in which the ability inheres to act by its own arbitration, this might be so understood that freedom is mere

[1] It is true that all good is not the work or product of man, and his freedom of itself apart from God, but is the impulse and work of the Divine Spirit, though not by irresistible constraint. Therefore the good effected by God still participates in freedom, it being possible to withstand the impulse of the Spirit of God who is at one with the true nature of man, and man being capable of falling out of the unity with God. For more on this, see § 130.

arbitrariness; the objection might be taken that freedom might then lay hold upon good in a merely arbitrary manner, *i.e.* it might not serve good. But freedom is not mere ability to choose; we are capable of allowing freedom not to issue in the ability to act arbitrarily; indeed, the latter constitutes only one moment of its idea. Man is never sheer absolute indifference, as Catholic theologians especially would say; a plurality of impulses and mental representations is in him, and possible evil is reprobated by what is innermost in him. It is only good which allows the will to become absolutely one with the essential being of man (with his destination) and with the good Spirit of God. Therefore in good alone is a pure unity and freedom possible that knows no discord. If man came pure from the hand of God, he had a good constitution, although not one ethically preserved and confirmed, such a constitution indeed as was nevertheless exposed to the temptation to desire to be autocratic by the disclaimer of humility. If now he remained in a good condition, and confirmed that condition by desiring to remain in communion with God, and by repelling the temptation, this would not be arbitrariness; for he allowed the good Spirit of God to rule within him, who stands in unity with the true nature of man; of the various possible grounds of determination he allowed the rational to work upon him, he did not wish to be self-willed or egoistical; he forbore opposition to the good Spirit of God. If, on the contrary, he yielded to the allurement of the temptation, that would be arbitrariness, freedom, which was allowed to sway, emancipating itself from commandment. In his freedom, man, although he cannot create any matter, but can only operate upon matter already given, has a power of decision purely out of himself as to what motives he will allow to become grounds of determination. There certainly lies therein, and this is the miracle of freedom, an analogy to the creative power which brings something out of nothing, only that here the products are acts, not things; these acts presuppose a material to which they are related, but nevertheless are determining forces over things, and therefore themselves belong to the sphere of being. It is therefore to be maintained that at the commencement, as it came from the creative hand of God, humanity did not begin with sin and sinfulness, but that the beginnings are to be thought of as pure. Man could then either continue in the good innate in him, could affirm the same, and thus advance from natural good to a good disposition by the suppression of false possibility, could advance, that is, to the moral stage which is ever ready for renunciation and sacrifice for the sake of the command, or he could follow the lead of the temptation, prefer the momentary selfish desire, and fall into arbitrariness and deceptive autocracy.

4. But now the empirical *universality* of sin confronts us, and, being undeniably an evil propensity not first incurred by the personal act of individuals, but natural or innate, not only forms a glaring contrast to that original purity, but suggests the question how it harmonizes with freedom and the idea of guilt as well as with the Christian idea of God. This problem calls for its separate consideration.

§ 82.—*Continuation.—Explanation of the Empirical Universality of Evil.*

As the individual free evil deed does not vanish without traces, but produces an evil state (*eine böse Zuständlichkeit*), so inherent evil (*das zuständliche Böse*) cannot remain isolated in such a species of being as man; the community is seized thereby, and that not simply by the agency of teaching, example, and a common evil spirit; a still more original mode of its continuous passage from one individual to another is established in the nature of man as a secondary causality, by which the origination of other human beings is brought about, as well as, on the other hand, in the nature of evil which perverts the various powers and functions of human nature, and having become inherent draws the coherence of the race into the sphere of its power. Penetrating generations and nations, inasmuch as they arise from sinful beings, and ramifying everywhere into new forms, sin takes its destructive course through humanity. From both causes together the empirical universality of innate evil results in all who have their birth within the coherence of the race; and since experience does not point to a sinless being within this circle, the Biblical statement is dogmatically verified, that the first men, though created pure, were sinners already, and it is from them that the sinfulness of the race proceeds. But with such a statement new problems disclose themselves, and it is requisite so to frame the doctrine of the universally innate evil propensity or of the universal human need of redemption, that neither the personal moral freedom, nor the truth of the idea of guilt, nor the ethical idea of God, may be violated.

*Observation* 1.—It will be again remembered in this connection, that the fact of the universal need of redemption has its substantiation in experience and in the Christian consciousness, itself essentially an experience of redemption, and by no means first awaits its substantiation from a dogmatic theory upon the origin of this universality. This need is certain even without an absolutely satisfactory derivation. But the correct derivation of the universal fact is of course of importance in another aspect, namely, in order not to violate the idea of God, or the idea of guilt, or the idea of the human genus by false derivations.

*Observation* 2.—The inquiry into the origin of evil has necessarily conducted us to freedom as the creaturely cause. But the universality in which sin enters does not seem to coincide therewith. For universality is not yet explained by freedom of itself, but requires another method of explanation. In close connection therewith, the two questions immediately open: first, if sin is universally innate, and not contracted by us individually in time by a free personal fall, how do *freedom* and the *consciousness of guilt* square in any way with such a view? Secondly, how does such universality harmonize with the idea of God, from whom only good can come? By the manner in which the first problem, the proof of the universality of sin, is treated, will the fate of the other two be conditioned. In order then to solve this first problem, we may either start from individual freedom, and thence seek to draw the lines which lead to a generic state of need of redemption; or secondly and conversely, we may start from the genus in order to reach guilt from that point, and the consciousness of guilt felt by individual personalities. Or, finally, in order to lay with certainty sufficient store by the generic life as well as by the personal freedom and guilt of individuals, we may regard the generic life and the personal life as two factors which are not to be derived apart, although pertaining to the idea of man and equally authorized. The two first inquiries are alike, in that they favour the one of the factors under consideration at the expense of the other,—in that in the first the generic character of humanity is from the outset left out of account, whilst in the second freedom and personal guilt are not accounted.

I.—*First Class.*

1. If we start from the personal *freedom of the individual*, or the *individualistic point of view*, the recourse to the power of evil example first presents itself as a means of arriving at the universality of evil in our race. Pelagius himself does not deny the universality of sinfulness; but he supposes moral freedom to be essentially and equally present at all times, and rejects both the passage of the actual sin of the individual into an evil state, and still more the passage of the sinfulness in the race to new individuals of the same. But if the universality of evil is not easily denied, the more frequent is the opinion that man comes forth from every act of his with his freedom intact, and in like manner the opinion of a *naturalis sanctitas*, with which children come into being. A certain reflection of paradisaic innocence does indeed rest on the age of childhood, on its joy, its ingenuousness and its gaiety. This attractive and loveable character is especially found in this age, because there are therein no conscious evil acts as yet; it need not therefore as yet bear within itself the scar of a sinful past. But when those, who feel themselves compelled to find all moral worth exclusively in freedom and its exercise, speak of an innate *sanctitas*, this is manifestly illogical. Worth and significance can only be ascribed in a moral sense to what is innate, if it does not depend upon freedom simply whether a thing has a moral worth, towards which opinion this first class tends. This class must in all consistency start from a state of moral

indifference in all. But there early shows itself as a matter of experience, and not only as a consequence of the misuse of developed spiritual faculties, an inclination to evil. Whence then the universality of evil, if every individual begins his life pure and fully free? If reference is made to the evil example of the community, that is to postpone the question instead of answering it.[1] Whence come then the suborners, if none are seduced but by the community? How can we really believe in a universal natural purity, or even in the inviolateness of the freedom of all, if there is not one who resists the seduction? By what right do we believe in a power which is nowhere evident? But it is also an internal *contradiction* to teach the universal integrity of freedom, and at the same time to wish to derive the universality of evil from evil example or the influence of the community. Either these influences produce an effect in a merely casual manner, and in that case they explain nothing, or they are an actual causality, as indeed no one can challenge the influence of education, of the common spirit, of custom. But if the latter is acknowledged, the conception of freedom is surrendered, which isolates the individual from the genus; and, as against Augustine, Pelagius has no longer any right to the initial opposition. Disputes may still occur on the manner of the derivation of evil, and on its measure; but the derivation itself, and the influence of the coherence of the race, stands sure. The principle

[1] The right must be conceded to decline any answer and simply to remain satisfied with the fact of the universality of sin, although such resignation may always be scientifically blameworthy. But when Ritschl, who formerly sought a gain in avoiding important theological questions by appealing to our ignorance, straightway asserts a knowledge both of the fact that every man is born even now pure and free, and also of the fact that each one is first drawn into the sin which is dominant in the community, we may pardonably ask on the one hand whence he has gained this knowledge, and on the other hand how he squares the two facts, or whence the community has become sinful, consisting as it does of these very individuals? So decisive an influence of the community is no more easily harmonized with the Divine government in its relation to freedom, than is the assumption of a natural abnormity of individuals. And as far as the Person of Christ is concerned, in order to secure sinlessness to it as opposed to so certainly efficient an influence of the community, as Ritschl maintains it to be, a special Divine endowment is scarcely more dispensable than in the case of the assumption of a natural abnormity in all those born of the race.

of freedom, as of that which alone decides everything, is given up.

2. That actual evil does not remain without consequences, but determines inherent being, is recognized by the PRE-EXISTENCE THEORY, as well as the universality of the need of redemption. Its more recent important advocates have also purified the theory from the imperfect form it had in Origen, who regarded this earthly life with this body of ours as a state of punishment, who indeed would have derived individuality generally from the use of freedom. For Julius Müller, in opposition to such a dualism of body and soul, assumes that corporeality belonged to the definition of man from the beginning, and that individuality was made by God. In like manner he repudiates Schelling's doctrine of pre-existence, according to which all in an intelligible act of freedom have so determined themselves beyond the limits of time, whether that act be good or evil, that they all bring with them into this life a character *indelebilis*. For he sees that in such a case some would not need redemption, and others would be no longer capable thereof.[1] Julius Müller has done the service in Dogmatics which should always be estimated highly, of having thought out to the end a scheme of solution wherein it must be manifest whether the adopted method is practicable or not. His theory already called for mention previously in connection with the question whether evil generally, and therefore at its commencement, is to be regarded as spiritual selfishness. We saw that if this question be answered in the affirmative, we *must* pass over to the theory of pre-existence, because spiritual selfishness is not the first thing in mundane development. Now its grounding of the universality of sin in man is to be proved, which seems according to it to lie in the fact that the spirits who did not declare themselves in their pre-temporal existence directly against God, but who gave to their love of themselves a preponderance over their love to God,—and with the exception of Christ these spirits alone,—have become transplanted to this earth. His leading positions are—(1) The actual fact of the universality of sin

[1] II. pp. 494-516, edit. 2; pp. 486, etc., edit. 1. According to Julius Müller, a relic of such *character indelebilis* may still be seen in the difference between demonic and human evil.

necessitates our acceptance of a disturbance and enfeeblement of freedom; (2) the ground of this disturbance might possibly be sought in the midst of this present life, in an act by means of which man passed from a sinless existence into one that was disturbed. But such an act no one knows how to indicate. We find ourselves in the midst of sin with an awakened moral consciousness, and we know not how. Nor does it aid us to seek in the commencement of the conscious life an individual fall for every one. We have no remembrance of such a fall, and remembrance could not be absent. Add the restricted measure of consciousness and moral force in childhood. Still every evil deed is reckoned by conscience as guilt, and guilt points back to an ability to do otherwise, whilst the whole temporal life shows, instead of this freedom, a mixture of freedom and dependence. (3) If therefore, notwithstanding, the testimony of conscience which attributes our sins to us, and the testimony of religion which says that God is not the originator but the enemy of sin, are true, and if, as distinct from a pure commencement by self-determination and self-decision without being necessitated in any way, the freedom of the temporal life which is so cloven and limited floats baselessly in the air, the course of the inquiry compels us, he concludes, to overstep the region of time. Freedom must have its origin in the sphere of the extra-temporal, where alone there is room for the pure and unconditioned self-decision of every one who is not found himself in the temporal life. Therein, he thinks, the unfathomable depths of our consciousness of guilt first reveal themselves, and there is here found the solution for the riddle of that inextinguishable melancholy and sadness especially in nobler natures which forms the hidden basis of all human consciousness. There also lies therein, he says, a guarantee for the immortality of man; especially is the antinomy thereby resolved between the universal rooting of evil in human nature, and the personal guilt and accountability of the individual.[1]

[1] This theory, expounded with seductive dexterity, is held more or less by Beneke, Rückert, Fichte the younger (*Anthropologie*, 1857), whilst it is combated by Bruch, *Die Präexistenz der Seele*, 1859, and others. Compare my notice of Julius Müller's work in Reuter's *Repertorium*, 1845.

But the following considerations stand in the way of this theory. The generic interdependence of humanity, as well as the bond between the body and the soul, would become something external, something contingent. There would be no common sin or no sin of the entire race, but only a sum of individual sins and trespasses. But why are parents ashamed for their children, and conversely? The slackening of the significance of the coherence of the race in reference to sin must also have important consequences for the *homousia* of Christ with us,[1] for the doctrine of atonement and that of the Church. Matt. xviii. 16 already intimates that our nature, as submitted to the influence of the coherence of the race, is an important element in our redemption. With the powers the race has inasmuch as Christ belongs to it, we shall enter into connection, becoming children again, in order to attain redemption by means of this association. On the one hand, the theory of Julius Müller endeavours to enhance the *intensity* of the personal consciousness of sin in reference to the innate evil inclination; and on the other hand, this enhancement takes place at the cost that no place is left for the sin and guilt of the race and the consciousness of such sin, and thus the *extent* of the consciousness of sin is diminished. That inextinguishable melancholy and sadness in the profounder minds, which he so beautifully describes, has certainly not merely our isolated personality in view, but is more completely explained from the consciousness that we are all a family bound together with solidarity, and at the same time a family which is deeply fallen and reduced. This is clear from the fact that the feeling does not vanish with personal redemption, but becomes a powerful impulse to render possible for our brethren the liberation of conscience from the consciousness of guilt and punishment.[2]

But, as has already been pointed out, it is inconceivable that we should have been endowed as ethical beings at the very commencement of our existence with such a power of freedom, and with so acute an intelligence, as this theory

---

[1] Even Christ must then have been pre-existent as to His humanity, either ununited with the λόγος (which would form a kind of Cerinthianism), or as the God-man, with which his birth of Mary would be inconsistent.
[2] Col. i. 24.

must necessarily presuppose, if that primary act, the transcendent deed, is to bear the whole weight of the fault attaching to the consequences which followed. The explanation of the Genesis answers far more according to its essential import to the nature of the case. It points to the first fall, which it does not transport into the present, but allows to have happened under earthly relations. In Julius Müller, Adam's fall only artificially retains a precarious significance for the whole race. The hypothesis of Müller does not really explain the universality of evil. It does not follow that because every one lives on the earth he must therefore be a sinner, for in that case the earthly laws and relations of life would be regarded as such as are only possible in sin,—a reasoning which would lead us to a superior connection between sin and the earth together with the earthly relations, and which might possibly in Rothe have a meaning. Müller must add a new element, the Divine ordinance which convenes only fallen spirits upon the earth. But this does not follow from the theory of pre-existence. If the transplanting of all to the earth is to have an internal basis, mortality must at least be regarded as a punishment and a means of education,—a view which would incline to the ancient view of Origen, from which Müller wished to keep himself distinct when he said that mundane corporeity had belonged to the definition of man from the beginning.

3. A THIRD theory of the first class is that, already referred to under another point of view, of Theodore of Mopsuestia. He applied himself to the solution of the problem by the *scientia Dei media*, and thought that God foresaw that men would become sinful, and He has therefore clothed them with this body ordained to decay ($\phi\theta o \rho \acute{a}$). But the disorder of the body taxes the spirit, cripples its freedom, and hence sin everywhere arises.[1] Attention has been previously directed to the Manichæizing of this derivation of evil. But even if it were said that God had been able to combine men in the coherence

---

[1] Similarly von Hofmann, who assumes with Reinhard and Hahn an infection caused by the eating of the forbidden fruit, Gen. iii., whereby the *peccatum originale* ceased to fall under an ethical heading and became a mere corporeal disease, whilst Zwingli thinks this disease at any rate spiritual. Comp. Philippi, vol. iii. pp. 218, etc.

of the race which produces sin, because He foresaw that they would have sinned even though they had remained left to themselves, still nothing would be explained thereby; the problem would simply be repeated. Indeed, such a view would lead to an intellectual existence of men before God, in which they could contract guilt and punishment. But this intellectual existence, to serve its end, must become a real pre-existence.

II.—*Second Class.—Theories where the Generic Character preponderates.*

The endowment with individual freedom not sufficing for the derivation of the universality of sin, others have turned to the opposite side. In this case also three forms are possible and have been prosecuted:—The theory of representation, that of solicitation, and lastly that of direct transmittal by virtue of the *scientia Dei media.*

1. The theory of REPRESENTATION by our first parents in its various forms has been previously criticized (see pp. 341, etc. vol. II.). It might suffice if we had existed as persons in Adam, a view which would present a special form of the theory of real pre-existence. And the former theory must also succumb to the same reasoning which was brought against the latter. The inconceivability of Adam's having the double significance of the totality of humanity and of a single person has been discussed. And were he regarded as the covenant-head, such a covenant, which should determine the sinfulness as well as the weal and woe of the entire posterity, could not exist without their conscious acquiescence. It would thus appear, to take the simplest case, that Adam is to be regarded as the head only, that is, as the real beginning of the race, who bequeathed what he had, not his actual sin indeed, but his sinfulness and his guilt, both of which are an evil inheritance. From the nature which was depraved and burdened with guilt by the Fall, the universality of sin would be derived, inasmuch as the new individuals of the race would merely be regarded as a continuation of that nature, as new leaves, so to speak, on the tree of humanity. Everything evil would accordingly be a mere effect of the inherited nature. The

Formula of Concord has passages of such a kind,[1] notwithstanding that expressions of an opposite nature which refer to the freedom of the individual are also found in it.[2] If we halt at the physical nature of man, man would not be thought of as a person or as a subject, but only as an individualizing or a special form of the manifestation of nature, without an internal self-existence, without a responsible centre of spiritual life; he would merely be a sheer exemplar or an accident in the human race. But this contradicts the lofty idea of personality, which the N. T., even Genesis and the Law, and the Evangelical Church especially, maintain; man would not in such a case be an ethical being. The subject for our guilt would also be wanting. Moral determination and responsibility belongs to the idea of man as distinguished from mere nature, and these require subjectivity and personality. Should the natural basis not simply be one element but everything in sin, a naturalism threatens us, as Julius Müller has rightly reminded us, which, consistently carried out, menaces the doctrine of the judgment of the world and of the immortality of the soul.[3] Redemption must also be transformed into a merely physical process. If all sins arise from the nature of Adam, then do his sins also arise from his nature? If not, but if they arise from his freedom, still his act is not ours. His personality cannot pertain to all his posterity. A physical constitution may be common to many, but not a personality. From Adam's nature, which we possess, his first sin cannot be derived without falling into some mode of deterministic thought already considered; that sin can only be derived from his free personality. All these theories of representation, though they may regard Adam as the *principium et caput seminale* or *federale*, fail to present an equalization of Adam and his posterity, and just as little present an actual explanation of the enigma. If the descendants were a mere act of the race, the warranted element of Creationism, as has been previously shown, would be excluded, the race would be constituted a kind of world-soul midway between God and man, or a kind of Deistic *middle-being,* and the immediateness of the connection between

---

[1] Pp. 577, 21; 640, 2.
[2] Pp. 619, 12; 640 b, 12; 808, 39. Conf. Aug. cap. xviii.; *De libero arbitrio.*
[3] J. Müller, vol. ii. p. 430.

God and man would be imperilled. But God has not abdicated His creative power in favour of the race, but He uses it through the race in such a way that every individual is a special Divine thought. Finally, *did all sin certainly come from the primary sin*, and were it simply an act of the physical constitution or of the race, unbelief in Christ must necessarily ensue; that is to say, whilst the universal earthly sinfulness made the manifestation of Christ necessary, it also made this manifestation fruitless, it made free appropriation impossible, it necessitated that none should believe; only those could be magically saved whom God had elected thereto. Those who did not believe would succumb to a necessity of nature, they were just the non-elect, and thus absolute and particular predestination would be the end.

2. THE THEORY OF SOLICITATION. For these and similar reasons, many have thought of original sin in such a manner that it simply opposes free will as an enticement to evil. Freedom acquiescing, sin and guilt arise. This is the doctrine of the Arminians, for example.[1] But if everything depends on free decision alone, it would follow that all natural and inward disorder and abnormity, which works to seduce, is not in itself sinful, and cannot be estimated in any way ethically; freedom is opposed thereto in a manner which is still indifferent, and it is only by the appropriating act of freedom that it becomes sinfulness. But impure or uncharitable and proud thoughts which casually arise also belong to the realm of sin; they originate in the ground of the heart, in a spiritual basis of disposition which belongs to our personality, and is not by any means a thing innocent and morally indifferent; it pollutes the man. Not merely is intentional evil sin, but there may also be unintentional sin; indeed, the two kinds often pass imperceptibly the one into the other. The assumption that evil absolutely arises only by the free act of acquiescence or of the intentional succumbing to temptation, would also include the

---

[1] Limborch, *Theologia Christiana*, bk. 5, cap. xv. 15, says that natural *impuritas* is *physica*, non *moralis*, and is not properly *peccatum*. So the Tridentine Canons already teach (edit. Richter, p. 15) concerning *Concupiscentia*, which is said not to be *vere et proprie peccatum*. Similarly Steudel, *Glaubenslehre*, p. 196; Reinhard, *Vorles. ü. Dogmatik*, pp. 287, etc. Comp. Philippi, vol. iii. pp. 56, etc., who, incorrectly however, attributes this opinion to Beck, *Lehrwissenschaft*, p. 291.

belief that it was also in the free power of man to abstain from all sin and all evil, which would be a contradiction both to the universal need of redemption, and to experience, which knows none who have abstained from all acquiescence in sin whatever. If the case so stands, there is no explanation presented by the theory of solicitation how universal sinfulness can square with individual freedom and responsibility.

3. FINALLY, the solution is not to be sought on this side by means of the *Scientia Dei media*. The descendants of Adam, it is said in this instance, have not their powers lessened by their dependence upon the nature which has been corrupted by him, *i.e.* in comparison with Adam, who had to choose freely. For God, it is said, foreknew that we should all have acted similarly in his place if it had been our lot to have been the first individual. In the empirical world, therefore, God has been able to bring all men into the position in which they were determined by the consequences of Adam's deed and became partakers of original sin.[1] But even if no one may venture to assert that he would not have fallen in Adam's position, it is still inconsistent with the moral consciousness, and with the true idea of moral responsibility, for God to treat men according to what they have not done, but according to what they might have done in Adam's place as foreseen by Him. If this view proves anything, there is latent therein the assumption of a universal necessity for the fall of all free beings; it thus recurs to Determinism. Supposing freedom to be guaranteed, this theory could only have a meaning if all persons had existed in Adam and had come in him to personal free decision.

Surveying our path, we have on each of the two sides,— the one of which starts from individual freedom and the other from the race,—three theories, and those of the one class answer to those of the other. To the pre-existence of all as spiritual atoms, corresponds as its most direct opposite the theory of the representation of all by one man Adam, assuming as it does a kind of pre-existence of all in the Adamitic unity of race. To the Pelagian attempt at mediation, which only concedes temptation by evil example, corresponds on the other side the theory of solicitation by the peculiar constitution of

[1] This is also contained in the theory of Adam as the divinely ordained covenant head.

the race, by the inherited tendency. Lastly, to the theory of Theodore of Mopsuestia corresponds the last-mentioned turn of thought;—because of the free sin of all, not really existent but apprehended by the *scientia media* of God, God is supposed to have made the empirical arrangement which draws us into sin, and to have given in the former theory the mortal body, and in the latter the natural evil propensity. But a satisfactory adjustment of the two factors, equally authorized as they are by the nature of man, has not been attained in any of these theories; indeed, the fact of the universality of sin and of the consciousness of guilt is so explained by them that either one factor or the other is deprived of its full weight.

### § 83.—*Continuation.*

III.—*Reconciliation of the Claims of the Generic Nature and the Personal Life* (comp. § 73).

There is a sin of the race in which we all participate as members thereof, and which is certainly the ground of a universal need of redemption, although it is not yet our personal guilt. This generic sin has the character of the morally exceptionable or of evil, although it is not decisive of the definitive worth or the fate of man. The members of the human race, on the other hand, are also destined to personal responsibility, and there is also a personal guilt which is not the effect of generic sin, and has not a universality equally referable to all, constituting them nevertheless from a new side needy of redemption, and also causing a common guilt. The definitive work and the ultimate fate of the individual are annexed to personal decision.

*Observation.*—If the aim were to regard the right of the generic and the personal consciousness as equal, it might appear unimportant with which of the two we begin. But seeing that it is a law for us to gain control over ourselves only gradually, because otherwise there would be no place for self-culture, we must not commence with freedom. Nature or the generic life either has a great power in the *origin* of humanity, or has no more than a contingent power. For the development, even the sinful development, always increasingly conducts to independent personality. To begin with the personal aspect, as Pre-existentianism does, is to make it difficult to find a secure place afterwards for the generic life. That, on the other hand, the reverse way does not necessarily turn out to be a menace to the rights of personality, a guarantee is found in the fact that the individual as a matter of experience gradually lifts himself up to independence from the bosom of the generic life, just as the moral influences of the race upon individuals, seen in customs, culture, and education, have personality for their goal. To master the matter we shall split the question into two problems; we must accurately distinguish the question as to the sinfulness of the innate evil propensity from the question as to its relation to guilt.

1. THE UNIVERSAL SPREAD OF SIN NECESSITATED BY THE CONNECTION OF THE RACE, SO FAR AS THE CONNECTION WITH SINFUL PARENTS REACHES.

Evil which has become inherent in the race (§ 78) passes over to the new individuals of the same not as personal punishment any more than actual sinful act, but as inherent abnormity and irregularity, which is not a mere physical evil, but evil with an ethical reference.

The transition in question follows as a matter of course from the secondary causality of individual human beings, through whom the origination of ever new individuals of the race obtains. The doctrine of the conservation of the race had to show[1] that the secondary causality ought not to be dislodged by virtue of the idea of creation (the element of creation). The individual, it is true, is not a mere manifestation of the race. God applies to the origination of every single man a special creative thought and act of will. But the individual is nothing isolated; being thought and willed in and with the thought of the race, the individual is consummated by means of the race as an original causality likewise at hand and endowed and conserved by God with power to act, although we are not in a position adequately to demonstrate the share taken by each of these factors. Supposing it certain that the human

[1] § 43.

race is willed by God to be a secondary causality which essentially co-operates to its self-reproduction in individuals; it is further equally clear that the secondary causalities can only work according to their own peculiar character. Should sin, inherent abnormity, penetrate therefore into the bearers of the generic life, there is only left the choice between such working as is possible and natural to secondary causalities according to their constitution and the withdrawal of the power of such working; therefore the permission of the destruction of the secondary causalities, whereby the class of beings such as ours, who are really bound to one another by the cohesion of the race, would be excluded. For a new establishment of our race by immediate creation, without the intervention of the connection with the race, would not be a continuation of this race of ours, but the establishment of a race wholly new. If the connection of the human individuals were done away with which placed them under the influence of the race, the human class of rational beings would vanish; only those would remain whom we call angels. If, therefore, the character of the reproductive powers of the race becomes sinful, the certain assumption is justified, that every product of the inherited powers will bear within itself the traces of its origin. To this conclusion Traducianism is not necessary to the exclusion of Creationism, but only the elements of Traducianism which cannot be wanting if there is to be any mention of secondary causalities. With this experience coincides, which always shows, in good and in evil, hereditary types in peoples, nations, races, families, in whom the sin of the race is made specific.

Now this inheritance, although it is not the act of the individuals who are physically connected with the race, is *to be attributed to the realm of evil*, even if the question as to its relation to the idea of guilt must still lie outside our immediate consideration. If nothing but what was originally at least the act of an individual's free choice, his desert or his guilt, were to be considered in a moral relation and in reference to the individual's worth, then education, indeed all culture of freedom by influence from without, only effects what was absolutely indifferent or worthless in a moral sense. But is man this subjective and self-reliant atom merely?

Has he not undeniably within him a side related to the race and to the influences of the common life? The eye of the Divine justice at any rate takes men as they are; but they are not atoms without relation, they have a generic character belonging to them. Such an isolation, according to which the moral, which is nevertheless implanted in us—in our feeling, our cognition, and our will—by the influence of others, has no application to us, is an untruth, not prompted by true personality and its interests. For the latter does not suffer by a recognition of the coherence of good and evil in the world, by virtue whereof even another's good and evil may harmoniously work for our future worth. Personality does not suffer by a recognition of a common or joint sin; rather does personal consciousness show a greater vigour if it accepts the recognition of a common and joint sin, where such exists. By means of the generic consciousness we are able to regard the victory of good in the world as a common joy, as a common honour of the race, and similarly we are able to consider as a concern in which we mutually share whatever has not so befallen by means of our personal choice or act. And the elements of both kinds, even those of the sentiment of a common sin (or guilt), are no base things, but have a greatness in them, and are required by the nature of Christianity and love, which do not isolate themselves. And this inheritance of which we are here speaking is no mere deformity, no mere physical evil; it is moral evil. It contradicts the normal constitution or moral soundness of mankind; it is a contradiction in its own nature which is to be vanquished if the morally normal is to be reinstated by moral action, not by a mere self-perfected development (which must necessarily be a development of sin), but by conversion and new birth. This constitution is therefore *displeasing to God*. God can have no pleasure in a constitution which sullies the rational being and distorts the Divine likeness; and such a constitution must be considered as devoting to death, excluding from the enjoyment of holy and blessed communion with God, and as making redemption necessary. Further, this constitution is evil, inasmuch as it originally arises from sin, and is a mere continuation of inherent sin, and will not be idle in displaying itself in new sins and in exerting an influence upon the conscious and actual will. And it is certainly not the proximate generations merely which are related to such inherent and inherited evil; an evil propensity of ancestors which has rested, so to speak, in the proximate parents, often breaks out in the descendants, so that the parents become the introducers of an irregularity slumbering in the natural ground of the family, and not merely of their own inherent state, whence the whole interlacing of the race into one joint sin becomes especially clear and visible.[1] He who would impeach this inheritance bequeathed by his parents, impeaches his parents also for giving him life. For, supposing them to give life, they could not do otherwise than transmit their own character. They could not give what they did not possess. Still more perverse if possible would be the impeachment of the Divine justice and holiness, seeing that it would gainsay that God should will a self-reproducing race, *i.e.* our race, at all. Only this can be said: God could only will to preserve this race after it sinned, together with its self-reproduction whereby it must bear this sinful character, if in spite of this sinfulness the preservation of our class of beings was not a greater evil than its annihilation, but rather remained a relative good. And this was the case, if sinfulness remained vincible. And thus we see that for this reason alone, or for the sake of the redemption which was still possible, God could preserve our race, could permit the propagation of the same, though sin was thus communicated. Even in this sense, the word that everything has its existence in Christ,[2] has its truth. But not merely does the holiness of God very well consist with the inheritance of sin, but it would be silly ingratitude to arraign God because we are not born without that inheritance. For the arraigner might, it is true, be born without the inheritance of sin; but in this case, as has been shown, he could not have come into existence as a being of the human race. Manifestly he speaks foolishly, who by what he says or demands annuls the presupposition under which alone he is able to speak. If I surrender myself as a human being, and surrender the conditions under which alone this being of mine could come into existence, I surrender my existence

[1] Comp. Schleiermacher, *Christl. Glaube*, I. § 71; comp. p. 402.
[2] Col. i. 17.

also, and therefore I cannot at the moment of surrender again presuppose my existence, or demand anything in its behalf.

§ 83.—*Continuation.*—*Relation between Generic Sin and the Guilt of the Individual.*

1. NECESSITY OF THE RECOGNITION OF DISTINCTIVE STAGES IN PERSONALITY.

If, as has been shown, the individual is unavoidably determined by generic sin, can we still speak of moral worth or of guilt? At this point the attacks of the Catholic system, and later those of Rationalism, especially array themselves against the Reformation doctrine. The latter doctrine, as we saw, is not yet satisfactorily settled; but in what direction its whole tendency points, is to be gathered from the fact that on the one hand in the interests of the universal need of redemption, as opposed to Pelagianism, the connection with the race is emphasized, and on the other hand personality is accentuated in the interests of personal assurance of the forgiveness of guilt and sin. The problem before us will be solved, when we have succeeded in so allowing the idea of personality to show itself or operate in the generic character described from which we start, that the doubts are thus resolved which arise from the moral idea, and especially from the conception of guilt, an opposition to the teaching of the Bible and the Church. At the end of our discussion we have again to consider that it is essential to human personality, and at the same time to the idea of guilt, to be allied to a development or a history. From lower stages in which it almost vanishes and is only potentially present, personality only raises itself to itself, to the actuality of the formal functions which constitute itself, conformably with the fact that every man is willed by God to be an individual who has to establish his moral worth or worthlessness by his own participation. *Every human being must become an actual personality, whether good or evil.* Man is created, it is true, for ethical good; but neither good nor evil attains its full precision and personal ripeness until the subject is in a position to participate freely in his self-culture, and at the same time to definitively determine his own fate. It is true that, if subjective freedom is made the sole principle of positive worth and blessedness instead of regarding it as a necessary link in the process, this is the Pelagian mode of thought. But, as has been shown, it is no less true that he who says that a mere inherited constitution can ultimately decide somehow or other upon worth and fate, falls absolutely into the standpoint of Predestinationism and a physical or magical doctrine of Grace.[1]

The doctrine of Man has already presented *individuality*, *subjectivity*, and *personality* as the stages through which generally the idea of man is realized. If this is so, corresponding stages must be given in the idea of guilt, and we are dealing with what is abstract and untrue, as well as with what is contradictory to Scripture, if we apply that idea equally everywhere. At these different stages the relation between the generic life and personality will be differently constituted. And the appropriate estimation will be most securely formed of the idea of personality, if we place the idea of *guilt* in relation to the different stages of personality. The scale of guilt will have to correspond with the leading features of the scale of sin treated previously.[2]

*Observation.*—The complete idea of guilt has a threefold application or relation. First it is related to the cause by which a thing is determined. In this sense the idea of guilt refers to the *past*. The second significance has reference to the *present*, and denotes the influential working of past acts, the continuous bond which unites the act even when long done with the doer, and confers on him responsibility, worth or worthlessness. The third aspect here comes in, which concerns the *future*, the aspect of the idea of guilt according to which man is subjected to righteous punishment for the evil deed, and is bound to do the good he did not do.[3] In our present inquiry we are pre-eminently concerned with the application of the idea of guilt in the first sense, which refers to causality ($\alpha i\tau i\alpha$), and which lays the foundation for the other meanings, itself, together with the idea of accountability, running through very different stages.

[1] See §§ 31, 40.     [2] § 77.     [3] Comp. § 78, 1, and § 88.

## 2. THE STAGES.

A.—*The First Stage, or the Time previous to the Awakening of the Moral Self-Consciousness.*

Man at his origin is not for a moment an individual outwardly self-existent. As an embryo, the child, still living a life preponderatingly associated with the mother, is assuredly a determination of the same; the mother is the higher logical subject, and rules the nature of the child. Although the soul is already existent, it is not yet a self-cognitive or self-willing soul; its personality is as yet not actually but only potentially existent; it cannot therefore as yet prove itself a moral being.

After its birth the child is an externally at least separate and self-existent life,—an *individual*; it is actually thus a separate bearer of predicates as a logical subject, and these predicates are actually to be attributed to it, because they together constitute it. The abnormity of the race which devolves upon the child, is now its abnormity attributable to it as a separate being.

In the further course of development the human individual apprehends itself as an intellectual "I," or *Subject*, and straightway learns to contrast itself with the world, to limit itself by the world. This illumination, this lighting, of the self-consciousness which is now permanent, is the commencement of the formation of personality. But intellectual individuality answering to that which is physical is not yet moral individuality. Now, how is the idea of attribution (*Zurechnung*), and therefore the idea of guilt or of punishment, related to this whole first stage? Logical and physical attribution and guilt will have to be definitely distinguished from moral.

Logical attribution is the relation between a logical subject and the predicates pertaining thereto. It is found, for example, when in human law debts of the testator are attributed to the heir, or generally when predicates without which a man would not be a man are attributed to man. So to speak, the determined nature of man as a generic being is answerable for his bearing these predicates. But there is no place for moral guilt in the individual who is not yet an actual personality. The subject of moral guilt still lies outside the individual—in the race, representatives of which are the immediate parents of the individual.

A more stringent application of the idea of attribution and guilt is already found where the individual is an actual causality, though merely *physically* so. As there is truth in saying that unhealthy weather is blameable for illness, similarly an attribution of guilt in the physical sense may exist relatively to man, if his powers begin to show themselves abnormal, as they are. The real and not merely apparent causality of the child, in self-will for example, is by no means unimportant or morally indifferent; rather is it the object of chastisement and education, although the abnormal evil, which is beginning to externalize itself thus, works according to a physical necessity which is not determined by the child. This physical causality is, it is true, an actual cause, though a determined one; it is not a cause of this being a cause, which still falls outside the man. It is therefore also not moral causation as yet, which must include the fact that the man is a causality at the second power, that is to say, is a cause of his causing this or that, or is himself a self-controlling causality, a godlike aseity not of being but action.

Finally, moral causality, guilt, and attribution are not yet given when the human individual becomes an *intellectual* Ego, for nothing is thereby affirmed respecting the volitional causality. Of the whole first stage up to intellectual subjectivity we therefore say inclusively, that the existent abnormity which contradicts the idea of man, and therefore deserves to be called an evil constitution, is in truth to be attributed to the individual so soon as he exists; indeed, even the acts which issue therefrom are to be attributed to the same causality, which pertains physically to the individual. But personal moral guilt and punishment are not yet thinkable at this stage, because infants are not yet actual persons, but are only a potential punctual existence, so to speak, of future personalities. On the other hand, it is impossible for them to be freed from the evils which follow as consequences of the entire sinful state in which they also participate. Minors could only be liberated therefrom by an illogical miracle. For, supposing them to actually be children of the race, interwoven in the compact structure of its life, they cannot be at the same time removed from that connection. Accordingly, as we see daily, children share corporeal evils, sickness and death; they suffer because of the totality of evil which has necessarily fallen upon the race because of sin, only the sting of punishment which pertains to the consciousness of the connection between evil and personal guilt, cannot touch them as yet; for as yet they have no moral consciousness, and still less have they moral guilt; of course there only lies upon them the obligation or the duty to become otherwise than they are, by giving effect in due time to the self-developing powers. The subject or the bearer of moral guilt is not even then wanting in the abnormity of his existence. There is the race, represented in the parents, and this recognition is salutary for the parents and fruitful for education. But if we regard the *relation to God*, it must be conceded on the one hand that all evil, and therefore also inherited evil, is displeasing to God, just as it must also be conceded that by a natural necessity this abnormity of itself, compared with normality, only leaves a more limited measure of receptivity for God and for blessedness;[1] still the Divine displeasure cannot be directed upon the person. It is not yet actually existent, it has not yet acted. On the contrary, the Lord, who does what He sees the Father do, has pressed the children to His heart and blessed them.[2] Of the whole first stage it holds, after what has been said, that as yet the moral subject is not existent; but a participation in the moral corruption exists, by which a holy development through all the ages of life such as corresponds with the idea of man is excluded, and a second birth is necessitated subsequent to the first; further, the inherited abnormity is a living potency which will make itself actually of force at its time. That this view does not conflict with the holiness and righteousness of God has been shown; whether it also harmo-

---

[1] And this detriment has been called by theologians *pœna damni*, as distinguished from *pœna sensus*, moral punishment proper.
[2] Mark x.

nizes with the Divine goodness, will be made clear in its due place.

*Observation.*—Luther says :[1] "Although little children bring inborn sin into the world with them, it is a great thing that they have not yet sinned against the law. For, because God is by nature merciful and gracious, He will not allow it to abound to their damnation, that (if) they have not had either circumcision in the Old Testament or baptism in the New." That the children of Christian parents, though they die unbaptized, are saved, is not doubted by our dogmatic theologians; they are more uncertain as to the children of non-Christians. Gerhard, Calixtus, and Baldwin would give no decision, because nothing is revealed thereupon, but the majority still hope the best for them, for the grace of God and the merits of Christ are universal. Dannhauer, Balth. Menzer, Musäus, Scherzer, confidently deny their damnation.[2] Buddeus together with A. Calov accepts a damnation of the children of non-Christians, although in a very light degree, —which would only have a meaning on the supposition that all have already sinned in Adam. But the friends of this hypothesis, in the question as to the damnation of the children of non-Christians, show no confidence thereupon. On the contrary, many say that God allows heathen to die as children and become saved, because He has known by virtue of His *scientia media* that they would have believed if they had heard the Gospel, a reason which would certainly have a far wider bearing than that contemplated. This reason is also two-edged. For others apply the *scientia media* conversely against the salvation of the non-baptized in this way, that God permits them all to be lost because He has foreseen that they would have rejected the Gospel if it had been offered them.

[1] *Werke*, Walch, I. 1529.
[2] Its fundamental principle is: *Analogia fidei constat, neminem absolute reprobari, solam resistentiam actualem mediis fidei adversam, solam incredulitatem damnare.* Nowhere, says Menzer, does the Bible teach that the *peccatum originale* in children outside the Church is the *causa adequata reprobationis;* comp. Scherzer, *System*, pp. 169, etc. ; Spener, *Theol. Bedenken*, iv. 57 : therefore Cotta says to Gerhard, *Loci*, 21, §§ 238, etc. : *Damnationis actu illatæ causa adæquata non est peccatum originale.* The *Augsburg Confession* of course says, Art. II. : *Quod vitium originis vere sit peccatum damnans et afferens nunc quoque æternam mortem his, qui non renascuntur per baptismum et spiritum sanctum.* Still the *damnatio actu illata* is nevertheless only pronounced upon children who die unbaptized if the *terminus gratiæ* for all men is shut in this life, which cannot be proved to be the doctrine of Scripture, and upon which the *Conf. Augustana* makes no utterance.

## B.—*The Stage of Moral Subjectivity.*

The intellectual Ego or self-consciousness is the basis for the dawning freedom of choice, which reveals itself at the outset merely as the so-called *liberum arbitrium specificationis,* that is, as the faculty of choice between different finite things which are therefore morally essentially equivalent, and comes into moral being with the entrance of the consciousness of good and evil, that is, of the law of a moral kind. This is the legal stage which, although opening the eyes to a higher existence of the spirit, does not of itself nullify inherent abnormity, this rather continuing as effective. Let us consider both these factors more closely, both the interworking of the first stage in the second, that is, of the power of the generic life, and the emergence of the principle of the second stage—freedom.

A man with a faculty of moral choice is not a new man, who leaves the abnormal condition behind him as a mere husk after he comes to exist: that condition still pertains to him. The organism of faculties, even of the psychical faculties whose unity is the heart, is still affected by the innate abnormity or evil tendency, and the subject must attribute this to himself, to the totality of his being; for it really belongs to him, and it is upon this the fundamental Reformation principle rests, that we are displeasing to God *non propter alienam culpam.* On the other hand, there enters with the actual νοῦς the consciousness also of the absolute obligation to annul the opposition between personal existence and law; and so long as this consciousness has not come, there is a debt still to be repaid, an obligation to be still fulfilled.[1]

*Evils* also now have a new sting, because of the consciousness that they stand in causal connection with sinfulness, and that sin thereon is guilt. Attribution [accountability] and consciousness of guilt is still more aggravated in reference to evil *deeds* consummated by the subject. For even if we could pay no heed to the influence of freedom at this stage, still the subject dare not say that his evil deed is of no concern, being

---

[1] The word debt occurs in this sense in Matt. xviii. 30 ; Luke xvii. 10 ; Rom. i. 14, viii. 12, xiii. 8, xv. 1-27 ; 1 Cor. vii. 3 ; Eph. v. 28 ; 2 Thess. i. 2, ii. 13 ; Gal. v. 3.

the effect of natural corruption. For not only is this corruption his own, but it will not do to pass over the nearest causality, his own, to emphasize a final causality lying indeed outside the subject, to ignore the personal evil will which is notwithstanding no seeming causality, and to improve which is a duty absolutely binding on man.

And at this period follows the manner in which the germinating *liberum arbitrium* is related to natural abnormity, according to the nature of the thing and of experience. In the *liberum arbitrium* lies the focus of a new and peculiar moral causality, by which the idea of guilt first attains its intensity. Man at the legal stage already has, in addition to a knowledge of good and evil, a share also in moral freedom of choice, although that choice is by no means alone decisive forthwith upon everything. There is no compelling necessity for the subject to fall into all possible vices and delinquencies because of original sin. Even the doctrine of the Church ascribes to the natural man the capacity for *justitia civilis*,[1] to which belongs not merely possible abstention from violations of law, but also the possible performance of the ἔργον τοῦ νόμου, of what the theocratic righteousness required in the O. T., *e.g.*, honouring of parents, reverence for the Divine name, a desire to live according to the fundamental principle of righteousness. Works of this kind even the heathen do, by virtue of natural moral tact and impulse.[2] Evil inclination may be quite combated at this stage, as the close of the Decalogue points out, although it cannot be extirpated. Man *must* not do the will of sin, if it lures to evil works.[3] But no one knows himself to be free from sins of omission, even if he is able to abstain from many an evil. Then, although works are done which are good objectively or materially regarded, still, inwardly or formally regarded, no single deed is perfectly pure and good, so long as the totality of man is not there. The ground which is not occupied by the love of God, is somehow possessed by false creature love, so that there is no mention of the extinction of the duty incumbent upon man; indeed, the free subjectivity allows itself to be entangled in demonstrations of the false creature love, in acts of sin against law and conscience, with

[1] *Conf. August* xviii.   [2] Rom. ii. 14.   [3] Gen. iv. 7.

more or less conscious free will and not compulsorily. Freedom in its initial occurrence is partly lamed and weakened for good by the inherited tendency even in things of mere civil justice, and allows itself to be captivated now more and now less by evil desire which insinuates itself, allied as it is to falsehood. Now, if the subject was already predicated to be in need of redemption because of generic sin, it now follows in addition, that after evil desire has won for itself the free will of the subject, the subjective guilt of the moral subject enters in the form of sins of commission and omission. Self-generated or fostered evil, and the inherited evil of his nature (likewise proper to the subject), in that case interpenetrate and commingle in a manner inconceivable. Now, therefore, a share must be ascribed to the subject in the total guilt of the race in a stricter sense, not merely because of his nature, but also because of the use of his conscious free will. If therefore the subject would know nothing of a common guilt, if in his self-isolating pride he says he would have no need of redemption were there no evil inheritance, there is shown therein already a stronger form of Egoism, to which the natural evil tendency does not impel, but at most tempts, namely the untrue denial of the personal share in guilt and of the real common life of sin. Endeavour after righteousness is still possible in spite of inherited evil; but the true kind of this endeavour, as we are, is only possible in the form of the acknowledgment of personal guilt, therefore in the form of penitence, which knows personal subjectivity to be closely interwoven with the total sin of the race in spite of moral freedom of choice, nay, even by virtue thereof, and does not wish to fancy itself better than Adam. And it is thus taught that aid for an individual or for individuals is insufficient, only an aid for the whole man and for all could suffice. The isolation of the generic guilt would, on the other hand, be a foolish abstraction as well as egoistical and untrue. For we would be man, and yet we should place ourselves in thought outside the connection of the race, by which we exist, with claims inconsistent with our membership in the race.

At this inconceivable commingling of the free and the inherited halt cannot be made, because neither on one side nor the other is this state as yet clear moral decision.

Although the principle of moral freedom of choice is not impotent to perform legal acts, individual good acts are not yet decisive of the total worth of man, because conversely only a good fundamental disposition imparts true worth to acts. It is one thing not to leave the will to evil inclination, and another thing not to have and put into activity an evil inclination, but a harmonious good disposition. It is one thing to impel oneself to good from a sense of duty (which presupposes an internal enemy to good, and therefore an evil power), it is another thing to do the same with free inward desire, because from love to God. Thus there is in all human good of the legal stage evil as well; there is in the highest respect no decisive good, because there is wanting the purity and power of a good disposition, which is the cotyledon of all good. The motives which would compensate for the love of God that is lacking, are rather diminutions and defilements of good. This is the view of the teaching of the Church when it decides against the *spirituale bonum* at the legal stage even in the noblest men (see § 78).

But as then evil is still associated with all good of the legal stage, and as pure decision for good is as yet not present, conversely there is at the legal stage of itself no pure, that is, no purely personal, decision for evil; but all evil remains intermixed with ignorance and immaturity, and therefore remains in a relative non-independence in relation to the entire life of sin and its influences. The law not yet being the highest revelation, at its stage good has not yet come spiritually near to man in its absolute revelation. Good cannot consequently be so rejected as yet, that what is rejected is known in full clearness. Good not being yet known in its absolute revelation, man cannot have so decided for the opposite of this absolute good, that he has consciously rejected the good as such, and has decided for the principle of sin. The degree of wickedness depends essentially upon the clearness and purity of the consciousness of good to which it is opposed; therefore the God-opposed will and the idea of guilt do not possibly attain their absolute height and decision at the merely legal stage, where good has not yet given itself its highest self-revelation.[1] And for this very reason, as far as

[1] Acts xvii. 30 ; Rom. iii. 25, etc.

## RECONCILIATION OF THE OPPOSING THEORIES. 69

*punishment* is concerned, the subject, although punishable, is not yet ripe for absolute judgment, because he is himself in process and in relative indecision. Otherwise expressed, he is not incapable of redemption, but he still stands prior to the proper crisis. Only absolute, that is to say perfect, personal guilt embraces in itself absolute condemnableness of the subject, nay, is in itself judged already.[1] This follows from the fact that we comprehend all the guilt of the legal stage, and the sinfulness which still possesses us under universal sin and universal guilt. For this is, it is true, *punishable* and *punished*. But because the evil of the subject and the evil of the race are still commingled, the same is, it is true, adequate in its unity extending to all to establish and to plunge ever more deeply into misery as well as sinfulness and guilt, if help does not otherwise come; is sufficient, therefore, to make redemption necessary, but insufficient, according to the decisive Divine judgment, to relinquish man or to definitively base his condemnation upon, in such a way as definitive unbelief directed towards the perfect revelation does; but is only adequate to hypothetically condemn him, namely, if evil advances to pure decision against good in definitive unbelief. On both sides, therefore, of good and of evil, the second stage is still that of unripeness, but it urges on to the crisis.

### C.—*The Third Stage, or that of Personal Free Decision.*

1. The creation of man having designed a free moral personality, the Divine order must be directed towards bringing all the forces of good and evil to decision. Indecision is itself an exceptionable state.[2] The crisis must follow, the pure, free, personal decision for or against good, and every individual has to give account for himself.[3] But at the legal stage there is in no respect as yet full decision; free self-

---

[1] John iii. 18–20.
[2] Rev. iii. 16, χλιαρός; Matt. vi. 24 (two masters), x. 34 (good is jealous); Jas. iv. 4, 5.
[3] Gal. vi. 5; Rom. ii. 6, xiv. 12; 1 Cor. iii. 13; 2 Cor. v. 10; 1 Pet. i. 17; Matt. xvi. 27.

determination, and determination by inherited nature or by the race, are still directly interwoven with each other; a chaotic state which must be brought to separation.

Now what are the features of this decision upon which depends the worth of man,—his eternal weal or woe? On the objective side, this, that good be placed before the eyes in its full clearness and truth, not merely as the voice of conscience or as γράμμα, but in its most lucid and attractive form as personal love, in order that decision for or against truth may have decisive significance. But side by side with the apprehension of this good, there is subjectively necessary, in addition, full freedom of decision from the innermost personality. For good and definitive decision, the possibility of evil must still stand open, otherwise it would not be free, so that the knowledge of good cannot yet be absolutely determining for the same. On the other hand, evil decision can only make ripe for the final judgment if it is in nowise naturally necessitated, for example by generic sin, but if the subject is somehow put into the position to freely strike the decision of himself, and therefore to himself incur the guilt of decided rejection of personal love, which is only possible by means of self-incurred infatuation and falsehood. Now this subjective and objective possibility of free decision is given by God through Christianity as the absolute religion,[1] and therefore Christianity is also the religion of freedom. The incarnate personal Love is the perfectly revealed good. The manifestation of Christ urges therefore irresistibly to decision for or against Him, and at the same time, in spite of original sin, makes free decision possible. His manifestation simply presupposes in the world those capable of redemption, in whom therefore evil is not yet consummated, not even by the misuse of freedom at the legal stage. Prior to Christ, sin has nowhere transcended the power of redemption; in no one is the possibility of good already destroyed by evil, but Christianity can fecundate this possibility, which though unfruitful is still extant, although it cannot actually compel a good decision in the personality. Christ does not condemn sinners, but seeks them out, and indeed was sent to that end by the Father; He straightway calls them to salvation. He often

[1] Comp. §§ 62, 70.

testifies that He has not at His first manifestation come to judge, that is, to condemn.¹ The whole world is to Him still capable of rescue, and is not ripe for judgment prior to its decision *for* or *against* Him.² But *He brings the crisis;*³ His manifestation has it in itself to necessitate every one to decide for or against good itself. All *crisis* is committed to Him; the Father judges no one but by the Son, and indeed because He is the Son of man, that is, the human manifestation of personal love, of good itself. He who therefore definitively rejects Him, has decided against good itself in its clearest revelation, and has therewith judged himself to be absolutely deserving of rejection. It is true that before Christ unbelief was possible, but only of such a kind as may be regarded as "not yet faith," and still has therefore in itself the possibility of belief, that is, the ability of redemption. Otherwise the words would be no longer true, that Christ has power to vanquish all sin before Him; pre-Christian sin would in some cases be *a priori* stronger than grace.⁴ Accordingly from the true standpoint, that of Christianity, it may be said that so long as the gospel, which must come to all before judgment,⁵ has not come inwardly near to man, and has not yet been refused therefore, it is possible indeed to predicate of him that he is punishable;⁶ he may even remain without Christ in progressive misery, but neither definitive condemnation nor the opposite attaches to him; he is, so to speak, still in a provisional state; the settlement of his entire worth or worthlessness is not yet ripe for sentence; even his ἁμαρτία is not yet ἀποτελεσθεῖσα;⁷ but advance must be made to the crisis, and with the separation of what was previously conjoint, of the necessary and the free,⁸ the man crosses in a moral and religious respect to the stage of personality as distinguished from the generic character. He now becomes an actual personality, whether evil if he consciously rejects in Christ good itself, thus willingly installing the opposite of good in the place of power over him, or whether it be a good personality, seeing that he

---

[1] John iii. 17, viii. 15, 16, xii. 47.   [2] Matt. xxi. 44.
[3] John iii. 18, v. 26, etc., xii. 48; Matt. xxi. 42, etc.
[4] Contrary to Rom. v. 20; Matt. xii. 31.   [5] Matt. xxiv. 14.
[6] Contrary to Ritschl, *Lehre von der Versöhnung und Rechtfertigung*, III. 1.
[7] Jas. i. 15.   [8] Matt. vi. 24; Luke xvi. 15; 2 Cor. vi. 15.

accepts with Christ good itself as the universal power within him; and starting from the entire good disposition, allowing the spirit of Christ to have power within him, he wills the good in free Divine living impulse. In comparison with the sin which knows and yet rejects Christ, all earlier sin is preparatory; however exceptionable in itself and punishable, it is still only an element in the process which has for its goal the making ripe for judgment. Sins prior to Christ, God regards as sins of partial minority. Therefore Christ could pray upon the cross, "Father, forgive them, for they know not what they do." The preceding times (even of the Jews) God has borne, nay overlooked, in long-suffering as times of ignorance.[1] The pre-Christian state, even that of the Jews, is several times called in brief ἄγνοια.[2] But from this position of Christ as the one who brings the crisis, and the one against whom alone the highest guilt can be committed, it does not follow that evil prior to Christ was not evil in a proper sense,[3] was not laden with guilt and culpability, though in a different degree or measure,[4] and did not therefore make atonement necessary.[5] It is only that ripeness for eternal salvation or misery cannot be yet yielded thereby. The definitive worth or worthlessness of the person cannot be proved, so long as it is still in undefined process, and the crisis is not at hand.[6]

2. From what has been said, it also becomes clear why, in contrast with the usual opinion, all evil before Christ is shown to be more malicious in degree simply as it hinders the acceptance of salvation, and favours the rejection of Christ. Christianity[7] constitutes a wholly new estimate of evil which deviates from the common civil estimate. What has been stated finds a special confirmation in the doctrine of *the sin against the Holy Ghost*. It is designated the only sin which is not forgiven either in this world or the next.[8] Those whom

---

[1] Acts iii. 17, xvii. 30; Rom. ii. 4, iii. 25, etc., ix. 22.
[2] 1 Pet. i. 14; Eph. iv. 18; comp. Acts xiii. 27, 28; Heb. v. 2; 1 Tim. i. 13.
[3] As Julius Müller (II. 560) fears, and Ritschl assumes (III. 323, etc.), in order to erect his whole doctrine of atonement thereon.
[4] Luke xii. 48.   [5] Against it Rom. iii. 25, 26; comp. ix. 22.
[6] As also must be acknowledged by Julius Müller, unless he would again annul the distinction between human and demonic sin.
[7] Matt. xxi. 31.   [8] Matt. xii. 31, etc.

Jesus warned thereof had attributed His works to the evil spirit, and had thereby calumniated Christ just as they afterwards crucified Him. For all that He says: Blasphemy against the Son of man may be forgiven, but not blasphemy against the Holy Ghost. With their sin against Jesus, therefore, sin against the Holy Ghost was not essentially committed, although they were to be warned of the near danger into which they were about to fall. Especially in the commencement of His Self-revelation He might be rejected in that ignorance for which He prayed on the cross.[1] But if the Holy Spirit, who takes of the things of Christ and brings Christ inwardly near to the heart, is blasphemed, that is, if His work within, the Divine impression of the Person of Christ which He arouses in man, is despised, is characterized as falsehood, there is no forgiveness more. For such definitive unbelief Christ even cannot have won forgiveness, for that would mean that Christ has wrought, that even in a state of unbelief in Him, after He has revealed Himself and testified to Himself in the heart, forgiveness of sin and salvation may be received.[2] For this sin, therefore, intercession is not to be made,[3] for such intercession would depreciate grace and might be called a degrading of itself to deny its ethical character and to legitimize unbelief. The sinful creature has as little right to the grace of God and to liberation from punishment as the administration of grace or punishment is arbitrary, rather is it bound up with ethical laws; and since the sin is undoubtedly more heavy and criminal which opposes itself with scorn and defiance to the highest demonstration of love, to forgiving, nay atoning love, it is conformable with justice that decision should be judged according to the relation to Christ.[4] Christianity cannot concede the right of crisis to any other power, not even to the Law; that must attach to

---

[1] Luke xxiii. 34.  [2] Heb. vi. 4, etc., x. 26, etc.  [3] 1 John v. 16; John xvii. 9.
[4] Matt. xii. 20. It is evident from this, at the same time, that if one can only put in the place of the atoning suffering and deeds of Christ, as is the case with Ritschl, his doctrine of the love of the Father and the institution of the community, in which faith in the eternal forgiveness of sins before God who regards sins as mere sins of ignorance is planted, the possibility has been removed of verifying why worth and destiny exclusively depend on the position towards the manifestation of Christ, and not merely towards God or the community.

itself, otherwise the contention must be surrendered that Christ alone is the absolute revelation. By this reasoning it is again conceded that prior to Christ there was no precise and decided personal character, whether good or evil.

3. If then, as we have seen, in spite of original sin, indeed even in spite of all other evil influences of the race, we are again brought by Christ to that freedom of personal decision (though not instantaneously) upon which dependence is finally placed, all doubts are wholly resolved which generic sin might arouse in its relation to freedom. Of course this only happens in so far as all pre-Christian differences in the entire worth of the man as contrasted with Christianity are still not firm decisive differences. For it can now be established that, in the decisive relation even, the posterity which inherits sinfulness, or which is sinfully determined by the race, has no curtailing of privilege as contrasted with Adam. It is true that, according to Scripture, Adam is the originator of the Fall, but we are only passively implicated in this fall at first; but in relation to definitive decision whether upon worth or destiny, we are not by any means less favourably placed than he was, who nevertheless was only to be tried by faith. It is true there is in us an evil tendency; but the attractive counter-influence which proceeds from the form and work of Christ, and the drawing of the Father to the Son (John vi. 44), remains as a complete equivalent to the drawing of natural sinfulness; indeed, through Christ it happens that the heritage of sinfulness may itself aid good and impel the consciousness of helplessness to the right source, to the redeeming power,[1] which even Adam needed for his perfection. Add to this that pre-Christian good, even were it not clouded by generic evil, may in its necessary initial imperfection[2] be as easily tempted to reject as superfluous in self-content and self-righteousness the perfect revelation, the good principle itself, as conversely, by the agency of Christianity, that evil common possession may become a wider impulse to form the saving decision for Christ, who is both the Perfecter and the only Redeemer. As definitive good decision was necessary for Adam even before the Fall, for he was not yet πνευματικός but ψυχικός, the same is still possible to us through Christ

[1] Comp. § 62.   [2] 1 Cor. xv. 45, etc.

in spite of our being determined by the common life of sin originating in him; and as definitive decision would still have been necessary for Adam even had he stood the first test, it not being given with his fall, so is it not given to us by our connection with his sinfulness; but as it is still possible, so is it necessary. If we reflect therefore how pre-Christian good, because it was still indeterminate, became a temptation to stationariness and self-complaisance, and conversely how the power of grace may itself change an inheritance of evil into an impulse to surrender oneself to the perfect revelation, the inequality between Adam and ourselves becomes an essential equality, though in the abstract none of us will assert that in Adam's place he would certainly have always remained sinless. For by the manifestation of Christ and its attractive power are we in relation to that wherein alone lies definitive decision restored to freedom, to freedom to accept or reject the redeeming as well as the perfecting grace of Christ, as if in this respect there were no original sin, and generally no divinely ordained dependence of any kind upon the race and its constitution for the settlement of entire moral worth. For the end of holiness and blessedness in the fellowship of God, though not in other respects, we are therefore in an essentially similar place and position to Adam, because the differences in pre-Christian life, however great they otherwise were, still, as contrasted with Christianity, bear within them an essential similarity or absence of distinction, inasmuch as they all have an essential indecision about them. Definitive good decision, which is the essential point, can be furthered by pre-Christian sin and even by inherited evil, just as it may be delayed by the incomplete and indeterminate good of the commencement or of the merely legal stage. This is the triumph of grace over sin,[1] that because of Christianity it is indifferent at least as regards the final result of the worth and destiny of the whole, whether a state of sinfulness produced by means of the race precedes the decisive free act for or against Christ, or whether every individual is in a moral and

---

[1] Which only the atoning love of Christ, and not a "love of the Divine Father," can establish, which sees in pre-Christian sin simply sin of ignorance and nothing worthy of punishment, and therefore also has nothing to pardon, but only an error to dispel and ameliorate.

religious relation once more an independent beginning not produced by means of the race and sinful, which latter alternative has been shown to be inconceivable on other grounds.[1] In another respect, indeed, the state of generic sinfulness is far from indifferent; it has brought with it a rich measure, as of sin and guilt, so of wretchedness and unhappiness. We are all in a state of punishment because of it, although we have not yet come into actual condemnation, and it makes the manifestation of Christ in humiliation necessary to our redemption. But the generic connection also aids the cure.

Thus the absolute character of the Christian religion saves us from the antinomies of the physical and subjectively legal standpoints. Starting thence, it is not only possible but necessary to allow its place to the personal free act and responsibility for final worth and eternal destiny as well as for an actual guilt which calls for atonement (§ 78. 1), in spite of the fact that prior to Christ a definitive decision upon worth and destiny cannot be asserted. Every other attempt at solution, which does not assume as its fundamental position the absoluteness of the Christian religion, creates new problems.

*Observation* 1.—In our discussion the ecclesiastical doctrine is partly expounded in reference to the degrees of guilt, especially the highest, and it has been attempted to image the progressive participation of personal freedom thereby, in opposition to a physical mode of thought as well as to absolute Predestinationism. The Formula of Concord (F. C. 577. 21, 639 b. 7) allows it to appear—an appearance which we must remove—that all sins, and therefore also definitive unbelief in Christ, must be regarded as necessary consequences of inherited sin. But that we have followed the lines traced by the Reformation standpoint, is not proved merely by the passages regarding a *liberum arbitrium in civilibus* (C. A. xviii.), but also by the moral endeavour of the Formula of Concord to establish, in opposition to the doctrine of a *decretum reprobationis*, the universality of the will of Divine grace, and to refer the rejection of the individual, although with some uncertainty, to resistance (*resistere*) to the universal gracious will instead of to that decree (F. C. 807. 38, 808. 41). But in this course of thought of the Confession the position is still to be added, that the final judgment can

---

[1] §§ 79, 83.

take place for none, before the Gospel has been so addressed to him that free appropriation of the same was possible. And this position influences therefore the form of Eschatology.

*Observation* 2.—After we have in the first place treated of the creaturely origin of evil (§ 81), then secondly have established the universality of sin, and have sought to solve the problem of planting securely side by side with this universality the right of personality, its moral worth and the idea of guilt (§§ 82, 83), the problem thus remains which has been but touched before, how all this coincides with the Christian *idea of God* (§ 83).

# TRANSITION TO THE THIRD HEAD.

§ 84.—*The Existence of Sin in the World in its Harmony with the Christian Idea of God and with the Divine Government.*

The realization of evil (§ 81) (not however produced by God), and its diffusion (§ 82), are embraced by the Divine conservation and government. In reference to the power of evil which has insinuated itself, neither the N. T., nor in the main the doctrine of the Evangelical Church, has recurrence to mere Divine permission; and there is as little seen therein a mere fate or a blind physical necessity; but it is held that this far-reaching power of evil is comprehended in the wise plan and government of Divine Providence. And here, by a most significant hint, the N. T. opens a wide path to Christian gnosis for bringing this existence of sin into unison with the goodness of the universal order.

1. The universal sinfulness which we perceive, cannot be divinely implanted in the race as inherent evil, but, as has been shown, is to be derived originally from creaturely freedom, *i.e.* from an act of sin; and seeing that the species exists in a state of sin not only in late races, but as far back as we can look, the opinion is justified that the first human pair was the first sinful pair. By this recurrence to the free act of Adam, the important point is gained that we are not compelled to make the Cosmogony coincide with the Ponerogony, as every theory inevitably does which supposes the first evil not to be a free act but an evil state productive thereof. But seeing that the further result follows,

that it was not the freedom of every individual man [1] which could be called the sole cause of the sin present in the world, but that by the mediation of the race-connection the first sinful pair exercised so far-reaching an influence upon all who had their origin in them, a new difficulty arises; the first pair almost disappears in the sum total of the race. That the whole of humanity was so involved in Adam's fall without its or his will, is so prodigious an effect, that the religious consciousness as well as science cannot be satisfied with the mere permission of the same, and cannot say that God as the Conserver and as Providence has as little to do therewith as with the original entrance of evil. The mere permission of so prodigious an effect would not merely lead to Deism, but in the face of the diffusion and the power of evil which good cannot obviate, we should come to say that evil has thwarted God, so to speak, in the concept of His counsel; that this is so inasmuch as that evil subjected those physical laws of the race-connection to its service, having possessed itself of government, so that it would appear that as to the effect God had ordained this race-connection for evil.[2] Thus the problem arises, to apprehend how, in spite of this universal realization of evil, the Divine government has not fallen a prey to evil, and that the natural order, together with the social ordinances which determine freedom, does not work like a fate outside of the Divine will and power, but how the evil which is not of Divine origin is embraced, after it has come to exist, by God's mighty, wise, and holy providence. Despite its power, evil cannot have frustrated a better Divine plan and have put a worse in its place; but if sin thought to make it evil, God has on the contrary made it good.[3] Only when we have understood this, is the problem of such universal diffusion of evil intelligible, and this diffusion does not depend upon Adam's sin as upon a weak support.

2. We have *first* to inculcate, according to the Scriptures, that God adopts the continuance of the evil which He did not cause into His conserving will, but for the purposes of the providence which combats, punishes, nay vanquishes that

---

[1] §§ 82, 83.   [2] Comp. Calvin, *Instit.* lib. I. cap. xvi. iii. 23.
[3] Rom. v. 12, etc.

evil. Because this providence is not concerned with a mechanical annihilation of the same by power, but with its ethical treatment, God long-sufferingly adopts evil into His conserving will as an actual potency in the world, but for the victory of good and for judgment.

*Secondly.* The irremoveable centre of gravity of the Divine plan must lie in the final goal. But this is not in the least dislocated by the variableness which is produced in the realm of means by creaturely freedom. This power of the communication and diffusion of evil God has allowed to the race-connection, because the same race-connection which might of course misuse freedom, was, according to the will of His grace, also fitted to become the means to incorporate as a member of our race Him in whom lay the power of the atonement of sin and guilt, as well as the ability to bring on the crisis and consummation.[1]

*Thirdly.* The sinfulness of the race, as embraced by the Divine conservation, and in reference to the work of the Divine providence which vanquishes it, is also applied thereby as the agent which must unwillingly be a servant to good by means of the supreme authority of Divine wisdom. "God has included all things under sin, that He may show mercy to all."[2] There does not lie in that fact a Divine origination of evil, but also there does not lie therein merely that God was in the habit of allowing all the children of Adam to fall into sin under the reservation that He would afterwards have mercy upon them all,[3] but a Divine purpose lies at the basis of this universality and diffusion of sin; it is not a merely naturally necessary course, but God has included all under sin ($συνέκλεισε$), that is, He was concerned in the fact that the working of this agent, the possibility of which was inevitable and necessary, and the realization of which was not of God, was incorporated in His world-plan. How far evil has become in the hand of God an agent applicable for good, the apostle gives a hint when he gives us to understand[4] that redemption has brought more good than Adam's evil. And indeed the adequate justification for such power

---

[1] Rom. v. 12, etc.      [2] Rom. xi. 32; Gal. iii. 22.
[3] $ἵνα$ is not "so that;" the apostle does not say $ἐπὶ\ τούτῳ\ ὥστε$.
[4] Rom. v. 12-20.

being permitted to sin, is only to be found if at least approximately this fact is known. We have previously seen [1] that pre-Christian evil generally, and especially inherited evil, is not yet ripened evil, as well as that pre-Christian legal good may lead into a temptation to self-righteousness, as conversely the corresponding evil may by its misery become an incentive to apply to God and His aid. If these two facts are put together, by the consequences of Adam's sin, at least in relation to the final decision, the world-order has not become worse than if Adam's sin had not had these consequences,—an impossibility unless our race of beings itself was to be annihilated. But the Scriptures do not even stop here; they teach that more good has been gained by Christ than lost by Adam.[2] How much may be learnt by starting from *God* and His *world-order* as well as from *man!* Starting from God in this way: the profoundest condescension of God is that condescension to beings who are not merely unhappy, but sinners. The most majestic revelation of the Divine love is that Christ died for His enemies.[3] Thus sin has become not the cause but the presupposition of the richest revelation of what is innermost in God, His love. Such a treatment of the world of sinners is also a revelation of the power of God on a new side, of the power of His love. It is further a beautiful and majestic spectacle, a revelation of the spiritual beauty of love, because of which the Son is rewarded by the love of the Church as the fairest amongst the children of men. Finally, judgment, the radiant revelation of the most indubitable justice, is assigned to this love. For that those who consciously reject or hate this love, who are unwilling to bend themselves and pay homage to this love, must be rejected, is manifest to every Christian conscience.—*Anthropologically*, the same thing is clear in this way. The bond of grateful love which knits a sinner to God and the Redeemer, must be far more intimate than where this ground of thankfulness is absent.[4] Similarly, aversion to

---

[1] § 83.

[2] For the sake of the connection it may be permitted to glance by anticipation at this point, whilst the thorough proof can only follow afterwards. Compare § 89.

[3] Rom. v. 6.  [4] Luke vii. 47.

sin and zeal in good must be more intense in the redeemed than if they had not passed through sin. A more secure establishment in good also follows from the fact that where sin has reigned, the turning-point, the recurrence to good will, has a more conscious form, and therefore a more penetrative significance. In this case also the knowledge of evil as to its effects and consequences is increased, and evil experienced has more and more lost for Christians its seductive power, because it has revealed its falsehood, and is known on all sides to be falsehood. Finally, it may just for that reason be said in reference to the *Divine government*, that this event must finally subserve its consummation. For a whole rich world would be lacking thereto, if the class of beings who were grateful for their redemption had no place therein.[1] And thus the previous theories [2] have their place, not indeed as deductions of the necessary origin of evil, but as elements in the Divine world-order,—a place ratified by the conserving and regulative will of God, although it included evil. This good world-order is not shattered by the evil which has entered. The wisdom of God has known how to make it so much the more magnificent foil to the revelation of His attributes directed towards its vanquishment. It pertains to the power and to the perfect victory of redemption to be able to vanquish all sin and all sorrow for sin, in such a manner that the remembrance of all the misery from which we are rescued by redemption becomes the earnest background, upon which joy in salvation and in God in Christ shows itself the more clearly, and gratitude gains a warmer tone. And thus we already survey the possibility that we shall not at a future time have cause to wish that the historical world-order had been different from what it was, and especially that we had not been brought into connection with Adam. For the reconciliation will be so complete, that with Paul [3] we shall wonder with untroubled joy and worship at the depths of the Divine wisdom and love, into which even the angels desire to look, and surveying the whole history of Adam's race even to its consummation, be able to regard evil as a power involuntarily of service to the kingdom of good.

[1] Luke xv. 4-10.  [2] §§ 79, 80.
[3] Rom. viii. 28-38, xi. 31, etc.; comp. 1 Pet. i. 12.

Therefore in an anticipative song of triumph the Church has sung in the liturgy of Easter-eve: *O certe necessarium Adæ peccatum, quod Christi morte deletum est! O felix culpa, quæ talem ac tantum meruit habere redemptorem!* Still we can only apply the predicate *necessarium* to the Divine world-order, inasmuch as it embraces the conservation and diffusion of the evil not originated by God, and therefore inherited sin, which was given with the conservation of our race, whilst we cannot speak of the necessity of Adam's sin, but conversely only of the co-determination of the Divine counsel by it. The profound thought of the apostle [1] must consequently not be understood as if evil had changed the Divine plan for the better, or as if a Divine error were rectified by redemption. No mention is anywhere made of a Divine error, and no thanks are due to evil if it is divinely transmuted against its will into a negative presupposition of a triumph of good which is so much the higher. Nor is it allowable to conclude that, a higher triumph of good being brought about by evil, God has Himself made evil for the end of this victory. If God Himself made evil, He would contradict Himself, the earnestness of His commandment and His veracity.[2] He would do evil that good might come.[3] Indeed, there would be no room for the resulting triumph. For if God were the cause of sin, His condescending love would become a kind of duty, the abolition of our sin would become a making good again of what had been evilly done, and scarce a ground for gratitude would remain. Every theory which refers the origin of evil to God instead of to creaturely freedom, only serves to weaken the idea of evil and guilt, to make evil a mere physical evil, to rob the conflict of the Divine Love of its intensity, its victory of its palms.—But if the place in the Divine world-order is to be left to freedom which belongs to it, it is of course to be said that the Divine world-order as it is has not been planned simply from the *a priori* of an immutable Divine decree, but that the Divine wisdom, surveying all possibilities, even that of evil, takes creaturely freedom into account as a modifying woof, so to speak, and also the manner in which it might decide and has decided. For the supposition of creaturely freedom is of course

[1] Rom. v. 20.    [2] Gen. ii. 17 ; Matt. v. 17.    [3] Rom. iii. 7, etc.

identical with the rejection of a Determinism, in the immutability of which God from eternity had "immured" (as Rothe says) His absolutely *a priori* decree, which conditioned itself by no reference to creaturely freedom.

*Observation.*—If the origin of human evil does not lie in God but in freedom, which brings responsibility with it and forms an essential moment in the world-order approved by God, the question still remains, Did sin first enter the universe through the sin of the protoplast? This leads us to Satanology.

# APPENDIX.

## THE DOCTRINE OF THE DEVIL.

### § 85.

The Scriptures associate with the evil in humanity an empire of evil which is not human, but which has invaded the world of man; and as the prince of this empire, they point to a created but lofty spirit, who has fallen from God, has become the enemy of God and man, and has power to show this enmity in action. After numerous preparations in the O. T., the N. T. especially thinks of Satan as operative for evil from the time of Adam's fall. He is the adversary of good who accompanies the kingdom of God in its whole development, and hinders it in ever new forms. Against Christ and the implantation of His gospel in humanity he exerts his concentrated might. Even after his overthrow by Christ, who vanquished him and won for the Church the possibility of vanquishing him, he still possesses a power which immediately before the second advent of Christ will be enhanced by means of the collection of all the powers inimical to God, and brought to decision by the working of the Gospel. But that advent will at the same time be the transition to the judgment of the returning Lord, by whom he is bound for ever, given over to punishment and sentenced to the second death, innocuous thenceforth to the saints and the blessed.

  The doctrine of the Church does not, it is true, present the doctrine of the Devil as a special article of faith, but it recognizes the Biblical statements.

LITERATURE.—Milton, *Paradise Lost*. Daub, *Judas Ischarioth*, 1816, 1818 (comp. Strauss, *Charakteristiken und Kritiken von Schleiermacher und Daub*, 1839). Erhard, *Apologie des Teufels* (that is, of the doctrine of the Devil), in Fichte's and Niethammer's Journal, vol. ii. 1795. Thomas Witzenmann, *Briefwechsel und Handschr. Nachlass* (amongst them the *Geschichte des Teufels*), edited by von der Goltz, 1859. Binder, *Studien der Würtembergischen Geistlichkeit*, 1837, 2. Romang, *Religionsphilosophie*, p. 430. Twesten, *Vorlesungen ü. Dogmatik*, vol. 2. Nitzsch, *System*, § 116. Sartorius, *Heilige Liebe*, vol. i. p. 99. Harless, *Ethik*, pp. 91, 93, 100 (on demonic temptations). Rothe, *Ethik*, edit. i. vol. ii. § 519, comp. § 487. Schelling, *Philosophie der Offenbarung*, vol. ii. pp. 257, etc. (Satanology) Philippi, vol. iii. Hahn, *Glaubenslehre*, edit. ii. vol. ii. p. 38. Martensen, *Christl. Dogmatik* (comp. Lücke's Review in the *Deutsche Zeitschrift*, 1851, pp. 57, etc.). Roskoff, *Geschichte des Teufels* (*i.e.* of the representations of the Devil), 2 vols. 1869 (harmonizing with Schenkel's *Glaubenslehre*). Biedermann, pp. 614, etc. *Evang. Kirchenzeitung*, 1859, Nos. 8, 9. Smaller treatises: Sander Jäger, Voss, Disselhoff, etc.

A.—*The Biblical Doctrine.*

THE OLD TESTAMENT does not give information concerning a special revelation of this doctrine, nor does it treat it in a special doctrinal statement; it rather presupposes the existence of demons or of Satan, where there is any mention of them, as a representation already current, and commences thereat. It harmonizes with this, that the features in the representation of the same have something of uncertainty about them, and this representation only gradually becomes more precisely fixed. In the older literature of the O. T. no traces are found of a doctrine of the Devil. In the later literature, especially in that which is post-exilic, it obtains a greater significance. In the O. T. there occur *in the first place* obnoxious or horrid beings, mainly of a predominantly physical importance, thus the Lilith,[1] the Shedim and Seirim,[2] dismal beings, who according to the popular representation haunt the night or the wilderness. They occur in poetical passages;[3] still a belief in their existence is presupposed in the people; for it is forbidden to

[1] Prov. xxiii. 7; Isa. xxx. 18, 14.   [2] Isa. xiii. 21.
[3] Jer. i. 39.

offer sacrifices to them.¹ Asasel ² also is to be thought as an impure being, who dwells outside the Theocracy in the wilderness. So far as these forms, which are manifestly taken for granted from the popular representation but are not known by revelation, have a religious reference, the profane world and Heathenism are personified in them; and as far as doctrine is concerned, so much at most is to be learned therefrom, that evil spirits are supposed thereby whose sphere is especially thought to be the wilderness and the extra-Israelitish world. The case is somewhat different with the angels or spirits who are messengers of evil, who have the mission of executing Divine punishment. To this class belong that lying spirit and the angel of death which visits Israel with plague or slays Sennacherib's army.³ They are *servants of the Divine justice*, who also punish with blindness and deceitful hopes.⁴ They might be good beings in themselves, serving Divine justice as they do; but since their function is simply to work lovelessly, and even to generate delusion, their idea inclines to that of beings who have their element and their joy in misery and evil. And thus they already form the transition to the representation in the Book of Job. Satan is here mentioned for the first time. He mixes with the sons of God (angels), amongst whom he no longer has any essential belonging; he arbitrarily roams about and seeks his own, but is still used as a servant by God, on whom he remains dependent. His independent activity is in this passage mainly that of the spy of evil, of the accuser of man to God, especially the accuser of the pious, and he maintains the assertion that even their fear of God is interested. Therein lies the expressed doubt as to the possibility of a kingdom of pure good, the suspicion that love of righteousness and piety, and virtue generally therefore, is a mere chimera, that the good law and God Himself can have no honest friends, that chance and selfishness are alone possible, and are consequently justified and rational. And doubt is thereby thrown upon the right of a higher stage than the eudæmonistic, than the heathen, the *right of the legal stage*, and Satan's endeavour is to withdraw from this higher stage,

---

¹ Deut. xxxii. 17; Lev. xxii. 7; Ps. cvi. 37.     ² Lev. xvi. 10.
³ 1 Kings xxii. 21; Isa. xxxvii. 36 ; 2 Sam. xxiv. 16, 17 ; comp. Acts xii. 23.
⁴ 1 Kings xxii. 21; 2 Chron. xviii. 20.

to seduce back into Heathenism, into unbelief in the revelation of law. But, nevertheless, as the accuser Satan upbraids God with the law, according to which He dare not spare even the pious, but, seeing that they are impure, must punish and bring their actual inward worth to light by trials. In this passage he maintains the standpoint of an isolated justice, but only in the hope that the trial will result in confirming his enmity against the law, and in the proof that the law contains an impossibility, and thus a contradiction to itself. Nevertheless, since he maintains the punitive justice, which is based in God Himself, in opposition to an arbitrary goodness, which is not strict with sin, he still has a right to be heard, he still has, so to speak, a foot in heaven, and therefore the poet rightly allows him still to be amongst the sons of God. God transfers Job to him, that he may carry out Job's trial. Satan's intention therein is to lead Job to apostasy and ruin; but God's will is only confirmation by trial, and Job's life he must spare. Satan is convinced that Job remains faithful, that disinterested fear of God may be a truth. The chastisement of Job is now changed into the greater blessing. The lustre of a fidelity and love which in the loss of all external goods regards God as the highest good, is revealed by Job as a triumph over Satan.

If already a secret joy in evil betrays itself in the heartless accuser, this is seen still more definitely when Satan appears as the adversary of the good, not merely of individual pious souls, but of the Theocracy itself. It is thus in Zechariah,[1] where after the exile he would hinder the reinstitution of Divine worship, asserting that Israel is rejected by the just judgment of God, and is not worthy of the renewal of the priesthood; it would be contrary to justice. But the impure garments are stripped off the high priest, and he receives festal garments instead, with the declaration that his sins are taken away. The vision expresses that the restoration of the priesthood after the exile is a victory of the gracious God over Satan, who maintains strict right. Similarly, in the N. T., in the apocalyptic vision,[2] the arraignment of Satan, the κατήγωρ of the saints, is overthrown by grace. The delight of Satan in evil and his enmity to the Theocracy is also seen in passages

[1] Zech. iii. 1. [2] Rev. xii. 10.

BIBLICAL DOCTRINE. 89

where he devises evil.[1] Still he never openly appears in the O. T. as the enemy of God Himself. Though he has his special purposes and aims, he is yet the servant of God for punishment or trial, the asserter or executor of the negative side of the Divine justice.

NEW TESTAMENT DOCTRINE.—Christ and the apostles adopt this doctrine from the pre-Christian time under different names, as ἐχθρός, πονηρός, διάβολος, βεελζεβούλ, σατανᾶς, ὄφις ἀρχαῖος. Mention is also made of a plurality of evil spirits (δαιμόνια, ἄγγελοι διαβόλου), with Satan as their head.[2] The demons, or the messengers of Satan, are πνεύματα, endowed with higher talents, power, and knowledge.[3] It has indeed been said[4] that there is no mention of the devil in the N. T. of a doctrinal nature; and that Christ only adopted the customary popular representation, which could not notwithstanding be called unimprovable, as a mode of expression. To Christ's official knowledge cosmological things did not belong. The passages in the N. T. are consequently to be understood as a figurative expression of the principle of evil and its power.[5] Undoubtedly the word Satan also occurs in a figurative sense.[6] But also where Christ gives to His disciples in a special manner the doctrinal exposition of a parable, and therefore of a figure, He says, the enemy is the devil.[7] The history of the temptation is no misunderstood parable.[8] It is true that in classical passages upon sin there is no mention of the devil,[9] chiefly from obvious causes where the side of human guilt is made prominent, and not man's miserable condition and penal state. But it also happens that ascent is made from personal human sin in flesh and blood to invisible, universal powers of evil,[10] to the enemy of men whose element is hate and falsehood. As he is a homicide

---

[1] 1 Chron. xxi. 1 (the census by David); in 2 Sam. xxiv. 1, it is doubtless referred to a Divine penal destiny.
[2] Matt. viii. 28, ix. 34, xii. 26; Luke xi. 19, etc., 24.
[3] Matt. viii. 29; Mark i. 24.   [4] Schleiermacher, *Christl. Glaube*, § 44.
[5] Similarly Schenkel, who thinks that no opposite evil being is taught in Scripture, but only a moral person, the collective evil in humanity.
[6] Matt. xvi. 23, and in xii. 43, the πνεῦμα ἀκάθαρτον is similarly treated.
[7] Matt. xiii. 19, 39; Mark iv. 15.   [8] Matt. iv. 10; comp. Luke xxii. 31
[9] Jas. i. 13, etc.; Rom. v. 12.
[10] Thus Eph. vi. 12; John viii. 44; 1 John iii. 8; Luke xxii. 31.

from the beginning,¹ so is he the enemy of the word of God and falsifies it;² he arouses hatred to Christ, and puts treason into the heart of Judas.³ Christ often speaks of the prince of this world.⁴ The world lies in wickedness, and wickedness ceases to touch him alone who is born of God.⁵ On the other hand it is said, it is true, that the world with its prince is already judged by Christ, or as Luke puts it, Satan is hurled from heaven,⁶ *i.e.* is inwardly and fundamentally vanquished. In Christ is given the personality pertaining to humanity, in which the devil can have no part, because Christ of Himself desires nothing of the world and is superior thereto,⁷ which is also for the advantage of His own. Still the victory fundamentally won is still to be carried out in realization. The whole history of the world subsequent to Christ is a struggle against the empire of Satan. Thus the Apocalypse especially depicts the history of Satan in the past and in the future.⁸ Prior to the death of the Lamb he still stands as the accuser of the pious;⁹ he still has a right, so to speak, to oppose God's merciful will. But his arraignment must grow dumb before the Lamb who has been slain, and he is expelled from heaven. Now he still works upon earth, and also in the Church, converts the empirical church into πόρνη by falsification of the Gospel and of the disposition, by lying prophecy, by falsification of the worship of God, and by alliance with the anti-Christian world-power. In the fact that pseudo-prophecy, pseudo-priesthood, and pseudo-kingship penetrate into the Church, and that all these unite against the office of Christ, the anti-Christian condition consists.¹⁰ According to the Apocalypse, Satan's fury increases with his losses, and finally, according to Paul, he collects his strength for one more effort in the ἀντίχριστος,¹¹ whom the returning Lord will annihilate with the breath of His mouth, and whose end is the burning lake¹² or the second death. Also according to Paul, Satan

---

¹ John viii. 44.  ² Matt. xiii. 19, 39.
³ John viii. 38, xiii. 27; Luke xxii. 53.  ⁴ John xii. 31, xvi. 2, xiv. 30.
⁵ 1 John ii. 13, 14, iv. 4, v. 19.  ⁶ Luke x. 18.
⁷ John iv. 30.  ⁸ 1 John iii. 8.
⁹ Rev. xii. 10.  ¹⁰ 1 John ii. 18 ; 2 Thess. ii. 3, etc.
¹¹ 1 Thess. and 2 Thess. ; Rev. xx. 7 is to be carefully distinguished from the Antichrist, 1 John ii. 18.
¹² Rev. xx. 10, xxi. 8.

still has in the present world-æon a power in the children of unbelief; he is called god of this world,[1] because he has the rule outside the realm of Christianity; therefore excision from the Church is called a giving over of the sinner to Satan.[2] Also according to Paul, he causes factions in the Church by false wisdom. From this usage is to be distinguished the designation in the Epistle to the Hebrews as prince of death,[3] whether because he is by sin the power of death, the prince of terror, especially the prince of the fear of death, or because he punishes sin according to the will of God and as His instrument. According to Peter, he ravens like a beast of prey after men,[4] as when alone he finds himself as in an empty desert or wilderness.[5]

If we combine all this, his activity is, first, temptation, sifting, and seduction;[6] secondly, he is the accuser of the seduced and fallen; thirdly, he brings destruction and misery, spiritual and bodily, to which class the δαιμονιζόμενοι especially belong. In this he is indeed thought of as the instrument of God, but he also no less proves thereby his joy in evil, and his hate. And all this[7] is united in the statement that he is the enemy, absolutely the adversary of God and man, the wicked one. As for his place of abode prior to Christ, it was until the coming of Christ still in heaven,[8] as is evident from the Book of Job. The thought is, that prior to Christ, Satan's right to accusation, his right also to be heard in heaven, is not yet extinguished, but that right is absolutely extinguished by Christ.

B.—*History of the Doctrine of the Devil and the Doctrine of the Church.*

As far as the origin of this doctrine is concerned, some (*e.g.* Lipsius) have considered Polytheism to be its source, *in*

---

[1] 2 Cor. iv. 4.   [2] 1 Cor. v. 5; Eph. ii. 2.
[3] Heb. ii. 14.   [4] 1 Pet. v. 8.
[5] Luke xi. 24; Matt. xii. 43, to which Eph. vi. 12 also belongs.
[6] Luke iv. 1, etc., xxii. 31.
[7] 1 John iv. 4, 5, v. 18; Matt. xiii. 38, 39; 1 Pet. v. 8 (ἀντίδικος).
[8] Luke x. 18; Rev. xii. 9, etc. 'Ἀήρ, Eph. ii. 2, and ἐπουράνια, vi. 12 point on the other hand to the earthly atmosphere; comp. Rev. xii. 12, etc.

*the first place* immediately and positively, the oriental religions commonly knowing evil spirits. It has been especially attributed to Parsism. Still Ahriman is not Satan, and the Book of Job is probably older than the contact with the Persians. This only is to be assumed, that in the time of the exile the Apocrypha, and especially the Book of Tobit,[1] have under the influence of Parsism introduced coarse superstitions into the doctrine of evil spirits.—*Secondly*, this doctrine has been derived from Polytheism, according to the law in the history of religion, that in relation to every new religious faith, the earlier world of gods is submerged as in a dark abyss, and these gods then become seductive evil powers. But if Satan is to be regarded as a relic of an earlier religious faith, it might be expected that he would have more significance in the earlier time than in the later, and the converse is the case. Others [2] attempt a *psychological derivation*. In Satan, it is said, man has sketched the awful ideal of his own end, if he persists in evil, just as in the angels he has sketched the majestic ideal of the true. But in this case a doctrine of the end of Satan would scarcely be wanting, and this is found nowhere in the O. T. Besides, Satan is not the evil ideal of individuals, but a principle of a more general kind ; indeed, as the adversary of God and His kingdom, he has no mere ethical significance, but one which is more comprehensive. The opinion, that the source of this doctrine is the tradition of the doctrine of the Fall,[3] which already contained a doctrine of Satan, that is, of a superhuman origin of sin, is deficient in foundation ; for the original record does not know the serpent as Satan,[4] and how should Satan have subsequently remained so long unmentioned ? But it may be said that the more joy in the theocracy, knowledge of the law, and zeal in its propagation in the world spring up, the more must man experience the eventful power of evil which is now seductive and now appalling, and which transmutes the evil conscience into fear and flight in the presence of God. The absorption into the

---

[1] Tobit iii. 8, vi. 9, viii. 3.
[2] Thus Binder, following the indications of Marheinecke's fundamental lines.
[3] For which von Hofmann decides.
[4] See p. 23 ; otherwise, of course, Book of Wisdom ii. 24.

## ECCLESIASTICAL DOCTRINE. 93

Divine thought of the theocracy, and on the other hand into the realization of the world and of the reign of evil therein, causes the knowledge of a combination of powers in alliance against God to arise in Israel, as happened upon similar grounds amongst the Persians; but in Israel not in dualistic form.

The DOCTRINE OF THE CHURCH[1] speaks of the devil in connection with the origin of evil and its punishment, and also with the general and final judgment.[2] He is brought into relation with natural sinfulness, and the impulse to evil thoughts and deeds is ascribed to him. The dominion of evil over men is also represented as a slavery to Satan, and this as punishment. He has his full power in the extra-Christian world.[3] But his power is broken by Christ, and by His word victory over him is to be won.[4] The power of creating anything is also denied the devil, and only the power of corrupting substances is conceded to him. But it is only at the Last Judgment that his power is wholly annihilated; he is himself delivered up to eternal punishment.[5]

THE MORE RECENT HISTORY OF THIS DOCTRINE.—It was very early laid hold of by scepticism, and many even now regard the denial of the existence of the devil as a necessary requirement of an enlightened mode of thought. The first assault emanated from the Cartesian philosophy, which conceded no influence of spirit on body; therefore the Cartesian Balthasar Bekker[6] explained the demonic as pertaining to sickness. Jesus, he said, accommodated Himself to the delusive representations of the sick. He does not deny the existence of the devil, but he is included in His servants. But if all his influences are denied, his existence becomes something indifferent. Semler[7] introduced this view into the Lutheran Church. The superficiality of the old

---

[1] *Conf. Aug.* xvii. xix.
[2] *Conf. Aug.* xx. § 32 (*Apology*, 50); *Conf. Helv.* I., edit. *Augusti*, pp. 15, 18, 19; *Belgica* 12.
[3] *Form. Conc.* 580. External misfortunes of many kinds are also ascribed to him, *Cat. maj.* 525.
[4] 405, 412. Similarly *Conf. Belg.* xii., where an express doctrine of the Devil is presented.
[5] *Conf. Aug.* xix.        [6] *Mundus fascinatus*, 1690, 1693.
[7] *De Demoniacis*. He also edited Farmer's *Letters on the Demoniacs*.

Wolffian and eclectic Rationalism did not know how to gain any advantage from this doctrine. It was otherwise with Kant:[1] he brings it into connection with radical evil, and regards the devil as its personification, and even the Fichtian Erhardt proceeds in a similar manner. Seeing that the earlier system of Schelling contained dualistic elements, a few of his pupils have endeavoured to attain a construction of Satan. Daub is of opinion, in his *Judas Ischarioth*, that a finite evil presupposes an absolute evil, just as a finite good presupposes an absolute good; and if finite evil is real, absolute evil must also be real. Finally, since good and evil can only be in a person, absolute evil must also be a person, and no mere personification. But granting that the reality of absolute evil followed from the reality of absolute good and finite evil, which is not the case, absolute evil would not be identical with the Biblical doctrine of Satan. There can neither be an evil Absolute, nor, as Rothe would have it, an absolutely evil being, because otherwise the God-created metaphysical being would become evil substance. Evil could only be in the metaphysically good. Eschenmayer coincides with the ideas of Schelling, adding that the universe consists in the opposition of two poles. As certainly as Christ is, His opposite pole is the devil. This also is dualistic. Philippi[2] is related to this opinion, when he thinks "*nullus diabolus, nullus redemptor:* If there were no Satan who seduced men, our sin generated without seduction would itself be Satanic, and would abolish the possibility of our redemption." But here too little consideration is bestowed upon human freedom and the possible stages of human evil (see § 83). It is no marvel that these constructions have not served for the establishment of this doctrine. Schelling himself, when he enters upon the question more closely,[3] regards the devil not as a person but as a spirit, a real principle. The devil is not to him a creature of God, but the limitless principle let loose by the freedom of man, therefore a spirit produced by man, whilst according to the Scriptures he is an independent power opposed to man, and not generated by him. The most acute

[1] Kant, *Religion innerhalb der Grenzen der blossen Vernunft*, edit. von Rosenkranz, pp. 45, etc., 92, 97, etc.
[2] *Glaubenslehre*, iii. p. 254. [3] *Philos. der Offenbarung*, ii. pp. 256, etc.

opponent of the doctrine of the devil is Schleiermacher,[1] and we therefore examine his dogmatic reasons against it. He attacks the possibility of his *idea*, secondly the possibility of his *fall*, and thirdly his *efficiency*. His idea, he says, is compounded of two or three non-coherent mental representations. He is the servant of God who spies out evil, then again he is the enemy of God, and finally he is the angel of death, who occupies the kingdom of the nether world. But it is not contradictory to say that Satan, although injuring and destroying with delight, is notwithstanding the Divine instrument in punishment. Especially does death stand in combination with sin. Indeed, more generally it has its internal truth to say that the seducer to evil desire incurs evil which is punishment. Even conceding the figurative character of some features, this does not annul his idea. "Persistent evil," continues Schleiermacher, "cannot consist with the most signal insight." But this insight is not of a religious kind in the devil. The understanding may easily be paired with an evil will. But Schleiermacher turns his especial attention to the idea of an empire of evil, which is self-contradictory, he thinks. Satan must be omniscient and must comprehend evil organically, whilst evil contradicts and limits itself. Undoubtedly a perfect kingdom is only thinkable in good, where each one seeks not his own but that common to all. But a kingdom is possible where there exists only a difference of powers; therefore a rule is possible though only based upon fear, artifice, and a common interest. And the unity of interest in the kingdom of the devil is certainly not thinkable as internal, but in opposition to good. Evil has doubtless a disorganizing power, but also a contagion and an affinity and an interconnection in its different forms. Certainly there cannot be a kingdom of evil which is without contradiction. Finally, Satan need not have omniscience to be a prince. It is not therefore to be said that the N. T. idea of the devil involves an impossibility. Next, as far as the *Fall* of the devil is concerned, Schleiermacher hesitates about its possibility, if he had "the fairest gifts." But endowments of intellect and power of will as little ensure against evil as physical endowments. If the fall of the first man cannot be shown to be impossible,

[1] Similarly Schenkel, Biedermann, Lipsius.

the fall of a higher finite spirit is also possible. When, finally, Schleiermacher says with respect to Satan's *Efficiency*, that "the problem remains to seek evil rather in self than in Satan, Satan only showing the limits of our self-knowledge," it is very right that the doctrine of the devil cannot possibly be applied to the diminution of human guilt, as is not seldom done. Were this the necessary consequence of this doctrine, it would have to be rejected. But little as human influences and temptations annul our guilt before the internal moral forum, as little can it be proved that the case needs be different with the efficiency of Satan. But we cannot of course give a more minute exposition of the manner of the same, just as generally we know but little of the mode of the influence by which spirits act upon one another.

Therefore also the most noteworthy theologians after Schleiermacher have not agreed with him upon this point. Even Lücke and Romang are not opposed to the supposition of fallen evil spirits, although they reject the possibility of an absolutely evil person or an absolutely evil kingdom. Nitzsch, Twesten, Rothe, Julius Müller, Tholuck, Lange, Martensen, as well as Thomasius, Hofmann, Kahnis, Philippi, and Luthardt, avow that not merely is sin found in humanity, but that a kingdom of evil spirits with a head over them is also to be inculcated. Romang[1] rightly satirizes the fond enlightenment which takes much credit to itself for being above this representation.

*Observation.*—According to Rothe, other spheres of creation with free beings preceded our world. That some of them have fallen can no more be called improbable than that they might persevere in an abnormal development as well as men. Instead of spiritualizing their nature, and so becoming pure and immortal spirits, they are only spirit-like beings. After their fall, they were, he thinks, subjected to a death of sense, like men, but have afterwards risen again to a sort of life, having attained the acquirement of a kind of animated body. But this organizing was a systematization of evil, and was united by a common opposition to God and His work; they have a head, although a shifting one, the devil. Like these spirit-like beings with an organism, they have a relationship with the material world, especially therefore can they influence

[1] *Natürl. Religionslehre*, pp. 389, etc., 430, 597.

the creaturely world of man, inasmuch as this presents a point of connection in its sinfulness. Thus, he thinks, humanity is exposed to the influences of demons, and even the demonic possession of human individuals is by no means an absurdity; it is part of the idea of demons that a mighty impulse attracts them to material life. But although the duration of their existence extend beyond their death of sense as far as it will, it must finally be extinguished by a gradual process of decadence.[1] According to Swedenborg, the devils are dead wicked men, and there is a world-struggle between God and the empire of Satan.

C.—*Dogmatic Investigation.*

§ 86.

Though the Biblical doctrine of the devil and the demonic powers is not capable of a perfect construction, it still forms a harmonious whole, of importance for the Christian idea of evil as distinguished from that of Heathenism or Judaism, as well as for the religious life; the doctrine of the Church therefore holds fast thereto, although it does not place the doctrine in the rank of one of the fundamental articles.[2]

1. It belongs to the full dignity of a dogmatic proposition, that it is not merely attested by the formal side of the evangelical principle, by the Scriptures (for much that is Biblical —rejoice though it may in perfect credibility—does not yet belong to Christian doctrine (*Glaubenslehre*)), but that it is also given by the material side of the evangelical principle, and is derivable therefrom. This is the case with sin, for the evangelical believing consciousness is a redeemed consciousness. But it cannot be said that the same immediate certainty of the devil is possessed by the Christian consciousness as is possessed of sin. It is true that Hofmann has sought to infer the devil from the Christian consciousness. Sin, he says, still left to man the need of redemption, consequently his sin is

[1] *Christl. Ethik*, II. p. 242; edit. 1, § 519, compare § 487; *Dogmatik*, I. pp. 232, 246.
[2] So Twesten also thinks, II. pp. 365, 378, etc.

not that of self-determination within himself, but he has allowed himself to be determined from without against God, not by impersonal nature but by the plurality of spirits (whose unity is originally the Holy Spirit), who, partly good, partly evil, rule for the purpose of evoking their individual manifestations in the corporeal world. Evil spirits can therefore determine the natural side of man.

But Hofmann and Philippi nevertheless hold man at the same time to be free and capable of selfishness; indeed, according to Philippi, all sin is selfishness,—an opinion which has little harmony with the view that all human sin is seduction merely. But it is also incorrect in itself to deny to Adam "a free determination of himself," or to think that the discovery of the thought of evil is only explicable as a demonic work. Rather, man could not will good even as such without the possible opposite of thinking evil, and the exclusion of it by thought as well as by will. The thought of evil as a possibility is not yet evil thought (p. 32), but may become evil if free will affirms instead of excluding it, undoubtedly not without self-delusion and falsehood; for everything evil is, as has been shown, foolishness also.[1] As far as Satan's mode of working is concerned, according to Hofmann, every influence of men and even of Satan upon man is an influence on the "natural side." But if by that the corporeal side of man is meant, it is obscure why Satan as a spiritual being is straightway supposed to work *only* upon the body of men, and not pre-eminently upon the spirit, or how far an incentive issuing from external nature upon the body is not supposed to be just as seductive for the spirit mediately, as the influence of a personal evil spirit.[2]

But the devil is as little capable of speculative construction as the realization of evil generally.[3] For construction demands that he or his wickedness be thought of as necessary. But Satan would no longer be the evil spirit of the Scriptures, if

---

[1] *Schriftbeweis*, Lehrst. III. 3. Philippi's view is partially related to this, p. 198.

[2] There seems in Hofmann to lie at the basis of his view a kind of theosophical idea of Satan as a power of nature—a relic of dualism.

[3] Daub and Eschenmayer have been already mentioned. An application of the law of polarity to the moral world is without justification. Both are dualistic. Schelling's evil spirits as the products of man, and of an impersonal kind, are not the evil spirits of the Scriptures.

he were not thought to have fallen by his creaturely freedom. It is consequently to be conceded that this doctrine, not being derivable from the Christian consciousness of itself as necessary, does not claim the full rank of a dogmatic article. Thus limited, the dogmatic task has to concentrate itself upon two points: (1) Is the Biblical doctrine of the devil harmonious, or does it bear the seal of error, namely internal contradiction? (2) Has the doctrine a significance for the Christian consciousness?

2. THE COMPATIBILITY OF THE BIBLICAL FEATURES IN THE DOCTRINE OF THE DEVIL.—Were the Biblical exposition of the devil essentially incapable of a perfect rendering, it must of course be supposed that the figurative is the main feature therein, and not the doctrinal. But, on the other hand, not merely has Christ spoken of Satan in a doctrinal manner in the Gospels, as has been shown, but this doctrine has received an important modification by means of Christianity. Satan appears in Scripture under four leading characters: *first*, as the tempter of freedom, who desires to bring to decision; *secondly*, as the accuser, who by virtue of the law retorts criminality upon man; *thirdly*, as the instrument of the Divine punitive justice, which brings evil and death upon men; *fourthly* and lastly, he is described, especially in the N. T., as the enemy of God and man. The first three predicates are not self-contradictory. They are rather homogeneous, inasmuch as Satan wills materially the same as God wills, and what is essentially comformable with the Divine justice. For it is also the will of God that the freedom of men should be brought to decision, and that evil should be impeached and punished. In all this Satan is still the servant of God, of the will of the Divine justice with which Satan coincides, in such a way indeed that all these revelations of the Divine justice may at the same time turn out for evil in man, and that what God wills may be willed by Satan for another purpose certainly, and therefore in another sense. These first predicates still dominate in the O. T. quite in accordance with its standpoint; for this is still pre-eminently that of justice. But with these three predicates of Satan as the servant of God and of justice the fourth does not seem to concur, and this is the most prominent in the N. T., namely, that Satan is the enemy of God

and of man, that he is formally and materially God-opposed. His service as depicted in the O. T. seems incompatible with this view. It is true that also the N. T. still preserves these three predicates.[1] Again, even in the O. T. Satan has pleasure in the suffering of men and the augmentation of evil;[2] indeed, he already assumes an ironical position towards good, treating spiritual life in righteousness and the fear of God as a chimera. But this only proves that both Testaments share the difficulty, although in a different manner. And this so much the more calls for solution that another difficulty enters. In the O. T. Satan still has a place amongst the sons of God, is still not severed or expelled from them,[3] whilst he no longer appears amongst the good angels in the N. T. and is no longer found in heaven,[4] so that he can no longer be called the servant of God in the same sense as in the O. T.—And here again yet a third difficulty arises, which appears to contradict the possibility of completing the representation of the devil as a unified whole. The dominant representation of him conceives him, namely, on the one hand as a power settled, immoveable, and complete in evil, and on the other hand he is supposed not to be an evil nature or substance, but to have become evil by means of freedom. It ascribes to him further a high knowledge, even a knowledge of God, for he is indeed the sworn enemy of God; thus there is not wanting in him a knowledge especially of Divine power,[5] though he does not believe or acknowledge the higher, especially the ethical, attributes of God. But the knowledge of the Divine power seems already sufficient to permit his appearing perfectly foolish in a quite hopeless opposition, as he must know, and in the thought of becoming, so to speak, an anti-God. But these new difficulties are possibly adapted to show us the direct way to the solution of the first. Creaturely freedom of course demands a development, a mobility, whilst the dominant conception, just as it is wont to think of inherited sin as an immoveable and fixed factor, proceeds in a similar manner with the evil spirits and Satan. But this is not to be supposed, and is not the Biblical conception; according to the Scriptures, Satan appears as

---

[1] Matt. iv.; Luke iv. 22, 31; Rev. xii. 10, 13; Heb. ii. 14.
[2] Job i., etc.; Zech. iii.    [3] Job i.; 1 Kings xxii. 21, etc.
[4] John xii. 31, xvi. 11; Luke x. 18; Rev. xii. 7, etc.    [5] Jas. ii. 19.

developing in malignity, as increasing in direct enmity and hatred to God, or, to look at the thing in another aspect,—he is urged to an ever more open self-disclosure by virtue of the augmenting Divine revelation; although from the time of his fall an internal alienation from God existed. Further, according to the N. T., Satan is not judged prior to the days of Christ; he is only then ripe for judgment after he has turned against the absolute revelation. Only with the manifestation of this revelation is he, as it is figuratively expressed, precipitated from heaven, and heaven is definitively closed against him.[1] Consequently the fourth predicate seems to harmonize thoroughly with the other three, and especially with the fact that he is amongst the angels as a servant of God in the O. T., whilst in the New he is compelled to serve the Divine will involuntarily and unconsciously. The correspondence follows if we suppose (in harmony with the Biblical representation of Satan) a change in Satan in the course of the history of the Divine revelation, in conflict with which he came step by step to be a sworn enemy of God and man, especially in the N. T. time, in which, on the other hand, his power is broken at the root by Christ. Such an increment of evil in him need not surprise us; even his fall would be unthinkable without the mutable principle of freedom. For him as well as for the good angels a progress was in any case necessary towards confirmation, and therefore an increase; but he fell, and thus an increase in evil was possible. For neither is it to be supposed that he rose by his one first act to the highest point of wickedness, nor that God immediately suspended His counter-efforts to bring him right. In Christ's treatment of Judas Iscariot we have a relative example, and he was not expelled from the circle of the disciples immediately the evil thought of betrayal found a place within him. But if, concurrently with a gradual vanishing of the higher Divine light in his apprehension, we suppose a gradual self-obscuration, so that he is now called ἐξουσία τοῦ σκότους, even the last difficulty might be approximately solved, how his opposition to God squares with his knowledge of God. It is possible to show that in his opposition to God he must only be foolish as all evil is inept. Satan well knows the Divine power, whilst

[1] Luke x. 18; Rev. xii. 7.

the ethical attributes of God have become darkened in his mind.[1] The pure monotheistic idea of God Satan will not have, but will only represent Him as does obscured monotheism, which only thinks of God as quantitatively exalted. Add to this that he may perceive in history that the *power* of God does not interpose in the present dispensation to annihilate evil forcibly. The righteousness and wisdom of God require this; for the Divine plan directed towards free and loving personalities would be surrendered by a mere struggle with the instruments of power. Apparently baffled, Satan would really gain what he desires. There would be no realm of freely loving spirits (as Satan, according to the Book of Job, doubted its possibility); there would only remain the void of an ethical nonentity. Since God, on the other hand, desires a free kingdom of good, He cannot exempt men from having their faculties brought to decision by temptation; and human evil being actually punishable, the Divine justice cannot simply annul the impeachment of Satan, although Satan seeks to drive to desperation by means of the same in the conscience. But God may desire to combat Satan in a spiritual manner during the course of the world's history, and not physically or magically. If the justice of God requires this, Satan has at once a hold, so to speak, thereon, just because God as an ethical being immediately renounces the use of His omnipotence for the annihilation of evil, and cannot wish to compel even human freedom, but must allow it to be tempted. Thus Satan can insert his wedge into the Divine world-order, the goodness of which he does not acknowledge, and can cherish hope because he sees the success. It is true that even in the world-judgment of history the Divine punishment is always directed against evil. But punishment has in itself the ambiguity that it may seduce to evil, and its increase by fear and mistrust, which darken and paganize the idea of God as well as impel to good. To the unrepentant sinner God easily becomes changed, if he does not seek wholly to deny Him, into a dark evil being, and the man's despair of God is Satan's road to apotheosis. Thus the world-order being in process as a moral order, permits breaches everywhere into which Satan can obtain entrance. During the present

[1] Jas. ii. 19. Rothe, *Dogmatik*, I. 233, ascribes to Satan an increase in evil.

course of the world, which he may imagine unending, he may rest upon that which, indispensable for goodness, still permits him actual hope of success. Hence the struggle so long as history lasts is so earnest, because God can only vanquish the temptations of the evil principle, which sifts and accuses and punishes, by the mediation of free powers, so far as these are willing to receive the Divine life into themselves, and cannot be willing to subdue Satan by sheer power. And thus Satan is able to hope, like any rival, although ever sustained by the Divine omnipotence, to snatch from God His own, the free creatures created in His likeness, and to rule them spiritually, which would be his highest triumph.[1]

Undoubtedly the Scriptures do not ascribe to the devil a power which compels to evil. According to them, there are sins—and most certainly is this true of the decisive sin

[1] Here a passage out of Milton's grandiose depicting of Satan may find mention (*Paradise Lost*, I. 138, etc.). After his first expulsion Satan speaks in a monologue, related to the place in which he is exiled (I. 252-363) :—

> Receive thy new possessor ; one who brings
> A mind not to be changed by place or time.
> The mind is its own place, and in itself
> Can make a Heaven of Hell, a Hell of Heaven.
> What matter where, if I be still the same,
> And what I should be, all but less than he
> Whom thunder hath made greater ? Here at least
> We shall be free ; the Almighty hath not built
> Here for his envy, will not drive us hence :
> Here we may reign secure, and in my choice
> To reign is worth ambition, though in Hell.
> Better to reign in Hell than serve in Heaven.

Compare Moloch's speech in II. 50, —

> Or if our substance be indeed divine,
> And cannot cease to be, we are at worst
> On this side nothing ; and by proof we felt
> Our power sufficient to disturb his heaven,
> And with perpetual inroads to alarm,
> Though inaccessible, his fatal throne ;
> Which, if not victory, is yet revenge.

And I. 610, etc. :—
> If then his providence
> Out of our evil seek to bring forth good,
> Our labour must be to pervert that end,
> And out of good still to find means of evil ;
> Which ofttimes may succeed, so as perhaps
> Shall grieve him, if I fail not and disturb
> His inmost counsels from their destined aim.

of unbelief—which issue purely from the personal freedom of man, and therefore not from Satan, and which are also not caused by the medium of inherited sin. Satan is no evil Absolute, but is at every moment sustained by the Divine omnipotence, which only allows him place for ethical reasons. Satan has power over man generally to work actual evil in him, not immediately, but simply by the mediation of sinfulness already existent, and of human volition.[1] If, nevertheless, Satan also occurs as the personal expression for evil in general, we shall soon see the ground of this. According to what has been presented, the biblical features of the picture of Satan are quite harmonious.

3. But this doctrine also has a validity of recommendation, from the fact that it serves, *in the first place*, to establish the intensive idea of the importance of evil and of its goal; *secondly*, to open an instructive glance into its far-reaching connections; and *thirdly*, because of both reasons together, to commend vigilance, and to allow of the redemption by Christ appearing in a new light of necessity and consolation.

FIRST. Whilst Pantheism is only able to deny evil, or to refer it to a dark natural basis, and therefore ultimately to God, the doctrine of the devil as the enemy of God and man is in its Biblical form a defence against this view, and points—in distinction from Determinism and Pantheism, which are both logically compelled to deny it initially—to freedom as the cause of evil, and in such a manner that there is placed before the eyes in Satan the way in which evil, if it develops itself without check, and attains the mastery over the will, attains to the spirit of denial, to the demonic form of delight in evil as such.[2] It is true that the possibility of hatred towards good and delight in evil has often been questioned in the creature; but incorrectly. Evil can be willed, it has been said, but not because it is evil. But God has placed in free beings nothing more significant than the possibility of proceeding in direct opposition to Him, and of directing their desire to anything they wish. Of course hatred of good as such is not arrived at in a

[1] Jas. iv. 7; 1 Pet. v. 8, 9; Eph. vi. 12.
[2] Rothe has depicted this advance from human to demonic evil with special force. *Theol. Ethik*, edit. 1, §§ 503-512, vol. ii.

moment, but gradually by a progressive blinding and exasperation towards that goodness which is always restraining and punishing self-will and selfishness.

As far, SECONDLY, as the more general connections of evil are concerned, Deism sees in evil not the religious but the moral side only, whilst its offshoot, Pelagianism, can only conceive it in its isolation. The Biblical doctrine of the Devil serves, on the one hand, the purpose of permitting a glance to be cast upon the universal combinations, upon the anti-Divine unity of evil. In this regard, that side especially of his idea in the New Testament comes into consideration, according to which he is not conceived as a *solitary* creature, but, of course with his empire of demons, as the hypostasized principle of evil generally; for he is thought of as kindling all evil, in addition to being present therein, although, as has been shown, not to the diminution of the idea of human guilt. According to the New Testament, Satan is not merely a single individual like others; a cosmic real principle of a universal kind is thought to be in him.[1] Whether it is consistent with this, to say that he is also a personal being, a prince in the kingdom of evil, we will inquire presently. But in any case, the New Testament already attests by this teaching an important fact of knowledge,—that it regards the evil represented by Satan as a universal as well as omnipresent power in humanity. There is, according to the New Testament, an accordant reality of evil and its power,—a secret conspiracy of the same, and Satan is, so to speak, the personal expression for a common will of evil, which is consistent in apparent inconsistency. And because of this fact the history of humanity receives its more profound earnestness; and its centre, the Christian religion, because of this fact comes into a new and clearer light. We say, therefore, that supposing the evil principle did not exist personally in one being (Satan), still a reality of evil and connected powers in the world would at least have to be assumed. Every advance of the better new dispensation has to do with a new concentration of evil forces, which are allied as if in silent concert against the renewal, and which on every occasion adapt themselves to the new position. At the time of the Law

[1] Martensen, § 102.

the evil spirit directed itself to drawing the people of the Law back into the heathen spirit and worship of nature, by decoying and by menace. Then it desired to oppose to the ethical principle, which applies itself to a world which is to be built up anew, the natural world as alone true, nay Divine, and to represent the endeavour after righteousness and virtue as phantastical and the dream of the enthusiast, to represent good as powerless, refuted by the reality of the world. In that dispensation, therefore, the evil principle installed itself in the place of the hiatus of revelation still to be completed, and combated the possibility of a realization of good in the real world. The non-presence of the consummation of the ethical realm is turned against right and the truth, even of the commencement in Law and conscience, in order to lead to despair of the problem, and to the fundamental position of heathen sense: " Let us eat and drink, for to-morrow we are dead." This is presented in the Book of Job. But when the Hebrew principle asserted itself by means of the knowledge that good thrives directly in conflict with reality in suffering and temptations, and proves its purity, nay, when personal good appeared in the form of a servant and brought revelation to completion, the evil principle assumed another form. It now necessarily appeared as enmity against good, and it is even thus again falsehood. It apparently no longer challenges the right of the Law, the Hebrew principle of righteousness, but from the Law argues against the Gospel. The arrows it now sends into the soul have their burning poison in a righteousness isolated from grace and voluntary love. The evil principle now seeks to lead the knowledge of sin and penitence astray, to produce mistrust, and despair of God and salvation, by means of the vindication of the Law, and to hinder faith in Christian grace. Christ is made an enemy of and rejected by the Pharisees as the enemy of the Law and of righteousness. To the heart which is called to faith, thoughts are whispered now of arrogant self-righteousness, which finds redemption superfluous (the Law being satisfied), and now of despondency, saying, like Judas, " My sin is greater than can be forgiven." [1] Thus the evil principle at this stage combats

[1] Compare § 11.

the Christian revelation by means of the lower revelation of the Law,[1] just as it previously combated the lower revelation because it fell short of the higher. The evil principle always aims at adhering in a reactionary manner to the earlier stage of the history of the world. It always has a tendency back towards nature in opposition to historical progress; for it desires no ethical growth to thrive, but aims at the decadence, at the nonentity (of the annihilation) of the moral world. Its art is to represent retrogression in every case as progress. The disorganizing principle of evil which is pregnant with moral chaos always arrays itself in a largely promising semblance of a more satisfying order than that which has been previously attained by the good principle. And thus we understand in how great a world-historical struggle humanity is involved.[2] Disorganizing tendencies are diverging and rival attendants of all higher organization, and support one another as in a well-organized campaign. The history of the world goes forward, not in a still and peaceful course merely; it has battles to join, it has to combat with a combination of hostile forces. In this cohesion of the inimical opposition to good, in which the latter aims at breaking forth in new power,—a cohesion which is not concerted by man and which is still a fact,—most are simply unconscious instruments of evil. Still a number of threads are united as if to form a net, a strong opposition. Not merely has evil its existence in individual acts or individual men as such; there is also a nameless, impalpable evil, which is especially present at certain points of the development of history as if it were in the air, and which reaches far beyond the evil tendency of individual men. It is a spiritual evil, πνευματικὸν τῆς πονηρίας,[3] of which it cannot be said, "See here, see there," for it is invisibly present like an atmosphere in the common evil spirit, for example. But it is not like a *physical* miasma, inhering as it does in persons in an *ethical* manner. In such an omnipresence and dominion evil possesses quite a different formidableness to that which emanates from any single individual. This coherence of evil

---

[1] Rev. xii. 10, 13.
[2] Compare Martensen, *Christl. Dogmatik*, 1856, pp. 170-187.
[3] Eph. vi. 12.

can be overlooked by no earnest thinker or profound observer.[1] The Church has fixed this knowledge in clear popular form in its doctrine of an empire of evil and the prince thereof; a knowledge which resists volatilization, inasmuch as the cohesion and unity of evil are established securely by the fact that, as evil generally can only exist in personal form, evil is thought to be concentrated in the intelligence and volitional faculty of Satan—in a word, in his person.

We are thus led to the further question, *Can Satan, seeing that he signifies the universal principle of evil, be thought of as a person?* Of course evil can never be so concentrated in a creaturely individual, as good is in God. Nor can the universal principle of evil be thought of as personal in itself. For in that case it would be a substance which does not originate in God; it would no longer be contradictory to the real basis to which it must attach itself, which can arise from God alone, and which must remain good in the metaphysical sense of the word. Otherwise evil might arrive at an existence which was free from contradiction. But it never attains to the constitution of an actual anti-God, it never comes to a complete existence. It must halt at the mere *endeavour*. Also so far there is the difference between evil generally and Satan, that the latter, not being evil substance, is not all evil generally. But hence there follows not an indifferent relation between personality and the evil principle; rather does the evil principle in the world address itself in general to personality, and seeks to become personal, so to speak, by means of the personal creature. Figuratively one may say with Martensen:[2] "What Pantheism ascribes to God, namely, that, Himself impersonal, He incessantly seeks to become a person, attaches, so to speak, to the universal principle of evil, which, impersonal itself and lacking indeed true reality, hungers and thirsts after the life-blood of reality, and seeks to step from its inner emptiness and nothingness into the living reality, which imparts to it the semblance of life." Love goes out and communicates of its fulness; remaining at home, it still exists in others. Evil is in this

---

[1] Therefore Schenkel, for example, recognises in this sense a superhuman evil, although he does not hold the devil to be a personal being.

[2] § 103, p. 176.

respect also its opposite, fleeing eternally from its own vanity, desiring not to see in falsehood the vanity with which it is affected, and seeking to amplify itself by something which does not belong to it. With this the phenomenon of the δαιμονιζόμενοι agrees. It may be figuratively said that the evil principle could not live in the world without personalities which it stands in need of as its organs and bearers, so to speak. And as accordingly it is always, as it were, seeking a new and personal existence, so conversely creaturely personalities may acquiesce in a union with the evil principle in various grades. Assent to evil desire straightway brings with it a participation in an evil principle, since the individual evil has a universal bearing and significance; and the more the free creature surrenders itself to the evil desire, the more has the universal evil principle a handle, so that man can no longer lay the evil spirit he has invited. Thus the person may become the organ of the evil principle, at first with an admixture of passivity, but soon with ever decreasing opposition and with a definite evil will. The supposition of a demonic power, which can seduce from stage to stage and solicit freedom, is not a diminution of the guilt of man, but only an imparting of a clear idea of the internal progress of evil and its danger. That there actually are forms of evil which cannot be called other than demonic, a traducing of God, and an execration of everything holy, a joy in the downfall of the good and a delight in destruction, he cannot doubt who has in historical crises taken a glance into the abysses which are there opened. One may sell oneself to evil, may become a prophet of the lying spirit in evil inspiration, and a priest of the same, initiated into the depths of wickedness. Such men even find adherents, and are able to confine in their circle by magical means a blind seduced mass which offers them an opportunity; they represent the far-glancing eye of evil. The spirit of evil intoxicates, inspires them, in order to guide by their means the multitude according to its mind, and to lead it into the conflict. And if the possibility cannot be denied, that a human person may receive the evil principle in such a manner into himself that he delights to be the bearer and representative of the same with its consequences, there is also no longer any right to deny that even in the higher spirit-world there may be one spirit or many, who fell before men, who gave themselves ever more thoroughly to evil, and who surrender their personality to become instruments of the evil principle, which was merely possibility before, but now found in them a personal existence. The fallen angel then, who, equipped with the highest gifts, energetically coalesces with the evil principle and becomes its bearer, nay, forms the thought of founding a kingdom antagonistic to God, and, so to speak, " devotes himself to it with the most disinterested surrender," neither shunning damnation nor annihilation, is adapted to become a rallying-point for all antitheistic powers, —so to speak, the most central revelation and realization of evil. This is the Satan who has become the prince of the evil spirits.[1] Those whom he seduces join him overpowered. They are not necessarily held down by his might merely; they may also be held together by his spirit, " his evil genius and admiration thereof,"[1] as well as by their common aim. And when an evil is unwatched and unresisted in man, the kingdom of evil is near, as if because of a secret elective affinity, " Where a carcase is, there the eagles gather together." It is easily thinkable that, by his most intense hatred to good and his very great and very far - seeing delight in evil wherever it is, he has constituted himself, so to speak, the *sensorium commune* for evil in the world, and became thereby indispensable to the other evil spirits. And even the confederates of evil won from amongst men, the more consciously they enter into evil as such, the sooner they become ganglia for the history of evil upon earth. And thus it comes about that we are filled at single passages of history with sudden horrors, inasmuch as we must turn a glance into the depths of a demonic abyss, or inasmuch as, perceiving the far-reaching and yet nonconcerted connections of evil, we are seized irresistibly by the presentiment of a guiding intelligence which gathers to a conspiracy, as it were, against good. We have therefore no right to deny a kingdom of evil with a prince at the head. Incomplete it must certainly eternally remain. It is condemned to constant endeavour. The unity of this kingdom may be broken through

[1] Martensen.

or menaced, as well as that of earthly empires, by tumults, but prudence and power may again restore a certain unity. It may nevertheless be said that the adherents of Satan's empire are in one respect more homogeneous than any earthly empire, in which there is a mixture of good and bad; add to this, that the baser forms of evil are most of all one against another, limiting themselves and dislodging unity, because their aims are purely particular and egoistic. But the delight in evil itself and opposition to good has again in the kingdom of evil a more uniting power, and is the antithesis of love. Just for this reason, therefore, the unity of this empire will the more seek to consolidate itself, the more it is threatened and confined by Christianity. Possibly even Satan first owes the willing recognition of his dominion to the approach and manifestation of Christianity.—In this realm the bond of trust also has its place. As an artist, nay virtuoso in evil, Satan can fill his friends with a kind of self-denial and enthusiasm, can reward their doings with approbation and honour, and attach their fidelity to himself by partial victories in which he has again and again succeeded. In the history of the kingdom of God it is not always clear sunshine; there are eclipses also, in which the elect themselves, were it possible, must be led astray, if these days were not shortened. These are the times of anxiety for faith, points of support for unbelief, festivals for the kingdom of darkness. Not merely has Christ experienced, as He says, hours in which the prince of this world has power and a free course; the life of Christ is in this respect typical for the Church. Although therefore Satan is never identical with evil generally, because there is evil which he does not work, and because the creaturely basis ever remains real metaphysically in him, still he is no mere image of universal evil, but represents it inasmuch as he is the spirit who seeks to become the central organ for evil, and to identify his finite personality with evil generally, in which he does not want a complementary companionship.

*Observation.*—The kingdom of Satan represents in the dogmatic system the antithesis of the kingdom of God.

Finally, this doctrine is, IN THE THIRD PLACE, adapted by both things, the knowledge of the intensity and the goal as well as of the connection of evil, to commend vigilance, and to permit the redemption through Christ to appear in a new light. The recognition that there is not an individual moral struggle merely, but a struggle that is world-wide, as well as that we are destined to take part therein, must, as cautious teachers of the Church themselves acknowledge, who think themselves obliged to deny a personal devil, exercise an influence upon an earnest conception of evil, upon the vigilance and exertion of the moral powers.[1] Therefore such teachers as Schleiermacher desire the mention of Satan to be maintained in the language of the Church. It deserves to be considered that they are very often morally lax times to which this teaching is most disturbing, times which are very little adapted to understand the depths and the extent of the opposition between good and evil; whilst energetic characters morally and religiously strong, of far-reaching glance, such as, to except the ancient fathers of the Church, a Luther and a Calvin, frequently maintain most decidedly the existence and activity of Satan. Supposing Satan indeed merely to have a place as a figure of speech in the language of the Church, this would not merely be unworthy of the clearness and truth of the Church, but even the figure of speech itself would immediately refuse its service if the doctrine itself were merely lowered to such an one. The possibility of a devil *must* be conceded ; to question the realization, therefore, because it is of course a disagreeable reality and out of tune, is not worthy of science (which has to make itself independent of moods), and decides nothing as to the thing itself. The wish that the devil did not exist, does not slay him.

But elevating and consolatory elements are not wanting to the New Testament doctrine of Satan. It is elevating, because we are accounted worthy to take part in this conflict, the importance of which, as this doctrine renders visible, is cosmical; and the conflict is one which brings us into communion with the whole world of good spirits and their interests, a struggle the final decision of which need not alarm us, because Christ is answerable for it, and He does not

---

[1] Martensen, p. 185 : the deep horror of the community of demons is the dark ground for the Christian fear of God.

surrender His world to Satan. The Church, which does not deny Satan's existence and might, because it has no right to do so, believes in his existence without fear, because it has the capacity to bear the thought. It does not flee before him or the thought of him, but courageously keeps him in view, and thus he flees before it. The *world* must either deny his existence or his power, for it cannot bear the thought that he is and works. That it denies him, is its artifice; at the same time there is visible therein a gracious dispensation, that the abysses of evil only reveal themselves to the eye in proportion as the glance is supportable and do not impel men to despair, because the saving power is not known as yet. But the Church does not need such a recreant-like denial of his existence. The world always wavers between the two extremes, either to make evil absolute, if it takes a glance into its depths and earnestness, or to deny its power and importance. To the Church, notwithstanding,[1] with the same glance which apprehends the depths of evil,[2] is disclosed the essential hollowness and falsehood of the same, as compared with the powers of redemption, and the reality of the salvation which alone is permanent. And thus it combats evil assured of victory, for Christ is born to it.

[1] Jas. iv. 7.     [2] τὰ βάθη τοῦ Σατανᾶ, Rev. ii. 24.

# THIRD HEAD.

## EVIL IN RELATION TO THE DIVINE GOVERNMENT.

### FIRST POINT: THE DOCTRINE OF DEATH.

#### A.—*The Biblical Doctrine.*

### § 87.

ACCORDING to the Scriptures, the spiritual and corporeal evil which is summarized in death, is not the natural fruit merely of sin, but is also its righteous reward or punishment; and just as pre-Christian sin and guilt also partake of the character of a common sin and common guilt, so the evil originating therein has the character of a common evil and a common punishment, which is distributed to individuals unequally, and as compared with others, not always in proportion to their guilt. But as the revelation of punitive justice is not without a trace of Divine love because of the Divine long-suffering, so the Divine love also counteracts sin in a positive manner by the consummation of revelation, which is conditioned by the holy justice, is not simply redemptive but pre-eminently atoning, and at the same time furthers the decisive judgment.

LITERATURE.—Comp. pp. 2 and 3, especially the works of Krabbe and Mau. Joh. Gerhardt, *Loci Theologici,* loc. xxvii. Ritschl, *De ira dei,* 1859, and *Die christliche Lehre von der Rechtfertigung und Versöhnung,* III. 1874. Weber, *Vom Zorn Gottes,* 1867. Kreibig, *Die Versöhnungslehre,* 1878, pp. 78, etc. Weiss, *Bibl. Theologie,* § 32, pp. 101, etc.; § 34, pp. 110, etc.;

§ 64, p. 222; § 50, p. 171; § 57, p. 194; § 98, p. 406; § 126, p. 536; § 129, p. 547; § 151, p. 657; comp. §§ 24, 25 of this work.

1. Just as God truly loves, so is He truly angry with everything contrary to His holy nature. He is a strong and zealous God.[1] His zeal has reference to good, which is His nature and honour, but also refers to evil in such a way that in His purity He excludes everything unholy. Thus the Old Testament in numerous passages.[2] The expressions often sound anthropopathic, but this is corrected by other statements which bear witness to God as an immutable ethical Self-identity, so that passages of this kind simply add absolute ethical livingness to the Divine Self-identity.[3] There is expressed thereby the energy of the Divine hatred to evil, as well as the energy of His love for good as such. The object of the Divine hatred is all evil, and the opinion will not stand the test of proof which says that in the Old Testament it is only apostasy from the theocracy or assaults thereupon, and in the New Testament only unbelief in Christ, which are the objects of the Divine anger or of the Divine punishment; the opinion, too, has as little authority, that in the New Testament all pre-Christian sins are not merely capable of forgiveness but pardoned at the outset, being regarded as mere ignorance (for which there is no need of an atonement through Christ, but simply of the revelation of the paternal goodness of God, in order that the representation of a punitive Divine righteousness, and consequently mistrust of God, may be dissipated). There comes here into consideration the teaching of the Old [4] and New [5] Testaments

[1] Ex. xx.
[2] Ps. ii. 12, v. 5, xxi. 10, li. 6, lxxvii. 10, xc. 7, 11, cii. 11; Deut. xxxii. 22; Isa. x. 17, xxx. 27; Jer. x. 10, xvii. 4, xxiii. 20.
[3] Comp. my treatise on the *Unveränderlichkeit Gottes, Jahrb. für d. Theol.* 1851, pp. 444, etc.
[4] The above is shown in Old Testament passages like Gen. vi. 1, etc., Ps. li., and the non-theocratical Book of Job.
[5] Matt. vii. 1, 2, x. 33, xviii. 35; 2 Cor. v. 10, ix. 6; comp. Gal. vi. 7, 8. This law of retribution is also recognised by John in reference to the wicked and those who stand in a living communion with Christ. Comp. Weiss, p. 657 and pp. 103, etc., 519, 259. The Divine punishment is an execution of the law, Rom. xiii. 4, a declaration of the Divine anger which is identical with zeal for good or the law.

of retribution according to the fundamental position of equivalence. The demerit, the exceptionableness, of evil provokes the Divine wrath, and indeed not merely the sin of definitive unbelief, but *all* unrighteousness.[1] The New Testament does not regard unbelief in Christ merely as punishable sin, and does not speak of a Divine ὀργή merely in relation to the final judgment; rather has it a special name for the latter,[2] and the world as it was before Christ is expressly described as the object of the Divine ὀργή.[3] Indeed, the long-suffering of God before Christ is itself in its way a proof that there were, according to the Scripture, even before Christ, sins amongst heathens and Jews which were actually culpable, to which the punitive justice of God had reference. Without the culpability of evil there could be no mention of long-suffering, but this could only be synonymous with the will to preserve. If indeed the ὀργὴ Θεοῦ were merely directed to the full and just execution of punishment, it would not consist with long-suffering (ἀνοχή), which embraces a postponement of punishment. But rather is the ὀργὴ Θεοῦ pre-eminently the inner Divine displeasure, the inclemency where evil is concerned, which is the spring of all possible punishment, the execution of which, however, may be delayed notwithstanding by long-suffering.

2. The effect of the Divine ὀργή Scripture phraseology summarizes in *death*, whereby all evil and mischief is described as a unity. Physical and spiritual misery and calamity bear this name.[4] But death is brought into the closest relations with sin.[5] It is consonant with the elevation of conscious-

---

[1] Rom. i. 18; comp. v. 13, 14. Therefore here, as in John iii. 36, the ὀργὴ Θεοῦ is thought of as present, and no refinement can succeed in proving that the New Testament only speaks of a future (or future possible) ὀργή.

[2] ὀργὴ μέλλουσα, ἐρχομένη, Matt. iii. 7; Luke iii. 7; Rom. ii. 5, 8; 1 Thess. i. 10; 2 Thess. i. 8; Rev. vi. 17.

[3] John iii. 36; Rom. i. 18, etc.; Eph. ii. 3; Rev. xiv. 10, xvi. 19.

[4] In the Old Testament (comp. Gen. iii. 15, etc.; Num. xvi. 28; Ps. xxii. 16, cxvi. 3, and frequently in the Proverbs, *e.g.* viii. 36, xi. 19, xiii. 14, xiv. 27, etc.), death is specially, yet not exclusively, physical death. Even in the New Testament, θάνατος is primarily physical death, Rom. v. 12–14; 1 Cor. xv. 21. But frequently it occurs in the spiritual sense, Rom. v. 21, viii. 6; Eph. ii. 1; John viii. 51, xi. 26.

[5] Gen. iii. 19; Ps. xc. 7–9; Rom. v. 12. It is regarded as a judgment, as a punishment of sin, with one consent in the Old Testament and the New. Rom.

ness above nature and its laws, as well as with the moral view of the world, that even the Old Testament derives the mortality of man only from a cause which lies in him, from his conduct in defiance of his idea; and it is not scriptural to say that death must have entered, even apart from sin, by virtue of a universal law of nature. His God-likeness would have preserved man from the fate of the animals, had he remained pure. We do not owe death to nature, we owe it to the flesh, inasmuch as it has become unnaturally lord over the spirit.[1] As men now are, death is indeed an event naturally necessary, as an effect resulting from the internal disorder, and under this point of view death is called the fruit of sin.[2] But the other aspect to be considered is, that the natural connection between sin and death is woven by the Divine justice. Death is also the wages of sin;[3] the naturally necessary process of death is also punishment, retribution. We must not stop at the punishment of the evil conscience,[4] nor at the consequences of sin resulting from the course of nature, but we must have recurrence to the ὀργή of God itself, which as inclemency is already punishment, and on the other side is the source of all just punishment.[5] The bond which knits sin to evil on the human side, and transforms it into punishment, is guilt.[6] Although the death which still affects Christians is no longer punishment or evil to them, it must not be thence concluded that it was not in itself and originally objective punishment for the sinner, but is only subjectively regarded as such by the unredeemed. Rather is it by the forgiveness of sins only that death has lost the character of punishment objectively as well as subjectively in relation to faith, and simply continues as a natural consequence which is incorporated in the purpose of

vi. 21-23, vii. 5, viii. 10 ; 1 Pet. iv. 6 ; Jas. v. 3, 5, comp. i. 15 ; Heb. ix. 27, comp. ii. 14 ; 1 Cor. xv. 56.

[1] Rom. viii. 12, etc.         [2] Jas. i. 15 ; Rom. vi. 21.
[3] Rom. vi. 23.         [4] Rom. ii. 15.
[5] The New Testament names which refer to the punitive justice are—δίκη, 2 Thess. i. 9 ; κόλασις, τιμωρία, Matt. xxv. 46, Heb. x. 29 ; ζημιοῦν, Matt. xvi. 26 ; ἐκδίκησις, 1 Pet. ii. 14.—In Rom. iii. 26, δικαιοσύνη in contrast with the long-suffering which does not punish as yet, the punishable is the exhibition of the justice which demands satisfaction, Rom. i. 18, etc.
[6] Matt. v. 21, 22, ἔνοχος τῇ κρίσει ; vi. 12, ὀφίλημα ; Rom. iii. 19, ὑπόδικος.

## 118   THE DOCTRINE OF EVIL.

salvation.¹ If now, as has been shown, the Divine ὀργή is directed towards all evil,² and sin in humanity is primarily sin of the race and common guilt, the evil answering thereto is also to be primarily regarded as common punishment which may apply as widely as the common guilt.³ And thence it also follows, that from the measure of the evil which affects the individual, the measure of his personal guilt cannot be inferred. Rather, as regards the distribution of the common evil, other factors intervene in the course of history.⁴ If in this distribution a disproportion comparatively at least exists, on the other hand the common punishment, which arises from the common sin itself, forms no disproportion in the sense that the sin is transcended by the greatness of the evil; but there is a disproportion of an opposite kind, so long as there is still a place for the Divine long-suffering, namely, inasmuch as sin must not wholly display in a moment its natural fruit, evil. Still this double disproportion between sin and evil does not apply for ever, but the New Testament refers to a compensating final judgment, and to an end to the provisional state in which there is still found a disproportional distribution of evil. There is a punishment which no longer has anything to do with the common punishment, with the hereditableness of wickedness and evil, but is of a purely personal kind, when guilt has also become purely personal. Here first, therefore, can punishment realize itself in strict proportion to guilt.⁵

3. According to the New Testament, DEATH has several STAGES. Sin itself, as a severance of the communion with the original source of life, is already regarded as a kind of death;⁶ its reverse side is that it is evil, for with sin man has taken into himself the principle of dissolution or death; and therefore θάνατος also has the meaning of spiritual decay. But through sin the unity of the human organism is essentially violated, and thus the second consequence of sin is *mortality*, by which man becomes subject to the necessity of the dissolution of the bond between soul and body which is only abolished

---

¹ Rom. viii. 1; Phil. i. 21.   ² Rom. i. 18.
³ Rom. v. 12–19; 1 Cor. xv. 22; Matt. xxiii. 35.
⁴ John ix. 1, etc. (the man born blind); Luke xiii. 4 (the tower of Siloam).
⁵ Gal. vi. 5; 2 Cor. v. 10.
⁶ Comp. Matt. viii. 22; Col. ii. 13; Eph. ii. 1, 5, v. 14.

with sin itself.[1] But from this corporeal death, by which the soul is stripped of its organ by virtue of the power now irresistible of the divinely ordained laws of the merely natural life, there is a progress, which is still unoriginated by a physical necessity, to a further stage, which is called the *second death*,[2] a death at the second power, which has something mysterious about it, and is at any rate the result of the concluding judgment, and apparently means a setting in impotence and ruinousness. But to this second death neither sin in general nor necessary mortality conducts. Both of these still leave room for the Divine long-suffering. The definitive decision of punitive justice is only brought about by the decisive rejection of the perfect revelation on the part of the person. This revelation is that of atoning love. As the justice of the Divine punishment and culpability are recognised by this love,[3] so is also the Divine righteousness brought thereby to full revelation, both with respect to unbelievers as well as believers.

B.—*The Ecclesiastical Doctrine.*

§ 87*b*.

In general, the doctrine of the Church agrees with Holy Scripture, only that conformably to its doctrine of original sin it bestows too little regard on personality as opposed to common sin and punishment. *Conf. Aug.* II. xvii.; *Apologia*, lviii.; *Anglicana*, 9; *Heidelberg Cat.* 10; *Gallicana*, 10; *Bohemica*, 4.

1. The doctrine of the Church does not merely recognize evil, with Holy Scripture, as the naturally necessary consequence of sin, but also the connection of the same with the justice of God, or its character as punishment; but just analogously to its doctrine of Sin, it stops at inherited sin or the punishment of the race, from which Christ has redeemed,[4] and

---

[1] Rom. v. 12, etc., vi. 21-23.   [2] Rev. ii. 11, xx. 6, 14, xxi. 8.
[3] Rom. iii. 25-28 ; Gal. iii. 13 ; Matt. xx. 28.
[4] Still, in opposition to the Catholic doctrine of satisfactions for sins after baptism, the power of redemption is also extended to actual sins, only that these again remain in too exclusive a connection with original sin.

treats of the difference between the generic and the personal without entering thereupon, simply expressing ingenuously the consciousness that the disfavour of God and punishment generally are related to the common sinful state of man as well as to the individual sins of individuals.[1] Still the Confessions associate the position herewith, that believers are free from all condemnation and punishment. For them also death is no longer punishment.[2]

2. The post-Reformation age of the 17th century already makes a more precise distinction between personal sin and generic sin, at least in reference to *Reprobatio*, in the measure in which it removes from the absolute *Decretum* (comp. § 83). But in the 18th and 19th centuries death was regarded by many as a mere natural necessity; the necessity of the connection between the Divine justice and penal evil was slackened or denied by the so-called amelioration theories, punishment being itself changed into a merely subjective representation, or wickedness simply described as its own punishment. But wickedness is the object of punishment, and the thing to be punished must not be confounded with punishment itself, unless the unethical volatilization of the idea of punishment into that of resulting evil is to threaten. Here also Kant, by his strong consciousness of moral evil and its necessary culpability, expresses himself on the other side.[3]

C.—*Dogmatic Investigation.*

§ 88.

The necessity for the punishment of evil (*Böse*) is based in the justice of the holy God (§§ 24, 25). It employs for

---

[1] *Scot.* III.; *Dordr.* III.; F. C. 641, 13: *pœnæ peccati originalis quas Deus filiis Adæ ratione hujus peccati imposuit, hæ sunt: mors, æterna damnatio et præter has aliæ corporales, spirituales, temporales atque æternæ ærumnæ et miseriæ, tyrannis et dominium Satanæ,* etc.

[2] *Apol.* 86, 125, 194. *Renatis et in Christum credentibus nulla est damnatio.* Upon the doctrine of later writers, as well as that of B. Menzer, see above, § 83. 2. A.

[3] Comp. *Ueber die Straftheorien,* I. pp. 287, etc. Kant, edit. by Rosenkranz, x. 168, etc.

that end both the good natural order and the peculiar nature of man, but in such a way that by means of physical and psychical evil (*Uebel*[1]), which are the divinely ordained consequences of evil (*Böse*), it points to a higher, an absolute evil (*Uebel*), the Divine disfavour or the wrath of God. This disfavour has reference not merely to the sin, but also to the sinner, and excludes a forgiveness at the cost of justice as morally impossible. Nevertheless the Divine love is not excluded by the Divine wrath; but as wrath as internally regarded is in itself and remains holy love to good, so God desires to change the sting of all punishment, the miserable sense of his just disfavour into an impulse to seek the satisfaction of justice by atonement, and the Divine justice imposes no necessity to permit those to be lost who are capable of redemption; but all who are born of Adam stand in need not merely of emancipation from sin, but also and pre-eminently from guilt and punishment, *i.e.* they all stand in need of atonement.

1. For the basis of punishment, *i.e.* of evil as an infliction of the Divine justice, reference is to be made to the doctrine of God, where the so-called absolute theory of punishment was established.[2] Pantheism and Determinism cannot consistently accept punishment in the stricter sense, but can only accept the logical or naturally necessary consequences of what passes for evil with them. But others also have scruples about the idea of Divine punishment. In the first place, there are METAPHYSICAL scruples. If the Biblical expressions concerning the Divine

---

[1] [Attention must be again called to the difficulty of translating into English the two words *Böse* and *Uebel*, the former of which signifies evil as the cause of punishment (wickedness), and the latter evil as the effect of punishment (the consequences of wickedness). The same word "evil" has to stand for both the German terms, leaving it to the context to suggest the more exact meaning.—TR.]

[2] § 24. 6, § 32. 4. Ritschl is in error in wishing to derive the idea of the Divine punitive justice from civil and political justice. Just on the contrary, justice in the state, according to reason and Scripture, has a religious and moral origin, and without these would be without a principle, and eudæmonistic merely.

punitive justice are not taken figuratively, and if more than a subjective meaning is given to Divine punishment, then it is said a mutability comes to be supposed in God, because His disfavour does not merely condition a changed relation to the sinner, but also points to a changed sentiment on the Divine part towards the sinner. God must rather be thought, therefore, in relation to man as well as in Himself, to be unchangeable and eternally self-identical.[1] But just because God is ethically unchangeable, He cannot treat or regard the evil and the good alike. He would be mutable just in His innermost ethical nature, if He embraced good indeed in Himself with the zeal of His holy love, but was on the other hand indifferent what relation men took to good, which in reality makes an unconditioned claim to prevalence.[2] Thus the Divine disfavour to evil and the wicked is simply the necessary self-assertion of His holy nature and His ethical immutability against all change in the world.

Just as little can the inference be drawn on ETHICAL grounds, *i.e.* on the ground of the Divine goodness and love, that God cannot will to punish because it is foreign to God to inflict an evil or pain. Rather is there no love in God, and especially no true goodness, which is not before all things just. Did God not hate evil, He would not love good: were there not in Him the fire of ὀργή against evil, there would not be in Him the holy flame of love; in zeal against evil, purity of love to good is preserved. Or is God to be supposed only eudæmonistically able to make the sensuous well-being of rational creatures the final end of the world, as contrasted with the good and the holy? This would also be degrading for

---

[1] One gladly refers hereupon to Matt. v. 45, a passage which utters Divine long-suffering for the sinner, but will not make good and evil an indifferent thing as opposed to the Divine justice (§ 32. 4).

[2] If the ethical be thought indifferent as to realization, it would itself be represented in a manner simply spiritualistic, and so to speak ghostly; it would remain a merely good thought, or a thought of the good, which lacked all power. Not for a moment would it be good disposition, for this aims with inner necessity at realization. And since the ethical desires objectivation, it cannot be indifferent to it, whether it has a value in realization. Indeed, it must also claim to be or to become the power over the physical; as absolutely powerless in reference to the same it would also be in opposition to itself, and must renounce the claim to be the supreme power, the power even above omnipotence (§ 26, § 32. 4).

man. That he can be punished, is a sign of his higher destiny.[1]

That the ethical must remain the final end of the world, others concede, but they will only recognize punishment as an *amelioration,* and they regard the addition of evil, inflicted as a punishment on the side even of human society, as justified only so far as its fruit is amelioration. But in this case, because of human freedom, the uncertainty would never be surmounted as to whether it is right to punish, or on the contrary to bestow further benefits, because they may also ameliorate. And if it is said that it lies open and certain to God what the final moral decision of the free man will be, it would follow, that if punishment is simply justified on the score of amelioration, the obdurate sinner, concerning whom God foresaw that no work of amelioration would influence him, must remain unpunished. If the amelioration theory would not remain without a principle, but would still leave a right to the sentiment of justice, it must maintain that, according to our psychological constitution, there is a necessity for us to bring evil as a righteous punishment into connection with sin. Now if this opinion shaped itself thus, that our psychical constitution does not correspond with objective truth or a Divine necessity, but simply generates a subjective and deceptive representation of a connection between evil and our sin, with the knowledge of deception the idea of punishment would be absolutely dissolved, and that psychological necessity itself would again be apparent merely. For the sake of justice what we assert must therefore be conceded, that our constitution originating *in God* is so framed that amelioration cannot enter without the experience of a corresponding evil, or without the recognition of the culpability of evil, and this of itself leads to the fact that the connection indeed between sin and punitive justice is a close

---

[1] If Schenkel and others simply adopt the position of Schleiermacher, "We have no wrath of God to teach," whilst notwithstanding they affirm, as Schleiermacher does not, a creaturely freedom, this is even logically blameworthy; and they despoil the Divine government of the counterpoise to the free powers which are inimical to God, unless their doctrine of Freedom changes again into a Determinism. Power must stand beside justice as the *ultima ratio,* which can reveal the inner hollowness and falsehood of evil, and divest the same of the assumed semblance of being the true reality. Without this the supposition of a free world would be something irrational.

and objective one. The actual recognition of culpability straightway contains the recognition of the objective significance of justice and punishment.

But FINALLY, OTHERS SAY, "evil must be punished, but it is its *own punishment*, and therewith justice is satisfied: no further punishment is needed." If the opinion here expressed is that sin, the punishable, is itself the punishment, the question is, wherefore punishment follows, if by hypothesis sin is itself punishment?[1] Actual sin or evil as guilt is manifestly not punishment, but works punishment. Of course the consequence of actual sin is sin, an evil state, and this, or the moral misery, is also punishment, namely as non-freedom or slavery. But even this is only the consequence of actual sin laden with guilt, which is not in itself already punishment. It is false and perilous to lay down absolutely, severed from the past and the future, the position that God punishes evil in order to increase it. Neither the commencement of evil, the act of sin, nor evil generally, so far as it is evil desire and not misery, is punishment; it is punishable rather. The punishment of sin by sin is never the immediate act or the direct aim of God, but is the effect of nature divinely ordered and destined for good. The position in question is also incorrect, because it is not evil which is punished, but the doers of evil, and just as little is evil itself abolished. With the position that evil is its own punishment, if it is to have a sense, the opinion must be held that evil is punished by evil, as the cause of necessary effects which are evil. In fact, who can deny that the evil-doer cannot enjoy the peace of soul of the righteous, that spiritual weakness and derangement are the consequences of evil—that, for example, sensuous sin necessarily by misuse destroys the body? All this is only the logically and physically necessary consequence of the fact that the nature of man is destined for good, and experiences because of evil a perversion which is pernicious. But by the natural necessity of these consequences, the recognition of a Divine punishment by that

---

[1] It approximates to this conception, when distance from God is treated at the same time as sin and punishment, particularly if God is thought to be near to man with His love in a manner eternally similar. In this case, what might be punishment in the remoteness of God vanishes into a mere erroneous representation, generated by the subjective Divine estrangement.

means ought not to be deistically excluded. For whence is this natural order? If punishment is not referred to the living God of providence, still the constitution of the physical and spiritual nature, through which this punishment necessarily enters, has its origin in God, who has ordered it in harmony with His justice. But He has never withdrawn from His creation, He dwells livingly therein. Add to this that God can only love and will the good He Himself is so absolutely, that He rejects what is unholy in offended reaction and disfavour, and cannot allow the same to be unmolested side by side with good, good being incompatible with its absolute opposite. So certainly as good is alone the unconditioned necessity, it must endeavour to exclude evil, that the world may pertain to good for which it was destined. It may be said, it is true, that this might happen by the vanquishing of evil, and that punishment is not necessary thereto. But first, as has been shown, no one can truly improve himself without recognizing the validity of his conscience, which describes him as culpable. Further, inasmuch as God created a class of free agents, He gave it the power to disturb the kingdom of good, He exposed His will to possible disregard. But this could only be without prejudice to His majesty and our creaturely position and absolute obligation, if at the same time God opposed to evil the punitive justice. Good, its victory over evil, cannot be effected by compulsion. Man can array himself in opposition to the holy God and to the means of salvation, nay can blunt his conscience, consequently the honour of good cannot be staked upon vanquishing evil by sanctification alone, but in opposition to evil the negative and also irremissible position must be retained, that good may at any rate make valid its rejected claims upon man by punishment. It stands thus: if thou dost not will good, thou canst not be compelled, but thou canst be punished. The blow which evil strikes against good by the misused means of good, demands, unless good is to be powerless, the inevitable counter-blow, which can only maintain itself and its honour securely by the fact that the arm of omnipotence is at its command and not at the command of evil, that the might and reality which evil arrogates are taken therefrom, and evil is divested thereof as well as of the pleasure the semblance of which it took to itself in order to hide its hollowness. Granting even that this counter-blow to evil, whereby it is robbed of its misused good things, advanced by no single step the amelioration of the sinner, there would lie in punishment itself not merely something absolutely justified, but a good, because it would reveal in the only way left the permanent absolute obligation of good even in spite of refractoriness, and would authenticate the stability of the good government of the world.

2. CONTENTS OF PUNISHMENT WITH ITS KINDS.—Punishments are first *physical* evils up to corporeal death, to which also all the disorganizing effects of sin belong. They also reach to the psychical sphere; for the human faculties are not equally good in the evil as in the good, but waste away until the end may be paralysis. Men originally highly gifted may become like extinct volcanoes by a life in sinful passion. A teleological view of the world must acknowledge that, were there no sin, possible evils would be permanently restrained.[1] In physical evil there is at any rate contained a reaction against evil of the good government of the world, and of the logic implanted in the world.[2] But there is also a reaction of the *moral nature* as a counter-blow to evil. To this category in particular belongs evil conscience, its impeachment and condemnation. Further, there are the moral forces which work in society and history; especially the divinely appointed practice of the administration of justice in domestic and civil life, which should be conscious of acting in the name of God, and which serves for the preservation of an existence worthy of man.[3] But to the judgment, which the good government of the world itself historically executes by its physical and moral forces, there

[1] Labour and effort would still retain their place; they are not evils. Even Schleiermacher maintained the connection of all evil with sin. To sin as the common act of the race evil answers as the common punishment, a view which Ritschl blames (III. pp. 208, 311) incorrectly. With a teleological view of the world such censure is only possible, if in the Kantian fashion homage is paid to a natureless ethics, and the constitution of nature is nursed therein not because of what it could and would give to the spirit in its normal state, but because it is simply asked, whether the spirit in spite of its limitations can maintain itself in its elevation, which is by no means a victory over the world.

[2] On the connection of Logic and Mathematics with Justice something has been said in § 24.

[3] Gen. ix. 5, 6; Rom. xiii. 1, etc.

necessarily succeeds the *Divine disfavour*, together with everything it includes in the withholding of communion with God, of peace and blessedness. The disfavour of God is the supreme source of all other possible and divinely ordained punishments, and it is itself also something *per se*, and a special further element in addition to these. So certainly as communion with God is a special good by the side of the harmony of man with himself and the world, so certainly is the Divine disfavour, which withdraws the Divine complacency from the sinner, is at variance with him, and puts upon him a ban or curse, a special, nay the supreme and most important element in punishment. We may call it the *Divine* punishment in the stricter sense. The other kinds of punishment are its proclamations or emanations.

3. But the physical, moral, and divine punishments in the stricter sense are to be considered in their relation to one another. They are ordained for co-operation. Punishment would not be ethical, it would only be a physical occurrence, a mishap, indeed it would lack that which is most poignant, and its inner meaning would be concealed, if man merely experienced an evil, without the strings of the moral self-consciousness being struck thereby in normal fashion, so that evils might be referred to sin and guilt in the inner forum. On the other hand, man is not concerned with self-condemnation in the conscience merely. The voice of the same would remain exposed to the grossest falsifications, were the natural order not the ally of conscience. Moreover, the human judgment in its limited sphere does not reach all that is culpable. It is now the art of the Divine punitive justice, which human justice can only imperfectly imitate, that it has ordained the inner ideal or spiritual side and also the real and physical to co-operate, although both do not always enter simultaneously. Man must himself, according to the good Divine order, contribute to his own punishment, for the accuser, witness, and judge of the evil deed is placed within him, and thus the blow is more than a mishap or ill, which may be avoided by art or prudence; it becomes, what it is in itself, subjectively in relation to man, *punishment*, and has its spiritual sting therein. On the other hand, in order that man may not stifle the judgment of conscience by self-

justification or by doubting the law, the physical evils (including the social) which develop themselves from sin, must always arouse in turn the careless mind, and thus aid in establishing the throne of the judgment of conscience. But as, finally, the physical evils already refer the sobered mind to God as the living originator and preserver of this world-order, the accusing and punitive conscience of itself points back to God. In the consciousness of guilt, which man knows right well, he has not merely to do with himself and discord in himself, and generally not with a purely subjective relation, but he is referred to an objective relation of God to sin and guilt. And neither conscience nor the God-consciousness says that God has eternally forgiven evil or regards it as ignorance. The judgment, in repudiation of evil made by conscience, is not something subjective merely, but by means of conscience, which is a knowing together with God, the judgment of God is made known; therein is the voice of God as well. For this reason, therefore, conscience does not say that its blame is the sole punishment together with the physical consequences of evil, in which the good continuity of nature is asserted, but in the judgment of conscience there is also contained the consciousness of guilt.[1] There is associated therein something of divination, something which points to the future, an "expectation of the Divine judgment."[2] The sense of the decree of conscience is: because it pronounces "guilty" by higher authority, the Divine disfavour is present, and culpability is present, and the punishment which follows is just. Consequently the state of punishment already essentially enters, the judgment has already descended, as it were. The disfavour of God hangs over the condemned.[3] He feels himself already apprehended, bound in the chains of fear, in a diminished life.[4] Although therefore for a time, by the falsehood of sin, the state of punishment may be denied and the consciousness of the

---

[1] Rom. iii. 19.　　[2] Heb. x. 17 ; ἐκδοχὴ κρίσεως, Rom. ii. 16.
[3] John iii. 36 : ἡ ὀργὴ τοῦ Θεοῦ μένει ἐπ' αὐτόν.
[4] Rom. viii. 10, 15, iii. 5, 19. That the judgment of conscience refers back to God, indeed receives from Him power and right, is on the one hand the most central and hard thing in punishment, and on the other hand, the basis for the fact that, when God has forgiven sin, conscience has no right to prosecute its accusation to punishment.

Divine disfavour forgotten or choked, a time comes in which falsehood is dissipated, and disfavour is so revealed that it cannot be denied any more even by the sinner, and in which the execution of punishment which only begins upon earth, must attain its wretched end, unless a turn for the better enters.[1]

*Observation.*—In what has been discussed is also contained the answer to the controversy as to whether there are only natural punishments or so-called "positive" punishments as well.[2] The contrast itself is awkwardly put. By "positive punishments" were meant punishments arbitrarily decreed by God and standing outside the effects of the system of nature, and the natural are not directly referred to the God who founds and preserves the world-order, but are regarded as works of nature without God. Both are false. We have to regard the natural also as the ordinance of God, and Divine punishment has nothing arbitrary in it, but corresponds with the immutable holy nature of God, as well as with the idea of man. Only this can be said, that the experience of the Divine disfavour as such within is the immediate experience of the Divine punishment, whilst the physical and moral punishments are only mediately Divine.[3]

---

[1] This is indicated by the Divine φυλακή or φρουρά, κόλασις αἰώνιος, 1 Pet. iii. 19; Matt. v. 25.

[2] Another ancient division is that between *pœna sensus* and *pœna damni*, the latter of which only denotes the withholding of the good things by which felicity is enhanced, the former the addition of painful evils.

[3] Evil may disturb the good order within and without us, the social and physical order, and that these disturbances in the objective world which react upon us as evils, bear the character of punishment, the uniform consciousness expresses with certainty; and this is not annulled by the fact that even these evils in the Divine economy may in turn serve the kingdom of good as means of exercise and stimulus. But they only do this with success when a higher moral power is attained, which they cannot themselves provide. Apart from the sinful weakness of the moral faculty, and apart from the disturbance or non-nature introduced into the world by evil, nature would be a willing organ for the dominion of the spirit and the realization of the moral therein. But actual punishment, and not a mere mistaken conversion of a subjective feeling of evil (ill) into a feeling of punishment, is to be seen even where at first nothing has been changed in the objective world by our sin, and no hindrance which was not previously existent is procured for us, but there has entered only a false relation of our power to the nature which is essentially good. For the resistance which disturbs us, and which the objective order presents, by the effect of our sin brings for us no mere imaginary evil with it, but an actual evil, which because of its relation to the evil in us, and by virtue of the world-order, which corresponds with fact and is just, is punishment.

4. The MEASURE OR THE STAGES OF PUNISHMENT are in general defined by the measure of the previous sin and guilt which is at first the common sin and common guilt. With these correspond the evil in the world, at least in such a way that evil as the common punishment does not surpass the measure of sin. In this common evil, which is at the same time punishment, every one shares who enters the circle of humanity, whatever its relations to his personal guilt. The physical and social evils have their relatively independent course, which does not depend every moment upon the present sin or guilt of the individual. The natural side of man and the spiritual have indeed, according to the unity of the world, a teleological passive relation to one another, and also a relative independence of one another. The natural side, ruled by the law of necessity, when it has experienced corruption, continues this disorder according to its own law; whereas the spirit can withdraw itself from the impelling effect of its past or of the generic life, and can make a new and better beginning. And hence it follows that participation in this evil cannot be determined by the measure of the sin or guilt of the individual merely, and consequently the latter cannot be measured by the former participation. As in sin, so more in evil, inheritance has its place. Thus, in reference to the distribution of the common evil by individuals, an inequality results which is not proportioned to the guilt of the same, to which doubts have at all times attached themselves as to the Divine justice, and whereby a problem is laid before us.

In this unequal distribution no single sinner indeed has the right to complain of injustice done him; for no one can show that too much has befallen him in relation to his sin. But relatively in comparison with others a disproportion of course exists, which apparently contradicts the reign of a pure justice in the world; and since the better spirits, because of the enmity of the world to good, have regularly much to suffer, the pious ones of the O. T. fell into great distress and vexation because of this disproportion.[1] Here again, the solution was only brought by the N. T., seeing that it allows the pre-Christian state to be understood as provisory in

[1] Comp. Ps. lxxiii., the Book of Job, the Proverbs, and Ecclesiastes.

relation to punishment as well as to sin and guilt. For, *in the first place*, to the Divine administration of justice the immediate equalization of worth and destiny is not requisite. The Divine justice relates exclusively to the collective worth of man, and under this aspect it harmonizes therewith that it should cause the judgment which is to be wholly adequate to the personal sin and guilt, to enter certainly when personal sin and guilt have definitively established themselves, but not before. As the mass of personal and common sin which is at the beginning indiscernibly intermingled is only brought to a separation at its own time, it is with this separation that the definite separation between the personal and common punishment is brought about. As definite unbelief, and it alone with certainty, is sin, which cannot be regarded as a mere effect of generic sin, so the punishment of this unbelief, condemnation, is the only punishment which is to be certainly excepted from the common punishment of the race.

If we are thus pointed as to the end to a definite expectation of an ultimately perfect equalization between worth and destiny, *secondly*, in the glance to the end the relative disproportion which remains *during* the world's course in reference to believers also resolves itself into harmony. For by means of the perfecting revelation it is possible that the entire evils of the pre-Christian state of punishment may be transformed into blessing. The sufferings which our fathers call "the holy cross," may loose from the world and draw to the cross of Christ; and this effect they produce on those who do not hinder the judgment of conscience, but acknowledge their culpability. And they also leave all comparison of envy or pride, as well as isolation from the common sin. The night and anguish of suffering can and shall turn in them[1] to be the birthplace of the new and free man, who, free in conscience from the Divine disfavour, and therefore also from self-condemnation, is able to change the sufferings which are still outstanding, death included, into a ground of holy joy,[2] for they serve the proclamation of birth and are the pains of labour. They were only by the Divine disfavour punishments indeed; and now there is the pardon of the person, they have lost the character of punishment, and con-

[1] John xvi. 19-22.   [2] Jas. i. 2; Heb. xii. 11.

sequently their sting; they are rather transformed into a good, to paternal chastisements or a means of education.[1]—Finally, it is true that the Christian has by personal faith broken through the circle of the natural cohesion of the race, therefore knows himself to be personally free from the common evils of the race, so far as they are punishments, and stands saved in contrast therewith; at the same time because of love, that active true consciousness of the race, new spiritual sufferings especially of a social kind multiply for him. But these sufferings through sympathy, through the participation of compassionate love in the misery of the brethren and the unbelieving world, are holy sufferings in the likeness of Jesus,[2] and no one who actually bears them is burdened with them or wishes not to bear them, so long as a cause for them is still extant. For these sufferings are deeds; the offerings which are brought in patience and meekness are the mightiest levers for the furtherance of the kingdom of God, and as they are in themselves quite compatible with the enjoyment of the highest good, with the peace of God and the blessedness of love, they also have the most splendid promises.

Thus the difficulties which arise from physical evil and its distribution in the world show themselves to be solvable, but only in the light of Christian grace, through which here also, as in the doctrine of sin and guilt, the relation between the species and the individual personality becomes clear, and consequently the Divine order shows itself to be harmonious and just.[3]—Another disproportion in the earthly course of the world is that punishment still lags behind sin. But this also is explained and ordered. The Divine disfavour rests, it is true, upon all evil, but not uniformly, as evil itself is not equal; there is a disfavour which guarantees respite, for God has no pleasure in the death of the sinner. This restraint ($\dot{a}\nu o\chi\acute{\eta}$) of the Divine justice also is neither arbitrariness nor weak goodness; it does not occur at the cost of justice, but answers thereto. Its law lies in the positively ethical final end; therefore it need not necessarily inflict forthwith all the evils deserved (§ 26. 1).

[1] Heb. xii. 5, 11; 1 Cor. xi. 32; 2 Cor. vi. 9; Rev. iii. 19.
[2] Col. i. 24.
[3] Gen. xviii.; Rom. iii. 25, 26; Acts xvii. 30; 1 Pet. iii. 20.

TRANSITION TO CHRISTOLOGY. 133

SECOND POINT.

§ 89.—*Transition from Ponerology to Christology.*

The punitive reaction against evil is indeed necessarily based in the justice of God (§ 88); but this necessity also leaves room for a revelation, which, arising from the depths of the eternal free-will of love, and acknowledging the right of justice, is reckoned to humanity, lost as it was without redemption, and yet capable of redemption. The new and concluding revelation has been realized by the manifestation of Jesus Christ, the Son of God and of man, in the fulness of times and in the form conditioned by sin, and realized in such a way that in His person the Divine justice and love, as they have their eternal union in God, have also come, in spite of sin, to perfect revelation and mutual interpenetration in the world.

1. Little as the assertion is to be made, that punishment can never and nowhere linger behind culpability,—on the contrary, physical punishments do not necessarily follow personal guilt as an equivalent,—nevertheless the punitive justice certainly has a necessity, and the universality of sin, the common guilt, is associated with a universal state of punishment. This was manifest in great measure even in the pre-Christian world. It lay in misery and ruin, in outward and inward decay, far more than it knew. Instead of the earlier delight and fulness of life, a feeling of decay and age had come; instead of the joyous security of existence there was a feeling of universal transience; side by side with the fear of death, the wish never to have been born spread, so that death was esteemed the highest good.[1] Thus the feeling of misery dominated even to despair, and there was therein a real revelation of the Divine justice.—In the Hebrew people the consciousness of the Divine justice was more purely present

[1] Nägelsbach, *Nachhomerische Theologie de griech. Volksglaubens*, 1857, Abschnitt VII.

because of the established Law ; amongst them the relation of misery to sin was more frequent, united as it was with the aggravation of the same by the consciousness of sin and guilt. Here also the sense of the approaching dissolution was diffused, unless by the agency of the light from above there broke forth from the night and winter of our race a new spring-tide. And as it was in the pre-Christian time, such is the present relation of every one in his pre-Christian state. For when a man has once reached the clearness of the religious and moral self-consciousness, and felt vitally the contrast between his realization and his vocation, he finds himself in misery and decay, nay, in a wretchedness which points back to a state of punishment, redemption from which is to be found in no other way than through the blessed, miraculous Divine act of the manifestation of Jesus Christ. But we must now realize more definitely, that, and why, redemption was impossible otherwise than by that manifestation. We consider therefore first, *anthropologically*, the need for this Divine act, and then we advance to the *theological* exposition, that this manifestation had its possibility, *i.e.* its necessity, in God Himself.

2. Through punishment of itself mankind would not become better. If it remained in the state in which it was,—entangled in the common sin and guilt as well as in the common punishment, in which every one also shares by his own guilt, and in which the presentiment of future punishment is at the same time included,[1]—humanity would eternally remain without redemption from its misery and decay, as well as without emancipation from guilt. For, *in the first place*, to punishment is not *given the power to atone or to improve*. To atone means to satisfy justice, and to change disfavour into favourable sentiment. But so long as the evil state is not broken, there always remains the source of ever fresh culpability, granting even that the earlier state were expiated by punishment. The evil state cannot be broken by punishment alone. Punishment may incite to gather up the strength for good resolutions, but these have no power over the basis of the soul. The apostle describes such volitions as a hopeless wrestling, as a shaking, so to

[1] § 88.

speak, of the chains of a prisoner.[1] And the reason is easily apprehended. True improvement requires, not abstinence merely, but positive love, which must come from the primary source of love, the Spirit of God. But sin is separation from the Divine source of life, and the consciousness of punishment fills with trembling, mistrust, and fear of God. Nor does it stand in man's power to open for himself the Divine source of life. On the contrary, the good resolution has an enemy in its own house. Opposed to the better will is the lower inclination, a fleshly will. And man being a living unity if a divided one, the will which does not wish evil is made impotent by the natural and fleshly will, and the stress of the better resolutions is ever enfeebled. And the better resolution, which punishment may arouse, is not yet pure besides, and this is one cause of its impotence. To will good in order to avoid punishment, is not yet love of good or God. The acknowledgment of culpability is good and necessary to improvement, but the consciousness of the same or of the Divine disfavour works fear,[2] and fear is opposed to love. Were the sense of punishment not moderated by rays of grace, it must darken, it must make reluctant in reference to God and intolerant of suffering as regards the punishment, which may of itself conduct to doubting the goodness of God, the obligation of the law, and guilt. Arrayed in the positive ethical attributes, God stands before the falsified consciousness as a hostile power, as a dark fate.[3]

Then, *secondly*, God does not punish immediately in such a way that the evil experienced is equal to the sin; He is *long-suffering*, and bears with the world even though sinful. He also still gives to the sinning world signs of His love.[4] He places a hindrance in the way of sin by means of Divine and human commands, law, threatenings, and promises. But even this long-suffering brings no redemption; it simply restrains the outbreak of the evil consequences.[5] The source of evil, the universal evil state remains; indeed sin, worked upon by the law and impelled within, easily clothes itself in

---

[1] Rom. vii. 15, etc.
[2] 1 John iv. 18.
[3] Rom. iv. 15 : ὁ νόμος ὀργὴν κατεργάζεται.
[4] Matt. v. 45.
[5] Gal. iii. 23, iv. 2.

finer and more spiritual forms, and is neither healed nor atoned by command or prohibition.[1] The law is even abused; legal observance may be taken for true righteousness and may generate pride; the knowledge of the law may foster false imaginations. Add to this, that justice cannot always and for ever be content with the merely provisory state, which is described by the Divine long-suffering. Therefore the Divine long-suffering would be aimless and impossible, because without fruit, if it did not with its forbearance reserve and prepare the human race for a fundamental cure which must come elsewhere than from the mere long-suffering conservation of the sinful state of the world.

And *finally*, sin cannot live itself out, man cannot become better of himself, sin exhausting itself perchance as a disease does. Amelioration can be no mere physical process. One kind of sin may, it is true, die out of humanity, if the power which is abused by it becomes exhausted, and thus the falsehood of sin is revealed. But a good disposition generally is not yet given. Evil remains, at any rate within, so long as the powers are there which it increasingly disorders, unless an opposite power intervene which so rescues, that with the blotting out of the previous sin and guilt of man the innermost volition turns from evil towards good. Sin cannot help us against sin.

Thus there is no hope for man, unless there enters from the primary source of good an overwhelming and victorious power, which breaks through the wretched circle leading from sin to punishment, from punishment and the sense of guiltiness to mistrust and despair, and thus to worse sin. In this circle we are confined, and we cannot escape therefrom with our impotent willings. The law shuts this iron circle around us, good in itself, for the law is holy, right, and good, as indeed punishment even is right and good in itself. But sin works through the good law an increasing evil result, augmentation of sin and death.[2] We are sinful, without the power of self-redemption from this ban. Still one course remains—we can call for the Divine act of redemption; as we are needy, so are we still capable of redemption. There is no compulsion forcing upon us despair of God and our

[1] See § 83, C.   [2] Rom. v. 20, vii. 13.

destiny. Despair would be practical *Manichæism*. The opposite Pelagian mode of thought finds little in the pollution of the existent state, and thinks it can easily loosen the Ego from the ban and curse of sin. It simulates a difference between the Ego and evil, which is non-existent. The Manichæan view, on the other hand, supposes that there is no longer any difference at all between the ἔσω ἄνθρωπος, the captive and sin, and imagines an identity in the two which is not present, an absolute distinction between God and good, which must cause the moral problem to cease. Thus both lead to the same result, to allowing the moral and religious destiny to lapse; Pelagianism in such a way that, in levity and superficiality, it regards the problem as essentially soluble or solved without a new birth; Manichæism in such a way that it regards a new birth as impossible, or supposes in the place of the new birth of the man, the new creation of a wholly different man. These are the two possible extremes by which men step out of the path which promises rescue, and the truth is denied which is still accessible to the sinner.[1] Should the sinner hold, however, to the road of truth, practically avoiding both errors, and thus combining the true element in Pelagianism and Manichæism,[2] this means that he takes to himself *repentance* on the one hand, and *the feeling of guilt* on the other. These two are not identically but relatively opposite. In repentance, man holds to the distinction between himself and sin in the only way still possible to him. He might not have done evil, therefore he withdraws from it in idea, or as far as his wish is concerned, and thus withdraws from the Manichæan error. By the feeling of guilt, conversely, he unites himself with evil as his own, as a real power still attaching to him, which exists and has a significance in spite of his better desire and repentance, and this is the rejection of the Pelagian error. But although repentance and the feeling of guilt both lie on the road of truth and are equally justified, still even together they are not redemption; but the more they arise and penetrate each other, the more are they simply a painful privation thereof. In the most favourable case they can only end in the exclamation of the apostle,

---

[1] John iii. 18, etc.    [2] Comp. vol. i. pp. 136, etc., 151, etc.

"Wretched man that I am, who shall redeem me from the body of this death!"[1]

3. But as improvement is not to be expected from the side of man either by means of punishment or the long-suffering of God, nor from the self-extinction of sin (and the negative verification of the necessity of redemption by Christ lies in this), the ethical grounding of the new revelation which breaks through the old world is now to be recognized on the *Divine* side. Its ethical possibility is clear from the fact that there is no necessity for God to make punitive justice the sole counter agent to evil, in accordance with the position, *Fiat justitia, pereat mundus*. Inviolable as may be the right of the retributory justice in itself, as is inscribed upon the conscience of every truly penitent soul, inviolable even in reference to the Divine goodness, still its exclusive dominion by no means follows. On the contrary, there is no justice in God, in which love for an empire of good and for its realization does not dwell (I. p. 310). So long, therefore, as there still remains in the race a capacity for redemption, so long the Divine activity is busy in realizing the honour and the kingdom of the good, and does not leave the field to punitive justice alone. But before Christ not merely were individuals capable of redemption, but the race, as has been previously shown, at least because the sin of definitive unbelief could not be committed before the perfect revelation.[2] Thus the deed of love is still possible therefore, which blots out sin and perfects humanity. If this deed of love could not enter because of the Divine punitive justice, and love left the field thereto, this would mean that generally the punitive justice is destined to be the end and goal of the Divine revelation, and therefore a pause at the standpoint of the law.[3] But seeing that God is love, although holy and just love, this would be to think of a justice sundered from God as love and turned against the will of love, a justice by which the love of God

[1] Rom. vii. 24.
[2] § 26. 1, § 32; Isa. xxxii. 16, 17, xxxiii. 5, xli. 10, xlii. 1-6, xlv. 23-25, xlvi. 12, etc., xlviii. 18, li. 1-8, liii. 11, liv. 14, 17, lvi. 1, lviii. 2, 8, lix. 16; comp. also Jer. xxiii. 6, xxxiii. 16, etc.
[3] Matt. v. 6, 10, 20, vi. 33, xiii. 43, xxv. 37-46 ; Luke x. 29, etc., xvi. 15, xviii. 9, 14; John xvii. 25.

is bound, and by which the absolute revelation that is possible and indeed is willed by it as love is restrained. If we have had to reject earlier the theories of amelioration, because the honour and self-preservation of the good requires a real revelation of justice in sinners, and because the force of the law cannot be furthered by defection therefrom, or by relaxation and suspension thereof, the other side is now presented. And it is only necessary in this aspect to think the idea of the Divine justice to the end to see the point where the perfecting revelation of the Divine love can be installed in the realm of justice, nay, where this revelation is, so to speak, expected and affirmed by the justice itself, as we shall conversely see later that justice attains by the perfect revelation of love to its own full realization.

In order to apprehend the perfect harmony of justice and the N. T. grace of God, everything depends on seeing how the Divine justice itself stretches beyond its exhibition as punitive, from which it cannot withdraw, and impels to the expectation of a higher exhibition, and how, on the other hand, that revelation which we rightly call the perfect revelation of love straightway guards the right of the punitive justice and helps to bring it to realization. Everywhere indeed the Scriptures proclaim such holy connection between · justice and grace, the total unbrokenness of the law and its inviolableness by the Gospel, and also that God had no need to become another in order to become the God of grace, and that He was not hindered therein by the law of His holiness, that rather already in the time of the law, indeed before the foundation of the world, the perfect revelation or the sending of the Son was included in the revelation of His holy will. Most simply and yet most strikingly is this harmony of the Divine justice and love expressed by the fact that in the transition from the Old Covenant to the New, from the economy of the law to that of love, the solemn expression is again only that of "the revelation of justice," and thus love is not put in the place of justice, but the Gospel itself is placed under the view-point of justice, and of the revelation now first completed of the Divine justice. The language of the Evangelists on this point had already had a precedent for this amongst the prophets.[1] With this usage of language the Lord had associated Himself, *e.g.* in the Sermon on the Mount; especially has Paul thoroughly adopted it; just as the idea which describes Christian grace in its centre, justification, rests [2] hereupon. The meaning of this the Evangelical Church has most clearly apprehended, when it describes the salvation in Christ by saying that Christ is our righteousness. That salvation is so often derived from the Divine justice, is not meant to concede a claim to salvation of any kind to man, even were it only on the ground of free and gracious promise; but the ground of this is, that the legislative and punitive justice do not yet exhaust the Biblical idea of justice (§ 26. 1), they are only imperfect manifestations of the entire justice of God. This gives a glimpse into the deeper ground of justice. It is not rooted in Divine caprice, but in the Divine love and zeal for the holy, for good, which is again God Himself.[2] This zeal desires also a good world as a place for the revelation of His ethical majesty, and requires all the evidences which serve the realization of good in the world. But these evidences the Scriptures often ascribe again to the Divine justice, which is therefore thought of as communicative and creative. God is also just in this, namely just to or in correspondence with Himself, inasmuch as He advances from the requirement to the gift and to communication to those who desire. The legislative justice already aimed at the realization of the law, which is compassed by means of the communicative revelation in those who are vitally receptive. Thus the Gospel, that gift, is the realization and confirmation of that which was willed from the beginning.[3] Indeed, even the *manner of the realization* of the law by the Gospel is in no way developed in opposition to the law, nor to the punitive justice even. By the fulfilling of the law in every respect (on the part of Christ), the way is opened to the Gospel. Even so grace or pardon in the Gospel is not the denial of culpability or of the right

---

[1] Rom. i. 16, 17, iii. 21, 22, 26, v. 19; Gal. iii. 11; 2 Cor. v. 21: comp. Heb. x. 38; 1 John i. 9, ii. 1, 29, iii. 7.

[2] See vol. i. § 32, p. 455.

[3] Rom. iii. 31, viii. 1–3. The moral law also needed for its realization the ὑπακοή to the νόμος πίστεως. Rom. i. 5, iii. 27, iv. 14, etc., ix. 31.

of justice, but, as will be clear in due time, its strongest affirmation, as is especially shown by the fact that the Gospel either serves to realize righteousness in man or to ripen for judgment. Thus even in the demonstration of His love God Himself remains the same and just. His holy will does not appear more weakly in the Gospel, but still more energetically than in the Law.

4. The creative new revelation, which breaks through the circle of the old natural life in order to make us sons of God, is THE INCARNATION OF GOD IN THE SON. The first part of our system had to demonstrate its necessity as the perfecting of revelation, and this part proved it unthinkable that man was not created from the beginning to be perfected, and that communion with God, internal or external witness or revelation of God, belonged hereto, in the perfection of which therefore that of man is conditioned. But the perfecting of the self-revelation of God is nothing else than the incarnation of God. Add to which, that the perfecting of humanity included from the beginning the idea of the perfect organism. Therefore we cannot think for ourselves the perfection of humanity, its destiny to be a perfect spiritual organism, unless he who was qualified to be God-man be its head and lead it to perfection. The idea of Christ, of the God-man, or of the counsel of the incarnating love of God, reaches back even to the foundations of the world, which was created not merely *through* the λόγος, but also *for* the λόγος, who was to become incarnate.[1] He in whose image humanity was created is alone in a position, after it has become ruined, to restore it again in accord with the internal bond which knits Him to humanity.[2] Little as is this necessity of incarnation of a physical kind, seeing that it is grounded in the free love of God (to which no man has a legal claim), just as little is the Divine freedom caprice, or its use of power chance. Rather is the free Divine love wise, and the plan of the final end of the world together with the instruments thereof are so articulated that the plan is in accordance with the Divine nature, which is contented therein and satisfied. Because of sin, as has been shown, the incarnation is necessary under a new aspect, and consequently proportionally as this is the case is still more

[1] Col. i. 16.    [2] Thus Irenæus.

verified, since it now appears as the only means, in which, whilst holding to the destiny of man, satisfaction can be given to legislative and retributory justice. It corresponds at the same time with the communicating creative Divine justice, as prophecy reveals it.[1] That the help can come from God alone, even the pure feeling of sin knows very well. That only a representation of men before God by a God-given mediatorship, and so far by God Himself, can avail and still the accusing conscience, that passage in Job[2] expresses with special beauty: "O lay down a pledge! Represent me before Thee! Who is at hand to become surety for me?"

[1] Comp. Jer. xxiii. 6.
[2] Job xvii. 3; comp. Isa. xxxviii. 14 and Ps. xlix. (according to the exposition of Gesenius).

PART II.—(*Continued.*)

# SPECIFIC CHRISTIAN DOCTRINE;

OR,

## THE DOCTRINE OF SIN AND SALVATION.

SECOND PART: THE CHRISTIAN SALVATION.

FIRST MAIN DIVISION : THE DOCTRINE OF CHRIST.

SECOND MAIN DIVISION : THE CHURCH, OR THE KINGDOM OF THE HOLY SPIRIT.

# FIRST MAIN DIVISION.

## THE DOCTRINE OF CHRIST.

### I.—THE BIBLICAL DOCTRINE OF CHRIST IN GENERAL.

#### A.—*The Old Testament.*

§ 90.

The revelation of the New Testament prepares a way for itself in the Old, partly in gross by means of the whole theocratic constitution, and partly in detail by the ideas of God and man from which it starts. Though the idea of the incarnation of God is not attained, still the Messiah promised is a Sprout of Jehovah or Immanuel, *i.e.* is the consummation of revelation, whilst at the same time He is a Sprout of David and the righteous servant of God, *i.e.* is the consummation of humanity. The Messiah is regarded as the Messenger of God for the founding of the eternal covenant, and as the Founder and Head of the Kingdom of God who brings the theocratic offices to perfection and harmonious presentation in Himself by His power, wisdom, and holy love.

LITERATURE.—Umbreit, *Der Knecht Gottes*, 1840. Oehler, *Der Knecht Gottes und A. T. Theologie*, 2 vols. 1873, 1874; *Die Grundzüge der alttest. Weisheit*, 1854. H. Schultz, *Die Theologie A. T.* Hengstenberg, *Christologie des A. T.*, edit. 2 (translated in Foreign Theol. Library); *Geschichte des Reiches Gottes im A. T.* (also translated in Foreign Theol. Library). Hofmann, *Weissagung und Erfüllung*, 1844; *Schriftbeweis*, I. pp. 84–163. Ewald, *Glaubenslehre*, 2d half, 1874, pp. 57–90

(The Creative Powers); pp. 303–403 (The Way to God by Christ, etc.). *Die Lehre vom Wort Gottes,* 1871, pp. 131, etc.

1. It is not in the Jewish people merely that we ought to see a preparation for the perfected revelation which is Incarnation. All religions strive more or less, consciously or unconsciously, after the idea of the Divine Incarnation, whether, like the oriental religions, they start from God and assume incarnations of the Deity, or whether, like the occidental religions especially, they start from man and see a deification in heroes.[1] But, since a sure law answering to the idea of holiness was wanting outside of Israel, the representations of God's becoming man or man's becoming God had certainly too little of an ethical character. The unity of the Divine and human was not morally brought about by either side, therefore that unity was only of a natural and confusing kind, and like a premature blossom remained unfruitful. It is otherwise in the Old Testament. By its precise distinction between God and man it seems remote from the idea of incarnation; yet that idea is prepared for therein, especially on the ethical ground. Its way is cleared really and ideally in the whole theocracy, inasmuch as in the Law and Cultus as well as in Prophecy a life of God is already begun in and with the history of Israel. Although God has not left Himself without a witness amongst the Heathen, it is only in Israel that the communion of God with man became a *covenant,* a secure, constant, and ordained relation. The communion had produced here a progressive growth by the agency of an exclusive selection, the earlier stages of which typically and prophetically revealed a higher, indeed the perfect, communion between God and man.

Passing to details, a THEOLOGICAL course of development is to be distinguished from an ANTHROPOLOGICAL. The two only come to perfect harmony indeed in the fulfilment.

2. In *the forefront* lie the Theologoumena of the Holy Spirit, the SPIRIT OF GOD, the WORD, and WISDOM, as well as the *Maleach.*[2] The SPIRIT of God is not merely thought of as an intellectual and moral but as a metaphysical and physical principle, consequently as creative and as a Divine communication.[3] He comes as a higher power over man,

---
[1] Comp. §§ 65, 66.  [2] Comp. § 28, vol. I. pp. 345–349.
[3] Gen. i. 2, ii. 7; comp. Ps. civ. 29, 30.

subduing him and at the same time raising him above himself, inasmuch as the Spirit of God weds Himself with man in a manifold and historically graduated manner, becoming the principle of all good, especially of all artistic skill within the Theocracy. But whilst the Spirit of God is a Divine principle immanent in the world, the WORD OF GOD, on the other hand (or God as speaking in the Word), is objectively contrasted with man. The history of the idea of God in the Old Testament does not begin with WISDOM (like the Hellenic philosophy from the days of Anaxagoras, which begins with νοῦς—the Divine Reason); but, essentially distinguished from idealistic Hellenism, commencement is made in Hebraism with the real principle, the creative will,[1] as the form of the revelation of which, or the medium, speech, the Word is regarded. Thus the word דָּבָר, λόγος, has at the first a realistic signification like ῥῆμα, quite conformably with the fundamental character of the two Testaments, which have for their fundamental positions the historically real Divine deeds.[2] As a real principle, the Word is not hypostatically distinguished as a thing spoken from the God who speaks; nor is it a special mode of the Divine existence; God Himself is not the Word, nor is the Word God, for God does not speak Himself, His innermost being, but individual thoughts. Nor is the world called in the Old Testament the Word of God (although this might be); by the Word is to be understood the command for the creation of the world spoken by the personal God; it is the mighty word, *by which* the world became. Therefore this Word does not itself speak in turn.[3] The Word is not a being self-existent and substantial, but speech is only thought of as the mediating function or instrument.[4] The matter of necessity assumes a somewhat different complexion in the revelation of the *Law*. The law is no longer a merely instantaneous means or action of creation and command; the product of Divine speech is now a Divine thing, in cosmical realization. The law, which is itself and is

---

[1] Gen. i. 3.
[2] This point of view must also be proportionally maintained in the exposition of the λόγος of John.
[3] Ps. xxxiii. 6-9.
[4] Thus Ps. cvii. 20; Book of Wisdom xvi. 12; Jer. xxiii. 29.

called a Divine word, is an established word, incorporated in the world; a Divine thing has consequently become a component part of the world's history. In the word of the legal economy, the speech of the holy and just God, and its spiritual contents, together with its own absolute teleology, attain to a permanent objectivity in the world. In the law there is therefore already contained an objectivation of the ethical will of God in the world, although not in a personal form, but rather in an ideal significance only as that which is supposed to be Divine, so that, notwithstanding, its reality in personal form is far from indifferent to this ideal. This ideal demands straightway a new and different existence in persons. At first, indeed, the Word of the Old Testament economy brings only a higher knowledge (wisdom), for it still lacks the realization it seeks. Still with personal knowledge there already begins the existence of the law in the intelligence of persons, and prophecy, which is closely allied with the law, promises the realization of the law also in the will of the people, especially in the righteous Servant of Jehovah. Since the principle of this human wisdom must be the Divine wisdom, it seemed natural that from the Word of God, which had by Divine agency received in the tables of the law and in the Book of the Law an objective existence, and in the knowledge of the law a subjective existence, there should in this manner frame itself the *Theologoumenon of* WISDOM.

The חָכְמָה has in the first place a relation to nature; it is poured out upon creatures; it is the principle which forms them with wise ends and which dwells in the world; it is the innate reason of creation; whilst the Word is the strong command which gives it existence. But besides this the Wisdom of God is related to the Law, and thus has an ethical character, absolute teleology. The sphere of its cosmical realization is not nature merely, but also the law in Israel,[1] and subjectively the souls of the pious.[2] To give special prominence to the new principle which is gained with wisdom, it is distinguished generally from God, but the distinction could scarcely be otherwise expressed[3] than by the spatial image

---

[1] According to Sirach xxiv. 12, 13, 32, etc. (the Book of the Law).
[2] Wisdom vii. 22-29; they became by Wisdom friends and prophets to God.
[3] Prov. viii. 22-31.

of being by the side of God (אֵצֶל), whereby it certainly cannot be meant that it is not in God, but that God Himself is not Wisdom. Neither in the O. T. nor the Apocrypha is the Theologoumenon of the חָכְמָה associated with the Messianic idea; this application and development is found in the N. T.[1] On the contrary, the Proverbs occupy themselves with the problem of the Theodicy, or with the question of apprehending how the good order of nature in creation harmonizes with the revealed holy will of God, with the harmony that is between the creative word and the word of the Law. The certainty is established, that he who answers to the Law has to expect a harmonious existence, "life." For the Creator and Lawgiver are one, and the earnestness of the lawgiver is directed to the real prevalence of the law. The solution of the problem of the Theodicy found in the Book of Job contains the knowledge that there is a suffering for the good of the world, and indeed a disproportionate suffering, in which pure love of good authenticates and reveals itself; this is therefore a distinction; a knowledge which culminated in the Messianic idea of the suffering servant of Jehovah. The Proverbs do not contain the fact, as they do not express the assurance, that the Law will attain to its realization in the world. This only appears in Prophecy; and with this is united the further knowledge that a new Divine act must enter to add reality to the good, to the *word of the law*, which only has at first an ideal existence in the world. Prophecy ever returns with definiteness to the realistic side of the "Word," seeing that, instead of halting at the covenant of the Law, it proclaims the consummation of the law and revelation by a new creative act.[2] It even attains the knowledge that the creative consummation of revelation, although it is of value to the universe, will be brought about by a God-given person of central importance, in whom all the gifts of the Spirit of God will find their point of unity, the Messiah.[3] In Him God is with us.[4] He is a Sprout of Jehovah as well as of David, originating in the

---

[1] Luke vii. 35, xi. 49; 1 Cor. i. 24; and the Prologue to John's Gospel, where the λόγος, who is described in ver. 4 as an ideal principle φῶς, in ver. 14 becomes flesh.
[2] Jer. xxxi.; Ezek. xxxvii. 11, 19; Isa. lv. 11; Joel ii.
[3] Isa. xi. 2, xlii. 1. [4] Isa. vii. 14, viii. 8, 10.

covenant between Jehovah and His people,[1] as in marriage; and the fruit of this marriage, the Messiah, is Himself presented in turn as the personal covenant, the personal union of the people and God.[2] Finally, the MALEACH of Jehovah comes in here for consideration, which, as has been previously shown (vol. I. p. 347), is characterized not merely as a creaturely angel, but also as a Theophany, a mission of Jehovah,[3] whether it now exist in actual or personal form. In Him is the name or the revelation of Jehovah, and He is even called the face of Jehovah, because the face reveals what is within and represents the person.[4] In all these passages there is nothing Messianic as yet, but the Maleach is afterwards applied in relation to the Messianic idea as the angel of the covenant, and the advent of the same in Messianic times is identified with the advent of Jehovah Himself.[5] With the Maleach, which is a visible sign of the presence of Jehovah, is associated the later Theologoumena of the Shekina or Jekara,—$\delta\acute{o}\xi a$[6] in the N. T., —by which the majesty, the brilliance around Jehovah is meant.[7]

Although in the preceding there is a disposition to distinguish between God who is revealed and God who is the medium of revelation, still the incarnation of the organ of revelation is not given therewith. Of the metaphysical nature of the Messiah there is very little mention at all; but notwithstanding, much of what has been adduced points to a superhuman

[1] Isa. iv. 2, xi. 1; Zech. iii. 8, vi. 12; Jer. xxiii. 5; Hos. ii. 19, 20; Micah v. 1, 2; Isa. vii. 14. Israel is the virgin which bears, the daughter of Zion.
[2] Isa. xlii. 6, xlix. 8.
[3] Gen. xvi. 7, xviii. 2, 3, xlviii. 16; Ex. iii. 2, xxiii. 20.; Josh. v. 12; Judg. ii. 1, vi. 11, xiii. 3.
[4] Ex. xxiii. 21, xxxii. 14. This may remind of $\varepsilon\iota\varkappa\acute{\omega}\nu$. Not ancient writers merely, like Tertullian, see in Maleach the Son of God, who has completed in His manifestation preludes to the incarnation, but also more modern writers.— It is a somewhat different turn of the same thought, when the Maleach, especially the angel of the covenant, is combined with an eternal humanity of Christ. To this class belong Barth, *Der Engel des Bundes*, a letter to Schelling, 1845; Brand's *Scholar's Bible* on John xvii. 5; Fr. K. Keerl, *Der Gottmensch, das Ebenbild des unsichtbaren Gottes*, Bâle 1866, pp. 208, etc., 230, etc.; Bartels, *Ansichten eines Freundes der Bibel. und Naturbetrachtung*, 1871.
[5] Mal. iii. 1.        [6] John xii. 41; 2 Pet. i. 17.
[7] Ex. xxiv. 15-18; 1 Kings viii. 11. In Matt. xviii. 20, Jesus applies a word to Himself which is used of the Shekina.

manifestation for the consummation of the Messianic kingdom, to an actually perfect being of God in the perfecting revealer. To this category it especially belongs that the Messiah is designated the Wonderful Counsellor, the Divine Hero, the Eternal Father, the Peaceful Prince.[1]

*Observation.*—The Apocrypha almost wholly allows the inner side of the Messianic hope to drop. They associate the "Word" of the challenging law with Wisdom, but do not go on to form it into the ethically creative Word, which first plants the law in the heart. The son of Sirach rather regards the law as the last and highest revelation, as the true Word and Wisdom.[2]

3. THE ANTHROPOLOGICAL SERIES.—Here belong the ideas of *the* SON *and* SERVANT *of God*, in which ideas the theocratic offices are also concerned.

That Israel bears the lofty name of *the* SON *of* GOD,[3] of course has its general ground in the fact that God is the Creator of all. The Creator is also called Father, and so far God is also the Father of the other nations, as may be inferred from the fact that Israel is called the first-born Son of God amongst the nations.[4] But in the word first-born lies a further distinction. It refers to Israel's special worth from its origin on. In a peculiar sense God has founded this people.[5] Already in Abraham has He chosen it for His peculiar people; its existence rests upon a special thought of God. Through this people salvation shall come to the world, and God has thought it and formed it as His organ for this end.[6] Thus Israel is also first-born in the sense that it is to lead the rest

---

[1] Isa. ix. 6 f. Micah v. 1 asserts, although not direct pre-existence, nevertheless the continuity of the Divine counsel from the days of the patriarchs even to the consummation. If Isa. xlviii. 16*a*, *b*, as well as 16*c*, is to be referred to the Ebed as speaking (and not to Jehovah), the sense would be that the servant has spoken from of old to Israel, and was present at the foundation of the earth (Gess, *Person Christi*, p. 41). But 16*c* is better referred to verse 17 as the word of the prophet.

[2] Sirach xxiv. 31, etc.; Baruch iii. 37, iv. 1, etc.

[3] Ex. iv. 22; Deut. xiv. 1, xxxii. 6, 18; Hosea xi. 1; Isa. lxiii. 16; Jer. xxxi. 9, 20. A name which the angels also bear, Job xxxviii. 7; comp. Luke xx. 36.

[4] Ps. lxxxix. 28, etc.; comp. Ex. iv. 22.

[5] Mal. ii. 10; Deut. xxxii. 6, 18; Isa. lxiii. 16; Jer. xxxi. 9, 20.

[6] Micah iv. 2; Isa. ii. 3; comp. Gen. xii. 3.

of the nations, to the end that they may become sons of the Highest. The term Son of God attains a still more intensive sense within the Theocracy in the bearers of office.[1] They are called gods,[2] because something Divine has descended upon them, whereby they have become organs of God,[3] not by virtue of their own nature, but by virtue of their office. Indeed, in the O. T. the person was far overtopped by the theocratic office. But just because the office is an eternal Divine thought which is indispensable to the realization of the counsel of salvation, it is preserved for the fulfilment to which it leads, and David's stem is the one to which this fulfilment will be attached. Thus David's race is designated the Son of God by special promise.[4] With power, wisdom, righteousness, with the true kingly spirit, David's son is endowed, and he always arises with increasing definiteness from David's race as the personal figure of hope, to build an all-embracing eternal empire, to execute the judgment of the nations, to found the eternal peace, and to bring the fear of God to universal dominion. In him also is the priesthood united with the kingship,[5] and even the spirit of prophecy will be in him, the spirit of wisdom and counsel and righteousness.[6] To the perfect empire of the king, which will indeed be the kingdom of God, there also attaches His blessing for all peoples, the universal realization of the true religion in righteousness. The time is prophesied when the people of God will serve in the garment of holiness, when even the heathen shall be the sons of God in righteousness. Even in this ethical sense the term Son of God appears.[7]—But the ethical side of the Messianic idea is especially presented in the idea of the *Servant* of Jehovah. On the one hand the name "servant" is lower than "son," but on the other hand the ethical relation is better expressed thereby. It is the correlate of the idea of the "Master," whose will has to prevail. The word has therefore its immediate relation to the will of Jehovah, as the same is also in the Law compressed into the promise. The servant is the organ for both, the enjoining and the promising will of God. He answers to the idea of the servant who, judged by the standard

[1] Ps. ii. 7.  [2] Ex. xxi. 6, xxii. 7, 8 ; Ps. lxxxii. 6.
[3] Comp. John x. 35, etc.  [4] 2 Sam. vii.; Ps. lxxxix. 27, etc.
[5] Ps. cx.; Zech. vi. 13.  [6] Isa. ix. 6, xi. 2, xlii. 1.  [7] Ps. lxxiii. 15.

THE OLD TESTAMENT DOCTRINE. 153

of the Divine will, is found right or righteous. Therefore the complete idea of the *Ebed* in the second part of Isaiah stands in the closest connection with that of righteousness, both that which enjoins and that which promises, or the creative righteousness.[1] It is true that, so far as the servant expresses an honourable engagement and duty, all Israelites have a share in the name of the servant of Jehovah.[2] And in a narrower sense this name is borne by the pious and the patriarchs, Moses, David, kings, prophets, priests.[3] But a further distinguishing selection exists in the prophets in question. Israel, even the pious and the prophets, must say in Him : our righteousness is as a sullied robe.[4] Therefore will Jehovah, who is zealous for righteousness, succour Himself in the universal unfaithfulness of man. As He Himself founded the earth and was the source of all revelation, so will He Himself plant righteousness upon the earth,[5] will call forth Him who is absolutely the Servant, the righteous One,[6] who is the truth and centre of the people, and who, as the personal bond between God and the people, will represent the people before God in substitutionary lowly love, in suffering and intercession, divested of kingly majesty. But when He has accredited Himself as the righteous servant by humiliation, He will restore the sure mercy of David,[7] consequently will represent Jehovah to the people as a Divine ambassador, will even bring the heathen near to atonement and salvation, will introduce a new heaven and a new earth,[8] as well as initiate judgment for everything ungodlike. The Messianic passages of this character, veiling as they do in suffering and endurance the exaltation and worth of the servant, have their highest ethical significance in this very fact, and thus the kingly majesty is, so to speak, born again out of lowliness.[9] Of itself the people has not the power to bear this servant, but only God Himself can give him.[10] Thus the anthropological method

---

[1] See above, § 26 and § 89. 3.   [2] Isa. xli. 8, 9 ; comp. xlii. 1-9.
[3] Isa. lxvi. 14 ; Ps. cii. 15, cxxxv. 14. Even the angels are called, Ps. ciii. 21, מְשָׁרְתִים, just as Moses is called in Wisdom x. 16 θεράπων.
[4] Isa. lxiv. 6, xlii. 18, etc., xliii. 22, etc., xlvi. 8, xlviii. 1.
[5] Isa. li. 16.   [6] Isa. liii. 11.
[7] Isa. lv. 3.   [8] Isa. lxv. 17.
[9] Isa. liii. 12, liv.   [10] Hos. ii. 19 ; Isa. xlii. 1-9, ix. 6 ; Micah v. 1.

returns back to the theological, to God. The servant of God, the perfected man, can only arise from the perfected revelation, which is thus described as a new coming of Jehovah to His people and His holy temple.[1] The true Mediator, who is prophet, king, and priest, a Sprout of Jehovah as well as of David, is Himself a revelation of Jehovah.

*Observation.*—To the Theologoumena of the Spirit, the Word of God, and Wisdom, by which the N. T. doctrine of Christ is prepared, Ewald adds (vol. II. pp. 63, etc., 319–324, 404, etc.) the doctrine of the "Man of God," out of which a peculiar metaphysical doctrine of the *Son of God* has been developed. He calls to mind that the passage concerning the Divine image (Gen. i. 26, etc., and ii. 7, etc.) distinguishes the empirical man from the ideal or the man of God. And indeed, he says, in the second record (Gen. ii.) the latter is to be regarded the original. This puts the primary man, he thinks, not merely as the being of highest worth, but he is also placed according to time at the head of creation as a witness of the same. The order in this record is:—the man of God, the stars, plants, animals; then the wife of the man, and marriage. With this thought of the primary man he imagines the Theologoumenon of the Divine Wisdom and that of the Messiah to be united. Especially was the Messiah, he says, as soon as he was thought in personal form, thought as the "perfect man," and consequently already referred to the Deity. A new advance he regards as made in Dan. vii. 13, where the empire of the world, that is, of God and heaven at once, is given to the Messiah, and that in heaven, where he stands amidst the angels. A further advance, after he was once transferred to the heavenly region, is seen when the Messiah, or the primary man and son of man, is thought to be pre-existent in heaven (and not, as Gen. ii., upon earth). This progress is completed, he thinks, as follows:—The necessity of the Messiah and his destiny have been necessarily brought into the closest connection with the original will of God. The majestic end, thought in the Messiah, has then been elevated above all contingency, so that the Messiah is thought of as the primary man, pretemporal and eternally existent with God, in order that he may appear at the right time. This transference of the Messiah to heaven is then further developed in the oldest part of the Book of Enoch, where the Messiah is called the chosen of the Lord, the son of man, the son of the woman, just as the expressions son of God and word of God are also applied to him. Now if the

[1] Zech. vi. 12, ix. 9.

Messiah were once thought to be the primary man or the son of man, and were transferred as pre-existent into the nearest presence of God, it would also be natural that he should be the son of God in the metaphysical sense. In this respect Ewald calls attention to a few interesting and little considered passages, which are found in the O. T. even, and which appear to speak of a mysterious son of God. In Job xv. 7, Job speaks of a wholly unusual man, who, born before all other men, is constantly with God as a son might be with a king. In Ezek. xxviii. 12-15 Ezekiel paints a being who is not a priest, nor a cherub, but is the highest pattern of all perfection and dwells in Paradise. In Prov. xxx. 4, in the seventh century before Christ, in a passage which speaks of the wonders of creation, this form is mentioned with the precise name of the "son of God." These representations are already partly combined in the second and third Books of Enoch and associated with the Messiah; they are perfectly combined in the N. T.

§ 91.

B.—*New Testament Doctrine.*

In the Person of Jesus of Nazareth the perfect revelation of God has appeared according to the N. T., and therewith the perfecting of humanity.

LITERATURE.—L. Th. Schulze, *Vom Menschensohn und vom Logos*, 1867. Nösgen, *Christus der Menschen. und Gottessohn*, 1869. Baur, *Vorlesungen über N. T. Theol.*, 1864. Gess, *Christi Person und Werk nach Christi Selbstzeugniss und den Zeugnissen der Apostel*, I. 1870, II. 1878, 1879. Schumann, *Christus oder die Lehre des A. T. und N. T. von der Person des Erlösers*, 1852. Hasse, *Das Leben des verklärten Erlösers im Himmel nach der eigenen Aussprüchen des Herrn*, 1854. Beyschlag, *Christologie des N. T.*, 1866. The *Biblische Theologie* of Schmidt and Weiss; treatises upon "the Son of Man" in the *Zeitschrift für wiss. Theologie*, 1860, 1863, 1865, by Baur, Hilgenfeld, Holtzmann, von Nebe, and Herborn. Messner, *Die Lehre der Apostel*, 1856. Lechler, *Das apostolische und nachapostolische Zeitalter*, 1851, 1857. Rich. Schmidt, *Christologie des Apostel Paulus*. Pfleiderer, *Paulinismus*, 1873. Frommann, *Johanneische Lehrbegriff*, 1839; on the same subject, Von Köstlin, 1843, and Weiss, 1862. On *James*, by W. Schmidt,

1869. On *Peter*, by Weiss, 1865. On *Hebrews*, by Riehm, 2 vols. 1858, 1859. Moll, *Christologia in Ep. ad Hebræos proposita*, 1854.

1. The historical manifestation of Christ in its uniqueness and grandeur could not be perfectly conceived by any one even of His apostles. They have all, it is true, conceived Him in the significance He has equally for the race, but according to their individuality and the stage of their knowledge they have appropriated one this and another that side of His portrait. Even Jesus Himself has not spoken in coherent and systematic manner upon His person or His work. The first thing was the impression made by His personal appearance, by His words, deeds, and sufferings; the doctrine of His Person was only the second thing resulting from that entire impression of His person. Still, in spite of the different stages in the conception of Him apparent in the canon, the fact is to be maintained therein that His appearance was accessible in certain relations, and indeed in the prominent circumstances to all who were spiritually receptive, to simple unculture and childlike dispositions still more readily than to those who were rich in knowledge and culture,[1] for what He especially desired to work upon was the intelligence of disposition. He worked through what He was, through His personality which corresponded to the whole man.

2. Therefore, notwithstanding all the variety of the stages of Christian apprehension in the early Church and in the N. T. canon, there is still recognizable in the entire sphere of sources accessible to us a series of common features in His likeness, in the recognition of which all who enter into inner communion with Him are at one.

All recognise Him to be the sinless holy one, who is not merely an example, teacher, and guide, but as standing in a unique and mysterious communion with God. Whatever names also the Divine principle within Him may have, He is the Son of God, the Lord, thereby; although man, He yet transcends all mere human proportion; He is not merely the organ of God as the prophets were, but He is acknowledged to be the subject and the realized end of all prophecy, with whom one epoch is closed and a new era is

[1] Matt. xi. 25, etc.

commenced which shall last for ever, the new covenant, that is, the new and permanent, and thus perfect, religion. Therefore His person had its religious significance for them. They not merely believe Him, they believe *on* Him, just as He Himself demanded not simply faith in God, but faith in Him as the One who could lead them to the Father. *Secondly*, He does not stand contrasted with them as the sinless holy one merely, but as the *Redeemer*, in no outwardly theocratic sense, but as the redeemer from guilt and sin, whose office of redeemer is the basis of His vocation, and who is therefore the Son whom the Father sent, and who leads to the Father. Add to this, *thirdly*, the popular and all-embracing conception of the *kingdom of God*, to which He likewise has a wholly unique relation. For with His manifestation and by virtue of His constructive deed the kingdom begins on earth, into which He gathers the members by penitence and faith in this person. And this kingdom of God is also His kingdom. He is its ruler; He leads it to victory and perfection. Thus He is the Messiah, the anointed One. He is a king, who stands pre-eminent on earth in inner spiritual majesty, suffering in lowliness and mistake. And, resting upon His words and His person, His own expect His *Second Advent* in outward majesty, for with His person the perfection as well as the redemption of believers is in their esteem interwoven. All, *finally*, even the Jewish Christians, believe in Him as the *Judge of the world*, whereby, once more raised above identity with men, He is again contrasted with them in unique manner. These features are common to the faith of the entire primitive Church. Only this faith in Jesus Christ, as that Church was distinguished from heathen and Jews, so was it united together,—however much or little definite knowledge it had of the higher Divine nature of Christ, however little was established concerning His atoning work, the Church and its sacraments, and the canon of the N. T.

3. Let us now consider the Christological features of the several writings of the N. T. They fall into *three classes*. To the first belong James, Peter, and the Synoptics; to the second, Paul and the Epistle to the Hebrews; to the third, John.

*First Class.*—*The Christological Creed in the Tradition of the Primitive Christian Church : James, the Synoptics, Peter.*[1]

It is to be expected at the outset that these writers would paint their portrait of Christ in its connection with the O. T., since they especially appropriate the sides which most clearly reveal themselves to be a fulfilment of the O. T. Very little that is Christological is found in JAMES. He also says nothing of the death of Christ as an atoning death, but He is to him the example of enduring obedience even to death.[2] Still the little he does say is significant. Christ is to him the bringer or bearer of the word of truth, which does not merely communicate wisdom from above, but is also efficacious, nay creative, which blesses or condemns ; at any rate it brings decision.[3] With this Divine power of the word of truth there is undoubtedly combined, according to our author, that the bringer of this word, Jesus, is Christ, the Lord of glory,[4] therefore the king of its empire in which Divine power dwells, who will come again to consummate the judgment of the world. The brief Epistle says little of the earthly life of Christ ; still Jesus is not to it a dead Christ ; it holds to the exalted living Lord, with whom His own stand in reciprocal communion. To James, prayer in His name is likely to be heard. Christ is therefore to him the Mediator, for whose sake we share in grace.[5] The grace that has come through Christ he so depicts that it perfects revelation. For the word of truth which comes from Christ he still calls "law," it is true, but the perfect law, it being perfect as the law of freedom. Since the word is implanted in the soul in faith, it is in a condition to bless, to remove the hindrances which discord brings in its train, and also to bring the moral law to realization, to beget man and make him the firstborn of creation.[6] The "word of truth" is therefore no longer a mere decree and doctrine, but life and power, so that the perfecting of revelation is at the same time the perfecting of

---

[1] Compare my *Geschichte der Christologie*, I. pp. 72-105 (*History of the Doctrine of the Person of Christ*, vol. I. pp. 51, etc.).
[2] v. 11.   [3] i. 18, 21, 25 ; comp. i. 5, v. 8.   [4] ii. 1, v. 7, 8, 9, 14, 15.
[5] v. 14.   [6] i. 18, 21, ii. 12.

man. With the authority of the law which demanded obedience, Christianity knew how to unite power and freedom, the free light of love.[1] Although the prophetic and regal offices predominate in James, nevertheless prayer in the name of Jesus is also the medium of the forgiveness of sins.[2] After all this, it is not to be denied that both in soteriological as well as in Christological form, James acknowledges the absoluteness of the Christian religion.

The SPEECHES OF PETER in the Acts of the Apostles[3] are mainly those of an evangelist, desiring as they do to outline the leading features of the entire image of Christ. This is certainly already done in such a way that an eternal significance is attributed to the historical according to Divine counsel. Jesus is often called in these speeches $\pi a \hat{\imath}_{\varsigma} \; \theta \epsilon o \hat{v}$,[4] connected with the *Ebed* of the prophets, which of itself is more nearly $v \iota \acute{o}_{\varsigma}$ than $\delta o \hat{v} \lambda o_{\varsigma}$. He is anointed with the Holy Ghost and with power, and after He had suffered, was made by the resurrection Lord and Christ, glorified by God, exalted to heaven, and appointed the judge over the living and the dead. Now He is the prince of life, Lord over all,[5] and throned in heaven until all His enemies lie at His feet.[6] Even in heaven He is regarded as the One who ever lives to work. He is the source of the miraculous power of the apostles, and therefore is in the possession of power to communicate His miraculous power. He is the initiator of life, being powerful over death;[7] He pours out the Spirit, and Christian baptism is a continuation of Pentecost. There is salvation in no other name; especially do we receive through Him the forgiveness of sins.[8] Stephen[9] also calls on the name of Jesus, whom he sees at the right hand of God; indeed generally the calling on the name of Jesus is described as the characteristic of Christians in the Acts of the Apostles.[10]

In the FIRST EPISTLE OF PETER everything is already framed in a more doctrinal fashion. The person of Christ is there placed in relation to the previous history of revelation, Christ not being so much accredited by prophecy (a position

---

[1] i. 25, ii. 12.  [2] v. 14, 15.  [3] Acts ii. iii. iv. x.
[4] iii. 13, iv. 27, 30.  [5] ii. 33–36, iii. 13, 15.  [6] ii. 24, 33, iii. 21, ii. 35.
[7] iii. 6, 15, etc.  [8] ii. 38, iii. 19, iv. 12, x. 43, xi. 15, xv. 8–11.
[9] vii. 59.  [10] ix. 14.

which the Gospel of Matthew especially attempts to prove) as that prophecy rather exists for the sake of Christ, in accordance with the counsel or plan of God, which has Christ for its contents. The prophets have the spirit of Christ,[1] consequently the earlier history is already determined by the idea of Christ, indeed by the principle, the manifestation of which He is. Still real pre-existence is not thereby given, as is the case with John or Paul, nor the definite distinction of the Divine in Christ from the Divine generally; but according to the Epistle, Christ, that is, the personal unity of the human and the Divine, has eternal ideal pre-existence before God.[2] More important still is the allusion to the O. T. doctrine of the *Word and the Spirit of God*, and the continuation of the same. Whilst the O. T. word did not yet create spiritual life, was inscribed on perishable tables, and was non-living, or was only momentarily effective in theophanies and prophecy, Peter calls the revelation in Christ, on the contrary, "the living and remaining word of God"—λόγος θεοῦ ζῶν καὶ μένων.[3] By this was not intended the fact of the evangelical proclamation, but its contents. The latter have lasting significance as contrasted with the thought of a revelation, or religion, which has still to follow on or become higher; the word, or the revelation of God, has attained in Christ to living and personal form, has in Him eternal post-existence,[4] although an immanent doctrine of the Trinity is not expressed in the Epistle, Christ being rather described according to the economic historical side. This word has its own power of salvation, inasmuch as when received into the soul it works like a seed of imperishable life, and brings the new birth. And the higher endowment of the person of Christ, Peter especially associates with the Theologoumenon of the *Spirit* of God. The prophets indeed have, according thereto, a share in the Spirit of God. But Jesus is Christ by His agency, or is anointed as it were by Him, which may in the first place be referred to His baptism,[5] but which does not exclude a special endowment from His birth.[6] And whilst, moreover, all de-

---

[1] 1 Pet. i. 11, comp. Jas. v. 10, where κυρίου itself (as v. 7, 11, ii. 1) is referred to Christ, in whose name the prophets have spoken.
[2] 1 Pet. i. 11, 20.   [3] 1 Pet. i. 22-25. λόγος is ῥῆμα in v. 25.
[4] 1 Pet. ii. 3, 4, i. 8.   [5] Acts iv. 27, x. 38.   [6] Luke iv. 18.

parted spirits have remained confined in the realm of the dead, by the abiding union of the Spirit of God with the pneuma, that is, the soul, of Christ,[1] His resurrection, that is to say, His living again by vanquishing death, was an inner necessity for His person.[2] This Spirit of God, who finds in the Messiah His goal and resting-point, has also ideally created the preparation for this revelation of Him in the prophets.[3] As compared with James, Peter goes still further, to bring the revelation in Christ as atoning into definite relation to the righteousness and love of God. Christ's death is to Peter a death of substitutionary love.[4] As the perfect man, not merely according to the body but the soul,[5] He sinlessly suffered death, as an innocent sacrificial lamb.[6] Thus His holy love has gained the power to purify, nay, to recreate into imperishable being.[7] In this there is already contained an approximation to the Pauline doctrine of the Second Adam; for the revelation by Christ generates a new race. He is Himself the contents of this revelation, which has eternal presence and realization in His person.[8]

The SECOND EPISTLE OF PETER makes Christians to be partakers of the Divine nature, who possess it not by birth or merit, but acquire it through Him whose majesty broke forth even upon earth on the mount of transfiguration.[9] His revelation is the decisive one, for it comes again to the judgment,[10] as the Epistle of Jude also teaches, which derives all salvation from Christ.[11]

*Observation.*—The doctrine of the "Word" in James and Peter shows already that the Johannine doctrine of the Logos has a related sphere of idea in the N. T., although Schwegler errs when he identifies Jas. i. 18 with the Johannine Logos.

THE SYNOPTICS.—However undeveloped the knowledge of the person and work of Christ in the congregation of Jewish Christians, it had nevertheless experienced that it had become a partaker of the Holy Ghost and of the forgiveness of sins

---

[1] 1 Pet. iii. 19, iv. 6.
[2] Acts ii. 24; 1 Pet. iii. 18.
[3] 1 Pet. i. 11; comp. Weiss, § 45.
[4] 1 Pet. i. 11, ii. 24, iii. 18, iv. 1.
[5] 1 Pet. iii. 18, 19, iv. 1.
[6] 1 Pet. ii. 24, iii. 18, i. 19.
[7] 1 Pet. i. 23, etc.; comp. John xii. 24.
[8] 1 Pet. i. 12, 23, ii. 3, etc.
[9] 2 Pet. i. 4, 16, 17, 18.
[10] iii. 10.
[11] Jude 1-4, 20, 21.

by faith in Christ, and had found in Him the mediator through whom it rejoiced in a living communion with God. Hence amongst those who did not, like a part of the Jewish Christians of the Epistle to the Hebrews, sink back into Judaism, there must have developed an ever higher knowledge of Christ, since they were in possession of the apostolic proclamation of Jesus, and the living tradition of the Gospel balanced inherited conceptions from which they had to set themselves free. The record of this tradition in the Jewish Christian circle or amongst the Hebrew Christians is the Gospel of Matthew especially, just as Mark stands in closer relation with Peter. Luke stands, it is true, as far as the doctrine of the forgiveness of sins is concerned, nearer to Peter, but manifestly has used many Jewish Christian sources, especially for the commencement of the life of Christ in His early history (Luke i. 1–4).

Matthew and Luke's representation of the person of Christ is given, in the first place, in the narrative of the *miraculous origin* of Jesus. He is born of a virgin by the power of the Spirit, who overshadows Mary without the intervention of man. The narrative reminds one of the narrative of the creation in Genesis;[1] it is a question here also of a creation. As Adam, according to the Genesis, became a living soul by the Spirit of God animating matter, so the Spirit of God is active in this case also, but on a higher stage, the influence now being not upon matter merely, but a living human being. On the other hand, the words do not permit us to regard the overshadowing of the Divine πνεῦμα as a mere potentiating of the powers of Mary, but according to Luke and Matthew there is within her a creative Divine act which forms a man, which of course coincided with her faith but was not produced by her causality, for of a holiness of Mary or of a noble line of holy and pure blood before her the Scriptures know nothing. Whilst the principle of the origin of Christ in John is called Logos, the Synoptics speak of the πνεῦμα ἅγιον. Is the Trinitarian πνεῦμα ἅγιον possibly meant, and is there thus an incarnation of the Spirit of God? This would be a dogmatic addition, and contrary to all Biblical and extra-Biblical analogy. For there are those, it

[1] Comp. Luke i. 35 with Gen. i. 2 and ii. 7; as well as John i. 1 with Gen. i. 1: comp. Matt. i. 20.

is true, who describe the Holy Ghost as the "Mother of Jesus," but they have no Trinity; they do not therefore take πνεῦμα in a Trinitarian sense. And if the angel spoke to Mary according to Luke, and to Joseph according to Matthew, of the Holy Spirit, neither of these would understand the words in a Trinitarian sense. If, notwithstanding (as happened in the Church), the Trinitarian Holy Spirit was thought of in Matthew and Luke, then, in order to unify the Johannine representation of the Logos therewith, another function than incarnation must be attributed to the Holy Spirit—the purification of Mary. But if the words of Luke are to be referred to this (for which there is no authority in the words), then nothing would be said upon the main fact, the principle of the origin of Christ. And in Matthew the words do not at all allow the action of the Spirit to be referred to anything else than the origin of Jesus from the πνεῦμα ἅγιον. Thus, there being no possible talk either in Luke or Matthew of a Trinitarian Pneuma, that which signalizes Jesus, the substantial, Divine power which originates Jesus, is Pneuma, and the word has here a more general meaning.[1] Even in John and Paul there is also a similar use of the word πνεῦμα.[2]

But Matthew does not stop at a creative act even. Adam is also created miraculously by the power of the Highest. But Jesus is no mere repetition of Adam, is no mere pure man after the fashion of the prophets, or endowed with powers of the Divine Spirit; according to Matthew, Jesus is "of the Holy Ghost,"[3] and therefore the embryo implanted in Mary is an ἅγιον and Immanuel. This statement implies that the Divine principle assisted in the constitution (*Mitconstituirte*) of this individual, and as much belonged to its substantial being as that which it had from the mother. Accordingly, since Divine nature originally belonged to the nature of this man, there is in him an original unity of the Divine and human supposed from the moment of creation, and therefore a theanthropic nature. We have consequently a union of the

---

[1] In Luke i. 35 the πνεῦμα is also called δύναμις ὑψίστου. Πνεῦμα is also in other places a more general designation of the Deity or His power. John iv. 24.
[2] Comp. John iii. 34 with John i. 14; Paul calls the Lord the Spirit without more ado, in 2 Cor. iii. 17; comp. 1 Cor. xv. 45; Heb. ix. 14.
[3] i. 20 : τὸ ἐν αὐτῇ γεννηθὲν ἐκ πνεύματός ἐστιν ἁγίου.

Divine nature with the human nature, although there is no mention of person, whether Divine or human. The ἅγιον being neuter describes a being which is not yet actually personal, in such a way indeed that with it the perfect ground for the person was laid, which it should become, saying, This holy one is to become the Redeemer, and be called Jesus.[1] Accordingly, Jesus in His twelfth year already knows God in a special sense as His Father, and Himself in a peculiar manner as His child or His son.[2] At that age His knowledge begins therefore to become theanthropic self-consciousness, as His being was theanthropic from the beginning. And with this the volitional side and its development which was well-pleasing to God runs parallel.[3] Jesus remains also true man, who knows and wills Himself to be the Son of God. In the cognitive and volitional aspect He remains in a process of development even up to His death. His knowledge was not yet omniscience.[4] He has first real problems to solve, which touch His innermost being,[5] as His life of prayer also proves.[6] His baptism was not epideiktic merely in relation to the Baptist, nor was it even a revelation simply of what was realized in Jesus; it bore witness, according to the simple sense of Scripture, to an epoch in the life of Jesus, which brought to His humanity a new and actual participation in the Divine powers, for which susceptibility was only then ripened. But the whole development He passed through without sin; from ἅγιον He became ἅγιος, as is attested, for the time before His official life by the word at His baptism, for the time of His official life by the history of His transfiguration as well as by His resurrection.[7] This leads to His peculiar characteristics.

Not merely does His *moral* character show no stain, but it displays virtuous power, unselfish love, in the richest and most living revelation, an undimmed harmony and identity [8] in all inward movement, in the relation to God and man. There is

---

[1] Luke i. 35; Matt. i. 21; comp. Schmid, *Bibl. Theol.*
[2] Luke ii. 49.  [3] Luke ii. 40, 52.  [4] Mark xiii. 32; Matt. xxiv. 36.
[5] Mark x. 18; Matt. xix. 17; Mark x. 38, etc.; Luke xii. 50, etc., xxii. 28.
[6] Luke iii. 21, vi. 12, xxii. 32, 41, etc.; Matt. xiv. 23.
[7] Matt. iii. 17, xvii. 5; comp. John xii. 28.
[8] See § 70; comp. my treatise on the *Sinless Perfection of Jesus;* as well as Luke iv. 22, 23; Matt. viii. 26, etc., xvi. 19–21, xi. 20, 25, 27, xxvi. 13, xxviii. 64, xx. 28; Luke xxii. 37.

no trace shown in His consciousness that, like others, He is athirst for penitence or atonement. For even His baptism in the Gospels is not regarded by the primitive Church as a confession of sin, but has its full significance for Him as a real equipment and consecration for His office. He is the first free man who has internally overstepped the stage of the Law, having perfectly adopted it into His will.[1] Therefore He moves freely therein as if at home. Every one stands in the legal stage who needs atonement. But He so transcends it that He stands in constant and innermost unity with God. He has by His appearance made the ineffaceable impression of a Divine purity and holiness upon the disciples, who saw in Him the Messiah, it is true, but were not accustomed to attribute to the Messiah absolute holiness.[2] And to that impression even His own utterances have contributed,[3] which would be inconceivable with His acknowledged moral elevation had His conscience accused Him of sin or guilt.

With His holiness His wisdom stands in close connection, which reveals itself in the most manifold ways, in reference to the relation between morality and religion,[4] law and religion; to the apparent antagonism between obedience to the theocracy and to constituted authority;[5] to the interpretation of Scripture for example as regards marriage, sacrifice, the laws of the Sabbath and of purification;[6] in reference to the harmony of all the revelations of God,[7] the future of His kingdom and the laws of its development;[8] lastly and above all, His knowledge of God. God was already known to be Creator and Lawgiver; the Son knows and reveals Him as Father.[9] He knows Himself to be the middle point of the history of the world,[10] to be the man who has the absolutely universal mission to humanity.[11] It is His unique union with God as the Son, by means of

---

[1] Matt. xv. 11, etc., xii. 1-13, xvii. 25; Mark ii. 27, 28.
[2] Matt. xii. 18; comp. 1 Pet. ii. 22-24; 2 Cor. v. 21.
[3] Matt. v. 17. In the fact that He describes Himself as the Judge of the world, is implied that He contrasts Himself with the whole of humanity as the holy one; comp. John v. 27.
[4] Matt. xv. 1-12, 17-20.   [5] Luke xii. 13, etc.; Matt. xxii. 15, etc.
[6] Matt. xix. 3, etc., xxii. 42, etc., xxiii. 26.
[7] Matt. xi. 12, xxii. 9, 29, etc., xxiii. 35, etc.
[8] Matt. xxiv. 25, xiii. 3-50.   [9] Matt. xi. 25, etc.   [10] Matt. xi. 11-13.
[11] Matt. v. 17, xiii. 37, etc., xxiv. 14.

which He has His knowledge of Divine things, a knowledge which is related to the Divine plan as well as to God and His peculiar nature,[1] to the kingdom of God and specially to the Church. And this coincides with the peculiar *power* and authority (ἐξουσία) which He ascribes to Himself and exercises. He is *the Lord* in the kingdom of God, in whom consequently right as well as energy dwells.[2] He is the Lord of the Sabbath, and higher than the most holy places in Israel.[3] He places Himself above the angels;[4] the greatest men of the Old Testament are related to Him as δοῦλοι to a son.[5] He has the power of miraculous gifts in such a manner that He can impart it to others.[6] He attributes to Himself a continuous power and presence even after death.[7] Although at the commencement, continuing the preparatory work of the Baptist, He allows the indispensable character of His person to but little appear, and speaks in many parables of the kingdom of heaven without direct reference to His person, still He ascribes to Himself the mission of bringing the law and the prophets to fulfilment.[8] On demeanour to His person eternal destiny hangs.[9] He describes Himself as the mediator between God and man, communicating Himself by the blessing and grace from above now and at the judgment.[10] Upon His exaltation the sending of the Holy Spirit is dependent.[11] The disciples are to pray in His name if they would pray acceptably. And His consciousness of being the Redeemer of mankind must be regarded as permanent from the commencement of His public ministry, for there never is seen therein uncertainty and wavering, but only a different procedure according to the need of the multitude inclined to carnal misunderstanding, which now demanded restraint or veiling, and now called for disclosure. And His disciples recognized the inner majesty of His nature ever more surely, and also received the external seal of the same in His transfiguration

---

[1] Matt. xi. 27, xvi. 18.  [2] Matt. ix. 6, x. 37, 40.
[3] Matt. xii. 30, 41, 42.  [4] Matt. xiii. 41.
[5] Matt. xxi. 33, 37, 43.  [6] Matt. x. 8, etc.; comp. Mark xvi. 17.
[7] Matt. xviii. 20, xxviii. 20.  [8] Matt. v. 17, xi. 12, etc.
[9] Matt. xxi. 42 ; Luke xx. 17, 18.
[10] Matt. xi. 27, xvi. 27, xviii. 20, xxv. 34, vii. 23 ; Luke xiii. 18, viii. 22, 32 (intercession).
[11] Luke xxiv. 49 ; comp. Matt. xxviii. 19.

and resurrection as well as in His miraculous deeds. Thus out of the lowliness of His earthly manifestation a Divine depth and height of His nature streamed forth, and this unity of the Divine and human in Him the disciples proclaim as the foundation of the salvation of the world.

To this unity all the special features they narrate concerning Him lead back. Therefore something is still to be said of the *self-consciousness of Jesus*, in which this unity must have mirrored itself as its conscious expression.[1] True, we have historical knowledge of Christ purely through the instrumentality of the apostles, and it might thus appear impracticable to distinguish the self-consciousness of Jesus from the apostolical faith and narrative. But in the Gospel narratives are found sufficient of the sayings of Jesus, which bear in themselves the stamp of originality, so that we have therein the firm starting-point as to what Christ knew Himself to be. To this class belong above all the designations "Son of God," "Son of Man," "the Son" simply, which He indisputably attributed to Himself, and upon which He has stamped His own self-consciousness. In these designations, which, seeing that He united them, express the perfection of revelation and humanity, these two series of the Old Testament, the theological and the anthropological,[2] arrive at unity and interpenetration. He knew this unity to be completed in His own person.

The predicate "Son of God" appears, it is true, in the New Testament as a mere theocratic official name. When, for example, the people call Jesus υἱὸς Θεοῦ, there is no reference to be sought in that term to His Divine nature. But He has applied the same not merely as a theocratic official name in the sense of the current popular representations, but also in reference to His nature.[3] As definitely as He describes Himself as true man, He at the same time beyond all doubt ascribes a superhuman position to Himself; for He contrasts Himself with all humanity as its Redeemer and Judge.[4] His

[1] Comp. Gess.     [2] See § 90.
[3] Most frequently in the formula "my Father" (first in Luke ii. 49), which is especially important, inasmuch as He never said in reference to Himself "our Father," but only taught us to say so (comp. Weiss, p. 59). With this harmonizes the history of the birth already considered, which undoubtedly goes back to the family circle of Jesus.
[4] Matt. v. 17, xi. 27, etc., xxv. 31, etc.

declarations concerning Himself remove Him in unique fashion into nearness to God; as when He says: "All things are committed to me by my Father;" "all power is given to me in heaven and on earth."[1] Instead of describing Himself as a Messiah, who is merely David's son, He describes Himself as David's lord, whose right it is to sit at the right hand of God as the King of the heavenly empire.[2] This saying of His, spoken to His opponents a short time before the final catastrophe, could not but be known to the Sanhedrim, in which case a peculiar light is thrown upon the transaction before them.[3] For the majestic confession before the high priest respecting His Divine sonship and His dignity of Judge of the world they could not now take in the sense of the current popular conceptions of the Messiah; they were compelled to see that He claimed much more, namely what appeared to them as blasphemy, a violation of the ultimate monotheistic fundamental principle. They could not possibly have called it blasphemy, if by His words He had merely attributed to Himself such a position as He must necessarily have claimed according to their view of the Messiah when He came. They rather held it to be proved that He was not the Messiah, because of His declarations concerning Himself which appeared to them to be blasphemy.[4] Jesus was sentenced by the Sanhedrim because He made Himself the Son of God. Consequently, that He thereby wished to attribute to Himself Divine nature and dignity, contradicted the abstract Jewish monotheism, which necessarily saw therein a lapse into Heathenism.[5]

The name *Son of man* appears about fifty times in the Gospels in the mouth of Jesus. It cannot be the designation

---

[1] Matt. xi. 27, xxviii. 18. The ἐξουσία of the former passage cannot be simply the power to conceal or reveal. Weiss incorrectly separates the moral unity and the unity of nature, a course which would not merely prove anti-Johannine, but would not agree with the early apostolic doctrine of the pneuma in Christ and the regenerate. Many sayings of Jesus transcended the point of view of His hearers, and necessarily what the people may have thought of the phrase can by no means *alone* be made the canon for judging of the sense of the designation "Son of man," applied by Jesus to Himself.

[2] Matt. xxii. 44; comp. Ps. cx. 1.   [3] Matt. xxvi. 64; Mark xiv. 62.

[4] To this John v. 18, and x. 36, etc. also refer.

[5] Upon this point John v. 18 is very instructive. By the fact that He called Himself πατέρα ἴδιον ἔλεγε τὸν Θεόν, i.e. the Son of God in unique fashion, they saw that He ἴσον ἑαυτὸν ποιεῖ τῷ Θεῷ.

of his Messianic office, since it was not adapted to that purpose.[1] The expression is partly His choice, partly His work, and has, because of its evident usualness, something oracular in it. The passage in Daniel,[2] strictly taken, does not give this *name* to the Messiah, but says, after the different empires of the world had been depicted under the figure of animals: "there came one 'like a son of man' up to the Ancient of Days." According to the context the true Israel is meant, in whom first human nature comes to be realized instead of animal nature, and raises itself to godlike dignity, a personification of the people, the reality of which must certainly be the Messiah. The passage in Daniel can therefore only be the occasion and not the source for that designation of himself.[3]—In this name there surely lies above everything actual humanity. Jesus knew Himself to be a perfect personal man, and would not have been able to call Himself Son of man if He only knew Himself to be a manifestation of God. Still He cannot merely have meant thereby *actual* humanity in opposition to *illusive*, but the phrase must also signify, especially with the definite article, the opposite to imperfection and defacement, the *truth* of man, *i.e.* the realization of His idea. If He only meant to express by the name that He was a real man like others, the definite article would be inexplicable. And even thus it remains obscure, why He used this expression so frequently in His ripe theanthropic consciousness. The phrase is intelligible from that profound

---

[1] In Matt. xvi. 13, Jesus asks: "Whom do the people say the Son of man is?" which cannot mean, "what I the Messiah am." For when Peter, in the 16th verse, makes the confession: "Thou art the Messiah, the Son of the living God," Jesus replies that His Father in heaven, and not flesh and blood, has revealed it to him. It is not therefore at all self-evident that the phrase long used by Jesus, Son of man, meant the Messiah. On pædagogic grounds Jesus not seldom interdicts the promulgation that He is the Messiah, whilst He Himself constantly and often called Himself Son of man. This would be inconceivable if "the Son of man" were the same as Messiah.

[2] Dan. vii. 13.

[3] Also so far the use of the phrase by Jesus does not agree with the passage in Daniel, seeing that He did not desire to be a manifestation simply "as a Son of man," but to be actual man. The definite article can also still less signify the well-known Son of man of Daniel, seeing that Dan. vii. has combined the phrase with the exaltation and glorification, whilst Jesus applies the same pre-eminently and on most occasions in reference to His own earthly present in the state of humiliation: *e.g.* Matt. viii. 20, xx. 18.

saying of the boy Jesus of twelve years old,[1] according to which He knew His peculiar home, His essential being, to be in the Divine. If He stood in the Divine element as in His own place, His immediate consciousness was that He was the Son of God in the sense of unity of essence with the Father. The foundation and centre of His person He knew the Divine to be, and this which was natural and nearest to Him He expresses directly where, as before the high priest, it was important to confess it. But because there lay therein His exaltation above sinful man, His love, which desires to belong to humanity, and to be reckoned therewith, chooses the phrase Son of man by preference for His customary designation of Himself. This does not preclude, and the definite article points in that direction, that He was also conscious of His humanity not as a merely ordinary or faulty humanity, but as the perfect manifestation of its truth as well as of its realization. This comes very near to the Pauline expression that Christ is the second and last, that is to say, the perfect Adam, all the more that He does not call Himself man simply, but *the* Son of man or of humanity. The sense of the passage in Daniel is thus obviously exceeded In Daniel the phrase is in the first place the symbolic designation of Israel (indirectly of the Messiah), and the theocratic limit is not yet overcome; but Jesus calls Himself the Son of man in preference to the Messiah. In His favourite name He allows every indication of a reference of His person to Israel only to be dropped,[2] so that the name expresses, as does the Pauline second Adam, that for Him and His universally human importance the differences between heathen and Jew no longer hold.

But since Christ applies both names to Himself,—and therefore the Divine and human sides in His person and His self-consciousness have arrived at unity, and in this unity the consummation of revelation and humanity is at the same time given,—this new personal living unity is to be thought as that which acts and speaks in Him. According to the portrait communicated to us by the Gospel, this man is no-

---
[1] Luke ii. 49.
[2] The relation to Israel still lies mediately for Him in the fact that as the truth of humanity He is also the truth of Israel.

where without the Divine, which constitutes His person, just as conversely humanity essentially belongs to the person who is υἱὸς Θεοῦ.[1] The frequent distinction made, therefore, that some expressions proceed from the Divine principle only, and others from the Son of man alone, is to be justified by preference in this way, that it is always the unity of person which speaks and acts, and that this person can fix the different sides which are unified therein by themselves, and can therefore now express itself upon the Divine side, and now upon the human, but in such a way that, by reason of the unity of both sides in Him, the whole Christ, and not merely the human side, is meant by the Son of man, just as it is not the Divine side merely which is meant by the Son of God. For the sake of this unity, at specially solemn moments He calls Himself the *Son* simply, in the Synoptics as well as in John.[2] This expression is analogous to the μονογενής in John, to the πρωτότοκος in Paul.[3]

According to all this, there rests upon Jesus the unconditional satisfaction of God;[4] He is the Son of the love of God, entrusted with the highest work of the establishment and completion of the kingdom of God on earth, and to that end endowed by means of His community of nature with God and the pneuma which personally constitutes Him in reference to His moral traits, His miraculous power and wisdom.[5] Still, neither omnipotence nor omniscience is ascribed to Him as God, and even in moral relations He is not yet remote from temptation or attack.[6]

The higher principle, whereby Jesus Christ is, is not to be thought merely as a charisma bestowed upon Him for a time for His calling, but rather as permanently associated with His person even beyond death. Still it is not yet so definitely distinguished from the Divine, and fixed of itself, that advance can be made to an express and definite doctrine of some kind of real pre-existence. It halts at this, that between the Johannine testimony and the Synoptic the fundamental differ-

[1] Both are affirmed by Jesus one after the other in Mark xiv. 61, 62.
[2] Matt. xi. 27, xxviii. 19 ; Mark xiii. 32.
[3] Col. i. 15 ; Heb. i. 6.           [4] Matt. iii. 17, xvii. 5.
[5] Matt. xi. 25, etc.
[6] Matt. viii. 10 ; Mark vi. 6, xiii. 32, xiv. 35, 36 ; Matt. xxiv. 36, xix. 17 ; Luke xxii. 28.

ence is, that the starting and middle point with the former is the person of Christ the Son of God, but with the latter the kingdom of God.[1] Nevertheless the step is not so great from the Synoptics to the Johannine stage, seeing in Him as they do the revelation of σοφία and the Judge of the world.[2] In every teleological view which holds to the unity of the world, that which shows itself to be in reality the power of consummation, according to the idea and power, must be the first, the all-ruling element from the beginning.

*Second Class.—Paul and the Epistle to the Hebrews.*

1. PAUL.

The remaining writers of the N. T. are, it is true, more important than those previously considered; still they only differ inasmuch as the following stage of doctrine shows the higher developed form of the earlier Christology, in which the impetus to such growth already lies.

In our Canon the Epistles of Paul are probably the oldest, and give us the earliest information concerning the primitive tradition of the Person of Christ. Probably Paul did not know Christ during His earthly life in humiliation. Still he must have heard much about the historic life of Christ both

[1] Gess, pp. 299, 300.
[2] In this point of view the passages in Matt. xi. 19 and Luke vii. 35 are noteworthy : ἡ σοφία ἐδικαιώθη ἀπὸ τῶν τέκνων αὐτῆς. Christ is there described as σοφία. And in Luke xi. 49 it is said of wisdom ; διὰ τοῦτο καὶ ἡ σοφία Θεοῦ εἶπεν, ἀποστελῶ εἰς αὐτοὺς προφήτας, etc., which Matt. xxiii. 34 reports in the words : διὰ τοῦτο ἰδοὺ ἐγὼ ἀποστέλλω προφήτας, etc. Many emphasize now the Gospel preaching of the *kingdom* instead of the person of Christ (although Christ unites both), in the opinion or hope of thus making the community of nature of the person with God superfluous or unnecessary. But a deeper and more correct conception of the kingdom of God would straightway lead conversely to this community of nature of the head of the βασιλεία Θεοῦ with God. The partners of the kingdom—certainly through *the Son*—are likewise sons of God, and have God for Father ; this is their designation from the beginning. Upon this point Gess (p. 327) has given some remarks deserving of attention, and has especially called to mind passages like Matt. v. 48, xvii. 26, etc. ; Luke ix. 35, xx. 36, compared with John xx. 17, iii. 5 (or 2 Pet. i. 4). To this point belongs also a striking sermon by Steinmeyer upon the Divine Sonship. According to Scripture, ethics stand in need of an ontological, or, if it is preferred, a metaphysical foundation. Ritschl also (iii. 351) gives correctly the point here treated.

as a persecutor of the Christians, and in his intercourse with his fellow-believers after his conversion. There is an additional point also which serves to characterize his Christology. The mere historical information communicated by human testimony which he had heard from others and doubtless believed, was notwithstanding not the knowledge of Christ in the true light. This he attained, according to his own asseveration,[1] not from men or through men; it came to him by an immediate contact with the personal Lord, who revealed Himself to his inward eye as the exalted Lord. It was thus natural for him to learn to consider and understand the whole earthly life of Christ from this elevation, and in the light which emanated from the glorification of Christ. The corrective to the offence of the cross, to the conceptions of the Messiah and the Messianic kingdom which filled him as a persecutor, lay for him already in the overwhelming first impression which led him to faith. It was the majesty of the Lord who had passed through death and suffering, who was glorified, and yet partook of human nature, which was revealed to Him.[2] In the Divine exaltation of Christ He did not lose His humanity, but this humanity is to Him the universal realization of the Divine image, and at the same time the true humanity.[3] Accordingly in his preaching he calls him Jesus, nor is He to him the mere Spirit of Christ. He calls Him the one man who is the second Adam,[4] who bore our flesh, yea the very weakness of it,[5] therefore He did not possess a natural immortality. He emphasizes Christ as the crucified, who, as he says, is his whole knowledge.[6] Altogether, Paul gives a multitude of historical traits of the earthly life of Christ, which wholly harmonize with the Gospels.[7] His humanity, to which he ascribes meekness, holiness, Divine wisdom, substitutionary sentiment for us and archetypal love,[8] he does not think He has laid aside in His exaltation, but Christ remains for Paul

---

[1] Gal. i. 1, xii. 16.  
[2] Acts ix. xxii. and xxvi.  
[3] 2 Cor. iv. 3-6; 1 Cor. xv. 45, etc.  
[4] Rom. v. 15.  
[5] Rom. viii. 3; 2 Cor. i. 5, xiii. 4.  
[6] 1 Cor. i. 17, ii. 2.  
[7] Paret, *Paulus und Christus*, Jahrb. deutsche Theol. II.  
[8] Phil. ii. 6, etc.; 2 Cor. v. 21; 1 Cor. i. 24; Gal. ii. 20; 2 Cor. v. 14; Rom. v. 19.

our intercessory mediator;[1] we shall also be united with Him, and become like His glorified body.[2]

Through what is higher in this man Jesus, He is then, according to Paul, υἱὸς Θεοῦ, Christ. He calls the same, so far as it is in Jesus, πνεῦμα ἁγιωσύνης;[3] indeed, he even says: The Lord is the Spirit whereby having is changed into being.[4] The name υἱὸς Θεοῦ also, it is true, embraces the human side; and he even calls believers υἱοὺς Θεοῦ. Still Christ alone is to him *the* son, even υἱὸς Θεοῦ ἴδιος,[5] and believers are sons of God because Christ lives in them. This higher principle is to Him truly Divine in nature. Paul regards it as pre-existent and distinct from God. God has, he says, sent His Son[6] in the fulness of times, namely, has sent Him from the invisible Divine sphere into visibility. This higher principle bears the name of Son in Paul even before the birth of Jesus, even though the name may be derived from His earthly manifestation. Further, Paul must have regarded the birth of the υἱός of a woman and His submission to the law, in short His appearance in the form of a servant, as not self-evident, considering the dignity which belonged to Him, or the mention of this would be wholly futile and meaningless. When he says, elsewhere,[7] we have a Lord Jesus Christ, through whom everything is, and we through Him, just as he had previously spoken of a Father, out of whom everything is, and we are for Him, the "everything" in the two cases must be the same, and cannot therefore be limited in Christ to the so-called moral creation. Paul also seems to have regarded Christ, especially the higher side in Him, as the spiritual rock of Israel in its journey through the wilderness.[8] It might, it is true, be

---

[1] Rom. viii. 34.
[2] Phil. i. 23, iii. 21. When Paul speaks of the glorified body of Christ, he cannot mean that He has wholly become Pneuma, that even His body has so become. 2 Cor. v. 16 cannot be understood of a disparagement of the humanity of Jesus, but refers partly to the opposition between the πάντις, *i.e.* the whole of humanity, v. 19, to which now His endeavour directs itself, and the narrowness of the Theocracy, in which He moved on earth by His birth from the stem of David, and partly refers generally to the fact that the apostle has now laid aside his earlier carnal conception of the Messianic idea.
[3] Rom. i. 4, not in a Trinitarian sense like 2 Cor. xiii. 13.
[4] 2 Cor. iii. 17.     [5] Rom. viii. 32.     [6] Gal. iv. 4.
[7] 1 Cor. viii. 6.     [8] 1 Cor. x. 4, 9.

thought that the passage through the Red Sea was a type or symbol to the apostle of Christian baptism, and the eating of the manna a type of the Lord's Supper; and consequently the words, "the spiritual rock" was Christ, would affirm that the rock which provided water in the wilderness was Christ in a typical sense—that the rock meant Christ, just as the manna meant the Lord's Supper. But Paul may also have supposed a real association of the Divine principle in Christ, to which he also gives the name Christ, with Israel in the wilderness, which is countenanced by the fact that the Israelites had in his view tempted Christ in the wilderness.[1] If, according to Paul, the υἱός is in relation to God the universal principle of mediation,[2] he would not have excepted the work of creation from this mediation by the Son.[3] Generally, such words are said of Christ as would be alone admissible if he really ascribed to him Divine nature. The words, "All knees shall bow to Me, saith the Lord," are referred to Christ, who in his esteem is the subject of Divine adoration, and to whom the judgment of the world is attributed.[4] In one passage of the older letters he calls Christ, according to the most probable exposition, God over all, blessed for ever.[5]

---

[1] 1 Cor. x. 9. The variant κύριον, instead of Χριστόν, is the easier and therefore the less commendable reading. To the Pauline circle of ideas the real relation of Christ to Israel in the pre-Christian time is not foreign. Heb. xi. 26.

[2] Comp. with 1 Cor. viii. 6, δι' οὗ τὰ πάντα, Rom. xi. 26.

[3] For which Heb. i. 2 is also an evidence, and Col. i. 13, etc., also.

[4] Rom. xiv. 9.

[5] Rom. ix. 5. A doxology to God would not fit in with the pain at Israel's rejection, to which Paul gives utterance in vv. 1-5 ; on the other hand, the words, referred to Christ, whom Israel rejected in spite of His dignity, give a reason for this pain. The continuation also of the sentence (ver. 6) with δέ does not suit a doxology to God, but to Christ.

What has been said shows that to the apostle the pre-existence of Christ was real and not merely ideal. But this cannot be applied in favour of the supposition of a pre-existing humanity or archetypal humanity, as was often done in earlier days, and has been repeated in many directions in more modern times (*e.g.* by Baur, Holsten, Pfleiderer ; by Bartels, *Ansichten eines Freundes der Bibel und der Naturbetrachtung*, 1871, pp. 19, etc. ; by Barth, *Der Engel des Bundes*, 1845 ; Keerl, *Der Gottmensch, das Ebenbild des unsichtbaren Gottes*, Bâle 1866, pp. 48, 96, 122, 144, 227, 246-258). Neither in such a way that the higher principle in Christ is in itself the primary man, the Χριστός pre-existing in the heavenly light-body, who then unites Himself with the earthly man Ἰησοῦς (Holsten, pp. 71-76, and 423), nor that He humbles Himself out of His pneumatic state for the sake of His earthly manifestation, and has transformed

In the later letters of the apostle, it is not so much that there is another Christology, as a development of the germs previously given. An overflowing exaltation is asserted of Him,[1] by virtue of which a universal adoration belongs to Him by all rational beings in the universe to the honour of God the Father, and this adoration is given to Him as a personal unity, to which humanity also belongs, which

Himself into the physical body (comp. Pfleiderer, *Paulinismus*, p. 152)—(a miraculous metamorphosis, for which the reverse change of the physical body into the pneumatic affords an analogy). The latter will not do, because Paul thinks of the body of Jesus as originating in the σπέρμα Δαβίδ. And the opinion that the higher principle—the Χριστός—in Him is nothing else than the archetypal man (as Baur, Beyschlag, and Hilgenfeld suppose) is not compatible with the fact that the Χριστός is rather to Paul specifically Divine, and is not created. According to Paul, Christ has neither brought a corporeality with Him from heaven (in Rom. i. 3, 4 he says nothing of a double body), nor had He in heaven a pneumatic body (comp. Weiss, *Bibl. Theologie*, pp. 296-300). The pneumatic body is in the world of men to which Christ is to be attributed as the second Adam, to Paul only the second, 1 Cor. xv. 46.—Barth, Bartels, and Keerl do not indeed deny that there is in the Pauline Christology room for a Trinitarian conception, but they think the Son a subordinate being *præter deum*, who represents the side of objectivity, intelligibility, "figurativeness," or "corporeality" in God, which is capable of being itself humbled and changed into our corporeality (so Bartels), or who, as the angel of the covenant, represents the side of the Divine being, by which the Divine manifestations become possible (after He has been personally associated with the first of all created things by incarnation—Barth) ; or finally, who, as Keerl thinks, being eternal humanity and the image of the invisible God, is indeed rooted in the inner Trinitarian essence of God, but in such a way that an element of the Trinity has projected itself out of the Father and exists independently with life in itself outside of (*præter*) the Father and Spirit, that it may be a middle being between God and the creature, and as a bridge between the finite and infinite may adapt itself to the work of mediation (pp. 170, 182, 227). This middle being, the eternal Son of man, has, he thinks, an original majesty with the Father, according to His corporeal mode of existence, and is the form of God, the archetype of beauty. Christ the archetypal man has brought the heavenly corporeality down, but He also assumed flesh and blood in addition, so that there was a becoming flesh but not a becoming *man*, Christ or the Son of God being Son of man. Thus Jesus had a double corporeality, as is also true of the regenerate. The main thing in all these latter theosophic views lies in the Divine nature of Christ as distinguished from the Father in the limitation of heavenly corporeality, which is supposed to capacitate Him for the position of mediator, and at the same time so to modify the Divine in Him that this in its unity with archetypal humanity only becomes a subordinate being outside of and side by side with the Father (Keerl, p. 495). But Paul speaks nowhere of Him who was pre-existent before the incarnation as a subordinate being ; he speaks as little of a corporeity in the pre-existent one.

[1] Phil. ii. 9-11.

indeed can alone be the subject of exaltation. An equality with God is ascribed to Him [1] (ἴσα Θεῷ ὑπάρχων). But the principal Christological passage [2] calls Christ the Son of love, the image of the invisible God, in whom everything is created and consists, through whom and for whom it was created. Were it only said "to Him," Schleiermacher's view might be admissible, that the reference is to His eternal idea which controlled creation, and not to a real pre-existence. But in such a case, the idle repetition "in Him" and "through Him" would be unexplained. Paul really says: He, the image of the invisible God, is before all, according to rank as the first-born, according to time as the co-existent cause of creation.[3] And He through whom everything was created, has also brought about the restoration of the harmony of the world through redemption. The world which had fallen asunder, and had indeed become reduced to schism, He has again gathered together, because He is the universal central point of creation and its innermost principle. He has ever remained the power of unity therein; the world has its existence in Him; and He therefore leads back to general consonance what had become disparted. The word "image," indeed, has in many places reference to His humanity,[4] but the Epistle to the Colossians speaks of the pre-existent being of Him who, as revealed in history, is the Son of love. This image is not merely a creaturely copy,[5] but the sense is: God, in Himself ἀόρατος, is manifest in the Son in perfect or adequate manner. The Divine principle in Christ is therefore supposed in this passage in relation to God generally. In relation to God He is the revealer simply, being His image. On the other hand, the word "first-born of the whole creation" forms the bridge to the world. He is not designated a creation thereby; the expression rather points to Sonship and unity of essence with God. And on the other side, as "the first-born of creation" He of course belongs to the world, and

---

[1] Verse 6. In Tit. ii. 13, Christ is also apparently to be understood by Θεός; the ἐπιφάνεια at the end of things is understood most consistently of the Parousia of Christ.

[2] Col. i. 13-20; comp. Eph. i. 6; Rom. viii. 32.

[3] Verse 17.     [4] 2 Cor. iv. 4.

[5] Col. ii. 9: the whole fulness of the Godhead dwells bodily, that is, in most complete reality, in Him.

that to such a degree that without Him the world would not be. In Him is the eternal idea of the world as well as its real principle, and both belong to the world in such a manner that if it abandons the world, neither its ideal value and unity nor reality remain. Still the passage does not call the world the Son of God, but distinguishes it from Him by saying that through Him, that is, through His will and intelligence, the realization of the world took place. He is thought of, so to speak, as a birth from God, in whom the ideal and real principles of the world are supposed.— The word λόγος is absent in Paul, he uses εἰκών; but what a word is to the ear, namely a revelation of what is within, an εἰκών is to the eye; and thus in the expressions there is only a translation, as it were, of the same fact from one sense to another. Nor does it contradict what precedes, if according to another passage the Son is subjected to the Father[1] at the end of the times. For the meaning can neither be that the Son has opposed the will of the Father, and will only become obedient in the future, nor that He will take a lower position in the consummation, absolutely and not merely relatively regarded, than during the period of the diffusion of the Gospel.[2] Relatively it is true that the redeemed, when they have become like Him, will be separated from Him by no such distance as before; in this sense, by virtue of His absolute loving will, He relatively decreases that they may increase. In reality, He sees herein, and has herein, His glorification. Rather than a degradation of Christ after His work has been crowned, we may permissibly see in the passage, that Christ is Himself only absolutely perfected with His kingdom, and that every possibility of the collision of the will of Christ and the Father will be excluded, as at any rate humiliation existed on earth without sin (Matt. xxvi. 39). The exalted Lord can certainly never abate His love, that being contrary to the entire N. T. portrait of Him. But this means that until the judgment He places Himself on the side of humanity by means of His intercession with the Father, and restrains the judgment, so to speak. It is the pitying, interceding, mediating will which mediates in the

---

[1] 1 Cor. xv. 24–28.
[2] Rom. v. 18, 19.

present æon between God and the sinner, and which would have the judgment postponed, and the work of redemption made fruitful, and which, finally, when mankind is ripe for judgment, acquiesces unreservedly in the Divine will, voluntarily lays down the mediating office of Redeemer, and surrenders or sacrifices, so to speak, His compassionate sentiment to the Father (ὑποταγήσεται), that the final decision, the judgment, may take place. Indeed, He will Himself execute this judgment in the name of God. Therefore it does not follow from the words, " that God may be all in all," that Christ will retire into a position of insignificance in the consummation. It is true that the intercessory mediatorship or substitution will cease, not merely in reference to unbelievers but believers, and that for the latter the relation to the Father will be immediate, just because the substitution of Christ has done its work.[1] But grateful communion with Christ need not therefore cease. If He no longer pleads as their substitute, it is only because He now lives and works in them and through them, so that there is in no way a resignation of His person. Even when it is said, " to the end that God should be all in all," Paul could not have meant to exclude Christ, for he thinks the Father undivided from the Son. In the dominion of the Divine will, whether of love or wisdom or righteousness and power, Christ also has His dominion; for with His humanity He is the sphere in which the realization of the Divine will is perfectly expressed. Did His βασιλεύειν generally cease, He would be in the Pauline view lower than believers to whom a βασιλεύειν is promised. And this rule is itself more accurately described as a companion-rule with Christ.[2] Christ accordingly remains the head, even in the consummation of things, when His mediating function has reached its goal. The kingdom of God, with its centre the Church, which is called the body of Christ, will not lose its head,[3] from which eternal life streams forth upon it; and in the idea of the "head"

---

[1] The passage in John xvi. 26 is of importance here: "I do not say unto you that I will always pray the Father for you, for the Father Himself has love for you because you have loved me."

[2] Rom. v. 17; Eph. ii. 6; 2 Tim. ii. 12; comp. Rev. xx. 4-6. xxii. 5.

[3] Eph. i. 22. The Epistle to the Hebrews also thinks of His kingdom as an eternal kingdom, i. 8, 12, xii. 28; 2 Pet. i. 11; Rev. xi. 15.

His humanity is also included. In the entirety of His person He is exalted to the right hand of God.[1] And the two sides, the Divine and the human, even in its humiliation, are, according to the apostle, embraced in the unity of the person of Christ. The Divine principle, that image of God, has so united itself with the humanity of Jesus that the humanity has come to express the Divine likeness.[2] And thus Jesus Christ, as realized in the world, is no mere transcendental image of God. The Divine in him is that which is all-deciding in this mysterious wedlock to which marriage is compared.[3] As the man is the head of the wife, God is also in another manner the head of Christ, because God is the determining element in Christ, this personal unity.[4] Nor will it be forgotten in this connection, that it is also said of the man who is the head of the wife, that he loves himself in his consort. To the apostle, the central or dominant element in this union is in any case the Divine. But in spite of this unity, according to which the Deity lives in humanity as the one person lives in the other in true marriage, there yet remains, according to this figure, the difference between the Divine and human side, that the latter is related to the former as the feminine or receptive nature is related to the husband; by receptivity humanity is, so to speak, lifted above itself. Jesus Christ is the pneumatic man endowed with power of life and animation.[5] Whilst, in relation to the person of Christ, God is the κεφαλή, that which is all-determining, the union of the Divine and human being perfect in Him, He is head of the body as this personal unity, that is, the head of the Church, the monarch of the kingdom of God exalted to the right hand of God. And this indwelling of God constitutes Him the second Adam, who as the perfection of the race[6] is at the same time called the last; for to the apostle Christ is not merely an individual like others, but has in his view a universal significance. Because the true humanity, the second and higher potency of Adam, is realized in archetypal manner,

---

[1] Rom. viii. 34.     [2] 2 Cor. iv. 4; comp. iii. 17, 18.     [3] Comp. Eph. v. 23.
[4] 1 Cor. xi. 3. If this dependence is referred to the Divine side,—which is otherwise called Θιός,—the unsuitable sense would arise, that God is the head of this Divine side. Rather is Christ the unique person in whom God is all-determining.
[5] 1 Cor. xv. 45.                      [6] Rom. v. 15; 1 Cor. xv. 45.

He is the progenitor of the new race of the children or sons of God.

This perfect unity of the Divine and human is conceived with comparative ease in reference to Christ in His exaltation. But how does Paul harmonize the humiliation with this portrait of Christ? In the Epistle to the Philippians there is a duality of states so distinguished, that the state of humiliation is a presupposition of the exaltation. Christ's humanity is exalted to full participation in the Divine majesty, as a reward for its confirmation in obedience.[1] He would not have been able to be so exalted had He not had a faultless development in a truly human growth and obedience. This growth Paul has not elaborated so strongly as the Epistle to the Hebrews; but he nevertheless says that Christ was only constituted the Son of God in power upon His resurrection, that previously, therefore, he was not υἱὸς θεοῦ ἐν δυνάμει, although he was υἱός.[2] Therefore the sonship of Christ, this personal totality, has a growth, and is not perfect from the beginning.[3] But if in Christ, as true and developing humanity, there was also the pre-existent Divine principle, how does Paul harmonize this with the unity of His person? It may be conceded that He does not expressly give an opinion upon this point, and that there remains by consequence a wide space for dogmatic investigation. Nevertheless, this much is certain, that inasmuch as the sonship including the Divine and human was not yet wholly completed, Paul must have definitely supposed a growth in the personal unity of life in reference to the relation of the body of Jesus to the unity of the person, because he thinks of this unity of the glorified body of Christ with His person in the exaltation as indissoluble, whilst it was previously dissolved by death. But it agrees with this fact but little, when many think that even for the state of humiliation Paul attained the perfect unity (or rather a responsive equivalence) of the Divine side with the human, by speaking in one passage of a self-emptying of the Divine principle (ἐκένωσεν ἑαυτόν),[4] by which He has humbled Himself to potentiality, and made Himself equal to developing man, so that we have to speak of a submission to the destiny of finitude, of a learning, of an

---

[1] Phil. ii. 8–10.   [2] Rom. i. 4.   [3] Phil. ii. 6, etc.
[4] Phil. ii. 6, etc.   οὐχ ἁρπαγμὸν ἡγήσατο ἶσα Θεῷ εἶναι ἀλλ' ἐκένωσεν ἑαυτόν.

obedience even of the Divine principle. Both natures have then, it is continued, developed themselves in perpetual unity, that is, have moved in a parallel and with equal steps. Whether the passage in the Philippians actually presents dogmatic instruction as to how the origin and existence of the unity of Christ's life is to be thought, will be decided if we ask, before everything, whether the subject of the passage is, as the point of view just mentioned would have it, the pre-existent Divine principle of itself or the historical Christ, who voluntarily submitted to humiliation, to renunciation of the use of power, nay, to self-sacrifice. In favour of the latter supposition, which the old Lutheran theologians maintain against the Reformed, whilst numerous more recent Lutherans abandon it, the fact speaks that Paul does not prefix " Christ," but " Jesus Christ " as subject, just as it is also acknowledged that he elsewhere ascribes to Jesus a life on earth full of self-sacrifice,[1] and `consequently there is no necessity present for the reference of the humiliation to the Divine side (for the end of the incarnation). The connection speaks definitely for this rendering. Jesus Christ wishes to be presented as an example of unselfish humility and of the most resigned obedience, even to the death of the cross. And an example must be historically cognizable, which that supposed invisible and transcendent act of a self-emptying of the eternal Son prior to the incarnation would not be; indeed, that supposed self-emptying, which consists in surrender of actual conscious life, in reduction to the state of potentiality, could not be performed by or required of Christians. Not for a moment could it be a question of the surrender of high and majestic powers or gifts on the part of Christ; for such surrender again does not belong at all to the surrender of self-denying humility. We say nothing of the fact that this view, maintaining as it does a theanthropic development, must still suppose for every stage of advance a progressive animation of humanity by the Deity, and consequently a momentary transcendence above humanity by the Deity, who is only communicating Himself. It might then be that this view might think of the humanity as completed spontaneously and without the influence of the Divine nature, in which case the God-human unity would be

[1] 2 Cor. viii. 9.

resolved into two lines of development independent of each other, and the human side would be thought of after the manner of Ebionitism. The passage will therefore be better translated, that Jesus Christ, although in Divine outline or form, and therefore being already in the likeness of God (ἐν μορφῇ Θεοῦ ὑπάρχων), held equality with God (τὸ εἶναι ἴσα Θεῷ), which is supposed to pertain to Him as the God-human unity, to be no fact of an arbitrary or powerful snatching for oneself, to be no robbery, which He has to drag to Himself of His own might, but in complete self-forgetfulness and humiliation He showed His humble and self-forgetful life of love.[1] Whilst the first Adam was disobedient, through the temptation of pride, which promised him equality with God, an equality he wished to steal, so to speak, the second Adam has actually attained to Divine majesty, inasmuch as He would not snatch equality with God of His own power merely; but although Himself exalted in dignity, He yet humbled Himself like another man, yea, even to the ignominious death of the cross.[2] —Accordingly, Paul speaks of a state of humiliation, which was the self-humiliation of Christ, on the side of majesty lacking at the beginning equality with God. But of a self-detriment of Deity the passage does not speak. The result therefore is, that Paul assumes a true growth in the union of the Divine with His humanity, but without describing more minutely the manner of this occurrence.[3] He only says that the personal unity of life was not already perfect from the beginning.

2. THE EPISTLE TO THE HEBREWS.

If, according to the Synoptics, Christ was on the one hand the sower of the "word" that brings healing and new birth, and was on the other hand the contents of the word or the

[1] Even Luther rightly expounds the passage of the act of incarnation. Comp. Hering, *Die Mystik Luthers*, 1878, p. 131, and explains the μορφή not of the substance (Divine or human nature), but of the constitution.
[2] The literature upon this passage is extremely rich; comp. the *Programm* of Tholuck; further, Meyer's *Commentary*; Keerl, pp. 144-184; Weiss, Köstlin, *Jahrb. für deutsche Theol.*, 1858, iii. 96; and my treatise on *Die Unveränderlichkeit Gottes*, in the same review, 1856, 1858.
[3] Rom. i. 4.

seed He sows,—the two ideas being harmonized thus, that the self-communicating revelation of God which was in Him had attained, as we already found in Peter, personal form,—the Epistle to the Hebrews in like manner starts from the point that Christ was not, like the prophets, the bearer of this or that individual Divine message merely. Rather is this person the decisive and perfect revelation of the word of God. The words of God, which were of many members and kinds, have now received their conclusion in the Son, in whom the revelation appears in personal form, and the Divine prototype Himself appears.[1] A part of the Jewish Christians, to whom the letter was addressed, were in danger of relapse to the synagogue, against which they are warned. Even where they did not hold Christ to be a mere man, a double declension threatened. The one was the angelological Christology which the letter definitely sketches, whilst the other (historically called the Nazarene, inclined to the so-called Patripassianism) supposed in Christ a manifestation of God, but, because, without a permanent distinction from the Father, a manifestation that was fleeting merely, and was therefore an individual theophanic act. The former is a prelude of Arianism, the latter of Sabellianism. The Epistle to the Hebrews is opposed to both.[2] Against the opinion that in Jesus a higher, angel-like, creaturely being has appeared, the Epistle admonishes how Christ, that He might be a perfect mediator, reconciler, and king of the kingdom of God, could not be a mere creature, but rather already took part in creation by the higher side of His nature.[3] Against the theophanic Christology which annuls the eternal import of the person of the humanity of Christ, the Epistle asserts in the strongest manner His true historical humanity, effective even in His exaltation by means of the high-priestly intercession, like to ours.[4]

As far as the former opponents are concerned, the Epistle paints Christ in detail as the goal of the whole history of revelation. Everything earlier therein is related as a type to Him in whom the heavenly archetype is realized. He is the Son in the house of God, as contrasted with whom a Moses

---

[1] Heb. i. 1–3, iv. 12, etc.  [2] Heb. i. 2, 3.
[3] Heb. i, 2, 3, 13, 14.  [4] Heb. iv. 15; chap. vii.-ix.

Himself has merely the position of a servant.[1] He is the king and priest of humanity; He perfects both offices, inasmuch as He unites them in His person.[2] He opens to mankind the innermost sanctuary of heaven by virtue of the eternal Spirit and the power of indissoluble life in Him, through which He has been able to present the sacrifice absolutely well-pleasing to God.[3] And he is especially superior to the Old Testament economy as not being its product, or as being accredited thereby; it is His product, He being the cosmical principle of revelation. Only in the personal form, indeed, it has in Him is it perfected; but the Epistle describes his relation to the Old Testament, and indeed to creation, in such a manner that it assumes no merely ideal, but a real and effective, pre-existence of the Divine principle, which in the last time appeared in Jesus. Therefore to the author Christ is no mere creature, even the highest, but a truly Divine being.

And indeed, *in the second place*, the Divine element of the Son is distinguished from God generally, nay, itself receives the name Son,[4] which name does not in the sense of the author apply to generation, but is meant figuratively, and is transferred from the historical Christ to that element.[5] Nor did this distinction enter at the incarnation only. The same Divine principle which appeared in the Son, is supposed to be present in relation to God generally. This is expressed by two ontological predicates. He is called radiance (not merely copy or reflection) of the majestic Divine nature, and thus in opposition to a merely creaturely conception an equality of nature is ascribed to the Son; on the other hand he is called a characteristic determination and an objective expression of the Divine nature. He is, so to speak, the delineation of His hypostasis, which includes that God is not merely the One who knows no distinction, but He has features in Himself which are imprinted and objectified in the Son as in an image.

[1] iii. 5, 6.     [2] v. 9, etc.; chap. vii.-ix.
[3] ix. 14, x. 19, vii. 16, 28.
[4] i. 8; comp. 5. The Son is here addressed as God.
[5] i. 2, 3, and v. 4, where the κικληρονόμηκε is to be considered of the name of son. The transfer of the modern idea of personality to this pre-existent Divine principle is a precipitate, dogmatic interpolation. Nor does the expression πνεῦμα αἰώνιον, in reference to the same, so far as it is in Christ, speak in favour of this interpolation.

The Divine image is that whereby God is cognizable or manifest as what He is; and that not only for the world, but objectively and *per se*, and therefore (although this is not expressly said) in or for God Himself.[1] Of this form of God, who also has the name Son from His revelation in humanity, it is then said that God has made the worlds through Him, and that the Son, who bears the universe with the word of His power, has seated Himself, after He has instituted the atonement, on the right hand of majesty, and has been as the first-born, appointed heir, that is, ruler, of all things.[2] In another noteworthy passage the word λόγος is also expressly applied to the revelation in Christ.[3] The supposition does not suit the predicates of the λόγος (iv. 12), that a glad message generally is to be understood thereby, for the λόγος Θεοῦ is called ζῶν, ἐνεργής, κριτικός; indeed, it is thought of as intelligence, for the reference is to His all-penetrating eye. Of course the passage does not speak of its pre-existence, but as to how it historically entered in the Gospel, and therefore in the person of Christ, as conscious, acting and productive of separation.[4] And it bears a didactic and not poetic character; and, however it may be with the personality of the pre-existent Divine principle, it may be thought of as personal in itself and without the one personal God, or only with and in Him (the author is silent on the matter); it is established both that the author supposes distinctions in God which are also relative to the world, and that the Divine principle of revelation pre-existent in God has its full existence in Christ, so that one may allowably say that Christ is to the author the personified λόγος.[5]

---

[1] Comp. the εἰκὼν τοῦ Θεοῦ τοῦ ἀοράτου, Col. i. 15.

[2] In i. 3, 4, 10, what is referred in the original text to Jehovah is said of Christ.

[3] iv. 12, etc. Πρὸς ὃν ἡμῖν ὁ λόγος, ver. 13, does not say, "to Him, namely God, we have to give account," but our evangelical proclamation treats of Him, who in ver. 12 is introduced and painted in detail as λόγος. Inasmuch as the radiance belonging to God and the form of His ὑπόστασις is figuratively called Son, an emphatic command (i. 3) may be ascribed thereto; for that radiance is to the author the Deity Himself, who is instrumental for God (δι' οὗ). It is quite in harmony that God as the Son or as the "Word" should also Himself again have or speak a command.

[4] This use of the word λόγος has a parallel in Rev. xix. 14; λόγος ζῶν calls 1 Pet. i. 23 to mind.

[5] I adopt this expression from T. Beck.

What is noteworthy in the Epistle to the Hebrews is further, that, elevated as are the expressions respecting the higher principle in Christ, these expressions are not allowed to hinder a more emphatic assertion of the perfect and permanent humanity of Christ, indeed of His humiliation, His growth, His struggles, and His temptations, than occurs in any other writing of the N. T. All docetic or merely theophanic representations of Christ are thereby rejected. At the same time this serves the latter for the proof that it has been possible to accomplish the atonement by the road of the high-priestly sympathy. Christ in His self-humiliation but absolute purity belonging to our race, it is brought about that we may have confidence in God and again approach the Father without fear.[1] Even the Son was like us in learning obedience, in standing in faith and not sight, in vanquishing evil by abhorring evil.[2] With supplication, prayer, and tears He turned to God in the days of His flesh; for awhile He was humbled beneath the angels for our sakes;[3] but He has remained in all without sin.

## Third Class.—The Johannine Christology.

There is a notable difference between the Apocalypse and the Gospel in reference to the doctrine of the Logos, which argues for the earlier composition of the former. The former says,[4] Christ has as the exalted Christ a new name, which no one knows but He Himself. This name is neither given before nor after. This means that in the contemporary sphere of ideas no name was to be found answering to the name of Christ. That sphere only knew the name of God on the one hand, and the name of man on the other, but not a being who is the unity of both, and so far unique in his kind. But the Apocalypse then adds the designation given to him in human speech which is notwithstanding a *nomen proprium* rather

[1] ii. 14, vii. 13, etc.      [2] vi. 20, xii. 2, v. 7, ii. 14, 17.
[3] ἡλαττωμένος (II. 9) refers to His form as a servant, in which He was like other men (vers. 6, 7), and to the progressive humiliation in the same; of a self-humiliation of God in Him there is no mention. Otherwise in the author's view pre-existence and kenosis must be affirmed of every man (see vers. 6, 7).
[4] Rev. xix. 12.

than *appellativum*. He is called "the word of God" (ὁ λόγος τοῦ θεοῦ). By this designation is by no means meant the pre-existent Divine principle of Himself, but the whole Christ, together with His humanity, in His post-existence and perfection. This passage is thus connected with the earlier series of thoughts of James and the Synoptics. It presupposes that it was already customary to designate the person of Christ as the Word of God (ῥῆμα, דָּבָר), *i.e.* as the revelation of God. The passages previously mentioned[1] are in fact evidences of the correctness of the assertion that the historic Christ already bore the name "the Word of God." According to the passage in the Apocalypse, the revelation of God in Him has attained personal form. Indeed, it thinks of Him not merely as the spoken word of God, but also as living and self-speaking, just as we also find the two united in the Epistle to the Hebrews (see p. 186). Therefore, immediately after reference is made to the two-edged sword[2] which goes out of His mouth, *i.e.* to His word. As certainly then as this noteworthy passage calls Christ, as historical, indeed, in His post-existence, the "Word of God," there are also in other passages of the Apocalypse references to His pre-existence, not merely His ideal pre-existence[3] in the Divine counsel, but also His real. For Christ is even called the real principle of creation,[4] and besides, the First and the Last, the Beginning and the End.[5]

If we turn to the Gospel of John, there are still many who maintain that this Gospel presents by its doctrine of the Logos a Christ who is wholly foreign to the other Gospels, and who as compared with the Synoptics is idealistic, docetic, nay, ghostlike, and lacking in true humanity.[6] Others seek an adjustment, by endeavouring to raise the Synoptic portrait of Christ to the elevation of the Johannine[7] (but against this the absence of an express doctrine of pre-

---

[1] Especially 1 Pet. i. 23; Heb. iv. 12, etc.; perhaps also Jas. i. 18.
[2] Rev. xix. 15; comp. i. 16.       [3] xiii. 8.
[4] iii. 14: ἀρχὴ τῆς κτίσεως, which cannot mean the first creature, for the adoration of a mere creature is prohibited in xxii. 9, whilst adoration is ascribed to the Lamb. Thus ἀρχὴ τῆς κτίσεως is analogous to the πρωτότοκος τῆς κτίσεως (Col. i. 15), and means the ideal and real principle of the universe.
[5] i. 17, ii. 8; perhaps also A and Ω, i. 8, xxii. 13.
[6] Thus Strauss, Baur, Köstlin, Zeller, etc.       [7] Thus Philippi.

existence in the Synoptics speaks); or else by attempting to reduce the Johannine portrait of Christ to that of the Synoptic,[1] which is interdicted by the doctrine of pre-existence presented in the Gospel. But it is already conceded by all unbiassed minds, that even in his older letters Paul has a doctrine of pre-existence, and that therefore the assertion is a weak one, that the pre-existence of Christ has only been introduced into the doctrine of the Church by means of the later Gospel of John and its doctrine of the Logos. It is already frequently acknowledged that Paul and John do not essentially differ in their Christology. On the other hand, others say that the "higher Christology" of both is a Theologoumenon which is to be placed to their account,[2] and which they have mixed up with the words of Christ and with the history, which they are to be supposed to have placed in the light of certain speculations, especially of Alexandrian origin. But Paul does not use the word Logos of Christ, and yet has essentially the same doctrine. And that the doctrine of the earlier Scriptures of the N. T. of the word of God ($\lambda \acute{o} \gamma o \varsigma$ or $\acute{\rho} \hat{\eta} \mu a$) was already a preparation for the Johannine doctrine of the Logos, is sufficiently evident from what precedes. As far as the Gospel of John itself is concerned, against the intermixture of speculations about the Logos in its Gospel history the noteworthy fact speaks, that the evangelist gives the prologue, in which mention is exclusively made of the Logos, as his own confession; on the other hand, when he makes Jesus speak, this word is not used at all,—a course which was, however, very usual with him when he was giving his own thoughts.[3] And against the borrowing from the Alexandrian wisdom, especially of Philo, the great difference between the Logos of Philo and of John speaks which becomes acknowledged with increasing universality.[4] Philo's Logos does not become $\sigma \acute{a} \rho \xi$ or man, and could not according to its nature. It is a false kind of harmony, to screw up the Synoptics to an equality with John, just as

---

[1] As Weizsäcker thought earlier (*Jahrb. f. deutsche Theol.* II. pp. 154, etc.), but he afterwards allowed the opinion to drop.
[2] Thus Reuss and Keim.
[3] Comp. 1 John i. 1, etc., with John i. and Rev. xix. 14.
[4] Comp. my *History of the Doctr. of Person of Christ*, vol. i. pp. 21, etc., 114.

conversely it is also a false harmony to apply the Gospel of John in such a manner that nothing peculiar is left thereto. Yet this individuality is not opposed to the rest of the N. T., but is only the most developed expression of what is already found therein.

The Gospel does not by any means depict Jesus as the God merely who steps down to earth, but makes Him walk in the closest living relations of love and friendship with man,[1] and permits us to glance into His rich and much-moved character[2] as no other writing of the N. T. does. If it is said that the fundamental passage does not speak of a human soul, but only of the becoming flesh of the Word, not of the becoming man,[3] so that humanity only appears to be the garment in which a God walks, mention is expressly made in other passages of a human soul of Jesus,[4] so that flesh must be taken in the wider sense of human nature or humanity.[5] The Epistle expresses itself in the strongest manner against Docetism.[6] Jesus calls Himself a man,[7] and affects all with whom He comes into contact as an actual man.[8] He is, according to the Gospel of John, subject even to human weaknesses, to fatigue, to hunger and thirst, to the interchange of disposition, of joy and melancholy.[9] The Johannine Christ is by no means an absolutely ready-made and perfect form, an immoveable living unity of eternally identical majesty and perfection. He rather speaks Himself of a future perfection of a continuing Divine teaching, showing and giving, of His learning, seeing, hearing of the Father, by which receptivity and petition His $\delta \acute{o} \xi a$ is communicated.[10] To the same class of facts His baptism belongs; indeed there is a mention of an inner struggle, which He sustains by means of prayer for the Father's help.[11] If

---

[1] ii. 1–12, chap. xi., xv. 15.  [2] Chap. xiii.–xvi. 17.
[3] i. 14, as Keerl emphasizes with special zeal.
[4] xii. 27, xiii. 21, xi. 34, 38.  [5] As iii. 6, xvii. 2.
[6] 1 John iv. 2, 3; 2 John 7.
[7] In John v. 27, viii. 40, without anything being said of the eternal Logos that He is in Himself humanity, as Keerl would have it.
[8] i. 30, iv. 29, vii. 46, ix. 11, 16, 24, x. 33, xi. 47, 50, xviii. 17, 29, xix. 5.
[9] iv. 35–38, xi. 33–38, xii. 27, xiii. 21.
[10] v. 19, 20, viii. 26, 40, xi. 41, etc., xiv. 10–16, xv. 15, xvii. 5, 7, 22.
[11] xii. 27 (Greek).

it is not the man Jesus Christ who speaks in the Gospel, but only God as the Logos, He could not say, I speak not of myself,[1] I seek not my own honour, I can do nothing of myself,[2] I do at all times what is well-pleasing to the Father.[2] The power to communicate the Holy Ghost becomes His only by His exaltation,[4] and He frequently speaks of the consciousness of the perfection which He lacks, but which He prays the Father for.[5] But His growth is of course a faultless development, and through all stages a constancy shows itself, a self-identity, His essential unity with God. Besides, from His humiliation there straightway streamed forth most for true contemplation the inner majesty of His love. It is characteristically Johannine to view His lifting up upon the cross as an elevation, namely, to the most majestic revelation of His self-sacrificing love.[6] This leads to the other side.

In numerous passages in John the consciousness of course finds expression of a unique exaltation of Christ which has its roots in His peculiar community with God.[7] Christ calls the men of the Old Covenant those to whom the Word of God came, and who on that account are already designated gods.[8] But He distinguishes Himself from them as the one who is consecrated by the Father and sent into the world, that is, who is singled out and absolutely equipped for His work by the fact that the Father is in Him and He in Him.[9] And the passages concerning the pre-existence of Christ [10] especially belong here. Further, that the first-

[1] John vii. 17, xii. 49.     [2] viii. 54, v. 19.     [3] viii. 29, 55.
[4] vii. 39, xvi. 7.     [5] xiii. 32, xiv. 28, xvii. 1, 5.
[6] iii. 14, viii. 23; comp. xii. 32, 33. This comprehension of Christ the Evangelist certainly did not gain at once. The idea of Christ in the Spirit was conditioned by the communication of the Holy Ghost, John vii. 39. Supposing the Revelation to conduct us mediately at any rate to the Apostle John, the vision of the glorified Lord in the first chapter may be compared with that which came to Saul, seeing that by both the objective figure of Christ the glorified and living Head became a part of their intuition, whence as a starting-point the inner and profounder understanding of the history and words of Jesus was gained by a retrogressive process. And the light, which fell upon the earthly course of Jesus from the glorified Lord, the Evangelist could not and dared not withhold from the Christian community.
[7] x. 30.     [8] x. 34.     [9] x. 38.
[10] John xvii. 5, viii. 56, iii. 13; compare 31, vi. 33, 38, 41, 46, 51, 62, viii. 42, xvi. 27, xvii. 8, 24. It is insufficient with Beyschlag to limit these passages,

mentioned passages which describe His true humanity and dependence upon God cannot possibly be understood as a mere equalization of Christ with others, is clear from the following consideration. With the being sent by the Father is contrasted the coming or the descent from heaven.[1] By the side of the sentence that the Father shows him His works, stands the other sentence that the Son makes living whom He will.[2] By the side of the sentence that He does not seek His own honour, but the Father's, stands this—all shall honour the Son, just as they honour the Father.[3] It belongs to the same category, when the Son calls Himself the light and life of the world, the way and the truth, the resurrection and the life.[4] He who sees Him, sees the Father,[5] who has given Him to have life in Himself as the Father has.[6] By virtue of His unity with the Father, He has the power to give His sheep eternal life, and no one can snatch them out of His hand.[7] Therefore the evangelist describes God as the ἴδιος πατήρ of Christ, and Jesus consequently a Son in a unique sense,[8] as is signified by the word "only-begotten."[9] Especially is the Johannine doctrine of the Logos to be still considered.

Whilst in the Apocalypse, Christ is called Logos, as glorified, and therefore in His post-existence only, this name is already applied in the First Epistle of John,[10] as well as in the Gospel, to the visible, historical presence of Christ. For the words: "What we have heard and what we have seen, what we have beheld and our hands have handled, of the Word of Life," are an expression of joy in the personal presence of Salvation. But from the present, retrogression is made to the pre-existence of the "Word of Life" (expressed in the Epistle in the neuter), which was in the beginning with the Father, but is now revealed.[11]

especially the first mentioned, to a mere ideal pre-existence, and therefore to find therein only God's eternal thought of humanity which must also have preceded the election of Abraham. So far Schulze "on the Son of Man" is right, as against Beyschlag.

[1] iii. 13, vi. 33, etc.   [2] v. 21.   [3] v. 23.
[4] xi. 25, xiv. 6, viii. 12, comp. xii. 36.   [5] xiv. 9.
[6] v. 26.   [7] x. 28-30.   [8] v. 18 ; comp. Rom. viii. 32.
[9] i. 18, comp. iii. 16.   [10] 1 John i. 1, etc.
[11] 1 John i. 2. Therefore ἀπ' ἀρχῆς is not to be understood of the beginning of the proclamation of the Gospel, but recalls the ἐν ἀρχῇ of John i. 1, as well as Rev. iii. 14.

This "Word of Life" which recalls the λόγος ζῶν of Peter and the Epistle to the Hebrews, is now, in the double prologue of the Epistle and the Gospel, fixed in His relation to God apart from the world and the history of revelation. If revelation is perfected in Christ, nothing is more natural than that in Him the principle of revelation should itself be seen and be brought into relation to God Himself. His relation to God is now first defined in the Gospel as equality of nature,[1] secondly as a relation of the difference between God generally and the Logos, who is also God, and therefore as a difference of God from God, which is not however of a dividing character; for the Logos is with God, directed towards God ($\pi\rho\acute{o}\varsigma$), just as it is figuratively said in the Proverbs of "wisdom," that it is with God or at God's side. The principle of revelation which was from the beginning stands in eternal relation to God, and is not therefore of a merely momentary, historical, temporal, or transient importance. The Logos is not the world, not even the ideal world, as in Philo, but He is thought of at first purely as a Divine principle. But He also has a relation to the world; through Him everything has become that has become. He is the real and the ideal principle of the world, in Him rests its life, and He is the light of men, in which lies the union of the דָּבָר and the חָכְמָה, the Hebrew real principle and the Hellenic ideal principle. But because the world arises from Him, He is also, and remains, in intimate union therewith, and it has need of Him and can receive Him. The Logos desires to be in the world from the beginning as life and light, and this is attained in perfect manner in Jesus. He does not merely put or call forth this man as He calls forth the world, as a thing extra-divine and different to Him; rather is He so perfectly united with this man, that the evangelist can say, the Logos became this man. Creation through the Logos has passed into the idea of the incarnation

---

[1] Θεὸς ἦν ὁ λόγος. The absence of the article does not prove that the Logos is merely a Θεὸς δεύτερος; comp. vv. 6, 12, 13, 18. The Logos is the subject of the whole verse, and Θεός is therefore the predicate; the Logos also was belonging to deity, of Divine nature. The ἦν denotes the eternal being which is at every moment a has been, and therefore the contrast to ἐγένετο in vv. 3 and 14. The ἀρχή in ver. 1 is not the beginning of the world (ver. 3 first speaks of the world), but rather describes the point, behind which it is impossible to go farther, *i.e.* eternity.

of the Logos. For it is not independent extra-Divine being, such as the world had by creation, and subsequently by the giving of the Law, which is the goal of His working, but union and living association with God. The grace and truth, which came to historical realization by means of the only-begotten of the Father,[1] aim at giving power to believers to become children of God.[2]

The two series of statements thus considered, those of the lower and of the higher kind, which belong to the one person of Christ, are nevertheless not yet unified, or apprehended in their compatibility, by saying that in the one class of passages the Logos is regarded as the person that speaks, and in the other the humanity is so regarded. This would only be a sharpening, not a solving, of the problem; and it would not be in accordance with the text. The naked Logos nowhere speaks as a person *per se* or "as a God who walks the earth."[3] Let it be wholly accepted that the humanity in Christ is impersonal, and is only the veil of the Logos who speaks and acts, then expressions like those mentioned above, "I speak not of myself," etc., or "The Father is greater than I," as well as His praying, are incomprehensible. There would also follow that the Logos Himself suffered, or else there would follow a mere seeming suffering; in that case the Logos must have transformed His eternal being into a temporal one, must have entered upon a mutation which does not agree with the fact that Christ knew Himself, even upon earth, as being in an ever similar eternal being.[4] Even the supposition[5] that the Logos has assumed the place of the human soul in Jesus, and has limited Himself to passivity in relation to the body, misses the mark, and is non-Johannine. For in that case He would not be actual man, but would only have adopted the *form* of the human soul by the side of the body, and this only temporarily, until in the consummation he became no longer a human soul, but the pure Logos, again restored to Himself

---

[1] i. 17.   [2] i. 12, etc.
[3] Nor is this the case even in the passages which assert His pre-existence, especially not in John viii. 58, xvii. 5. Even here the speaker is the man; the object of His speech, and therefore also of His consciousness, is the eternal, Divine side of His nature, which stands in His consciousness as the fundamental element of His person.
[4] John iii. 13, etc.   [5] Von Gess (and Wörner).

and only clothed with a body. An actual human soul would then be denied, which nevertheless the Gospel teaches. Finally, the Gospel as little declares for the view,[1] according to which the Logos has temporarily laid down the Divine attributes relative to the world, in order to be in harmony with a truly human and developing life. For this modern Kenotic theory the words are quoted from the Gospel of John: "And now glorify me, Father, with the brightness which I had with Thee before the foundation of the world was laid," and they are understood thus, that Christ as the Logos implores the restitution of the majesty of the Logos laid down for the sake of the incarnation. But the one who prays is Jesus, and prayer is a creaturely human function. Since the sense which lies grammatically nearest cannot be that Jesus, this man, has already existed before the world and has then had majesty, but has it now no longer, the pre-existence is of course to be ascribed to the Divine principle. And further, the Jesus who is praying *not yet having* this majesty, the sense will be that He implores for His humanity what it does not as yet possess, and not that the Divine side implores glorification for itself, inasmuch as nothing is said of a previous humiliation of the same. The speaker, Jesus, knows Himself to be united with the Logos in a manner which is fundamental as regards His person, has a knowledge of the same and of His majesty, but has not as yet the possession of the majesty, the hour of deepest humiliation being at hand. The Kenotic meaning would only follow if the speaker were exclusively the Logos, and if Jesus were not the praying person, who did not as yet know Himself to be wholly united "with the eternal Logos," with His δόξα. It is nowhere said that the Divine side, with which He is conscious of being in actual, but not yet absolutely perfect union, must have humiliated itself and abandoned heaven. On the contrary, according to other passages, Christ knows Himself even on earth to be in heaven [2] in such a way indeed that a knowledge of this as well as of the unity of His humanity with the Deity belongs to the humanity. And this

---

[1] Von Thomasius and others.
[2] John iii. 13. Similarly His continuous communication to the world is represented as His continuous condescension from the heaven where He is to the world. John vi. 50.

knowledge assigns the goal of the theanthropic development. His descent to earth, that figurative expression, describes the beginning of bringing heaven to earth, and of making earth into the kingdom of heaven, but does not mean an abandonment of heaven.[1]

Surveying the whole Johannine Christology, there is evident what is often indeed overlooked, that even by John, different stages in the person of Christ are distinguished, to which corresponding predicates belong, and to which the lower predicates even cannot be wanting if the humanity of Christ is supposed to have full truth, and therefore also a development. It is thus conceded that the whole fulness and majesty of the Logos could only gradually be assumed, and consequently that the Divine-human unity itself was conceived to be still in increase. And *next*, for the high predicates which are ascribed to His Divine-human unity of life, the fact forms an elucidating fulcrum that He has not merely a true humanity as we all have, but a humanity so constituted, that, when it has wholly become what it is capable of becoming, the Divine principle, which the evangelist calls the Logos, can dwell therein in His complete fulness and majesty. Therefore is He called not man merely, but also the Son of man.[2]

According to what has been advanced, it would be unhistorical to deny that there are considerable differences in the primary Apostolic Church. But these differences are only various stages in the development of the common faith which we have stated in a preparatory fashion above. This common element is already so rich, that the characteristics of the lower stages lead onward of themselves to the higher.

B.—*The Ecclesiastical Development of Christology.*

## § 92.

The entire apostolic testimony is partly appropriated by the Church in a manner always more complete, and is partly unfolded and dogmatically verified in a manner always more comprehensive; hence the ecclesiastical develop-

[2] Comp. i. 52.   [1] John iii. 13; comp. v. 26.

ment of Christology begins at the lowest canonical stage, and under the guidance and stimulus of the Spirit of God and of the Word of the canon, attains the principal elements of Christology, and establishes their internally sure connexion. The history of this doctrine falls into three periods.

The *first*, to A.D. 381, establishes the two sides ("natures") of the Person of Christ according to their main elements.

The *second*, to the end of the 18th century, seeks to lay down the unity of the Person and the relation of these two sides to each other, but without a closer investigation of their nature; rather under a conception of the same, by which the one side must necessarily be abridged by the other, as happened at different epochs in opposite fashion.

The *third* period, from 1800 on, has for its problem, after the two sides have again attained recognition in their equality of authority, to allow the distinctions in the Person of Christ their rights in so uniform a manner that, in the interests of the unity of Person, the compatibility, nay, the inner living relation of its distinctions to one another is also exhibited, and therefore an image of Christ is sketched which is actually and truly human and Divine at once, that is, is theanthropic.

LITERATURE.—George Bull, *Defensio Fidei Nicænæ*, edit. Grabe, 1703; comp. Dan. Whitby, *Disquisitio modesta in Bulli defens.* 1720. Dionysius Petavius, *De theolog. dogmatibus*, 1644, etc.; J. Gerhard, *Loci Theologici*, iv. (with Cotta's Treatise *De Persona Christi*). Baur, *Die christliche Lehre von der Dreieinigkeit und Menschwerdung Gottes in ihrer geschichtlichen Entwickelung*, 3 vols. 1841–1843. Matthias Schneckenburger, *Zur kirchlichen Christologie ; Die orthodoxe Lehre vom doppelten Stande Christi nach lutherischer und reformirter Auffassung*, 1848, 1861; the same, *Vergleichende Darstellung des lutherischen und reformirten Lehrbegriffs*, edit. by Güder, 2 vols. 1855. Al. Schweizer, *Die Glaubenslehre der evang. reform. Kirche aus den Quellen belegt*, 1844–1847. H. Schmid, *Die Dogmatik der evang.-luther. Kirche*, edit. 3, 1853, § 31, etc. Fr. Frank, *Die Theologie der Concordienformel*, vol. iii. 1863.

No dogma has had a history more transparent, more logical, and freer from ecclesiastical aberrations, at least on its productive side, than Christology. The ecclesiastical tact which eliminated what was morbid, which recognized and sanctioned what was healthy, could nowhere guide more surely than here, where the heart of Christian faith was in question. With this dogma the six oldest Œcumenical Synods pre-eminently busied themselves, and the times in which the common faith of the Church has again occupied the position of the heartiness and certainty of the beginning, have erected the landmarks for the development of this doctrine on the right and on the left. The ecclesiastical consensus, which even within the divided Church is far-reaching upon this dogma, and has survived the two great divisions in the Church, undoubtedly owes its stedfastness to the circumstance that the great Christological fundamental propositions, at least of the four first Œcumenical Councils in the years 325, 381, 431, 451, do not gainsay the intimate connection with Christian faith, but must be enlightening to the Christian consciousness. In the first centuries every earlier stage was transcended under the guidance of Holy Writ, because the common understanding of the Church had convinced itself by its thorough treatment that the only choice is to fall back behind this stage or to bestride a new stage equally prefigured in the canon. The decisive motives in these advances were so weighty, and were so taken from the nature of Christianity, that Christology, whilst preserving its memory, remained conscious therein of its own dogmatic verification. And the factors which condition the endeavour of the Church after an ever more defined Christological apprehension are two—one *subjective*: the faith of the Church or the consciousness of redemption by Christ, and therefore of His work, from which there necessarily follow conclusions upon the nature of the person who accomplishes the same; and one *objective*: the variously graduated, and yet concordant, testimony of the apostles, the appropriation of which forms and augments faith more and more, in order that faith may attain to strength to unfold the apostolic nucleus of doctrine accepted by it. To these two factors of a productive kind, to the Scriptures and to faith struggling after knowledge (both of which again refer back to the Holy Spirit, the Spirit of Christ, as their higher unity), there is still to be added as the soliciting element the spirit of the world and of the wisdom of the world, which coming into the Church now in Judaic and now in heathen form, seeks to draw it back into its own customary mode of thought, a danger it only withstands by an ever clearer self-consciousness of its faith, and by an ever more happy solution of the contradictions which the wisdom of the world thinks it can discover in Christian faith. In this relation the radical character of the course the Church has followed is specially to be considered. For the oral and written word of a Paul and a John the Church long possessed; but for a long time, until need and receptivity were awakened, it was upon many a point a sealed treasure. And if we regard that which was not merely inherited legally, so to speak, because of apostolic authority, but was always known according to its truth and its internal connection with faith, and therefore could be freely evolved therefrom, we may say that the dogmatic apprehension of the ancient Church begins with the lowest stage of canonical Christology, in order under the guidance of the canon from within outwards to attain the actual elements contained in the higher canonical forms more and more, and to co-ordinate them more certainly.

§ 92*b*.—*Continuation.*

FIRST PERIOD TO A.D. 381.

*Introduction.*

The impression which the appearance of Jesus and His works made upon mankind was so profound that, on the one hand, He laid the strongest hold upon reflection, imperiously demanding the harmonizing of the pre-Christian modes of thought with the facts upon which Christianity was founded. On the other hand, the ideas of God and man in the heathen and Jewish world were of such a nature that this appearance was inconceivable under the customary categories, and indeed was contradictory thereto.

To rigid *Judaism*, which esteems itself orthodox, as it is represented in Phariseeism especially, legal righteousness is the highest thing, and therewith the standpoint of law in which God and man are externally opposed to one another. To it, therefore, the doctrine of the incarnate Logos necessarily appeared a violation of the supreme monotheistic principle, a scandal and a capital crime,[1] as is recognized in the discourses of Christ.

In *Heathendom*, indeed, the representation of *sons of* the gods was frequent, but, with analogies which mingled god and the world in an unethical way, and which denied Monotheism, it was not a service to Christianity. Moreover, the doctrine of gods had for intellectual heathendom sunk into a nonentity, and only a certain philosophical Monotheism was left to it, which, if it was not rigid and lifeless, had a pantheistic character, the Divine being to it the unknown and unknowable Being (τὸ ˮΟν). To the widespread pantheistic modes of thought the world was the manifestation, the body or the realization of this Divine Being. Nor was it difficult to think of man at the same time as Divine. But this immediate apotheosis of the human was opposed to the ethical character of Christianity, which remembers the fall of man from God, and does not tolerate a self-redemption by a self-actualization of the Divine nature of humanity instead of a restoration by condescending grace. Both—the hardness of the Judaic idea of God, which inclined to Deism, and the extravagant treatment of the Divine in which Heathendom delighted—were equally opposed to Christianity. For Deism and Pantheism, unless they allow themselves to be elaborated in a Christian manner, there only remains the denial of the fundamental Christian fact.

But the internal untenability of both standpoints had already revealed itself prior to Christianity by the fact that Judaism had laid hold on the heathen wisdom, Hellenic and oriental, and that Heathenism had given many proselytes to Judaism, especially that it allowed itself to ferment with monotheistic opinions. Thus arose those mixed forms in Alexandria and East Syria which sought to adjust the Solity, Unapproachableness, and Incognizability of God to the heathen

[1] John v. 18, x. 31, etc.; Matt. xxvi. 63-66.

apotheosis of the world by means of manifold theories of emanation of a monistic and dualistic kind.[1] Between God and our world they interpolated a series of higher beings, æons or angels, to fill up the chasm between God and man.[2] These are the presuppositions for the heresies with which the Church had to struggle in the first centuries, mixed forms which arose through the introduction into Christendom of well-known extra-Christian elements. In these struggles the essential thing was to break the common fundamental presupposition of the heresies on both sides, the belief that the highest and truly Divine nature could not unite itself with man to form a true unity, because of its Sublimity and Simplicity, and that man did not need this union, whether because he enjoyed immediate Divinity, or because man simply needed a self-procured legal righteousness in order to correspond with his idea.

The first thing necessary for Christology was the recognition of two distinct sides in Christ, a knowledge which was gained in the struggle with Ebionitism and Doketism, both of which so abridged one of these sides, that, strictly regarded, only the other remained. We therefore consider, first, the main possible forms of the Ebionite and Doketic tendency, in the first place moreover singly in the interests of the dogmatic and not the mere historic knowledge of these conceptions, and therefore also not under a strictly chronological point of view, although in such a manner that in reference to the dogmatic ideas we fix our eyes upon corresponding historical forms.

1. THE EBIONITE MODE OF THOUGHT. — It has for its characteristic essence, the seeing in Christ a merely creaturely nature. It may follow as well from a Deistic as a Pantheistic concept of God. The principal forms are the following :—

*First:* the oldest Judaic form regards Christ as a man filled with the Holy Spirit, who has arisen either as son of

---

[1] Comp. H. Ritter, *Die Emanationslehre, ein Uebergang aus der alterthümlichen in die christliche Denkweise*, 1847; also, *Die christl. Philosophie*, 2 vols. 1858. E. Zeller, *Geschichte der Geischischen Philosophie*, vol. iii.

[2] Those who were educated in a more Hellenic fashion saw therein moments or categories of the idea of God, whilst the Orientals found there real births as a rule. Comp. Franck, *Die Kabbala oder die Religionsphilosophie der Hebräer*, translated by Gelinek, 1844.

Joseph or by a mysterious creation, just and holy in His behaviour. The special endowment with the Divine Spirit, which is wont to be attributed to Him by this view after the manner of the prophets, is either dated from His birth or from His baptism, and even then as a reward for His righteousness and virtue. Thus Christ does not essentially surpass the series of prophets by what He is. At His first appearance He is a *teacher* by word and example. Customarily a state of exaltation after His earthly life is added.[1] As exalted, or because of His Second Advent, He becomes the king of a new world, but this world is thought of by the Judaists in a manner pre-eminently eudæmonistic.[2] But the Christian consciousness knows itself redeemed, and Christ endowed with the power of atonement and mediation, and not as a second higher Moses merely. If Christ were only a creature, upon whom the Spirit of God worked in a manner stimulating and animating without being one in nature with Jesus, his person consequently could not possibly remain an object of religion. Therefore this form of Ebionitism was early overcome, in spite of its reliance upon the Old Testament doctrine of the Spirit of God.[3] The primitive Church undoubtedly devoted to Christ a religious adoration. The Christians are ἐπικαλούμενοι τὸ ὄνομα τοῦ Κυρίου.[4]

A *second* form of Ebionitism might be called *Hellenic*, because its fundamental conception is not Jewish, but Pantheistic. It concedes Christ's unity of nature with God, but in such a manner as straightway to take human nature generally for Divine on the score of reason. To Christ is then conceded a quantitative distinction in the circle of humanity as a genius, perhaps. Thus Carpocrates and Epiphanes, who consecrated a *sacellum* for Christ side by side with other great men. Similarly also Theodotus, Paul of Samosata, and Photinus.[5] Even this cannot satisfy the Christian consciousness; for in this case Christ could only be the object of

---

[1] So still in Socinianism.    [2] By the Socinians only legally.
[3] Which, as we saw previously, is also found in the New Testament, for example, in Matthew. To the same category belongs the "conceived of the Holy Ghost" in the Apostles' Creed.
[4] Thus, according to the New Testament, see p. 160. Similarly, according to Pliny, *Epistola*, 95 : *Christo tanquam Deo carmina dicunt*.
[5] In modern times the so-called cultus of genius belongs to the same category.

religious faith at the cost of idolatry. In this case also, there is ascribed to the nature, or the substance, more value than is ascribed to the moral element.

In order to the attainment of a higher position for Christ, whilst maintaining the pre-Christian monotheistic ideas of God, it might be thought, *in the third place*, that a superhuman, God-related, but still creaturely being, who had a pre-existence in heaven, had appeared in Jesus. According as this view is represented in a more Jewish manner, he is an angel, or archangel, just as the same point of view is already combated in the New Testament.[1] This is the *angelological Christology*. According as it is applied more pantheistically, or ethnically, the higher being may be represented *emanistically* as an *æon*, which, however high it be thought otherwise, and decked in majestic attributes, stands, notwithstanding, without the peculiarly Divine sphere. This mode of thought, which is no longer Ebionite in the stricter sense, has found its most developed form in Arianism, which partly sought to amalgamate the more Jewish angelological doctrine and the more ethnic doctrine of æons. Arianism also sought to appropriate the doctrine of the Logos after a manner; it described the Son as the Creator of the world; indeed, like Semi-Arianism, it condescended to acknowledge ὁμοιουσία, God-like nature, in the Son. In this case the higher being who appeared in Jesus was thought as a specially God-like being, but always as a finite person, who is, notwithstanding, supposed to be the object of adoration. But since, according to Arianism, the pre-existent Son is supposed to have become in time, to be mutable, and to be excluded from the essence of the Father, which consists in ἀγεννησία, Christ is not essentially distinguished from the creature, is rather the perfect creature ideally thought, and in this sense the First-born of creation or its unity. For a human soul, besides, there remains no place in this theory. For God, it is true, can, in self-communication, unite Himself

---

[1] Heb. i.; Col. ii. This Christology proves, from the Judaic side, how early the supposition of a pre-existence of the higher side in Christ existed. The angelological Christology cannot attain to true humanity, and therefore participates straightway in Doketic features, as does the Christological doctrine of æons.

most closely with the creature, whose principle He is; but two created spirits or souls cannot become one person. Accordingly, therefore, the Subordinationist modification of the Ebionite tendency has something Doketic in it; indeed, in this view, the beginnings of the life of Jesus stand below the stage which the exalted spirit, supposed to take the place of the soul of Jesus, already occupied before, and consequently a self-kenosis of this pre-existent Son must be affirmed in order to the possibility of being born as man.

2. THE DOKETIC SERIES.—The opposite to this is to maintain the true humanity according to its individual elements. This series has, likewise, *three* main forms: the *Theophanic;* the *Gnostic*, which treats the body of Christ, and therefore His sufferings and death, in a Doketic manner; and finally, the *Apollinarist*, which does not attain to a true human soul and person. That the Doketic line, so early entered side by side with the Ebionite, may afford us a historical proof that Christ produced the impression of an appearance which reaches beyond mere humanity, and awakened the feeling that the Divine world itself has in Him approached humanity. If then we start with the idea that it is unworthy of God to enter into so close a union with mortal suffering man, it might be supposed, *in the first place*, that there has been given in Him the point of the highest Divine revelation or presence, but only in such a way that we have to see in Him a Theophany of longer establishment. He might, accordingly, have momentarily received not humanity, but only a suffering body; of a human soul there could be no mention. This is the so-called Patripassianism, already extant long before Praxeas, about 190,[1] amongst pious Jewish Christians,[2] who wished to hold fast to the intimate nearness of God in Christ as Emmanuel, without receiving a true and permanent God-humanity. But in this case the action of Christ would not be human, but only Divine. The supreme God walked in Christ for a time upon earth; but the

---

[1] Comp. Lipsius, *Ueber Praxeas, Jahrb. f. d. Theol.* 1859, iv.

[2] For example, in the Testament of the Twelve Patriarchs; comp. also Schneckenburger, *Das Evangelium der Ægypter*, and also compare my *Entwickelungsgesch. der Christologie*, i. 253, etc.; [*Hist. of Doct. of Person of Christ*, vol. ii. p. 15, etc.]

human manifestation, as well as the revelation in Christ, would thus be transitory. The refinement of so-called Patripassianism in Sabellianism,[1] by Sabellius, Noetus, and Beryllus, sought to give Christ a share in the Divine essence without making the Deity suffer. But its Monarchianism or Unitarianism allowed no distinctions in God. Sabellius only reaches to a distinction between the hidden and the revealed God, to a repeated interchange of the self-expansion and self-contraction of God. The revelation in Christ is indeed a self-expansion of the self-revealing God (Logos) into the man Jesus, but of a transient kind. According to Noetus, God of His own will has given Himself for a time in Christ a mortal living form, and according to Beryllus has allowed Himself to be partially circumscribed and limited by finite humanity or corporeality. None of these leave any place for a human soul, but think God as somehow limited in Christ, or as suffering, whether from without by means of the body, or by His will. Finally, in order to wholly exclude the capacity to suffer, Marcellus limited the Divine presence in Christ to a mere powerful working upon him or in him ($\delta\rho\alpha\sigma\tau\iota\kappa\dot{\eta}$ $\dot{\epsilon}\nu\dot{\epsilon}\rho\gamma\epsilon\iota\alpha$). Thus every possibility of change or condition in God in His revelations, because of the world, is excluded, and at the same time room for a human soul. But if a mere powerful working upon Christ, or in Christ, is assumed instead of the being of God in Christ, there would follow hence an anthropocentric Christology, just as in Paul of Samosata; and the pupil of Marcellus, Photinus, definitely completed the transition of the Sabellian Christology into the Ebionite. Jesus is to him only a human person, in whom the Divine power and influence work. Thus the Sabellian line either fails to attain to a full and permanent humanity, which at the same time includes a soul, especially if it accepts an actual presence of God in Christ, or it sinks back to Ebionitism.

Even before this, the truth of a human body, therefore also of the mortality and death of Christ, and generally of the history of His earthly life, was combated by Gnosticism. To it the union of God, nay, even of the æon $X\rho\iota\sigma\tau\acute{o}\varsigma$, of that high emanation from God, with a material body, bringing

[1] *Gesch. der Christologie*, i. 518, etc.; also see § 29.

with it birth and death, appeared an unworthy representation, from which it sought to withdraw itself by the supposition, in different ways, of an apparent body and an apparent suffering. The ideal Christ as æon can find no essential relation to a human corporeality and soul, and, generally speaking, to history, but can only be loosely associated with a man who is thought of in an essentially Ebionite manner (κάτω Χριστός). The Doketism of Valentinus endeavours to come a step nearer to the ecclesiastical teaching, since it at least aims at gaining an actual body for Christ, but, holding the higher principle to be incapable of union with a material human body, it lays hold upon a heavenly ideal humanity. The æon Christ might pass through Mary, with a purely pneumatic body, which was worthy of Him, as through a canal, or as a gleam of light through a coloured glass, which communicates its darkness thereto. But here again the truly Divine principle is not ascribed to Christ, for the supreme God is to him the unapproachable abyss (βυθός). Similarly there is no perfect humanity.

The finest form of Doketism is *Apollinarianism*. It is free from the Gnostic aversion to matter; indeed, it teaches that the profoundest entrance of the Logos upon humiliation and suffering is the highest sign of love. In this respect it speaks quite Theopaschitally. Further, it has no desire to at all abridge the higher principle in Christ, or the Logos, of His deity, but, in order to gain an intimate unity with humanity, assumes Trichotomically that he has received from the humanity in Mary only the material body and the ψυχή as the power of life (not as the rational, free soul); on the contrary, the Logos, who is immoveable and immutable in the ethical relation, has taken the place of the human Pneuma. But in the feeling that thus the humanity seems to be abridged, and the Logos to be added thereto as a foreign element, it supposed that there was in the Logos an eternal drawing to humanity, indeed, that the eternal true humanity is in God Himself; the Logos is Himself eternally man, namely, the prototypical man.[1] But then the incarnation

[1] This thought has often been repeated later. In more recent times I mention Keerl, *Die Gottmensch, das Ebenbild Gottes*, 1866, who, on pp. 246-258, cites a great number of ancient and modern writers who think likewise. Even

would be eternally absolutely present in reference to the principal fact, the human spirit, whereby the historical incarnation in time would be depressed in its importance. And seeing that the human spirit is supposed to be represented by the immutable Logos, there would be no place left for a human development, except for the body; rather would the spiritual growth be reduced to a gradual showing of what the Logos eternally is. An actual development was only attainable if a depotentiating self-transformation of the Logos or the prototypical man was assumed for the purpose of the earthly incarnation,—a view which, in the Apollinarist school, was frequently asserted, of course, in addition to the position already mentioned of the capability of suffering on the part of the Logos out of love.[1]

3. THE ECCLESIASTICAL DEVELOPMENT IN THE FIRST PERIOD. —To the three principal Doketic forms—to Patripassianism, or the Theophanic Christology; to Gnostic Doketism, which denied the truth of the body, and therefore of the developing history of Christ in earthly human personality; and to Apollinarism, which at least denied the human soul to be of an identical nature with ours—the Church opposed the true and permanent humanity, the full historical reality of His birth, death, and resurrection, and finally also the truly human soul of Christ, the former in the Nicene Symbol and the older portions of the Apostles' Creed, from the birth even to His return to judgment, and the latter after the example of Origen and the Council at Constantinople by the later addition to the Apostolic formula of the Descent into Hades. The guiding canon thereto was: What was not added, would be neglected.[2]

As opposed to the various forms of Ebionitism, the faith of the Church, becoming ever more master of its own contents, expresses the avowal of the Divine side with increasing definite-

Beyschlag touches this view. Further, as it seems, J. Müller has also assumed a pre-existence of the humanity of Christ in the original holy state (vol. ii. p. 510), although he has not expressed himself more exactly upon the relation of the same to the Logos.

[1] The beginnings also of the modern Kenotics in Liebner and Thomasius have started from the Apollinarist circle of ideas, in which many of the present Kenotists have remained standing.

[2] Τὸ ἀπρόσληπτον καὶ ἀθεράπευτον.

ness. A merely creaturely being would be a dividing mediator. The Divine communion faith enjoys could only be established through Christ's person by the fact that with Christ we are not associated with a creature merely, but also with the supreme God. Thus it could only suffice if we had in Christ, not a just man only, or a prophet, or a man animated by the Spirit of God, but God Himself in the highest Self-revelation. Therefore even the Patripassian mode of thought had something attractive, because it, at any rate, comprehended the presence of God Himself in Christ. And the doctrine of the Trinity has shown us [1] that the interest of having God Himself present in Christ, without permitting the conservation and government of the world to be destroyed thereby, irresistibly impelled to the acceptance of eternal distinctions in God Himself, in opposition to an abstract simplicity of God, and to every form of Monarchianism, the Sabellian form as well as the Subordinationist. In the third century it is opposed to Monarchianism, that God is in Christ not merely as a power, but in the highest thinkable form, in the concentrated totality and fulness of a special mode of his own being, which has not been first put on him from without (as Beryllus had it), nor has first arisen in time, be it even by his own will, as Tertullian and Hippolytus, for example, taught. Instead of the expression "Logos," which had become ambiguous, and which meant to the Apologists partly what was immediately one with universal reason, and was partly distinguished from the Father with insufficient definiteness (especially as λόγος ἐνδιάθετος), by the agency of Tertullian, Hippolytus, and Origen, the expression "Son of God" became the dominant one for the Divine principle in Christ, in which there was a definite consciousness, especially at the beginning of the figurative character of the expression, as well as of the related words, "Generation, birth." This "Son" was described as a pre-existent "hypostasis" of like nature with God, but which, for the sake of the Divine unity, was represented by the three Fathers named as subordinated to the Father. Tertullian and Hippolytus even allow the Logos first to become Person, *i.e.* "Son," and to issue from God into self-existence for the end of the creation of the world

[1] § 29.

(just as Sabellius and Beryllus in their manner for the end of the incarnation). Origen, in order not to make God mutable, first took the great step to stating the procession of the Son from God to be not temporal only, but eternal (as of course creation also was). But the subordination of the Son, which he distinctly maintained, did not harmonize with his doctrine of the Divine equality of nature of the hypostasis of the " Son," but introduced into the Son an element of finiteness and creatureliness. Therefore his school split asunder. Some sacrificed the eternity and equality of nature of the Son with God to the subordination of the same, and this is *Arianism*, which regards the Son as the world-principle it is true, but as a creature who has arisen in time, and consequently sinks back to the Ebionite series, the summit of which it forms, to a kind of angelological Christology. If this was not desired, as the Church could not desire it, Subordination must be changed into *Co-ordination*, and this is the sense of the Nicene " Homousia " of the Divine principle in Christ with the Father. But because of the Divine unity, this has the effect that the differences between the absolute Father and the Son cannot be thought so deep as Arianism would have them, nor as three separated individuals comprised under one generic concept. Thus Christendom knows its religion to be so grounded in the Divine sphere itself, that it has in the same its imperishable as well as original special principle. Rigid and lifeless Monotheism, Monarchianism, whether of the heathen or Jewish form, was thus broken through by distinctions in the Divine nature. These indeed are not supposed to be of a merely temporal and transient kind. But, on the other hand, Athanasius will not have the eternal Son thought as without the Father, nor as an individual Ego like another finite Ego, still less does he desire by the Homousia to introduce a duality or triality of Gods. Rather does the one Divine personality in his esteem eternally arise by means of the distinctions in the Godhead, that is, by means of the fact that God stands opposed to Himself in the Son, the image of God. This image of God is not to him eternal humanity, but the Divine prototype of humanity, who is therefore called to its restoration and completion. The same Athanasius, who has set the crown on the doctrine of the Divine side in

Christ by means of the idea of the Homousia, has also fought against the abridgment of the human side in Christ, and maintained against Apollinaris the true human soul, which was then in the year 381 accepted into the Confession of the Church. But after the two complete sides in Christ had thus become the common conviction of the Church in the three first centuries, the problem arose how to associate with these two sides the unity of the person, which had been previously presupposed, but not dogmatically investigated.

§ 93.—*Continuation.*

SECOND PERIOD (381-1800): CHRISTOLOGY UNDER A PREPONDERANCE OF ONE OF THE TWO SIDES, DIVINE OR HUMAN.

*First Epoch (to the Reformation), or the Attempts at unifying the Two Natures under the Preponderance of the Divine.*

Nestorianism and Monophysitism are indeed rejected by the Church at large, but they are not internally vanquished; rather does there rule until the Reformation an abridgment of the true humanity, because the hypostasis of the Logos is supposed of itself to form the bond of unity.

*Observation.*—At the outset a word must be said upon the dogmatic term "two natures," in which the double outcome of the first period was compressed on the Divine and human side. In the first centuries there was no mention as yet of the two natures in the Person of Christ itself. The two sides, the Divine and the human, were not opposed to each other in the person of Christ itself as two distinct natures, each of which was of itself a complete whole. Athanasius especially did not teach two natures *in* Christ, but his formula was μία φύσις Θεοῦ λόγου σεσαρκωμένου, to which also Cyril of Alexandria, and still more decisively the Monophysites, held. Nor had Athanasius as yet thought of the idea of God and of man as absolutely distinct in essence, any more than Irenæus or other ancient Fathers, who rather reckoned his deification to be part of perfection, and therefore part of the idea of man. But the more completely the main elements of the two sides in Christ's person gradually came into consciousness, the more thoroughly the *distinctiveness* of the two sides came into view. The rejection of Apollinarianism by the Church, which curtailed the differences in the interests of their unity, further opened a free course to the Antioch school, who most zealously maintained the duality in Christ, the difference between the Divine and human, in fear of any admixture of the two, which seemed to them heathenish. The leaders of this tendency, which received the name of Nestorianism, are especially Diodorus of Tarsus and Theodore of Mopsuestia. The equally one-sided emphasis laid upon the unity in the Monophysitism of Cyril, Dioscurus, and Eutyches, put itself in opposition to them, until the Council of Chalcedon established the permanent duality of the natures, but side by side with the unity of the Person (Hypostasis) they formed. We proceed to consider the dogmatic importance of these three attempts, which refer to the mode of the *unio* of the Divine and human, after the two had been established in the fourth century.

1. NESTORIANISM may assume, it is true, different forms: the essential point therein is this. It so compresses the elements of the humanity, the "human nature," into a totality different from the Divine, that it has in the humanity of itself a rounded and completed whole, a personal Mikrotheos, so to speak,[1] from which consequently the need and receptiveness for such a union with the Divine as the incarnation supposes is absent. Besides, let a man start, according to the ruling ideas of God and man generally, from the fact that both are only absolutely distinguished and divided from one another by their *nature*, and it would be purely impossible to regard them as associated in one unity, such as faith desires. And this exclusive idea of the nature of God and man appeared most definitely in Nestorianism. But, on the other side, Christian consciousness demands the unity of the Person. For it also Nestorianism by consequence seeks to provide. In this respect, however, no real addition is made, if the two natures were only verbally united in Christ, or were added in Him as in a numerical sum, so to speak. For in such *unio verbalis, nominalis, nuncupativa,* or *arithmetica,* the unity, which was

[1] Compare my *Programm über die Lehre des Theodor v. Mopsu. vom göttlichen Ebenbild.*

not presented in the object as real, would exist only in the consideration of the subject in this theory. The unity sought for could, on the presuppositions mentioned, only lie either in a principle external to the two natures, or it must be expected from a union of the factors immanent in Christ, which originate it, inasmuch as lines of union between the two natures are drawn, or finally in such a way that a higher unity is sought above the two, as a new centre as it were, in which they coalesce.[1] The *unio* is attributed to a merely external principle if the community *of place*, where the natures run together, is supposed to effect or produce the *unio*—*unio localis*. In this case it is said that the Deity dwells in the man Jesus as in its temple. But if the Logos is omnipresent, in such physical being of God in the man Jesus nothing of a distinctive nature has yet been said in reference to Christ. This *unio* will only become of some importance if this being of the Logos also work somewhat in this man and communicates something to him.

On the presupposition of the difference of the two natures, secondly, the union which they are able of themselves to evoke, can only consist in *lines of union* being drawn between both, which express a reference or a relation of the two to one another, *i.e.* the *unio relativa*, ἕνωσις σχετική. If both natures are thus thought to be co-ordinate, personal wholes, and therefore the human as well as the Divine will is thought to have a special and independent will, unity can only consist in their volition of the same contents in spite of their being formally two wills. In this case, by virtue of the similar volitional contents, they are united by a συνάφεια—*unio moralis*. In free obedience the humanity wills what the Deity enjoins. In this case also it is assuredly taught that the humanity is recompensed for its virtue by a higher dignity (ἀξία), whereby it is as to majesty approximated to the Divine nature, although without participation in the Divine essence. Thus the old Antioch school teach. But if this virtue is not again brought into connection with a Divine endowment, but

---

[1] The demand to make the *unio* thinkable cannot be removed or settled by the appeal to the Divine Omnipotence, which can make one from two. For if the two natures are first thought absolutely disparate, their union by the Divine omnipotence is an impossibility, because a self-contradiction.

is thought to be a purely human product, we have a recurrence to the Ebionite Christology, which treats all participation of humanity in the Divine as its simple due. Conversely, were the human nature thought without any self-determination and as passively determined by God, therefore simply as an instrument, as an organ or garment of the Deity, this would lead back to the theophanic Christology. Historical Nestorianism holds itself between both in an indefinite wavering, with a preponderating inclination for the former alternative.

ADOPTIANISM finally seeks so to find the unity of the person that the Divine *Sonship*, which is thought to be the higher idea embracing both natures, is shown to be the product, so to speak, which both natures of the person of Christ form, and wherein both harmoniously coincide. The Divine nature, it is supposed, constitutes the Logos, and therefore Christ as well, so far as the Logos pertains to Him, the *filius Dei naturalis;* and the human side, by reason of its virtue, is elevated likewise to become the Son of God, namely the *filius Dei adoptivus* by the Divine judgment—*unio forensis.* But if this is not to become again a mere unifying of the divided by means of a similar title or name (*unio nuncupativa*), it re-conducts to the doctrine that the man Jesus has only gained the *unio* supposed to exist in the "Sonship," by means of His virtue,—a view which would straightway presuppose in Christ a becoming man prior to the *unio,* and therefore Cerinthianism. The thought of Adoptianism would only prevent this and become significant, if[1] the idea of the Divine image and the Second Adam were added in reference to the *filius Dei adoptivus,* and it were said that through the indwelling of the prototypical form or the Logos, the Son of God, the man Jesus became the second Adam or Son of man, the realized image and Son of God. But this already presupposed an advance beyond that original distinctness of the two natures; instead thereof, communicativeness on the side of the Logos and receptivity on the part of man would have entered.[2]

[1] Attempts at which are found in Theodore of Mopsuestia, comp. my *History of the Doctrine of the Person of Christ,* vol. iii. p. 31.

[2] The later Nestorianism in Syria likewise assumed a higher unity, which combined the two persons into one total personality, in which these two were elements simply, possibly as we say that the State is a higher personality, a unity consisting of several persons, or as two become one in marriage (a figure

All the Christological theories, according to which the two sides must remain essentially or internally distinct and independent of one another even within the *unio*, were fundamentally rejected by the Council of Ephesus by the repudiation of Nestorianism. Cyril recognized that the thought of the incarnation of God would be annihilated, and that it could neither be said that the Logos became man, nor that man was exalted to Divine dignity, if the two natures essentially of themselves remained in friendly relation to each other simply.

*Observation.*—By the Lutheran party Nestorianism is wont to be cast in the teeth of the Reformed. But the Reformed creeds expressly repudiate this, and acknowledge the Council of Ephesus. They do not teach two persons in the one Christ; nor do they leave the two natures standing outside each other without relation; they think this relation to be an absolute determination of the humanity by the will of the Logos, which is also the hypostasis of the humanity, and disown the communication of essence of the Lutherans.

2. MONOPHYSITISM.[1]—Much as Cyril and the Council of Ephesus were in the right as opposed to Nestorius, nevertheless their positive expression left much to be desired. Cyril stopped at that Athanasian formula of μία φύσις, and this μία φύσις has the sense of his ἔνωσις φυσική (*unio*

which appears even in the older Nestorianism). But how is a higher than the Logos to be thought? In Him, inasmuch as He is creative, there also lies the possibility of humanity. This reflection must lead to a wholly different treatment excluding the simple co-ordination of two independent persons. Nestorianism consequently becomes a duality of eternally separate "Egos," two personal wholes complete in themselves, whereby the unity of the person is shattered, although Nestorius, as Luther rightly acknowledged, had no such desire. The clearest and most permanent form of Nestorianism, which has also returned from time to time, is that of the moral *unio*, in which, instead of the unity of person, the similarity of two essentially distinct unities is supposed,—a view which also influences redemption, inasmuch as this cannot be any longer thought to be a united Divine and human work. The Nestorian mode of thought did not die out of the Church after the repudiation of Adoptianism at the Council of Frankfort in 794. Duns Scotus again approximated thereto, and in more recent times Günther, to whom Christ is a united being. See my *History of the Doctrine of the Person of Christ.*

[1] Ebionitism also assumes one nature. But the development of the Church had passed beyond it. Ebionitism is never called Monophysitism in the Church, only the one-sided domination of the Divine side.

*naturalis*). The doctrine of the Antiochenes, that even within the union two natures must continue, appeared to him to be the root of all the errors which divided the person of Christ. Only prior to the *unio* did he allow two natures. But even he thought of these two natures as exclusively opposed to one another, though in his own fashion. This presupposition, which is common to it and Nestorianism, Monophysitism so applied, that, in order to bring the two natures notwithstanding to one unity, the human side is abridged if not absorbed by the Divine. Cyril himself stopped at the more indefinite expression, that the human nature is allied to the Divine as an *accidens* to the substance, is, so to speak, implanted in the Divine, a view which assuredly permits a better meaning (*consubstantio*). Monophysitism proper might assume a threefold form.

*In the first place,* a change of the Divine nature into the human, a self-humiliation of the Logos to become man by the self-emptying of the Logos that He might present the human form of a servant. Thus taught the Valentinians of the fourth century, who approximate to a part of the Apollinarist school. But such self-transformation of the Deity into a lower form for the sake of the incarnation is too much at variance with the immutability of the Divine essence. There may be traced therein a Pantheistic commingling of God and the world with a heathen tang. God being unable to deny His absolute essence, if the Logos were able to become transformed, He could no longer be thought a participant of absolute Deity. Preferably to this ἕνωσις κενωτική, an attempt might consequently be made to obtain the union *in the second place* in a converse manner, by the change of the human nature into the Divine—*unio magica*. But if the humanity were annulled by the *unio*, the incarnation would be retracted, and there would at best remain a doketic appearance. This theory is that of Eutyches, who does not simply maintain with Cyril μία φύσις since the incarnation, but will no longer acknowledge in Christ a humanity of like nature with ours. Finally, *thirdly,* by the combination of both views a partial transformation of both natures may be assumed, the one being, so to speak, tempered by the other, to the point of equalization in a third (*unio chemica*). Eutyches already compared humanity to a drop of honey falling into the sea of Deity. Still more frequent was the figure of the ἤλεκτρον, of an alloy of silver and gold. Thus said Severus (Xenaja) at the beginning of the sixth century. Christ is said to be a composite (*zusammengesetzte*) person (σύνθετος), who has all attributes Divine and human, but the substance bearing these attributes is no longer a duality, but a composite unity.

*Observation.*— A section of the Monophysites, convinced of the untenableness of their attempt to unite the truth and completeness of the Divine and human sides in Christ with the supposition of one φύσις only, conceded later the duality of the natures, but sought to secure the unity of the person in the actual life of Christ by the rejection of two series of activities in this one person; they therefore supposed but one will in Christ. Thus, for example, Pope Honorius. But this monothelistic formula of union, maintained by Heraclius and Zenon, retained no place between Dyophysites and Monophysites. Maximus Confessor showed that Monotheletism, the unity of the series of activities, also presupposed a unity of the nature which formed their foundation, and must therefore re-conduct to Monophysitism.

3. The *Council of Chalcedon*, of the year 451, did the service of opposing the doctrines of mutation or commingling as well as Nestorianism, the latter by the formula ἀδιαιρέτως, ἀχωρίστως,[1] the former, together with the Antiochenes and Leo the Great, by the formula ἀσυγχύτως, ἀτρέπτως.[2] Thus the bias towards the doctrine of transformation, which subsequently laid hold of the dogma of the Lord's Supper, was opportunely diverted from Christology. As opposed to all identification as well as division, a unity was demanded by the Church, together with a preservation of the distinctions. The formulas mentioned, which concern the relation of the two natures to one another, are all of a negative kind, although they fix their limits on opposite sides. A positive description of their relation is not found as yet in the Creed of Chalcedon, except in the description of the result of their union, the ἕνωσις ὑποστατική—*unio hypostatica* or *personalis*. This formula is irreprehensible, for the unity of the person of Christ every one must maintain to be the result of the *unio*, just as he always thinks that personal union brought about, whether by means of

[1] Later still, ἀδιαστάτως was added.   [2] Later still, ἀναλλοιώτως,

the *uniting of the natures*—with reference to their two-sided special mode of being (hypostasis)—or by means of one of the hypostases, namely the Divine, which does not merely seize the initiative in reference to the work of union, but also constitutes the Ego in the result of the same, in the complete person, which is the person proper. In reference to this double possibility also, the mode of the formation of the person of Christ, the tone of the Council of Chalcedon is beyond cavil or blame. *It starts from the two natures,* and says: the ἰδιότης of the two φύσεις συντρέχει εἰς μίαν ὑπόστασιν or εἰς ἓν πρόσωπον ; that is, seeing that the two distinct "natures," with their peculiar mode of being, coalesce, the one "person" Jesus Christ is to be thought the *result* of the union. It does not say that the human nature was united with the *person* of the Logos, or was joined to its hypostasis (this the Antioch school, who were still so influential at Chalcedon, would not have conceded), but the two "natures" in their peculiar mode of being are thought to be in movement towards one another (not the Divine hypostasis merely in movement towards the human nature); but with their ἰδιότης both are thought to be incorporate in the one complete person, Jesus Christ, the result of the union, who is here called ὑπόστασις or πρόσωπον. Thus Monophysitism is supposed to be excluded, and by virtue of the μία ὑπόστασις the duality of the person to be avoided. It may be said with justice, that the manner is not thus made clear in which the two natures with their two-sided ἰδιότης can unite to form one ὑπόστασις or one πρόσωπον. But it is indubitable that the Chalcedon formula in itself contains nothing of an abridgment or still less impersonality (ἀνυποστασία) of the human nature. Nor does it say that the hypostasis of the Logos is the Ego in this person. Indeed it does not give an account as to how each of the two natures contributes to the unity of the person. Later Dogmatic theology has produced more adequate definitions, but they have allowed themselves to miss the caution of the creed of Chalcedon. The main points are the following.

That the initiative in the *Unio* belonged to the Divine side was self-evident. But it is not merely Divine *nature* (called οὐσία, *substantia,* and earlier ὑπόστασις even), but also a special mode of being of the Deity, which bears the name Son, and is called *the persona*, πρόσωπον, and even ὑπόστασις of the Son. When later, subsequent to the Council of Chalcedon, the point was to attain the unity of the Divine-human person or hypostasis, it was inviting to apply the hypostatic nature or the hypostasis of the Son for this end. And a departure was thence made to considering the person in Christ solely as the result of the union of *the natures;* or rather it was now ascribed to the hypostasis of the Son, not merely that it effects the result of a *Unio personalis*, but that it is or constitutes the person in the God-man. Thus resulted the doctrine that the *Unio personalis* arises because the person of the Logos assumes a human nature, in order to be therein the Ego or the personality. But thus Christ is only the personal Logos, who has a human " nature " in itself, in relation to which, as well as in relation to Himself, He is the Ego. Therein there was a double supposition, which was not contained in the creed of Chalcedon. *In the first place,* such a conception of the hypostasis of the Logos, according to which it could be in a position to assume immediately the place of the Ego for the human side of Christ, that is, according to which it would be an individual Ego after the fashion of a separate human personality. *In the second place,* such a conception of the humanity of *Jesus*, by which—as was not previously done—it was excluded from having its own personality, endowed with self-consciousness and self-determination. For if the Logos was once thought after the manner of an individual personality, the concession of a human personality would have again led to a Nestorian double personality. It was now said by theologians in preference, that the human nature is without its own hypostasis, is in itself impersonal, but is implanted in the Divine hypostasis, which is thus supposed to represent the place of its own hypostasis.[1] This position of the *anhypostasia* or impersonality of the human nature has passed indeed into no Church creed, but only to a moderate extent become the common doctrine of theologians; nor did it bring any gain, but rather involved it in the greatest difficulties. On the

---

[1] But it has ἀνυποστασία together with ἐνυποστασία in the Logos, which is an excellence for it. Thus John Damascene.

one hand, Dyotheletism did not consist therewith, which in the interests of the vitality and truth of the two sides in Christ aimed at maintaining in Christ a series of actual human acts of consciousness and volition side by side with the Divine actuality.[1] For thus again self-consciousness and self-determination were demanded as a consequence in reference to the human nature, the unity of which is a human personality. Next, if a Divine Ego is supposed to take the place of the human, there is necessarily an abridgment of the humanity according to its complete idea, a more subtle kind of Apollinarianism. If a Divine Ego merely is the Ego of the humanity, the latter must become the selfless organ of the Deity, a mere Theophany, a view which tends back to Doketism.

Thus the position had now become as follows:—If the humanity was to be thought completely endowed, and therefore also endowed with its own self-consciousness and self-determination, in brief with personality, and if the Logos was at the same time to be thought to be upon an equality with a single human personality, there resulted a Nestorian double personality. If, on the other hand, in the interest of the unity of the Divine human person, the personality of the humanity was to be surrendered, and its place to be taken by the Logos, there was by consequence a lapse into a confusion of the Divine and human sides, and into a more subtle kind of Doketism. In these difficulties the ancient Christology remained. They could only be solved, if inquiry was made and it was established, in what sense the Logos may be called *persona*. But a development of the doctrine of the Trinity would have been implied therein, to which the ancient Church had not yet come. Only this may be said, that it rejected the conception of God as a mere impersonal unity of species, and that of the Trinitarian distinctions as specific individuals (ἄτομα), because it rightly saw Tritheism therein;[2] further, that, at any rate, it fundamentally put away Doketism, and desired to see the perfection of the true humanity preserved. In opposition to all theories of confusion, the Church held to Dyophysitism and Dyotheletism,

---

[1] Ecclesiastically sanctioned in the year 680.
[2] Comp. Nitzsch, *Dogmengesch.* I. pp. 303, etc.

and sought to make provision for the unifying of the two sides, at least in their confessions, not by the hazardous means of the supersession of the human personality by a Divine Ego, but in another way. To this belongs, in the first place, the decision of the Dyothelitic Council of the year 680: "The human will remains in unity with the Divine, because it is always determined by the omnipotent drawing of the Logos." Certainly such an application of the category of omnipotence would leave to the humanity self-less passivity merely. John of Damascus deserves more recognition. He endeavours to provide for the unity by means of lines of connection between the two natures, and speaks once of an exchange (ἀντίδοσις) of their *names*. Because of the unity of the entire person, it is supposed possible to attribute Divine names and predicates to the human nature. But nothing is thus done for the union of the natures themselves. Just as little was done by the Περιχώρησις, or his doctrine that the two natures penetrate each other; for this is only a fragment of the *unio localis*, so long as the natures themselves are not somehow defined. To this latter the two further ideas of the Damascene might seem to conduct, the deifying (θέωσις) of the humanity and the appropriation of the human on the part of the Divine nature (οἰκείωσις). But the "deification" is no more than a rhetorical expression, seeing that a real communication to the humanity, together with appropriation of the Divine by it, is repudiated.[1] So, in reference to the Divine nature, the οἰκείωσις really considered means no more than the ἀντίδοσις ὀνομάτων. A real *communicatio idiomatum* the pre-Reformation doctrine generally does not know, although scattered sentiments of that kind are to be found in the more ancient teachers, such as Ignatius, Irenæus, Origen, Athanasius, and Cyril.

By John of Damascus the Western Church of the Middle Ages was determined, his *System of Doctrine* having been translated into Latin, and used especially by the Lombard. In the main, that Church remained at the point, that the unity of the person of Christ is supposed to be secured by

[1] John of Damascus: Ἔκδοσις τῆς ὀρθοδόξου πίστεως, iii. 17; the human nature, οὐ κατ' οἰκείαν ἐνέργειαν ἀλλὰ διὰ τὸν ἡνωμένον αὐτῇ λόγον τὰ θεῖα ἐνεργεῖ.

the anhypostasia of the human nature, and the representation of the human personality by means of the Logos, the consequences of which view are very evident.

Surveying, therefore, the Christological theory of the Middle Age up to the Reformation, it clearly betrays a mixed character, as is also seen in the Roman Catholic theology of this present age. Whilst in the sphere of the personal life the humanity is thought to be selfless, indeed after the manner of Monophysitism to be absorbed by the Deity, in the sphere of the natures the difference between them has remained preponderant after the Antiochene fashion, and a real union of the natures themselves has not been 'attained. It may therefore be said briefly, that in this Roman Christology the two previous opposed Christological systems are welded together as by a compromise, according to the procedure of the Roman Theology in other respects, *e.g.* in reference to the relation between nature and grace. But the unnatural character of such dovetailed Christology was necessarily made manifest by the fact that, immediately the one side was earnestly regarded, the other was seen to be inconsistent therewith. When, in accordance with this doctrine of the natures, the true and perfect humanity was fixed, the point of juncture for the Divine nature was lost, and from the humanity regarded as a totality of a different nature and self-enclosed there arose again the theory of the adoptive Son. Thus it happened in the *Adoptianism* of Felix and Lipantus, as well as Duns Scotus. On the other hand, if the selflessness of the humanity, according to that doctrine of the person, were seriously taken, there followed Alcuin's position that the human Ego comes to naught because of the Divine.[1] But the consequence of this selflessness of the man Jesus is that Christ is not so much a man as the Son of God, who makes the human form He has assumed a symbol of His revelation. This consequence of a mere theophany in the garment of the humanity is drawn by the so-called *Nihilianism* of Peter Lombard, which was rightly rejected likewise by Pope Alexander III. Seeing, then, that these attempts to free the dominant Christology from its disparate elements were wrecked, and only led back to old

---

[1] *Perit;* according to Innocent III. *consumitur;* according to Thomas, *impeditur,* namely, at the entrance into existence.

heresies, whilst a satisfactory union of the natures was not possible, so long as they were themselves thought to be thus disparate, it cannot astonish us that the endeavours of the Middle Age to frame a Christology failed and wavered insecurely in an alternating resuscitation of Adoptianism and of a more subtle Nihilianism, then fell lame, and Christology ceased to be a guiding light for other dogmatic labours. All the more unhindered, therefore, the already existent tendency worked to install the Church and its prototype, Mary, in the place of Christ, and to create surrogates for what Christology had to do, partly in the saints (they represent the true humanity in Christ, lost because of the preponderance of the Divine side, but Pelagianizing at the cost of grace by the apotheosis of human nature), partly in the mass, which, by means of transubstantiation, magically recovered for Christ in the present (the Lord's Supper) that which was agreeable to the spirit of the Middle Age, but was restrained by the decrees of the Council of Chalcedon. And to this day there remains in the Roman Catholic system of doctrine this inability to free itself from the contradiction of an external combination, — of Monophysitism in the sphere of the Ego, and of Nestorianism in the sphere of nature. Bound as it is, every noteworthy Christological movement to attain a thinkable image of Christ either leads back again to the Antiochenes, or to Monophysitism and Nihilianism.[1] In the practice of the Church the latter has the upper hand, and consequently the living God-man is partly pushed into the background by the worship of saints and the mass, and is partly snatched from us by a Doketic and mythicising doctrine of the origin, birth, and youth of Christ. Christ has again become for the mode of thought of the Middle Age an exalted God, an almighty lawgiver and judge; according to the decrees of the Church, there remains no essential place for His humanity. By her intercession, Mary represents the Divine love in human form. Indeed, the Greek Church has as little known how to find a necessary significance for the humanity of Christ, for Christ is to it pre-eminently only the $\Sigma o\phi i a$, the bringer of the true knowledge, which pertains to $\pi i \sigma \tau \iota \varsigma \ \dot{o} \rho \theta \acute{o} \delta o \xi o \varsigma$, for

[1] The former in the school of Hermes and Günther (to whom Christ is a combined nature), the latter by Lieber, Clemens, and others.

which it is evident an inspired man, and not a God-man, might have sufficed. Because the Greek and Roman Churches find no essential and permanent importance in the humanity of Christ, the consequence is that they ever place the Divine side in a position of preponderance, and incline to a Doketic treatment of the humanity.

For a more intimate relation between the two sides, *the German Mysticism* of the Middle Age alone showed a disposition. It expresses the thought that the Ego of the Son of God does not despoil the humanity, nor is there merely an honour conferred upon the latter, but that the desire of the human nature after personality finds superabundant satisfaction in the person of the Divine Son. Only this desire is not yet free from a magical tang, inasmuch as it was wont to be thought a surpassing of its idea, as a transport of the humanity beyond itself, instead of as a fulfilment of a receptivity for God peculiar to the humanity of Jesus, and as a realization of its idea not yet perfectly realized in the Adamic humanity.

§ 94.

*Second Epoch.—The Time of the Reformation, and its attempt to think the Unity of the Person, together with an equal authorization of the Divine and human sides.*

Both the Evangelical Confessions are at one in opposing to the volatilization virtually dominant in the Romish Confession, the reality of a perfect humanity of Christ, and also in seeing in Christ not merely the revelation of the wisdom of God, or the king, lawgiver, and judge, but pre-eminently the revelation of His holy love. For the atoning work of Christ only then entered for the first time truly into its dogmatic position. But in respect of the unifying of such actual humanity with the true Deity, the result of the discussions was different in the two Evangelical Confessions. Only the Lutheran doctrine entered upon the problem of applying to the unity of the Person of Christ an internal relation of the two natures, and not a mere hypostasis of the Logos (§ 93, 3), whilst only the Reformed doctrine bestowed lasting attention on the true development of the humanity of Christ.

### I.—*The Lutheran Doctrine.*

1. LUTHER AND MELANCHTHON.—It was not the controversy on the Lord's Supper which created Luther's Christology in its most important features. Long before that time Luther gave utterance in his *Haus und Kirchenpostille* to a fundamental Christological view, whence flowed the fundamental thought of his subsequent doctrine of the Supper. That view stands in close connection with the nobler German mysticism, and is as speculatively as religiously important, although not dialectically formulated. On the contrary, the Supper controversy encroached upon this view in a disturbing and obscuring manner.[1]

A closer consideration shows that Luther made an advance upon the old Christology, inasmuch as, *in the first place*, he sought the bond of union of the person of Christ, not in the person of the Son, but in the sphere of the natures, and adduced for this end a different idea of the Divine and human nature to what had been previously advanced, namely, he recognized that they do not repel or exclude, but seek each other according to their innermost nature; inasmuch as,

[1] It is true Philippi (iv. 273) thinks it is a prejudice that there was an essential advance made in the Lutheran Church upon the ancient ecclesiastical Christology. Christology, as well as the Doctrine of the Trinity, was, he thinks, the problem which the ancient Church busied itself with, and solved once for all. The Lutheran Church, he further thinks, does not strive after the glory of development, but appeals, without adding material, new fundamental thoughts, to the testimony of the Fathers. On the other side also Schenkel (*Wesen des Protestantismus*, 1862, pp. 182, etc., 193, etc.) thinks that Luther was entangled wholly in the Chalcedon positions, especially in that of the impersonality of the human nature, seeing that only the Divine in Christ was to him the person. We have seen above that the Chalcedon formula does not speak of the impersonality of the humanity, does not once speak of the person of the Logos, but starts from the two natures, and the

*secondly*, he did not wish in the sphere of the Person to do homage to Monophysitism, nor to regard the humanity as impersonal; and inasmuch as, *thirdly*, he acknowledged a human and true development and two states of Christ,—this, of course, not without fluctuations.

Luther sees above all things, as far as the first point is concerned, that in respect to the unity of the God-human person as it eternally stands before the eye of faith as living, little is said, if a Divine Ego is alone the bond therein. This bond lies for him pre-eminently in the *unifying of the natures themselves*, and he starts from this point, as does also the creed of Chalcedon. The possibility of this unifying lies, in his esteem, in the fact that the two natures tend to each other —the humanity, in that it is able (as he sees by virtue of his profounder conception of faith) to become a partaker of the Divine nature; the Deity, in that he knows that the dignity and glory of the Divine nature consist before all things in the ethical essence of God, in righteousness, holiness, and love, not in that infinity which is foreign to the finite, and that God does not find it to be opposed to this His ethical nature to condescend in love, to lower Himself most profoundly into our flesh, " in order to exchange our misery with us, that we may change with Him in faith." In the love, which he ontologically takes to be being, he finds it based that God should assume in Christ so very close a share in humanity as to class humanity with Himself. Even prior to 1517 he had made speculative attempts in this direction, in which he now looked upon the humanity as the form or impression of the Divine image in the reality of the world (Phil. ii. 7 ; 2 Cor. iv. 4), and now regarded the Deity as the

Divine-human person is to it the coalescence of both natures. Schenkel further thinks that, in the interests of the unity of the person, Luther has assumed the dissolution of the humanity in the Deity, with which he also combines the opposite reproach, that he makes God capable of suffering. Schenkel himself indeed denies the Lutheran position of the receptiveness of the humanity for the Divine nature, as well as the immanent Trinity, and finds Zwingli also to blame because he maintained the Chalcedon formula. On what follows compare my *History of the Doctrine of the Person of Christ*, where rich appendices will be found from Luther's works in reference to the following positions ; compare therewith Thomasius, *Christi Person und Werk*, ed. 2, vol. ii. pp. 307, etc.; and Frank, *Die Theologie der Concordienformel*, iii. 1863, pp. 165, etc., 319, etc.; Hahn, *Christliche Glaubenslehre*, ed. 2, 1858, vol. ii. p. 183.

formative power or the form for the matter of the humanity, in reference to which he quotes the Aristotelian position: *materia appetit formam*. But later he relinquishes these categories, inasmuch as they are inadequate in their generality and indefiniteness. In his last years he required new categories for Christology, the old ones being insufficient: "Christ must be spoken of in new tongues and speech, the new humanity revealed in Him." For, in his view, Christ is to be conceived under an idea of humanity, according to which it has nothing foreign to the Divine nature, but has that by which it can first attain its own perfection and truth. As *capax divinitatis* it longs to be impregnated, as it were, with the Divine nature. This new speech, indeed, he has not created. Nor has Melanchthon,[1] who rather clave to the pre-Reformation and not real *communicatio idiomatum*.[2]

As opposed to Nihilianism, Luther further attaches an importance to the humanity and the human personality, where he says[3] that there cannot be anything more heretical than to call the *humana natura* the garment of the Deity, for *non vestis* or *corpus et Deus sed Deus et homo constituunt unam personam*. Therefore also pure Lutherans, like Th. Thumm and Calov, suppose a communication not merely of the Divine attributes, but also of the *persona* of the Logos, and thus attribute a communicated personality to the humanity of Christ. On this side the Lutheran Christology has sought to reach the humanity of Christ more perfectly than the Reformed.

And, finally, apart from the question on the personality of the human nature, Luther has insisted on the perfect reality of the humanity. This is clear from the characteristic feature of his Christology, the comparison of the figure of Christ with that of the believer, in which the metaphysical treatment is at the same time raised to the ethical and completed.[4] And

---

[1] Comp. Herrlinger, *Theol. Melancth.* 1879, pp. 172, etc., 182, etc.

[2] At an earlier date Melanchthon had for a while spoken in his letters like a few of the more recent Kenotics.

[3] See his Christological disputation, 1538, Thesis 36, etc.

[4] Comp. Hering, *Die Mystik Luthers*, 1879, p. 130: "The humanity of Christ is treated (by Luther) ever more evidently not as a mere determining of nature, but at the same time as a determination and direction of his life,"

this is also especially shown by his position in reference to the *growth*, to the human development of Christ.[1] The previous Christology thought Christ, even as a child, ever omnipotent, omniscient, and a performer of miracles, not growing within, but only revealing more and more an inner being which was always equally perfect. But Luther says: "The humanity of Christ, like another holy natural man, has not at all times thought, spoken, willed all things, although some make an almighty man of Him, and unwisely mingle the two natures and their work together. As He did not at all times see, hear, and feel all things, so has He not regarded all things at all times with the heart, but as God has led Him and brought them before Him." And on Luke ii. he says: "The words, 'He increased in spirit and wisdom,' must stand fast, and all peculiar imaginary articles of faith, which would put themselves in opposition to this word, are to be allowed to go: one must understand the words according to their simplest signification. Whether He was at all times full of spirit and grace, the Spirit did not at all times move Him, but now urged Him to this and now to that. Whether He was in Him from the commencement of His conception, still, just as His body grew and His reason increased, in a natural manner, as in other men, so the Spirit rested upon Him ever more and more, and moved Him more and more. That there may be no dissimulation, Luke says 'He became strong in spirit;' but as the words sound clear, it also follows most plainly that the older He became the greater He really grew before God and in Himself and before the people, and the greater the more rational, and the more rational the stronger in spirit and wisdom, and no gloss can be tolerated here. And this understanding is free from danger, and there is no force in the fear as to whether it conflicts with their imaginary article of faith." To this point he refers also in Phil. ii. 7: "Paul also teaches," he says, "that He has grown like another man. Of course both (Luke and Paul) assume that He was a peculiar child. In his complexion He was nobler, and the grace and gifts of God were

whereby He is the prototype of our life, as his first interpretation of Phil. ii. 6, etc., of the year 1518 shows.

[1] *Works*, Erlangen edit., vii. pp. 185, etc., on Mark xiii. 22, and x. 300 on Luke ii. 52.

richer in Him than in others."[1] If afterwards the Lutheran doctrine maintained the truth of the humanity of Christ less than the Reformed, passages such as those quoted show that in these writings Luther did not come short. But certainly the Supper controversy hindered the quiet development of Luther's Christology and that of the Lutheran Church. The real presence of the Lord in His Holy Supper lay on the conscience of Luther. Instead of basing this presence upon the state of His exaltation, he thought himself compelled to recur to the idea of the *Unio* generally, upon which the inquiry was no longer made as to whether this idea could possibly or necessarily have been realized at one time by one act, and therefore from the beginning. He held the *Unio* of the two natures to be such a means of proof for his view against his Swiss antagonists, that he thence derived generally and universally, and therefore also in reference to the earthly life of Christ, all the attributes which, in respect to the humanity of Christ, he thought applied to his doctrine of the Supper. But seeing that this means of proof dated back to the first beginnings of His theanthropic existence what could only have its place in the state of His exaltation, his previous doctrine of the true growth of the humanity of Christ was thus impaired. And even as regards the Supper too much was proved. For if the humanity of Christ of itself is everywhere by virtue of the *Unio*, the Lord's Supper no longer has any superiority objectively and in itself. Nevertheless it is wrong for any one to regard these positions, which Luther made trial of in the great confession of the Supper of 1528 *as a means of proof* for the real presence of Christ, as forming the peculiar Christology of Luther, and that exclusively, and as denying the actual growth of Christ, or as purposing to dissipate His humanity.[2] He has also thought

---

[1] *Luther's Werke*, von Walch, xi. 389.

[2] As Schenkel thinks. That it is necessary to distinguish here what is doctrine and what means of proof, also follows from the fact that in his treatise on Councils and Churches of 1539, and in his small Confession of the Supper of 1543, he does not again return to that demonstration from an eternally similar *Unio*, but notwithstanding maintains unchanged the doctrine of the real presence of Christ. The Supper controversy certainly caused amongst the Gnesiolutherans the rejection of the three important Christological thoughts of Luther's mentioned, and they formed their Christology after Luther's doctrine of the Supper,

the omnipresence of the body of Christ not to be infinite extension in the universe or diffusion, but to be the power to make everything present to Him, and Himself present to everything dynamically.

2. JOHN BRENZ AND M. CHEMNITZ.—The Swabian school has done the service of having saved a few at least of the great Christological thoughts of Luther. In striking fashion Brenz criticised the different Christological theories, in order to show that everything depended upon forming a new and higher idea of the *humanity* of Christ. To the formula, " God is in Christ," we may rightly reply, he says, " God is everywhere." Should it be said, " God dwells in Christ," that is also true of all saints. Even if it is taught that God is in Christ according to His whole fulness and power, it is to be said by preference that God of Himself is everywhere wholly. We might hope to express what is specific and pertinent to Christ, by saying that God is in Christ *personally*. But again, God and the Logos are everywhere, where they are only personally. Nor does the indissolubility of the union of the Logos with the man Jesus belong to Christ alone, but to all the perfected saints. Consequently, he says, what is distinctive of Christ is not yet described in the *Unio hypostatica*. This must rather lie in what the *humanity* of Jesus has received by the *Unio*. We are consequently referred to the unifying of the *natures*, and its consequences for the humanity. With Luther the road is again opened, first to the completion of the unity in the sphere of the natures, and as a consequence only thence to the permissible resulting of the unity of the divine-human person.[1] Only thus, he thinks, is the thought of the incarnation reached, which finds a still quite insufficient expression in the *Unio personalis*, namely, when it is acknowledged that in Christ the humanity attains by means of the Logos to a unique existence ; that is to say, this thought, the

or rather after his attempt at finding a basis which he had surrendered for a long time. But even Melanchthon and his school have not cherished what was new and important in Luther's Christology, because in their view it was buried under the doctrine of the Ubiquity.

[1] Corresponding with the words of the creed of Chalcedon. It was there thought to be of itself consistent, that the Logos communicates His Ego to humanity, as later teachers expressly said. But the *Communio naturarum* is thought to be the first, although by the deed of the Logos-Ego.

possession of Deity in an inseparable manner as something which has become its *own,* so that in this sense it may be said that this man is also God, Deity pertains to Him. In this Luther's thought was again assumed, that advance to the *Unio* of the natures should be made within themselves, and that the *Unio personalis* should thus be the result, instead of making the union of the Divine person with the human nature the foundation, and seeing therein the theanthropic unity. Thus, at any rate, the words "man," "humanity," receive a new importance, which seems to condition that it belongs to its truth, that it has the Divine as its own and its proper right. The possibility of this, Brenz finds a basis for thus: the humanity is *capax divinitatis;* from the beginning this humanity is the goal of the world in the idea of God.[1] Therefore the susceptibility of humanity for God is first satisfied by the Divine self-communication perfected in Christ. And this also corresponds with the essence of God. According to His power over Himself, and according to His love, He can and will wholly communicate Himself. It is true His self-existence is not communicable, but His whole nature besides is. And unless the Divine nature were given to humanity, the communication of God, and its goal-incarnation, would be an impossibility.

But these most excellent positions of the Swabian Christology Chemnitz[2] opposed. Especially would he know nothing of a *humana capacitas* in the sense that the actually Divine can become man's own; he would only know it in the pre-Reformation sense, that humanity is the sphere in which the Divine fulness is, and that God can work through it. He does not teach an inner longing (*appetere*) of human nature for Divine self-communication, to use Luther's phrase, nor an inner self-inclination of the Logos towards humanity; it is simply that the omnipotence of the Logos has completed the hypostatic *Unio* with human nature *contra* as well as *supra naturam humanam.* Start is made by him from the *Unio hypostatica,* not from the *Unio naturarum,* and consequently various new predicates attach themselves to the God-man, but not in such a way as to make the Divine a property of

---

[1] *Opp.* viii. pp. 984, 1006. He has similar thoughts to Irenæus, Hilary, etc.
[2] *De duabus naturis in Christo,* 1570.

the human; rather the Divine remains a property of the Logos. The opposite assumption was, he thought, *confusio*. Thus it only remains that the Logos inhabits the humanity, and works through it, mysteriously augmenting its forces; and the question soon suggests itself, with what right mention is still made of a *communicatio idiomatum*, seeing that a communication, which confers nothing as a possession, is no communication. Chemnitz remained satisfied with the fact that the *Unio hypostatica* is established, and that the hypostasis or person of the Logos represents the Ego in the human nature assumed, in which he overlooks that either thus he inconsistently still allows a Divine thing, the Ego of the Logos, which means more than the communication of Divine attributes, to become the property of the humanity; *or*, that he thereby abridges the human nature, inasmuch as that the Person of the Logos may become the Ego for the humanity, he assumes a loss of the proper human personality;[1] to say nothing about the Person of the Logos being necessarily thought to be equal with a human individual Ego, if it is supposed capable of occupying the place of a human Ego. Nevertheless everything in the Incarnation is reduced in his view to the *Unio hypostatica*, which does not merely mean to him that the (personal) Logos accomplishes the incarnation, but also that its result is essentially nothing else than that the Logos places Himself as the person or Ego of this man, whereby the humanity is lowered to be the mere garment of the Deity, and a mere theophany necessarily becomes the consequence of the Christology.[2]

But the Swabian school is certainly not without obligation to this opposition of Chemnitz to a more earnest *communicatio* of the Divine, because of exaggerations which it allows to become faults. What was for a time a means of proof for Luther of his doctrine of the Supper, namely, that the *Unio*

---

[1] In fact, he teaches a *dimissio propriæ subsistentiæ humanæ naturæ*. Compare my *History of the Doctrine of the Person of Christ*.

[2] The laborious and skilled defence of M. Chemnitz in Frank's *Theologie der Concordienformel*, iii. 1862, pp. 164–396, has not been able to set aside the considerations adduced above, and has not exactly conceived in a historical manner the fundamental difference between the plan of the Christology of Chemnitz and that of the Swabian school. Comp. my *History of the Doctrine of the Person of Christ*.

*naturarum* was from the first complete, they have sought to transform into a dogma. This is their doctrine of the *status majesticus* of the humanity of Christ from the commencement of His life, seeing that the school almost wholly omitted to distinguish between the idea or the ideal of the *Unio* and its realization, and imported what can only be the result of a truly human process into the initial stages of the life of Christ. In a word, they dated the state of exaltation back to that of humiliation. Thus they arrived at the monstrous propositions, that the humanity of Christ is by the act of the *Unio* already exalted to the right hand of God, that the ascent into heaven has already happened therewith, and that the later narrative of the ascension only shows by symbol what existed from the beginning. On His human side, they say, He has always possessed absolute omnipresence, and was in Athens whilst He was in Jerusalem; hanging on the cross, He ruled the world by His omnipotence; whilst He lay in the grave He was also everywhere, etc. In this it is still to be specially noticed that, contrary to Luther's meaning of 2 Pet. i. 4, they see the Divine *Majestas* in physical attributes pre-eminently. For the ethical attributes they would have conceded a development. Seeing, then, that they thus ascribed the Divine majesty to Christ from the beginning, namely, His omnipresence, omnipotence, and omniscience, and opposed themselves to Luther's position of a true development of Jesus, the only course open to them was either to change all development in the whole state of the humiliation of Christ into a mere appearance, or to suppose a double humanity in reference to the state of humiliation, an absolutely perfected, side by side with a developing humanity.[1] On this side, Chemnitz, as the head of the Lower Saxons, has done the service of having preserved important positions, especially belonging to Luther's earlier time. We may not, it was said, volatilize the truth of the human development of Christ; during its time a relative repose of the Logos in Christ must

---

[1] When Frank (p. 210) maintains, in opposition to the above, that the Swabians had *no wish* to deny a true development, he forgets that we are not in scientific things concerned with mere desire. And when there appear, side by side with the expressions mentioned (Frank, p. 337), passages which expressly assert the growth and development of Christ, they directly prove that they pertain to a double humanity.

be assumed in spite of the *Unio*.¹ By the act of the *Unio* the fulness of the Divine powers does not flow over even into the human nature by a physical necessity, but it depends upon the will of the Logos how much He will communicate. Even Luther, it is asserted, afterwards abandoned the *omnipræsentia absoluta* of the God-man.² The Logos has ever maintained and used at His own disposal His Godhead and activity of government. And with the humanity of Jesus He has only been so far united as the state of humiliation admitted. In this a relative separation was assumed for the time of growth between the eternally perfect Logos and the still non-perfected man, and the full idea of the God-humanity was distinguished from the stages of its realization. Indeed, this full idea was thought insufficient by him, for even in the state of exaltation the predicates of majesty are supposed never to become the property of the humanity.³

§ 95.—*Continuation.*

*The Christology of the* FORMULA CONCORDIÆ.—In the two tendencies in the Lutheran Church, the Swabian and the Lower Saxon, the factors which are found together in Luther's Christology are separated. Had they been brought to a scientific union, a satisfactory Christology might have been hoped for. As a matter of fact, both parties united in the work of concord;⁴ but before inner agreement and collaboration had been attained, haste was made to a premature formal conclusion, which neither elicited for the common good

¹ Cap. xxx. says that the Logos has restrained Himself, has suspended or retracted His influence upon the humanity, in order to remit thereto its own laws of development.
² Cap. xxx. p. 193.
³ Only he assumed inconsistently, from love for the doctrine of the Supper, that, because of the *Unio*, prerogatives which are superior and opposed to the human nature were communicated to the exalted Christ, namely, the ability to be and to work where He wills—*omnipræsentia hypothetica*. On the contrary, even the Swabians assumed, for the state of humiliation, a miracle which Jesus has performed of Himself sometimes in order to limit His humanity in knowing and working, *e.g.* to limit His presence to one place. But the more stringent stood to the secret *use* of the Divine prerogatives (κρύψις τῆς χρήσεως).
⁴ The result lies in the *F. C. Epit.* 605, etc., *Sol. Decl.* 761, etc.

all that was good in both sides, nor excised all that was incorrect; rather did weakening and mutual concessions (partly in equivocal expressions) conceal dissonances still existing, which soon broke out again, and at once the *F. C.* failed to find universal recognition. Upon the genuine sense of the unifying formula there soon arose a second controversy. Nevertheless the *F. C.* saved a few of Luther's important thoughts.

The *Unio*, it teaches, is a *Unio naturarum*, and does not consist in the unity of the *person* who includes the natures.[1] It boldly stops at the position that in Christ the most distant extremes, God and man, have combined into a unity, on the one side by the love of the self-communicating Logos, and on the other by the receptiveness of the human nature. *Humana natura capax divinæ*.[2] Mary did not bear a mere man, but a man with whom the Logos Himself was essentially united, and there is a real communication of the one nature to the other.[3] Not figuratively merely, as the Reformed and Catholic Churches customarily teach, does the one nature contain the predicates of the other, as though they had not actually everything in common; but the *proprietates essentiales* of both natures, nay, the natures themselves, have intercommunications, in so far as this is at all possible without detriment to their permanent duality. Only the substances of the two natures remain of themselves unchanged. Within the *Unio* the two natures cannot be united mechanically merely like *duo asseres conglutinati*, but their

---

[1] The formulas are: *Divina et humana natura in Christo personaliter unitæ sunt*, 606, 5. *Divinitas et humanitas in Christo unam personam constituunt*, which is also called *hypostatica unio*, 771, 41. Nothing is taught by the *F. C.* of an *impersonalitas humanæ naturæ*, nor is it said that God as the Word has accepted the position of the personality for the humanity of Christ, but the formula is: *utriusque naturæ una tantum est persona*, 770, 36; *Deus et homo unitus est in una persona*, 772, 44; it is the end and result of the unifying of the natures, *unitæ sunt* ad constituendum unum, ὑφιστάμενον, 606, 9. *Divinitas cum humanitate unita est in unam personam*, 785, 85; *ut—Persona Filii Dei incarnati*—sine humanitate sua non sit integra persona, 763, 11.

[2] 611, 34; 774, 52; 775, 53. But the Divine endowments were never *naturales* for the humanity, so that it had them *per se* (781, 71), they remained as that which was conferred; this humanity remains *sub Deo* (777, 61), there is never found an *exæquatio divinæ et humanæ naturæ*. Nevertheless the Divine predicates became the property of the humanity.

[3] *F. C.* 605-612; 761-788.

inexpressible alliance lies in the fact that in Christ man is God and God is man, which would be impossible, if the natures had not actually communicated something to each other. Without this communication, which according to the ancient figure is compared to the fire in glowing iron as well as to the union of body and soul, the Son of God could only be with us upon earth in word and sacrament, and in all our need, with His naked Deity. His human presence would no longer pertain to us. But in this case all that was most consoling would be taken from us. His pure Deity would be for us a consuming fire.[1] Conversely, without a participation of his Divine nature in the human, Christ would have merely suffered for us as a man. His Divine nature certainly cannot suffer of itself. But it can lovingly participate in the humanity, together with which it has become a person.[2] In spite of its participation in the Divine nature, the human remains limited, finally, in itself, continues in its lineaments.[3] This also deserves honourable mention, that, although not elaborated purely, the doctrine of a double state of Christ has been introduced into Dogmatics, the *status exinanitionis* and *exaltationis*. Upon this point there was unity, namely, that in the state of exaltation the humanity no longer stood in the mere possession of the Divine predicates, but has entered upon the open exercise of the Divine majesty. But upon the exercise of the Divine prerogatives on the part of the human nature during the *status exinanitionis* there was not an actual unanimity, although Chemnitz made the rash concession, that from the first moment the humanity had by virtue of the *Unio* entered into the *possession*—although not the exercise—of all Divine predicates.[4] On both sides the continual exercise of the Divine predicates was ascribed to the Logos, and all self-

---

[1] *F. C.* 786.    [2] 607, 13 ; 608, 14 ; 771.

[3] 606, 6, 8 ; 610, 27-29 ; 786, 89, etc.

[4] He certainly did not understand the possession to be a property which he should have, like the Swabians, but yet he consented to the proposition in the *F. C.* 764, 13 : *Quod ad hanc majestatem attinet, ad quam Christus secundum suam humanitatem exaltatus est ; non eam tum demum accepit, cum a mortuis resurrexit et ad cœlos ascendit. Sed tum, cum in utero matris conciperetur et homo fieret, quando videlicet divina et humana natura personaliter sunt unitæ,* 767, 26.

renunciation of the same was denied for the *status exinanitionis*.¹ But whilst Chemnitz did not regard the exercise of the Divine predicates by the humanity as a natural consequence of the *Unio*, but subjected that exercise to the will of Christ, the Swabians held fast to a continual latent exercise of the possession of the Divine attributes. Ordinarily, thought Chemnitz, Jesus in His *status exinanitionis* did not make use of His possession of the Divine *majestas* on the side of His humanity, but when He so willed, He could do so at any moment, and similarly He also made in reference to the state of exaltation the presence of Christ in the Supper dependent on His will, whilst the Swabians regarded His perpetual Omnipresence as the necessary consequence of the *Unio*. To the concession, that the humanity was from the beginning in possession of the Divine attributes (therefore also of the Omniscience, for example), he allowed himself to be driven by the Swabians, who knew how to break through the acknowledgment of Luther's so-called great Confession of the Supper,² but at the same time not merely lost the possibility of precisely distinguishing the two states, but his strong position generally;³ for, with the possession of the Divine attributes, *e.g.* omnipresence and omniscience, as the Swabians maintained, their exercise must be indissolubly associated.⁴ This possession from the human beginning must manifestly

---

¹ That since the *Unio* all operation of the Logos has also become the act of the humanity of Jesus, was therefore not accepted. If after the *Unio* the Logos still has His freedom, His operation transcending the humanity, this would not agree with the later proposition : *totus Logos in carne*, etc. To this only the Tübingen theologians had a right for the earthly life, because they maintained a latent exercise of the majesty on the part of the humanity.

² *F. C.* 761. 3, 784. 81, 786. 86 (in this passage Luther's Great Confession upon the Supper is raised to a Symbolical importance). Comp. Planck, *Geschichte der Protestantischen Lehrbegriff*, vol. 6, pp. 453, 459.

³ Frank seeks to defend Chemnitz, because from the beginning he assumed a *Unio hypostatica*, and that in it, according to the principle, all Divine prerogatives have become the possession of Jesus. But this possession would thus have been a physical necessity logically following from the *Unio hypostatica*, which would not agree with what Chemnitz teaches upon the repose or self-retraction of the Logos (see above, p. 232).

⁴ Which even Frank is compelled to acknowledge. Therefore the case is little improved when Chemnitz broke through the view that 782. 74 only appears to refer to the exalted state : *jam etiam secundum humanam naturam omnia novit et potest.*

make all spiritual growth Doketic. But even the Swabians conceded, not to the benefit of the case, the formula of Chemnitz of the *supra vel contra naturam humanam*, which does not consist with the former *capacitas* for the *Divina natura*.[1] It is clear that these definitions of the *F. C.* either volatilize the humanity or conduct to a double humanity, a perfected by the side of a developing humanity.

It was no wonder that the oppositions in the controversy between the Tübingen and Giessen theologians, which were only silenced, broke out again. The former (Thumm) taught a κρύψις τῆς χρήσεως of the Divine prerogatives on the side of the human nature, whilst the Giessen theologians (Feuerborn, Balthasar Menzer, and others) taught a renunciation of their exercise (κένωσις τῆς χρήσεως). With them the Saxon *Decisio* of 1624 agreed in the main, and still more the further history of the Lutheran Christology. Both sides accept the uninterrupted actuality of the Logos in the government of the world, and reject as a βλασφημία the opinion that the Deity empties Himself in Christ, or that the Deity is to be thought as humiliated,—an opinion which the *F. C.* had already repudiated.[2]

Thus the *F. C.* brought no settlement, indeed a stagnation soon intervened, and by consequence a relinquishment of the problem. The gradual decomposition of this Christology began even in the seventeenth century. At first the acknowledgment seemed compulsory, that not the quiescent attributes of God, the *æternitas, infinitas*, but only the active, are communicated. Further, instead of the doctrine that the Divine attributes became the property of the humanity, the so-called συνδύασις of the two natures was supposed, in virtue of which the Logos works in and through the humanity.

The main doctrinal activity in the seventeenth century was

---

[1] 773. 50.
[2] *F. C.* 612, 773. 49, 781. 71. This would lead to Arianism, *i.e.* to the denial of the Deity of the Son as equal in essence to the Father, which Philippi rightly gives prominence to as opposed to Thomasius, 4, 129–137, 257. Even Hahn, *Lehrb. des christl. Glaubens*, recalls that this mode of teaching swerves from the doctrine of the Œcumenical as well as the Lutheran Church, II. p. 187, etc. Frank vainly tries to come to the help of this passage of the *F. C.* as opposed to the Kenotic view of Thomasius, and to vindicate its ecclesiastical character, p. 265.

to distribute the *communicatio idiomatum* into different classes, according to the suggestions of Chemnitz. These are three. The two natures give, *in the first place*, their predicates of the one person (*genus idiomaticum*); *secondly*, the person acts through the two natures (*genus apotelesmaticum*). The Reformed Churches also concede these two kinds, whilst they deny the *third*, the *genus majestaticum, i.e.* the communication of the attributes of the Divine nature to the human nature and person.[1]

The *status exinanitionis* the Lutheran Dogmatics was wont to regard as an act of the humanity of Christ, consequently as a self-abasement on His part, for the Divine nature cannot be abased, even by its own agency. But the very first element of the earthly existence of Jesus is humiliation. If, notwithstanding, the latter is to be thought as initiated by Christ's humanity, we are led by logical sequence to the belief that the humanity already existed *in unio* with the Logos before its conception, and indeed in the state of majesty, *i.e.* we are led to a pre-existence of the humanity of Christ.[2]

§ 96.—*Continuation.*

II.—*The Reformed Christology* (comp. the introductory paragraph of § 94).

Generally speaking, the Reformed Christology abided by the positions of the Creed of Chalcedon, rejecting both Monophysitism and Nestorianism, only that it did not merely accept a unifying of the natures to form the unity of the person as the result, but regarded this unity of the person as given purely in the Logos, who assumed humanity, and even constituted the Ego thereof. Still it definitely sought to avoid the volatilization of the humanity. Zwingli halted at an external relation between the Divine and human. He was only able to

---

[1] The Christology of the modern Kenotics would have, side by side with the *genus majestaticum*, a ταπινωτικόν, *i.e.* a communication to the Deity of the human abasement,—a view which, according to the *F. C.* (612), is absolutely inadmissible because of the Divine immutability.

[2] Comp. Schneckenburger, vol. ii. pp. 202, etc., 207, etc.

distinguish the natures as the infinite and finite. In order to avoid the perfect communication of the Logos to the humanity, he expounded the passages of Scripture which point to an internal relation of the two natures in a figurative manner (as *Allöosis*).[1] Calvin, on the contrary, halted at the position that adoration and the power of redemption do not belong to the Logos only, but to the God-man, seeing that he asserts the main idea to be that of the mediator between God and man. The leading Reformed theologians, such as Beza, Olevianus, and C. Ursinus, Zanchi, Grynæus, Peter Martyr, Sadeel, accepting as they did a co-operation of the Deity and the humanity in the production of the work of redemption, held that fast which was of immediate and indispensable importance for faith in Christ. On the other hand, the elaboration of christological doctrine effected by the stricter Reformed theologians swerved in an important manner from the Lutherans, especially the Swabians, whilst they approximated more to Chemnitz. When Chemnitz said that the Divine *idiomata* essentially transcend the receptiveness of human nature, — being *supra et contra eam*, — they accepted the statement most seriously. Their canon was: *finitum non capax infiniti*.[2] As a finite magnitude, the humanity of Christ must, they said, be confined to a space in heaven. But whilst Chemnitz coincided with the Swabians, for the sake of the doctrine of the Supper, that the humanity of Christ received what was *contra et supra naturam*, and was thereby exalted above itself, the Reformed theologians found an inconsequence in this, a magical *donum superadditum*, and assented to the fundamental position of the Swabians, that what was actually communicated by the Divine nature to the human, must actually become the property thereof, and not be superior or contrary to its idea.

The Reformed theologians certainly conceded an elevation of the powers of human nature by the Logos, who communicated to it powers of the Holy Spirit or anointing (*unctio*), and they therefore laid a great stress upon the Holy

---

[1] John i. 44 means, he says, Man has become God, *Luther's Works*, vol. xx. pp. 1496, etc.

[2] As opposed to this, the Lutherans say that the measure of receptiveness is dependent on the almighty will of God.

Spirit and the baptism of Christ in reference to the Person of Christ. But they halted at the position, that the Divine communication must observe the limits laid down by the receptiveness of the human nature. But it is only finite, they say. Finite and infinite wholly exclude each other (in which statement no difference is made between extensive and intensive infinity).[1] With this axiom they operated no less than the Lutheran did with the opposite axiom. Therefore the controversy necessarily remained unfruitful, and agreement impossible, so long as an inquiry into the essence of the human nature in relation to the Divine had not decided this fundamental question. But to this metaphysical inquiry advance was not for a long time made; and it is only the philosophical investigations made since Kant which have directed themselves to the ideas of the infinite and finite, of God and man, and which have brought a wide-reaching agreement into the more recent Dogmatics. Consequently at that time the only course open was to show the consequences of the two-sided axioms, and to maintain them against opponents. The Lutherans considered it in many ways a touchstone, so to speak, of Lutheran orthodoxy, whether it was recognized that the Logos is *totus* or *totaliter in carne*, not in order to confine him, but to expand the humanity, without wishing, nevertheless, to volatilize its limited form.[2] Some said that

[1] Even Chemnitz concedes (comp. Frank, p. 358), that the natural grounds do not permit the *finita natura* to be *capax infiniti*, but Almighty Wisdom can nevertheless make it *capax infiniti*, in which view it is certainly to be again considered, that to Chemnitz this *capacitas* does not mean the ability to have the Divine as a property (see above, p. 230).

[2] Various theories were attempted, to show how the humanity could take part in the omnipresence of the Logos, upon which more will be said in the doctrine of the Lord's Supper. A few modern writers, also, especially those who are attached to the modern Kenotic theories, love to regard it as the result of Lutheran orthodoxy, that from the moment of the *Unio* not merely are Deity and humanity inseparably associated, one not being without the other, but also that the Logos is and works in no way *extra carnem* any longer, in which case it necessarily breaks with all Christian antiquity, with all passages of Scripture and in Luther which speak of a growth of the human nature, and with the positions of Chemnitz upon a *Retractio* of the Logos for the purpose of this growth, indeed even with the common Lutheran doctrine that prior to the exaltation the humanity of Christ had not the *plenaria usurpatio* of the Divine endowments, and therefore did not actually work everywhere and always with the Logos, who on His part exercised the Divine prerogatives eternally unchanged.

the omnipresent Logos has everywhere the assumed humanity of Christ present itself, as the humanity has Him present (*præsentia intima*). On the other hand, the humanity of Christ is not present in relation to everything, therefore, in the whole world. It has not, it was said, *præsentia extima*. Philipp Nicolai thinks that the Logos takes the universe in His hand as a web of dust, and that He is in the humanity of Jesus. Since, then, the soul of Jesus gazes into the Logos, who embraces the world omnipresently in Himself, the whole world is present to it, which view seems to lead back to a mere omnipresence of knowing. *Others* said that the humanity of Christ is omnipresent, but only *actu personæ*, not *naturæ*. But then it is their *persona* of the Logos who is omnipresent. It is evident that even the Reformed theologians might say this, inasmuch as no omnipresence was found for the human *nature*, but at most for the person of the humanity, when, namely, the *persona* of the Logos was communicated thereto. The Helmstedters and others who approximated more to Martin Chemnitz supposed a hypothetical omnipresence, or more exactly a *multipræsentia, multilocatio*, for the sake of the Supper.[1]

The Reformed theologians said, on the contrary, that the Logos has indeed become incarnate, whether with His *persona* alone as the majority thought, or with His *natura* as well. They also said it was inseparably associated with the humanity, and never after existed without it since the *Unio*, as the humanity did not exist without the Logos. But it also eternally is and remains omnipresently active outside of the humanity and its limitation. Since the humanity must remain finite, the infinite Logos could never be *totaliter in carne*. It is, they said, everywhere wholly, and therefore also *totus in carne* of Christ. But it is also *extra carnem*, and remains so. His *divina natura* transcends the human eternally and infinitely, although it rules the world omnipotently from the human nature as the world-centre. An

---

[1] Chemnitz had insisted upon the position, that the exercise of the Divine prerogatives depended on the free will of the God-man, a position which was also broken through by him (*F. C.* 767. 26, 782. 74), and which the Swabians could only grant in the sense that what is self-evidently given in the *Unio* is also willed by Christ.

impartation of the properties (*zueigengeben*) of the Divine to the human they would not have; but then, strictly regarded, no adoration of the God-man could be permitted, but only of the Logos in Christ.

If, in conclusion, we survey the two-sided Christology according to its fundamental character, the strength of the Lutheran lies in the prominence it gives to the ideal or goal, but it acknowledges too little that this goal is only to be attained by a development, especially of an ethical kind. The strength of the Reformed Christology lies in emphasizing this development, and in the delineation of the true humanity, so far as its constitution is conditioned by growth. But both Confessions disagreeing with each other, the consequence is that the Reformed Christology does not advance beyond a distinction between the idea and the reality, and does not attain the perfect interpenetration of the natures so as to form a unity, a failure which appears to the Lutherans to be an eternalizing of the state of humiliation; whilst the Lutheran Christology refers the state of exaltation to the very beginnings of Jesus, and does not reach a true state of humiliation and growth. If the Lutheran Christology approximates too closely to Monophysitism and its after-effects, the Reformed Christology, not in the doctrine of the person but in that of the natures, approaches too near to Nestorianism, although neither do so intentionally, and in this fact there lies for both an impulse and obligation towards an adjusting progress.

The goal of the further labour of the Church is accordingly laid down with clearness beforehand. It would depend on uniting the true and actual humanity — development included—with the close coherence of the essence of the two natures. The former must become prominent for the state of humiliation, whilst not the identification, but the perfect union, must be the result of the process of the two factors. It is of importance to take the distinction of the two states seriously, but to think the former state in its movement to the goal, the absolute God-humanity in exaltation. In order to attain this goal in a way satisfactory to faith, it will be requisite to understand and to construe the *religious motive* of the two Christologies, side by side with the investigation into the essence of the two natures. That of the

Reformed Christology is reverence for God, desiring to guard carefully against confusion of the Divine and human, against idolatry. It measures the self-communicability of God to the world by the necessary self-preservation of God in distinction from the creature. The Lutheran theory lacks the Divine self-communication according to the love of God, which wishes for complete and intimate union. But reverence and love coalesce in Christian piety, and so in God do self-preservation in His holy majesty and loving condescension. Rightly conceived, they cannot contradict each other. A love which would exalt the humanity indeed by self-communication, but which absorbed it in the process, would be no longer love, but the opposite, the revocation of the incarnation; so that it is in the interest of the love itself to guarantee distinctions even in the unity. Again, it cannot be contrary to reverence for God also to ascribe to Him the power of, and the will of, self-communication. The justice or self-preservation of God must also preserve His communicability, otherwise since God is also love, as the Reformed theology itself does not deny, the self-preservation of God would not be complete.

§ 97.

*The Third Epoch of the Second Period (from* 1700 *to about* 1800).

The stagnation, into which the solution of the existing problems of the Ecclesiastical doctrine fell, passed over into the gradual resolution of the two-sided Christology. In the preponderance of the *human* side the latter was now so placed as to recur even to Ebionitism.

1. It was after 1700 especially that the consequences worked themselves out of the disharmony latent in the Christological positions previously considered; and this fact stimulated the attempt to eliminate the elements step by step which were regarded as disturbing, or as likely to disturb, and partly to introduce elements as well which had been overlooked. We may distinguish three stages.

IN THE FIRST PLACE, the bond which had been knit between the Deity and the humanity by the *communicatio personæ, naturarum*, and *idiomatum*, was loosened, because the true humanity seemed inconsistent therewith. After the quiescent attributes had been already accepted from the *communicatio* in the 17th century, the structure of the *communicatio idiomatum* was broken through in the 18th century step by step. About 1700 it was combated by Pfaff and others that the *persona* of the Logos gives itself to be a property of the humanity; there thus remained a mere *determinatio* by the Logos, and the humanity might be thought to be in itself personal or otherwise. Further, if the having of the Divine idiomata, the μέθεξις of the same, was changed into a mere συνδύασις of the two natures, as a result the contro versy with the Reformed theology upon the *tertium genus* was already as good as objectless. The denial of the *communicatio* of the Divine *nature* soon followed; finally, the communication of the Divine *attributes* generally, without point of connection in the absence of the *natura*, was so weakened that the possession of the same was reduced to a title (thus Heilmann and Reinhard). Retreat was increasingly made to the two first *genera*, which even the Reformed theologians acknowledge. Long before the influences of philosophy, therefore, an Indifferentism was widely diffused to the high and powerful structure of the old Christology.

By the elimination of the elements mentioned, the aim was—and this is THE OTHER SIDE of the matter—to make a way for a *true humanity;* the process of the decomposition of the old Christology was also advanced by the aid of new points of view. In the 16th and 17th centuries, scarcely enough had been thought in the *communicatio idiomatum* of the ethical predicates, but only of the *majestas* of the human nature because of the Divine, of the metaphysical and physical predicates of the omnipresence, omnipotence, omniscience. But when, subsequently to 1700, holiness was also introduced into the consideration of Christology,[1] the point was reached, in which demand was peremptorily made for a humanity of Christ which was not selfless and impersonal,

---

[1] In connection with the Spener movement, as the Hymnology of the time shows.

but which was in itself holy, particularly as holiness, although a Divine attribute, cannot transcend the idea of human nature. To this end there was assumed, after the Reformed fashion, an *Unctio Spiritus Sancti* (Walch), by the side of which the *communicatio idiomatum* could only hold a precarious, external position. But since ethical acts, like prayer and obedience, could not pertain to the person of the Logos, and are nevertheless of a personal kind, as Haferung, for example, maintained, the human nature was thought with increasing universality to be personal in itself, and not first by a substitionary Ego of the Logos.

But this independence of the human personality soon appeared to many to be only possibly substantiated, if, IN THE THIRD PLACE, a deduction was made from the Divine side. One stone after another was now removed from the structure on the Divine side. Subordinationist or Arian theories revived (*e.g.* by the influence of Samuel Clarke and others in England, Clericus, Töllner, Döderlein, Flatt), partly in the form of a pre-existent heavenly humanity of Christ (Paul Mathy and Goodwin); Sabellian views also revived (Swedenborg, Urlsperger); and finally, Ebionitic views (Gruner). The old Socinianism had not merely forced itself into the Church, but was outbid by Rationalism, which clave indeed at the outset to the sinlessness of Jesus, a point which in its Pelagian mode of thought could have only a limited importance. G. S. Röhr, in his letters on Rationalism in 1813, went further; he denied that Christology belonged to Christian doctrine as a dogma. Many even abandoned the moral impression of the holy personality (*e.g.* Reimarus, Venturini). It is true that in the Church the old confession of Christ as the God-man continued, but the circles of the pious whose faith and Christian life nourished itself upon the God-human Redeemer became ever more limited and silent. Theology itself, always withdrawing more and more from the structure of the old Christology which had become uninhabitable, stood helpless and without power and trust, without religious breath, and now held to these, now those, wrecks of the old. The reins fell from her, and for a time philosophy took them, at first completing the process of dissolution and anon reconstructing, for it ventured upon the consideration of the points previously neglected,—of the ideas of the infinite and finite, of God and man,—the exclusion of which had been an ancient detriment, and the fruitful source of untenable intellectual positions.

2. Even prior to 1800, Philosophy had rendered important services to Christology. In the positive part of his system Kant did not venture to abandon the Christological idea. He conceives Christ as the idea of humanity well-pleasing to God, through which alone we can be justified before God; but he distinguishes this ideal Christ from the historical Jesus, who is in his view the founder of the purely moral community, upon whose person, and especially upon whose sinlessness as a philosopher, he makes no definite statement. Further, it is especially worthy of note, how the philosophy of Subjectivism of Kant, Jacobi, Fichte, in seeking to find a basis for the nature of man, upon which it could stand, found in this nature points of connection for the idea of the Divine, nay, for Christology. If in the previous teaching since the 5th century the human had only remained an *accidens* in the Divine, the human was now certainly thought to be the substantial element in the person of Christ; but in this human element, thought according to its idea, the investigation straightway found traces of the Divine, an internal relation thereto. According to Kant and Jacobi, man is finite according to his empirical constitution; but there is in him something infinite; according to Kant in the practical reason, in freedom and in conscience, which are co-ordinated; in the feeling of the infinite, according to Jacobi. "Were the eye not adapted to see the sun, how could we perceive light; were there not living within us a peculiar power of God, how could the Divine transport us?" An infinite worth, something Divine therefore, does not lie beyond the range of what is attainable by man, according to these thinkers. Similarly has Fichte answered on the side of cognition, as well as on that of the moral faculty, that truth as well as freedom is for man. Before them all there rises the image of an ideal man different from the empirical man, who may be, nay, should be, free and holy, wise and full of God, without therefore ceasing to be man.

The theologians also soon saw their advantage, and sought

to give these theories of Subjectivism an application favourable to Christianity. Especially did many theologians connect themselves with Kant, less for the sake of his critical, nay, sceptical, position towards a metaphysical knowledge of Divine things—which might also become a very perilous method of recommending faith—than because of his earnest, moral spirit. As a proof, we give the view, which is not so well known as it deserves, of the theologian, who has possibly achieved the most important results in this field, the Wittenberg Director, Professor and General-Superintendent Carl Ludwig Nitzsch, who died 1831.[1] He divides the main thoughts, which Kant has especially given utterance to in his *Religion within the Limits of Pure Reason*, into the indispensable self-certainty of the moral consciousness for the ethical, further also the acknowledgment of an evil and a good principle in us, and the distinction between the moral and the historical, the intellectual and the empirical. But his task then advances thence to knit more closely the connection between the moral world-aim of God and historical Christianity. The "community of social life," from which all spiritual culture starts, is destined and adapted to arouse and foster all germs of the good and the Divine, whilst, on the other hand, experience shows that it favours the outbreak of internal corruption and its external dominion. Help now for entire humanity must consist in bringing the better elements to voluntarily associate to form a community, which Nitzsch at first calls the Church, but later the kingdom of God; further, that the sublime moral aim be set before such

---

[1] His son, K. Immanuel Nitzsch, has already made reference to him in his *System*, ed. 6, pp. 65, 71. We consider his *Prolusiones academicæ* (from 1805 to 1807) *de revelatione religionis externa eademque publica*. The first treatise (pp. 3–34), treats *De Jesu revelationis interprete*, the second of the inspiration of the apostles, which the author thinks to be the fruit of the external and public revelation; the two following treat of passages of Scripture which refer to inspiration; whilst the fifth treats of the practical, and the sixth of the theoretical exercise of the idea previously proposed of revelation not as internal and private, but external and public. Add to these two collections of "Programs" of the year 1830, which he issued under the collective title *De discrimine revelationis imperatoriæ et didacticæ*, and which were composed from 1796–1813. Finally, his Jubilee treatise at the festival of the Reformation, 1817, *Ueber das Heil der Welt, dessen Gründung und Förderung*, deserves mention.

society, and a just as voluntary, earnest endeavour be facilitated as much as possible. To this end must that help first impel the heart to arouse its own feeling and consciousness of the truths of the conscience, and be adapted to occasion a union in a religious respect, and to stimulate to voluntary accession. The *main aim* of the help for humanity must be to check the internal and external corruption of man and his social life, and to advance the dominion of the Divine Spirit over the human feelings, the thriving of the holy impulses which had been suppressed, by means of voluntary fraternization to this end, and consequently *to found an invisible kingdom of God upon earth by the agency of external arrangements.* This help lies in the *Divine revelation,* which must be an external revelation as well as public. It is the substance of the Divine facts, by which according to the decree of God, and under His guidance, the true religion becomes so known, and so proper to a number of men at a certain time, that it may become in the sequel the property of all. And everything depends in his view upon distinguishing precisely the contents, or that which is to be revealed from the form or the mode of revelation.

That which is to be revealed by God externally and publicly cannot consist in mysteries, can be nothing else than just the truth, which might and ought to develope itself in every man by the assistance of education, and proceed from what is within him, but which is suppressed in and without him by corruption. That which is suppressed must then present itself from without and come openly into light, in order that the conscience may be moved, the heart touched, and a voluntary agreement with the better self or the Spirit of truth which stirs in every heart produced. The *main object of revelation* can only therefore be the true godliness itself, good presenting itself as pleasing to God, *humanity as well-pleasing to God* or the *God-man.*[1] The right knowledge

[1] See the last-mentioned work, pp. 15-20. Jesus is to him a "representative" of the eternal Word or of the "Son of God," a relation of identity he does not teach. Jesus is pre-existent in the Divine counsel. P. 57: In the symbolico-practical sense the true Saviour of the world must, of course, be the Creator of the world, inasmuch as the creation of the world is to be deduced from the complacency of God towards the humanity which is like Him, or towards His Son. Comp. *De Jesu,* etc., p. 13, etc. He himself needed no

of the latter, his message, raises and animates by humiliation the holy impulses of the hearts; it belongs to the encouragement that the message is a glad one, embracing the pardon of the sinner. The revelation may well be a doctrine of grace, if this is only ethically grounded, namely out of the holy complacency of God in the truly childlike disposition towards Him, to which man can still lift himself. That which is prevenient, therefore, in pardoning grace is simply the announcement that God *will* forgive us, if our disposition is truly childlike,—an announcement which already shows the goodwill of God in spite of our guilt.[1] Add to this, that Christ is not merely a teacher, but His life and sufferings are more important still. By the purity of His virtue and His love to His own, He is to us as a God-given representative of the love of God, a personal pledge (or symbol). But for the most part His being well-pleasing to God is a guarantee to us, because He makes a successful beginning of the execution of the world-aim of God, namely, the establishment of a kingdom of God from men of a candid moral endeavour, by collecting a circle around Himself. The full certainty, indeed, that He has the Divine call to establish the kingdom of God by the promulgation of His own true contents, can only arise when His word and work find recognition and belief in humanity; for if the idea of the kingdom of God were still not actually received into spirits, its promulgation would not be as yet complete. But Christ has at least built so strong a moral fraternity, that there lies the power in it to expand itself over the whole of humanity; so that out of the success of His vocation, our security as to its Divine destiny increases. This becomes still more clear, by considering the manner in which He built so firm a holy fraternity. It is His bloody death which has especially effected this. For His death shows His love and fidelity in its full radiance; as a martyr, He is also a guarantee of His doctrine of the pardon of the

revelation of His dignity; but the Divine seal of His mission lay first in His success.

[1] On the contrary, according to Nitzsch (p. 54), the eternal grace of God to the guilty must not be made dependent upon a temporal fact; such a fact could not be supposed to be a satisfaction in the common judicial sense of the word, but only an external pledge of the reconciliation on the side of God, a sign of grace, which powerfully invites men to be reconciled with Him.

sinner; as the death of the love which offers itself for the good of humanity, He kindles an inextinguishable love in the community founded by Him, and Christ remains its centre.

Although, then, looking at its contents, the Gospel does not, according to Nitzsch, communicate any new mysteries, but its contents are merely the moral contents which lie in the universal reason (therefore he calls his view *Material Rationalism*), nevertheless the whole arrangement made to bring these eternal contents to power and life has been the product of historical facts, so that, formally regarded, he leaves a place for Supernaturalism, although in limited measure. It belonged to the vocation of Jesus to announce Himself as the Saviour of the world *publicly* and *externally*, in order that the image of His holy person might arouse the germs of good, and might show the power of the gathering of a community which was itself the beginning of the kingdom of God. Therefore Jesus, from the moment when He had found this confession of Himself suitably made, could not yield a step in order to spare His life, not indeed giving provocation, but continuing according to His vocation he had to await what His enemies were preparing for His destiny. His miracles served to make Him fully certain of His vocation, and also to direct the glances of receptive hearers upwards to Him who is accessible in His name. This gives to the faith in revelation its consummation and intensity.

It is certainly no light thing that C. L. Nitzsch, in opposition to the subjective, ethical Idealism of Kant, so strongly argued for external, historical revelation; but the impression of an artistic apparatus can scarcely be banished from the working out of his idea. How far a sinless being dying as a criminal can represent the love of God to humanity—especially if he is not in a special sense a gift of God to humanity—will always remain unthinkable without the thought of a God-given means of atonement. But especially does Nitzsch remain standing in the contradiction, that on the one side he allows the atonement of man, the forgiveness of sins only to follow upon the purity of childlike love which is never perfect, whilst on the other hand he well knows that comfort and trust in the forgiving grace of God are indispensable to moral courage.

And, similarly, all the different forms of subjective Idealism remain standing in a Dualism between the idea and the reality of man, between obligation and being, and they confess this. Whilst Christianity is able to vanquish this Dualism in the person of Christ, Kant points to an infinite progress in the approximation of the empirical to the ideal man; Jacobi is imprisoned in the Dualism between heart and understanding. They stop also in empty longing and endeavour; nay, they insist that the empirical and the ideal can never be equivalent. They remain in conflict between freedom and, what ought not to be, radical evil, between the thing in itself or νούμενον and the φαινόμενον, between the infinite which is anticipated by the heart and the understanding which makes the same finite, nay, denies its existence. And inasmuch as they thus consider the two worlds, the ideal or intellectual and the empirical, as mutually exclusive magnitudes,—just as the theology of the Middle Age with a similar effect had emphasized the Divine exclusively,—they consequently make the absolute right of the ideal world to reality itself waver. It ought to be shown as a consequence, that subjectivity cannot assert itself, if it thinks to exclude or dispense with the Divine objectivity, and to be able to present the pure humanity purely from itself, and to bear of itself the Divine, whether from freedom or from thought or from the noble nature of the heart. The old Dualism must therefore be banished from the standpoint of human nature, because of the fact that its ethical and metaphysical need of God are manifest, and the knowledge has been won, that the human and the Divine cannot be thought as exclusive of each other, because the former dwindles into contradictions, if subjectivity desires to rest purely on itself instead of seeing in the Divine its basis and the indispensable elements for its own perfect realization. Subjective Idealism had sought to develop the Divine from the Ego in the form of Divine activity, Divine feelings and thoughts. But at this extreme point the reverse process must begin, and the powerlessness of the subject become evident apart from the Divine objectivity. This reversion appeared in the philosophical sphere through the influence of Schelling and Hegel especially, and in the theological through that of Schleiermacher.

## § 98.

### THIRD PERIOD (FROM 1800 TO THE PRESENT).

With the exception of the time of the Reformation, in which there was no sequential elaboration of its Christological thoughts, a one-sided preponderance, now of the Divine and now of the human side, had hindered since 451 the erection of the dogma. The Christological problem of the third period is therefore defined by saying that by the aid of a more correct idea of the nature of God and man, the unity of the person is to be so delineated, that in the entire image of the same both sides may receive their full due, assigned, however, according to the difference of the two states.

*Observation.*—The common knowledge of the newer Christology is the advance beyond the opposition of the Divine and human, the acknowledgment of the internal relation of the two to each other, their mutual consistency or compatibility.[1] But even upon the common basis which has been won, the God-human unity may also be thought in very diverse ways, not merely according as one or the other factor is abridged, but also (the initiative arising with the Divine side) according to the different categories of the idea of God which lie at the base. Thus the different Christological attempts of the present classify themselves as the physical, the logical, or the ethical *Unio*, and they themselves may again assume different forms. Especially is the latter divided in its imperfect forms again into the direct contrast of the juridical and kenotical, according as justice, the guardian of distinctions, or self-surrendering love, is the more considered. None of these theories being of themselves adequate, but the lack of the one being disclosed by the truth of the other, the problem results, to combine what is true in them all as elements of the *Unio* correctly and completely understood.

1. It may be said that in the present century our dogma has again come to the front in its exegetical, historical, and

[1] Comp. Acts xvii. 28.

dogmatic sides, and has been seized by a more profound movement than at any time since the early centuries. The most vital need is widely spread, to gain a true and living view and knowledge of the person of Christ. The conflict of theological and ecclesiastical parties moves increasingly around the person of Christ, as an earnest battle may finally gather around the person of the general. For centuries the objective dogmas remained almost unmoved, corresponding to the directly anthropological starting-point of the Reformation. Now the former sphere has again come in for most vivacious regard, as the rich recent literature shows. As the gain of the more recent science since Schelling, the knowledge that finite and infinite do not exclude each other has become demonstrable. Human nature is not finite merely, but has something infinite in it, at least in the form of receptiveness. That which is of infinite value — the moral and the knowledge of truth, originally resting in God alone—does not transcend the idea of man, but belongs to his reality, although derivatively. Man is also essentially in need of God, and is therefore destined for the Divine, and for living communion with God. Conversely, if the Divine, to guarantee its own idea with purity, must maintain itself in an exclusive attitude with respect to what is human, then the finite, as Hegel has shown, would be a dualistic limitation which God could not transcend. And thus God would straightway be made finite. With this knowledge of the internal relation or coherence of the Divine and human according to their essence,[1]—which is already expressed in the doctrine of Holy Scripture of the Divine image, or of God as the archetype of man, and which is essentially strengthened by a correct estimation of the importance of the ethical for the idea of God and of man,[2]—the spirit of the more recent speculation again turned with delight to the problems of the Trinity and the Incarnation of God, which had been neglected though not dropped by the later Supernaturalism of the 18th century.

But if for a time it was thought that, on the theological side also, these problems had been already solved with those general positions upon the relation between Divine and

[1] Even Schenkel confesses it in his *Christl. Dogm.* I. §§ 7, 8; II. 2. 679, § 80.
[2] Matt. v. 48.

human nature, the joy could only be of short duration. For new contradictions arose on the new ground, which are especially defined by the different conceptions of the idea of God, and just for that reason may permissibly be considered as ascending steps serving for the knowledge of the different sides of the object. Let us then survey briefly the present state of Christology, in the consciousness that by the ancient creeds, especially by that of Chalcedon, the problem was not yet solved, but also with the confident trust that so great and so rich a history of ecclesiastical labour has not been unfruitful, and cannot remain without consequences.

2. As far, in the first place, as the FACTORS are concerned, with the union of which our dogma is occupied,

*Firstly*, the whole newer time is true to the lead of the Reformation, in emphasizing earnestly the *perfectness* of the *humanity of Christ* in body and soul. Only a few permit themselves to change the Logos into a human soul;[1] this is to make the soul a mere temporary form or manifestation of the life of the Logos. No considerable theologians, further, any longer think of the humanity of Christ without personality;[2] all own a truly human *development*, a growth of Jesus according to body and soul, and distinguish to this end with precision the state of exaltation from a state of humiliation, in which Christ is not as yet in possession, or not as yet in the exercise, of the Divine power, omniscience, and holiness raised above temptation.[3] But not merely is the reality and perfectness of the humanity of Jesus, and therefore His equality of nature with us, commonly acknowledged, but all the more important dogmatic theologians confess no less that the humanity of Christ was also pre-eminently distinguished by perfectness of an unparalleled kind, and not seldom the doctrine of Christ as

[1] Thus Gess, Ebrard, Wörner, Plitt, Godet, Bushnell.

[2] Philippi himself ascribes to the humanity of Jesus self-determination and self-consciousness (vol. iv. pp. 121, etc.), therefore a proper self, or personality, if the unity of the two is understood thereby. In his treatise on the active obedience of Christ, Philippi had certainly introduced under the impersonality of the humanity of Christ the meaning that Christ is not an individual man, but that humanity in general was assumed by Him,—a view which does not agree with the former. Against the *anhypostasia* of humanity, compare Gess, p. 322, etc.

[3] A main motive for the more recent Kenotic views is just the interest in making room for the true humanity of Christ and its growth.

the second Adam, or the Son of man,[1] is associated herewith. This leads—

*In the second place,* to the *Divine side.* Here, first of all, those are to be excluded who pantheistically call everything human Divine, and therefore leave nothing unexampled for Christ, though they call Him God-man. Such physical or substantial unity of the nature of humanity generally with God, which forgets the self-existence of God, is not at all allied with the fundamental Christian fact, but makes that fact foreign and superfluous. The doctrine of the " universal" incarnation of God ignores sin and the need of redemption, and, seeing that according to Pantheism God neither has self-determination nor self-consciousness in Himself, the incarnation of God cannot be called a free act of love, which is the Christian fundamental postulate.

Nor is this postulate satisfied if in Christ only a specially high Divine *manifestation of power* is seen. This view does not go definitely beyond Ebionitism and the type of prophecy, but makes Christ so very much upon an equality with us that His redemptive power would be inconsistent therewith, whether that manifestation be derived from influences of the Spirit of God upon him from without, or be represented as the development of a purely natural—it may even be an ethical—power.

*Schleiermacher* stands higher. In a Sabellian manner he seeks, indeed, to think of the universal being of God in the world as articulating itself according to the receptiveness of the latter. God has, in his view, a threefold manner of revelation, —in creation, redemption, and the work of the Holy Spirit. In His revelation God has a being. Especially in Christ, he thinks, has the God-consciousness become the perfect being of God in Him, which was not yet the case in the first revelation, the creation. Christ alone is He in whom the peculiar being of God is found; the perfect indwelling of the highest essence in Him he supposes as His individual essence and His innermost self.[2]

---

[1] So by Schleiermacher, Neander, Rothe (*Dogmatik,* II. p. 120, etc.; *Theol. Ethik,* ed. 1, § 562). By some in the form, that they see in Christ the manifestation of the archetypal humanity which pre-existed in God, whether potentially (Beyschlag) or in heavenly reality (Keerl).

[2] *Christl. Glaubenslehre,* II. 43, § 94.

The central intensity of the receptiveness for God, which conditions the being of the living God in Christ, has received its fulfilment, and makes Him the organ through which God has resolved to communicate all His grace to humanity, and makes Him the head of humanity, in whom the power of redemption and the communication of the Holy Spirit dwells.[1] That this special mode of being of God in Christ corresponds in itself to an eternal mode of being of God, he certainly does not assume,[2] although, as compared with all other men, it is a special mode and inseparably associated with Christ. There corresponds to it in God an eternal thought which becomes real—indeed, in this reality God has a being; but from passing over to an immanent Trinity, his idea of the abstract simplicity of God proscribes him. Similarly *Weisse*, although, moreover, he accepts distinctions within God, sees in Christ only the realized image of God, the perfect realization of His eternal thought of the world.[3] By the Logos, says *Redepenning*, only the sum of the Divine thoughts relating to the world is to be understood;[4] in this sense the ideal world, which may be also called the ideal counterpart or image of God, because thoughts of God answer to His essence. The archetypal personality or the Father may also express this whole of thought, and bring it into existence outside himself in time and the world in a personal form, which stands opposite to God and is the archetype of man. From the beginning that whole of thought, he supposes, has begun to pour itself out into humanity; in Christ, the second Adam, it is perfectly realized. He is, to him, the express image of the Deity, which embraces the Divine fulness of essence, shares it with God and portrays it. The Divine Logos, previously a purely ideal existence,

[1] With this may be compared the treatise, "Ueber das höchste Gut," *Sämmtliche Werke*, Div. iii. on Philosophy, vol. ii. p. 491, where he states as possible, that "the (Divine) reason as absolute lives in an individual being, which may evoke a type of life which dominates the whole race."

[2] § 30*b*.

[3] Weisse, *Philos. Dogmatik*, vol. i. pp. 437-556; also Schleiermacher's Sermons on John i. belong here; further, Bunsen, *Hippolytus und seine Zeit*, 1852, vol. i. pp. 279, etc., 289, etc.; Ewald. *Geschichte Christus und seiner Zeit*, 1855, pp. 447, etc.; partly also Schenkel, *Dogmatik*, II. 2, pp. 717, 724.

[4] Redepenning, *Protest. K. Z.*, 1854, pp. 200, etc. Compare my *Geschichte der Christologie*, II. pp. 1213, etc.

has now become a human personality.¹ This theory does not satisfy the statements of Christ Himself upon His pre-existence, referring as they do not merely to an eternal thought or a mere Divine power, but to a substantial mode of existence of the higher nature dwelling in Him. To this, also, this theory itself leads; it would not see in Christ a mere man, but would think the real Divine fulness of life to be eternally and inseparably embraced by the humanity of Christ. If, then, God is not supposed to change Himself in time, the ground for the special mode of the existence of God in Him must lie in the internal nature of God, and this leads back to the immanent Trinity. If it is desired to repel this inference, the particularity of the being of God in Jesus must be derived from His humanity, from its finitude. It must be said that the Divine, on entrance into humanity, suffers a limitation, and becomes by the περιγραφή of His humanity a separate Divine being different from the Father (a commencement of Theopaschitism or Kenoticism). But it is inconceivable to suppose the same determined by the world and passive by its agency;² rather does it determine the world, and indeed dwell therein. Redepenning would not think God generally, but Christ to be the Redeemer, the one who is to make all partakers of His Divine nature in state and will. But much as this corresponds with the Christian consciousness and the Scriptures, there is thus at the same time conceded that a man as such, stand he ever so high, cannot attain such a position. Only if God is united personally in Him, and inseparably

[1] Inasmuch as God has a special mode of existence in Christ, which lasts for ever, this may also be so applied that, since the humanity of Jesus existed, God has a special permanent existence in time and in the world, *i.e.* in Christ Himself. This Christology again arrives at the stage of the ancient ecclesiastical development, which is shown in Beryllus and others, whilst Hippolytus and Tertullian already make a special permanent mode of existence of the Divine, which appears at its own time in Christ, to issue from God with the creation of the world, as at the present Hofmann and others allege. But in this case the world would produce a change in God Himself, and His nature would undergo change in time, although through His own will. If a distinction of the modes of being does not contradict the Divine Essence, and if it is supposed to actually exist from a definite time, then it is more in correspondence with the immutability of the Divine essence to suppose these distinctions to be eternal, as the N. T. also recommends.

[2] At this point the theories related to Sabellianism show a connection with Theopaschitic representations, the precursors of Sabellianism.

with Him, can such lofty assertions be made about Christ, as Schenkel especially clearly recognizes and presents at length.[1] Should, moreover, by the humanity, a division in the Divine nature be supposed (ἀποκοπή), then the Divine fulness of nature would no longer be in Jesus, but the God-humanity would simply collapse into a rhetorical expression for an essentially Ebionitic mode of thought.

To this place belongs the so-called anthropocentric Christology,[2] which has found many friends, since the time that the necessity of a human personality of Jesus was acknowledged. If the figurative expression " centre " is meant to show what is dominant, this would be Ebionitism, which this view repudiates. Conceding as it does, that in the human person it was the Divine which was the determinant, it would be more correct to show the *latter*, with Schleiermacher, to be the innermost fundamental essence or " self," and consequently the centre. If, because the humanity of Jesus is personal, it is thought compulsory to show it to be that which is innermost or the centre, it is, on the contrary, to be remembered that elsewhere also the individual person must—for example, in the state or the Church—cease to desire to be the centre, being received into a higher reality which determines it. The individual personality is rather capable, without losing thereby, of accepting a higher spiritual principle, and having its animating centre therein.—Beyschlag,[3] finally, has acknowledged that a self-communication of God of eternal duration, such as we have to suppose in Christ, must also affect and modify the idea of God. We must, he says, suppose a self-distinguishableness in the Divine essence,—indeed, the eternal principle of self-distinguishing,—although this principle only becomes actual in time or in relation to the world. There is, he thinks, an ontological Trinity, or a Trinity of essence, and not merely an economical Trinity; but the former is only actually present in the latter. The economical Trinity itself is to be thought as a Trinity of essence, seeing that God as love to the world distinguishes Himself from Himself—His love is the principle

---

[1] Schenkel, *Christl. Dogmatik*, II. 2, 1859, pp. 724–730, a passage which stands on the threshold of a doctrine of an immanent Trinity.

[2] Comp. Weiss, *Sechs Vorlesungen*, etc.

[3] *Christol. d. N. T.* 1866, pp. 249, etc.

of self-communication or self-surrender. It is the essence of God to reveal and communicate Himself. Not that He loses Himself therein, rather does He rest His self-communication upon inalienable self-preservation. God as changeless and self-enclosed ($ἀόρατος$) is the Father. But as love He also wills His self-disclosure, nay His self-denial. From the beginning He wills Himself in a second form of existence, in that of another being, not again as a perfect whole, but as a principle capable of development, the summary or principle of all creation, the archetypal humanity in God, another to Himself, a real image of Himself, which is at the same time the archetype of the world and especially of humanity. God makes Himself, says Beyschlag, capable of growth (which therefore embraces a mutation, a renunciation of self), and in so far a creature, but only in order to put Himself at one in free fashion with this other being, penetrating and sanctifying it, which points to a third form of the existence of God as Holy Spirit. In Christ, he says, the second form of the existence of the Deity has become perfectly real. As perfected, Christ is of like nature with God ($ὁμοούσιος$), but this only takes place by means of a process, and by His means or in Him the Divine essence in its second form of existence first attains personality. This theory has in its Trinity, properly speaking, only the distinction between the God who is concealed, and the God who is revealed in the world in a double manner. Not in the inner Divine essence, already apart from the world, is there a Trinity in this view, but God is only a Trinity as mediated by love. Beyschlag thus endeavours to think ontologically the economical life of God; but this view, failing to think of God as a Trinity in His eternal inner being above all, must make God mutable, and introduce a species of Kenoticism out of love for the end of creation. For God, the Absolute, in order to be capable of growth, must degrade Himself in His other being to a potential existence at least for a time. And the world being to Him not a God opposite something else, but another being of God Himself, there is in this view a tendency to the obliteration of the distinction between God and the creature. Instead of creation we should have an evolution of the Divine life produced by the agency of self-denial. In this way we should arrive at no other

Trinity than that of the process of the world, in which God is passively implicated, although by His own means. Since, also, the self-conscious love in God is eternal according to Beyschlag's view, it is insufficient to assume in God apart from the world mere reserve or self-preservation; rather is He already in Himself disclosed to Himself, which points back to eternal actual distinctions in Himself, even apart from creation.

Similarly, Schelling's philosophy of revelation teaches three historical forms which God assumes. First, there is, he says, in God the Tautousia of the Son and of the Father, which is the truth of Sabellianism. Secondly, God places opposite to Himself His other being, as the world, as Heterousion. This Heterousia is the truth of Arianism. And, finally, after the perfecting of Christ, the time of the Homousia of the Father and the Son begins.

Other theologians, on the contrary, certainly acknowledge that even apart from the world a distinction of God from God in His inner essence is to be supposed, that an eternal Trinity which does not first become successive and actual is to be taught. But in such a way that they ascribe to the Son, who is thought to be really pre-existent as an individual Ego, Divine fulness of essence, it is true, but they think Him ontologically *subordinated* to the Father, and to be without a participation in the Divine self-existence, consequently as dependent in His existence upon the will of the Father. Thus Thomasius, Kahnis, Gess, Keerl, and others. Inasmuch as they, like the Arminians, ascribe self-existence to the Father alone, and subordinate the Son to Him, they desire to establish thereby the possibility that the Son Himself may subject Himself to mutation and growth, conformably to which He is considered to be τρεπτός.[1] We shall only have to insist in this matter, that what is posited by the free will of God, and has not in itself necessity of being, is a creature and not God. Therefore the majority of the more prominent recent theologians[2] stop at the position that we are united in

[1] Just as Arianism taught. Many of this tendency desired, indeed, to maintain in that doctrine the identity of essence of the higher principle in Christ with God, but without bringing it to cognition that to this principle self-existence belongs in the last resort.

[2] *E.g.* K. J. Nitzsch, Twesten, J. Müller, Martensen, Sartorius, Liebner, Lange, Voigt.

communion with Christ, not merely with a subordinate being, but with God Himself.

3. But whether the two sides, the Divine and the human, are perfectly thought or not, the main problem remains, the UNION OF THE FACTORS themselves, which must take place diversely, indeed according to the categories under which the Divine side, to which the initiative attaches, may be thought.

*First.* THE PHYSICAL UNITY.—The formula of Daub and Marheinecke is: " the Divine is the truth of the human, the human is the realization of the Divine." Since the identity of the two is presupposed, the Divine is thought to be the potency, the human the act; and only the substantial pretendedly Divine, and not merely the nature of man as receptive of God, is regarded, a position which would not be essentially different from that of Strauss. For although to the latter every man is of God-human nature, he still seeks for Christ a progressively higher position, inasmuch as he calls Him a religious genius. The distinction between Christ and all others will of course only become more earnest, if, whilst Strauss does not for a moment ascribe sinlessness to Jesus, the acknowledgment is made with Vatke that actual sin did not attach to Jesus. Yet better Marheinecke and Daub, on the contrary, deny even His inherent sinfulness. Strauss merely gives us a renovation of the ancient Hellenic, *i.e.* Pantheistic Ebionitism. The physical, unethical character of this mode of thought is shown in the fact that, on account of the nature or the capacity, it would have all men thought to be God-human, as if the actual personality of man, his moral character, were not essential to the definition of his worth. But the nobility of man cannot lie in that alone which is his nature; he is a historical nature (a being with a history). If the worth of man is measured by his substantial nature simply, the fool would be as the wise man, and the saint as the transgressor. But the physical character of Strauss's mode of thought is also shown in the fact that he regards God as a quantity which divides itself into individuals, so that God is not supposed to be able to pour out His fulness into an individual, unless others are supposed to be diminished in spiritual contents. He would rather have it that the individuals together supplement each other to form moral perfection, or rather the æsthetic beauty of the world, whence, if the necessary need of completion is also related to the disposition, and not merely to the work, it would follow that moral perfection generally surpasses the idea of human personality.

*Secondly.* The LOGICAL UNIO would be when the human and Divine become one in *knowledge*, inasmuch as the Divine nature is conscious of itself in the human form, and thus knows itself as human and the human as Divine. But the question arises, whether an identity of the two is meant by such a view, or simply a unity of distinct natures? If they are distinct, the consciousness which embraces both must mirror this distinctness, and we do not thus learn how they are united. If they are not distinct, the identity of nature is presupposed, and this would merely be the previous view in a logical application.[1] But the Divine and human are not immediately one, as the doctrine of creation already shows. Higher stand—

*Thirdly.* The theories which, presupposing a distinction between the Divine and human natures instead of their identity, seek an ETHICAL UNIO. As we know, the ethical may be either thought in a one-sided manner under the type of the justice which guards distinctions, therefore of self-preservation or the preservation of distinctions, or may be thought just as one-sidedly under the type of self-communication, unless a way be found which unites both. As far as the first is concerned, God, according to Günther, is distinguished from man, and therefore the Divine nature of Christ is distinguished from his humanity, as the lord and lawgiver from those who are under obligation, without a relation of nature between them. Instead of the absolute self-communication of the love of God, who does not lose in communicating Himself, we simply come in this case to relations or references between the two natures, not to an actual unity of person. To Günther Christ is only a "joint-nature (*Vereinwesen*)" of two persons, the Divine and human,

---

[1] To this place belongs the Christology of Hegel, inasmuch as he sees in Christ the man who first recognized his nature to be Divine, and in whom God first knew Himself within humanity.—Even Biedermann might claim his place here; but we devote to his noteworthy inquiry a special investigation later on.

who coincide in the two-sided will and consciousness. They include each other, the Logos knowing Himself to be the Lord of this man, and this man knowing the Logos to be his Lord. But halt is made at a merely external relation between the two, as is suitable to the stage of law or right: a self-communication to humanity is not reached; therefore we may call this Nestorianizing Christology the *juridical*. Though, therefore, for the time of growth the distinction of the human side and the Divine may appear strongly, still this process must have the perfect union, the absolute God-humanity for its goal, and this process must from the commencement start from the fundamental fact of the self-communication of God to the human nature. Finally, also, the process of the unifying must not be regarded one-sidedly as the work of the humanity of Jesus, or as a reward for its virtue. This would be false ethicism. The *Unio* is rather to be considered at every step as a Divine act as well, which saturates the ever open receptiveness of the human nature of Jesus by means of the self-communication of the Logos.

If the juridical *Unio* points back to earlier standpoints, because it knows no real self-communication of God to humanity, and thus allows both to stand apart from each other, the MODERN KENOTIC VIEWS would, on the other hand, assert the more strongly the other side of the ethical nature, the self-communication or surrender of God to humanity. A series of notable theologians[1] attach themselves to this view with manifold variations. The most simple form of the Kenotic theory, which also appears the most appropriate, in order to vanquish the ancient Dualism with which the doctrine of the two natures was commonly infected, and to attain an actual living unity in the person of Christ, taught that the Logos is capable of growth and is mutable according to His essence, being thereby distinguished from the Father, who alone has self-existence; that the Logos has passed into

---

[1] *E.g.* Liebner and his pupils, Hasse, Thomasius, Gess, Ebrard, Kahnis, König, v. Hofmann, Luthardt, Delitzsch, Besser, Gaupp, Schmieder, Steinmeyer, Hahn (junior), Oehler, Plitt, Wörner, Bushnell, Godet, Edm. de Pressensé, and others. Exegetes: Meyer, Weiss (Phil. 2), Riehm (Heb. ii. 4, 10). Comp. my treatise *Ueber die Unveränderlichkeit Gottes, Jahrb. f. deutsche Theol.* i. pp. 377, etc., and Rothe, *Dogmatik*, ii. § 22, etc., pp. 149, etc., 154, etc.; Hahn, *Dogm.* ii. pp. 187-189; Schenkel, *Dogm.* ii. 2, pp. 693, etc.

human form, has Himself become the Son of man, who appears in the form of a servant.[1] He has, it is thought, by emptying Himself, brought Himself into the form of existence, from the commencement of which He has lived wholly according to the laws of human development, until, having attained its end, this development re-conducted Him to His original form. This would be the theory of the *self-mutation* of the Logos into a man.[2] Such a conception of the distinction between God and man would lie at the basis of this view, that God is only the perfect man, and is at least in Christ the man who becomes God, and the distinction would therefore be merely a quantitative one. For a human soul, and for an actual humanity generally which is itself more than the bare form of the manifestation of the Deity itself, there would remain no place. This Christology does not rise, therefore, above a theophany in human form. In order, then, not to regard a mere adventitious addition in Christ, the human form with the laws of development of human nature, to which the Logos has subjected Himself,—as the humanity, it is said by some that the Logos is in Himself—because He is the archetypal form of humanity—to be called the eternal humanity in God (a view which Apollinaris also held), which, after the previous self-emptying, entered into the form of growth.[3] Although, in improved form, this theophanic form is Apollinarian. The actual, substantial humanity, assumed from our race, would in this case, side by side with the human laws of development, be merely the body with which the humbled Logos arrayed Himself. In this case it was of course no longer necessary to ask how two unities thought as persons could become one person. In a mere theophany the Logos alone is presupposed as internal in Christ. But after it had been noticed[4] that in Apol-

---

[1] So Ebrard, *Dogm.* ii.    [2] Comp. above, § 93. 2.
[3] So Plitt and Gess. Even Liebner and Thomasius did not teach at first a human soul of Jesus. Gess wishes to distinguish himself from Apollinaris. Certainly, according to Gess, the Logos did not so represent the human soul that He was Himself mutable, but this will only make a distinction to the favour of Apollinaris.
[4] *Reuter's Repp.* 1846, in my review of Thomasius. Comp. also my treatise, *Ueber die Unveränderlichkeit Gottes*, in the *Jahrb. f. deutsche Theol.* 1856, pp. 378, etc.

linarianism no actual humanity appears, but that, when the growth of the humbled Logos has attained its end, then necessarily a return of the self-restored Logos into the Deity has to be assumed, and the becoming *man* has therefore to be withdrawn (because it is supposed to exist nominally side by side with the body, in the form of the self-renunciation of the Logos); further, that Christ would thus be of a nature foreign to us, because without a human soul; later on, Thomasius and Liebner came to the resolution to accept a human soul of Christ as well, whilst retaining the Kenosis of the Logos, and consequently to renounce that very gain of their Kenotic theory which they had in view in the same theory, namely, the advantage of attaining in the manifestly easiest way an actual God-human, living unity, and of removing the difficulty of thinking a personal human soul in unity with the Divine hypostasis. Others, on the contrary, like Gess and Plitt, persist with more consistency in the standpoint essentially of Apollinarianism and Theophany.—The theory of Thomasius and Liebner was framed, after their acceptance of a human soul, in the following manner. The Logos, they say, by virtue of His almighty love, has emptied Himself to the point of the humiliation, which could make itself equal to the beginnings of a human embryo, and did not exist any longer thenceforth outside of man.[1] But in the measure in which the latter developed, and parallel therewith, the Logos has again exalted Himself to actuality at the prompting of the Holy Spirit, until He was restored to Himself. The Holy Spirit is admitted, because, if the impulse to His self-restoration originates in the Logos, His self-humiliation would not be perfect, and the Logos must rather stand at all times above Himself as depotentiated.

But in this theory the humanity and the humiliated Logos stand opposed to each other in Christ with a parallel development; and since parallels never join, as is known, nothing at all is done in this theory for the unity of the person, and the self-renunciation of the Logos accordingly appears as an idle as well as forcible addition, only adapted to destroy the Trinitarian conception of God. If one member of the Trinity for the time of the growth of Christ stoops to mere potenti-

[1] This will require an *exæquatio* for the *Unio*, which the *F. C.* rejects.

ality, and therefore suspends His preserving and governing activity, the Logos becomes not mutable merely, but also superfluous in reference to the Trinity, and holds therein a merely casual position, all which leads to a subordinationism. Others therefore say, as Besser does: the act of self-kenosis is not to be thought as momentary, but continuous, so that side by side with the emptied Logos, who is growing to potency, there always stands, not an emptied, but an active and self-emptying Logos. But although this is not a self-destructive thought, we should have thus a double Logos, and the humanity would not be united at any rate with the actual, but at most with the emptied Divine. In this expedient Thomasius has sought to interest himself, seeing that, even after the Kenosis, he speaks of a Logos above the line "of the God-human development." But in such a case there is simply repeated, in reference to the Logos, what happened with the Swabians in the time of the Reformation with respect to the humanity. For as they arrived at a double humanity instead of the unity they sought,[1] so we should have here a double Logos, one who has renounced Himself to enter into humanity, and one "above the line" who has not so renounced Himself; the formula "*totus Logos in carne*" would be surrendered in a more suspicious manner than when it was assumed that He was not from the beginning *totaliter in carne*, and is also not divided into the duality of a renounced and a non-renounced Logos. In order to meet the objection that his theory, instead of serving the living unity of the Person of Christ, even annuls the unity of the Logos Himself, Thomasius subsequently restricted his view to this: The Logos has only surrendered the relative Divine attributes, *i.e.* those which have reference to the world, for the state of humiliation,— the omnipresence, omnipotence, omniscience, etc. But the objection to this is rightly taken,[2] that omniscience does not permit Him to remain standing half-way; for it is also knowledge of God and the world. If the Logos then had surrendered the knowledge of God, He would not have surrendered a merely relative attribute, but one essentially

---

[1] This double humanity Gen. Sup. Brömel von Lauenburg assumes anew in his letters to Thomasius, 1857.

[2] Gess, *Lehre von der Person Christi*, 1856, p. 312; Philippi, iv. 363.

Divine, and it would violate the idea of God; but if He had retained His absolute knowledge, self-kenosis and its aim would be surrendered, according to which the Divine side is supposed so to empty itself, until it no longer reaches beyond the human, but rather is perfectly equal thereto. For the human soul cannot have from the beginning perfect knowledge of God. A renunciation of knowing by volition is also in itself unthinkable. For by willing to forget a knowledge I have, I have thought it again. So is it also unthinkable that actual love should surrender itself from love. And generally the opinion, that the Logos can retire to sleep, is contrary to the doctrine of the universal Church of the ἀναλλοιώτως and ἀτρέπτως. It is an error when Thomasius thinks this theory to be new; rather has it been proposed by the Valentinians and a section of the Apollinarists, and in the Reformation time by the Anabaptists; and it has always been repudiated, in specially severe manner by the *F. C.*[1] Nor does it lie in the straight line of the Lutheran development, seeing that it fails to attain the living unity of the person side by side with the true humanity. For although the Logos might so diminish Himself that He might no longer extend beyond the humanity of Jesus, we should only have in such a case, as has been said, two equal wholes and two parallel series of developments side by side, but the actual bond of unity would only have to be still sought. The whole apparatus of the supposed self-kenosis is therefore unfruitful. This bond is rather to be sought directly in the Logos as self-communicating, and therefore surpassing the humanity, whilst Thomasius seeks to set that aside with much trouble as the presumptive hindrance to the *Unio*, which is alone in a position to form the starting-point for a

---

[1] P. 612: Rejicimus etiam damnamusque, quod dictum Christi, Matt. xxviii. 18: "mihi data est omnis potestas in cœlo et terra horribili et blasphema interpretatione a quibusdam depravatur in hanc sententiam; quod Christo secundum divinam suam naturam in resurrectione et ascensione in cœlos restituta fuerit omnis potestas—perinde quasi, dum in statu humiliationis erat, eam potestatem, etiam secundum Divinitatem deposuisset et exuisset. Hac enim doctrina non modo verba Testamenti Christi—pervertuntur, verum etiam dudum damnatæ Arianæ hæresi via de novo sternitur, ut tandem æterna Christi divinitas negetur, et Christus totus—amittatur, nisi huic impiæ doctrinæ ex solidis verbi Dei et fidei nostræ fundamentis constanter contradicatur. Comp. 773. 49.

living union of one who is at once communicating and receptive. Therefore there are ever more and more who withdraw from this bypath,[1] which, in order to gain for every element of the life of Christ, not so much the complete living unity as the absolute balanced equality of the Divine and human, imputes the most violent sacrifice to the idea of God itself, makes God as Son a τρεπτόν, and forgets that the aim of the incarnation cannot be an always complete and perfect living unity, but rather the self-communication of God as Logos to the humanity. Self-evidently this communication is governed by the measure of the receptiveness for the latter at the time, but demands for the entire process, that the Logos as communicating should have more than the receiving humanity in its growth. The absolutely perfected God-humanity can only possibly be the result of this process.

It is not much to be wondered at, if from the perplexing thicket of the thorny hypotheses of a Kenotic theory, in opposition to the 18th century Christology of the Church, many should long to be free, and to seek to reach the open by recurring to the simple lineaments of the dogma, whether on the ground of feeling, or cognition, or will.—The justifiable opposition of Jacobi and Schleiermacher to an intellectualism which was beclouding religion, side by side with conceptual thinking, has not remained without influence,

---

[1] *E.g.* Kahnis, *Lutherische Dogmatik*, ii. 82, acknowledging the objections to the laying aside of Divine attributes, thinks that the Logos has retained these, but that the idea of finitude has an elasticity, the Logos can also contract, finitize His infinite personality, and He exists in Jesus as a finitized Ego. The answer to this is : either this Ego must be a person in an equal sense with the humanity, in order to be perfect ; but we have then two Egos : or the Divine Ego is the substitute of the human, which view again inclines to Apollinarianism. Besides, if Kahnis for the unity of the person will not be satisfied with the fact that the finitized Divine Ego is in the stead of the man Jesus (*Unio localis*), he has to give an account how the totality of the Divine attributes, in the possession of the exercise of which the Logos is supposed to remain, agrees in the unity with a growing man, ii. pp. 597, etc. The same is to be said of Zezschwitz, *Zur Apologie des Christenthums*, p. 335. If, finally, it is said (Keerl, Nösgen) that the Logos has only surrendered His δόξα, and maintains His Divine actuality, the peculiar problem would not yet be touched. If a Christology is possible without a surrender of the Divine attributes or personality, even the surrender of the δόξα of the Logos is not requisite, which is not taught in John xvii. ; were it necessary, what the common Kenotic views require, would be far more requisite.

to which the fall of the great speculative systems at the commencement of the century not a little contributed. Thus it has happened that to many all knowledge of Divine things appeared impossible, nay, that the banner of Agnoeticism (if not of a double truth) was raised to avail with a certain pride, and at the same time with a claim to humility. Thus it has been, not merely in England where this tendency has been long spread,[1] but also in Germany.[2] But when war was declared[3] with metaphysics, whether generally or at least in theology, the only sphere still left for knowledge was the empirical, although, since Kant could not be forgotten, such empirical cognition limits itself only to a knowing of our mental representations, and therefore became subjectivistic enough. The empirical itself may be thought materialistically or ideally. German science is always striving after the ideal. But if a *knowing* of an objective ideal world or Divine world[4] is still denied, what is left of knowing is reduced to investigation and description of certain psychological facts which, without containing in themselves what is true, may be mere phantasmagorias arising in us.—In order, therefore, not to permit all objective truth to vanish in the abyss of Nescience, or to fall back on the mediæval contrast of a double truth, *others* again make an earnest endeavour to gain a firm standpoint for knowing, whether it be that, starting from the certainty and inner objectivity of the Christian spirit, an attempt is made to avoid what was blameworthy in the speculative method at the beginning of this century;[5] or whether it be that a knowledge is built in a Neo-Kantian manner upon the empirical deliverances of the moral consciousness, and even a kind of doctrine of God is sought to be derived from this empiricism.[6]

---

[1] The pupils of Sir Wm. Hamilton, who were so regardless of consequences, may be mentioned, Dr. Mansel (*The Limits of the Religious Thought*, comp. my remarks on him in the *Jahrb. f. deutsche Theologie*, 1861, pp. 320, etc.), and also Stuart Mill and Herbert Spencer's *Unknowable*.

[2] To this class Lange, *e.g.*, belongs (in his work on Materialism, vol. ii.), Lipsius, H. Schultz, Hermann, and many others.

[3] Pre-eminently to release Christology from the Trinitarian connection as well as from the relation to the world-whole.

[4] As, *e.g.*, happens with Lipsius.

[5] The most noteworthy defender of this former tendency is Biedermann.

[6] Thus A. Ritschl.

There must still be some delay upon Biedermann and Ritschl;[1] and that the more indeed that both have regard to the more recent critical movements which have originated in Strauss and Baur, and regulate their dogmatic positions upon Christology by what they regard as historically tenable, in order that a harmony may be shown between the empirical, or the historically demonstrable, and the image of Christ which faith includes. We first inquire into what is characteristic of the Christology of Biedermann.

The idea of the incarnation of God was brought into recognition by the philosophy of Schelling and Hegel in the third and fourth decades of this century. This was wont to be thus expressed: It is essential to the idea (or the Deity) to enter into finitude, to sink itself into finitude as its other being, but in order to elevate itself again eternally thence and to restore itself to itself, which process is completed by the finite spirit coming to itself in its absolute essence, or consciously apprehending itself in its essential unity with God, and thus by knowing itself to be God-human. The Deity, inasmuch as He submits Himself to this universal and continuous process, and undertakes the lot of the finite, but in order to eternally posit Himself as Spirit and as absolute knowledge, is also then called the ideal Christ. But in such a conception of the incarnation the historical importance of the founder of the Christian religion was manifestly dissipated, and His historical personality was made something incidental, contingent, similarly to what Jesus was for the Kantian idea of humanity as well-pleasing to God; at most there remained for the historical manifestation the meaning that it was a symbol of that universal and eternal idea, which was alone thought to be the effective, acting power in history—by no means merely within the limits of Christendom.

If, then, Christology was thus dissipated in the universal, ideal Christ, the necessity was, on the other hand, given for the Christian Christology, — of emphasizing the historical personality of Jesus, and for a few decades the watchword was: "The '*historical Christ*' in opposition to the '*ideal*

[1] Not in Lipsius, who in all leading Christological formulas appeals literally to Biedermann in spite of the hiatus between their standpoints.

*Christ,*' or rather to the Christ of Idealism."[1] To this the whole tendency of the spirit of the age was favourable, since this was beginning to turn from Idealism, indeed from all speculative Philosophy, and to put its trust in empirical methods and investigation simply. This direction of thought has created for the life of Christ, and the historico-critical investigation of its sources, a literature of such an extent and richness as has been seen for the first time in the history of the Christian Church. According to the nature of the case, the human side of Christ—the person of Christ and its historical efficiency[2]—must come into the foreground in these inquiries.

The prevalence of this empirical, historical tendency had as consequence, that even Idealism itself could not wholly forsake its influence. The remains of this doctrine, which of course always became more sparse, itself repudiated as inadequate the formula of the "ideal Christ;" it approximated to the "historical Christ," inasmuch as, within that process which embraced humanity, it sought a unique position for the historical Jesus of Nazareth. Thus Biedermann. Jesus is not to him merely the first man who has attained to conscious unity with God; by means of His person, His self-consciousness, which He transmitted to men by His teaching, or even by means of His example; He has also become the originator and founder of the new community which knows itself to be in unity with God. The formula, which would express this significance of the historical Christ, " the historically primitive realization of the union of God with humanity in Jesus,"

---

[1] Remembering the universal significance the Church attaches to Christ, and also in traceable connection with the previous lines of thought of Idealism which depreciates history as such, and puts the idea in its place, some have sought an attachment to the historical Christ, by seeking to think of the latter in Himself as the race or humanity, and not as an individual, in a manner analogous to those coruscating, vague representations which were presented previously concerning Adam as the generic unity or as humanity. To this class belongs Göschel, according to Marheinecke; even Philippi sought to so far share in this view, in order to give a substitutionary significance for the race to the obedience of Christ, and gave the anhypostasia of the humanity of Christ the meaning that he became no individual, but humanity. Still he did not repeat this later.

[2] In which the distinction between the idea of Christ κατὰ σάρκα and κατὰ πνεῦμα is too frequently forgotten. Comp. my letters to Dr. Ehrenfeuchter and Dr. Martensen, *Jahrb. f. deutsche Theol.* 1874, especially pp. 575, etc., 609, etc.

was now: the *Christian principle*, or the basis in fact (*Realgrund*) of the Christian religion, *i.e.* the union of the Divine and human nature, in order to the realization of personal human life into history, or more accurately, has entered with His consciousness of the Divine Sonship or the "Fatherhood of God."[1] The relation of the historical person of Jesus to the efficiency of the Christian principle which has entered with Him into history, and which historically starts from Him, and consequently the significance of Jesus for entire Christianity, is not merely external and accidental, but internal and permanent. For that principle, he thinks, not merely consisted in a doctrine newly handed down by Jesus, and the person of Jesus did not give the impulse to the entrance of that principle mediately simply. Rather does it seem to him that the personal religious life of Jesus is the first self-realization of that principle so as to form a world-historical personality, and this fact is the source of the efficiency of this principle in history. He regards Jesus as the historical revelation of the redemptive principle, as the historical Redeemer. Therefore the person of Jesus is immediately for all time, he says, the world-historical guaranteeing example of the efficiency of the principle of redemption, for which reason he attains the permanent place in the doctrine of the Church and of the means of grace, seeing that the exposition of the historical Gospel of Jesus Christ is the fundamental vehicle of all Christian proclamation of salvation.[2]—Nor does Biedermann wish to favour an Intellectualism, so high does he place the true and certain knowledge, that is that which originates in the innermost self-consciousness and unites itself with the Spirit of God, as compared with mere theories of feeling and mere Empiricism. He would maintain the right of phantasy, mental representation, nay of heart, to a place in religion. But, on the other hand, he also certainly says, that Jesus Christ is not to be called the principle of Christianity, but the new, *religious* principle of the Divine kinship or Divine sonship. This new principle has, he thinks, of course been able to reveal itself merely as a new *personal* self-consciousness. Therefore it happens, he says, that in the com-

[1] Biedermann, *Christl. Dogmatik*, §§ 788–844, especially § 800.
[2] *Ibid.* §§ 815, 816.

munity of believers the consciousness of what is newly opened for them in the personality of Jesus must express itself in the form of statements upon this person himself, as if this individual, finitely historical personality were *identical* with the principle of Christianity. But the identification of the Christian *principle* with the person of Jesus Christ, is, as the history of the dogma shows, the fundamental contradiction upon which every solution of the Christological problem must be wrecked.[1]

This theory admits the Divine kinship or the Divine Sonship of Jesus in time prior to all other men; but the principle of the same, wherein the essence of Christianity is contained, seeks the same realization in all men. The same thing is to be indeed conceived, it is said, as pre-eminently a religious principle, not a metaphysical truth merely concerned with the ideal cosmical relation of the absolute and the finite, or the anthropological relation of the Divine to the human. But still this religious principle is also, it is said, of a metaphysical kind, and this metaphysical consideration is requisite for the adequate conception and expression of the contents of the Christological idea.[2]

Human spiritual life is supposed to be already in itself a God-human life; but it is only in the human personal self-consciousness of the absoluteness of the spirit, in the absolute religious self-consciousness, that the principle of God-humanity enters, which is in itself immanent in man as finite spirit, into the actuality of the life of humanity.[3] This actuality of the absolute religious self-consciousness, or of the Divine kinship, is certainly not the work of Jesus Christ; it is not He, but the Christian principle, which is the redeeming agency; but also the religious community, or the Church, is not to him the Redeemer, nor the efficient bearer by itself of the principle of redemption; he requires for the existence of the actual

---

[1] Biedermann, *Christl. Dogmatik*, § 817; comp. §§ 790, 602, etc.

[2] *Ibid.* § 793.

[3] *Ibid.* §§ 797, 798, 802. The unity of the Divine and human in the finite spirit which exists of itself does not yet satisfy Biedermann, and rightly; with such a unity we only have natural humanity, which with its religious destiny falls into a naturally necessary discord (see vol. ii. p. 367), from which it cannot of itself issue. In this strait only the effective power of the Christian principle can help, which then becomes the principle of redemption.

Divine kinship the efficiency of the absolute spirit, *i.e.* of God as Father, and an immediate union with Him in consciousness, feeling, and will.[1]

In close connection, therefore, with speculative philosophy, especially that of Hegel and Schelling, Biedermann has striven to frame by that means a Christology of a more satisfying kind for the Christian consciousness in this way, that he thinks the Christian principle of Divine Kinship or Divine Sonship enters as the living power into the historical personality of Jesus, and sees therein the revelation in fact of the principle of redemption for natural humanity, of course independent of His individual person, of the Divine will, of love and the Divine Fatherhood.[2]

Finally, the Christology of Ritschl is to be discussed.[3] He would hold it as pure as possible from the speculative standpoint or metaphysics, inasmuch as to him the world of the *will* is rather the main fact, and knowledge a somewhat subordinate matter, and therefore he is wont to be numbered amongst the Neo-Kantians. What is characteristic of his Christology consists in this, that in order to commend again or to make accessible a higher estimation of the person of Christ to the common consciousness of the present, he cuts

---

[1] Remark, § 800 : In the absolute religious self-consciousness the absolute spirit is the generative ground of a spiritual life realizing its own absolute spiritual nature outside of it in the creature ; on the other hand, man finds in the same the ground of his own nature and life in the Divine self-exclusion of God in reference to him (*i.e.* in the kinship, comp. §§ 803-805).

[2] The distinction of the "Christian principle" from the historical Christ, and the designation of this principle as the Divine kinship or the consciousness of the Divine Fatherhood, many recent theologians have appropriated, *e.g.* Lipsius, *Lehrb. der evang.-protest. Dogmatik*, ed. 1, 1876, ed. 2, 1877, §§ 552, etc., 620-655, and my notice of the same in the *Jahrb. f. deutsche Theologie*, 1877, pp. 177, etc. Further, Hermann Schultz, *Die christol. Aufgabe d. protest. Dogm. in d. Gegenwart, Jahrb. f. deutsche Theologie*, 1874, 1, and my reply, 1874, 4. (In a more independent manner, Lang, *Versuch einer christl. Dogmatik*, § 35, ed. 2, and Pfleiderer, *Religionsphilosophie*, 1878, pp. 683, etc.) A special presentation of the Christology of Lipsius is, after what precedes, superfluous. It is true that Lipsius is distinguished from Biedermann by the resuscitation of the æsthetic Rationalism of Fries-Jacobi. But scientifically considered, Lipsius offers a far less clear and independent position than Biedermann. The case is similar with H. Schultz.

[3] In reference to what follows, Book iii. cap. iv. and vi. pp. 170, etc., 339-410, of the *Christl. Lehre von der Rechtf. und Versöhnung*, especially come into consideration.

off from the established Christology everything which could bring it into collision either with the natural sciences, or with the laws of historical writing or with historical criticism. Therefore not merely is the pre-existence of Christ combated *retrospectively*, but even the so-called early history is abandoned to criticism; indeed, a dogmatic assertion on the origin of the person of Christ, or its peculiar, original constitution, is not ventured for a moment. We should, he thinks, merely have the materials therein; and this is a bare possibility; and the rough sketch would still not explain the reality of the Christian life. The latter may suffice, if every one becomes what he becomes by himself absolutely—possibly taking into account external historical influences. — And *prospectively* he renounces the whole Christological eschatology, —the Second Advent, the doctrine of Christ's personal judgment of the world. His positive significance, he says, is not to be apprehended from His person, but conversely His person is to be apprehended from His work, which is to be placed under the ethical point of view of the call He followed, substantiated as it was by the issue as pertaining to Him.[1] This call, according to Ritschl, had for contents the grounding or founding of the Church or the kingdom of God, *i.e.* the uniting of men for the purpose of a conquest and domination of the world, therefore for freedom and for communion of love amongst each other. From the consideration of His works, which corresponds with the Divine purpose of the world, there follows immediately, it is true, only the *ethical* estimate of Christ; He is the man, whose will is perfectly in harmony, nay, is identical with the Divine purpose of the world, and who in the most persevering surrender has prosecuted His call. But this ethical conception passes over, he thinks, into the *religious* conception, such as is maintained in the New Testament and in the Christian community. The religious conception does not look to the fact of human freedom, but presupposes the act of God. The same conception guides to transferring to Christ the attribute of God-humanity, in the first place, namely, in the sense that in Him the loving purpose of God in the world has come to full

---

[1] Ritschl overlooks the fact that the self-presentation of Christ, as well as His work, reveals Him.

revelation, and is continued in the community which pertains to Him, and therefore He is called the Word of God which has become a person. Secondly, the attribute of Deity is also ascribed to Him in the religious conception, in the sense that what fulfils His will is destined to become an impulse and power over the whole of humanity, and therefore the meaning of that attribute is dominion over the world.

Certainly these expressions lose much in importance, if thought is bestowed upon whether a Divine act is actually to be *known* in the manifestation of Christ or only to be believed in the power of the religious conception. For the latter the repeated definite statement speaks, that we have not a knowledge of a doing of God, nor can we have. Further, the peculiar dignity of Christ is limited in no narrow measure by the oft-repeated canon, that we cannot ascribe Divine attributes to Christ simply analogically from the attributes applicable to ourselves. For Christ, he thinks, there is always thus assured the historical position pointed out,—as the first, who can have no second after Him, even granting there may be a successor fully equal in himself to Him. In this statement it is betrayed with special clearness, that it cannot be regarded as the proper sense of the often varying speech of Ritschl to say, that an original and permanent uniqueness belongs to the person of Christ as contrasted with the whole of humanity, which stands over against Him, as its Redeemer, as that which is to be redeemed, but that, as in the case of Biedermann and Lipsius, so in that of Ritschl, the person has only a contingent significance side by side with what the former more clearly designate the Christian principle.

And if the further question is asked, whether Ritschl presents us with a better scientific guarantee at least for this image of Christ which has been so reduced, this is scarcely to be answered in the affirmative. It is certainly well said that Christ has chosen the Divine purpose for His life-purpose. But whence has Ritschl a *knowledge* of what is the Divine purpose in the world, seeing that neither Scripture, which he partly subjects, *e.g.* in the case of Paul, to a sharp dogmatic criticism, and would have judged in relation to canonicity by the Old Testament, nor the doctrine of the Church, nor immediate experience, which has to him but a small value as mystical, nor philosophical speculation, can communicate such certainty? Thus, to establish that the life-purpose of Christ was identical with the world-purpose of God, no other course is left, than to find with Kant the scientific necessity of the idea of God, or more accurately, " Of the scientific hypothesis of the idea of God," by the method of moral proof.[1] In the subsequent course of his argument the good Divine will becomes for him the will of love; indeed, he protests that the " Essence of God " is love, although this essence must still belong to Metaphysics. And it is also insufficient to stop at the fact, that he does not place the love in a clear relation to the remaining Divine attributes, and that he is unable to give to justice its appropriate place, with which it is connected, that his idea of the fatherly love of God contains something of weakly, general benevolence. (Compare iii. 238.)

But has Ritschl laid a strong foundation for the *ethical* dignity of Christ at any rate? He acknowledges this without dubitation, and sees in Christ the archetype or primitive norm. But whence comes this knowledge to him? If all knowledge of Christ's person comes to us from His working, and His life-work is the founding of the Church of God, there is no course left to him but to build the conviction of the dignity of Christ and of His constitution upon the fact of the founding of the Divine community and the Church. But what is this Divine community which he would distinguish from the Church? If he is unable to specify as a historical magnitude precise limiting characteristics in reference to it, by which it is recognizable and that as actually existent, it remains, like his " kingdom of God " too, a hazy idea, standing scientifically far beneath the Evangelical idea of the *Ecclesia invisibilis*. Again, where does the Divine community show upon earth its archetypal character in recognizable manner? So far as it appears in the empirical world, it shows schisms and unresolved contentions upon what constitutes the essence of Christianity.

[1] The preferable course of proof Kant rests upon the fact of our spiritual life, that although nature follows other laws than those of the spirit, still the spirit esteems itself the power over nature, and nature as its means. This must be a false imagination, unless the spirit so leads in harmony with the supreme law which prevails in nature. "For then the ground of this can only be recognized in a Divine will, which creates the world for the final end of the spirit's life," iii. 192.

These dissonances cannot be passed over dryshod, as if they were unimportant, or without testing according to fixed principles can it be brought to decision scientifically what is Christian truth, and in what the benefit Christ brought consists.

But as accordingly the image of Christ left to Ritschl is by no means securely placed, we must also say finally, that it is itself adequate neither to the New Testament nor the faith and need of the Church. The most disturbing feature in this view is, that by Ritschl's image of Christ no care is taken to preserve a living continuance of working of Christ, which would be more than the after-working of His doctrine and image. Rather are we confined in the historical past of Christ by the excision of the Christological eschatology, instead of fostering the living connection of His person with the Church of the present and future, and faith in His abiding presence with His own in the Word and in the Holy Supper. If we regard the living continuous influence of the person of Christ merely as an enthusiastic representation, all mention of the attributes of Deity pertaining thereto, of His universal dominion, etc., becomes an unmeaning hyperbole.

It remains worthy of notice, that Ritschl asserts with energy the ethical in relation to the image of Christ, His call and the connection of His person with the kingdom of the good, *i.e.* of God. His opposition to a *merely* physical or metaphysical or one-sidedly religious conception of Christology is well grounded. Only on the other side two things are to be remarked. *First*, in his work the peculiarly religious relation, the reciprocal living communion between God and man, recedes very far, side by side with the relation of man to the world and humanity, equally as piety does not itself form again an essential side of the moral life. It may, generally, have connection with his rough refusal of Mysticism. On the whole, religion pre-eminently appears to him to have the significance pertaining to heart and trust only, which, where the consequences are independent of us, form a condition of joyful work and success. *Next*, he is unable to really unite the religious and the ethical consideration. The religious view regards the humanity as the form, in which the Divine material, so to speak, was coined, so that this form might be looked upon as the revelation and manifestation of the Divine essence, *i.e.* of grace and truth. In reference to the ethical consideration (according to which the human side of Jesus is the *self-dependent* form of all its functions, and in correspondence with the historical reality as well as with a necessity of thought (iii. pp. 381, 382)), the dependence of the free and self-dependent does not come into view, he thinks. We are not in a position to know enduringly the dependence of Christ on God from the Divine standpoint; we must alternate between the *moral* judgment, which expresses the ethical self-dependence of Christ in the scheme of human freedom, and the *religious*, according to which God is not merely with Him, but in Him, His acts are Divine effects, His love is identical with God's love.—This exposition, which requires that we see alternately now (and indeed customarily) only the man Jesus and His ethical Ego, and now, on the contrary, that we see the dependence on God and the Divine act in Jesus only as in a means of revelation, itself confesses by consequence its imperfection and incompleteness. At least the compatibility of the two modes of view must be explained by Ritschl, in order to make their objective consistency clear. Wherever he makes a few attempts, as in passing, to establish the compatibility of the ethical and religious view, there is much in Ritschl's exposition which approximates to a pure theory of immanence, or to the opinion that all human morals are identical with the Divine life, without its becoming clear how the permanent distinction between God and the creature still maintains its right.

### C.—*Dogmatic Exposition.*

### § 99.—*Survey.*

We must endeavour to avoid the evils in the customary arrangement of the Christological material, in order to gain as simple and consistent an image of Christ as possible.

1. The customary mode of treatment divides Christology into the doctrine of the Person of Christ in itself, into that of

the two states, and into that of the office or work of Christ. But the doctrine of the Person would be incomplete without a doctrine of the two states. And the separation of the office from His Person favours a conception, which darkens what is given to us in Christ, because it does not regard Him Himself as the centre of His gifts to humanity, as the highest good of the world. Even His personal perfection extends through His official life, so that it is evident that the doctrine of His Person cannot be brought to an end of itself, and apart from His work.

2. These shortcomings will be avoided, and the doctrine of the Person of Christ will be presentable in a more connected manner, according to its fundamental features, if we divide the material in the following manner:—

FIRST SUBDIVISION.—The PRE-EXISTENCE OF CHRIST on its *Divine* side.—Here we treat of the eternal Word of God; next of the efficiency of this Divine principle in creation and in history, especially of religion and revelation.

SECOND SUBDIVISION.—The PRESENCE OF CHRIST ON EARTH, or His temporal Parousia in the state of humiliation, in increasing external humiliation, together with increasing internal Transfiguration.

*First Head.*—The act of the incarnation of God in Christ, or His *God-human nature.*

*Second Head.*—The *ethical God-humanity*, or the doctrine of the holy God-human personality.

*Third Head.*—The *official God-humanity* of Christ, or His God-human functions on earth, in which He presents Himself as the Redeemer (His prophetic, high-priestly, and kingly vocation).

THIRD SUBDIVISION.—The POST-EXISTENCE OF CHRIST, or the Person of Christ after His earthly course (Descent into Hades, Resurrection, Exaltation to the right hand

SURVEY. 281

of God, in which the continuation of the threefold
office in heaven ends in the consummation of His work
and in the universal judgment).

LITERATURE.—Compare pp. 257, etc. Bertholdt, *Christologia
Judæorum*, 1811. Schleiermacher, *Christl. Glaube*, ii. Göschel,
*Beiträge zur speculativen Philosophie von Gott und dem Menschen
und vom dem Gottmenschen*, 1838. Jul. Schaller, *Der historische
Christus und die Philosophie*, 1838. Casimir Conradi, *Christus
in der Gegenwart, Vergangenheit und Zukunft*, 1839. Frauen-
städt, *Menschwerdung Gottes*, 1839. König, *Menschwerdung
Gottes als eine in Christus geschehene und in der christlichen
Kirche noch geschehende*, 1844. Wegscheider, *Institutiones*,
ed. 8. Carl Hase, *Evangelisch - protestantische Dogmatik*,
1826; ed. 5, 1860. Hahn, *Lehrbuch des christlichen Glaubens*,
ed. 2, vol. ii. pp. 140, etc. Nitzsch, *System*, ed. 6,
1881. Beck, *Christliche Lehrwissenschaft*, 1840; ed. 2, 1877.
Peip, *Christosophie*, 1858; compare also his article on the
Trinity in Herzog's *Real-Encyklopädie* and his *Religionsphilosophie*. Thomasius, *Beiträge zur kirchlichen Christologie*,
1845; *De obedientia Christi activa*, 1846; *Christi Person und
Werk, die Person des Mittlers*, ii. 1855; 2d enlarged edition,
1857. Liebner, *Die christl. Dogmatik aus dem christol. Princip*,
i. 1, 1849. Von Hofmann, *Schriftbeweis*, 1857, 1859. F. A.
Philippi, *Der thätige Gehorsam Christi*, 1841; *Kirchliche
Glaubenslehre*, iv. 1, 1861. F. v. Rougemont, *Christus und
seine Zeugen, übers. von Fabarius*, 1859. H. v. d. Goltz, *Die
christl. Grundwahrheiten*, 1873, pp. 134–255. Pease, *Philosophy of Trinitarian Doctrine*, 1875. H. B. Smith, *Faith and
Philosophy*, ed. Prentiss, 1877. Goodwin, *Christ and Humanity*,
1875. Horace Bushnell, *Christ in Theology*, 1851; *God in
Christ; The Person of Christ; The Trinity*, etc. (compare my
*Geschichte der Christologie*). R. Wilberforce, *The Incarnation*.
Const. v. Schätzler, *Das Dogma von der Menschwerdung Gottes
im Geiste d. h. Thomas*, 1870. Weisse, *Philosophische Dogmatik*,
iii. pp. 795–885, 1862. Schenkel, *Christliche Dogmatik*, ii. 2,
1859; *Lehrstück*, xiii., xiv. pp. 643–790. Schweizer, *Die
christliche Glaubenslehre*, i. 1863; ii. 1, 1869. Biedermann,
*Christl. Dogmatik*. Lipsius, *Lehrbuch der Dogmatik*, 1875; ed.
2, 1879. Rothe, *Theologische Ethik*, ed. 1, vol. ii. pp. 279,
etc.; his *Christliche Dogmatik*, edited by Schenkel, 1870, ii. 1,
§§ 13, etc. J. P. Lange, *Positive Dogmatik*, 1851, pp. 595, etc.
Martensen, *Christliche Dogmatik*.

*Observation.*—The incarnation of God is a mystery, as is
the relation between soul and body, and still more the

relation between God and the world, the most speaking expression of which is just the incarnation. No theory therefore will be quite adequate to this matter, and after having critically surveyed so many theories and found them unsatisfactory, we have moreover a strong warning for ourselves against surmises and premature satisfaction. But the critical survey has yet undeniably shown a manifold augmentation of knowledge, and thus no age ought to hide its talent. It is faithful if it does honestly what it should do. But it does so, if it removes those difficulties, which are the pressing ones for the given stage of knowledge, and which disturb the origin of faith or its certainty, and places that side of the image of Christ in clearer light, for which the eye is open. It is true that in all the uncertainty upon the more delicate definitions of dogmatic Christology there is also still a series of positions which the Christian Church of all times holds to be unquestioned, whilst others belong more to the school, and therefore their recognition may not be demanded by the Church. And, indeed, the establishment even of the former for the planting and fostering of faith may strike most gravely upon seeming contradictions, and faith can neither endure contradictions in itself nor with intelligence, rather must a restless reaction against the formation of faith issue therefrom. It is therefore the life of faith not to suspend inquiry until the perfect solution is found. As little as we postpone the taking of meat and drink until we have perfected beyond contradiction the theory of assimilation on its objective and subjective side, dare we delay the laying hold of spiritual sustenance, do we delay faith until the work of science is completed. This work is still itself dependent in turn upon an even more perfect standing in the element of truth, which faith lays hold of so far as it commends itself to its moral confidence, not as mere thoughts, but as a reality. Faith is not a mere product of cognition (*credo quod intellexi*), it has its own self-dependence also as opposed to cognition (§ 12); its religious certainty does not arise from any theory, but from the experience of the power of the object with which faith brings into connection. The contrary would be an intellectualistic conception of Christianity. Simple faith is to be presupposed, as for the whole of Christian doctrine, so especially for our subject, and the same may continue in spite of seeming contradictions, because frequently enough a higher stage of knowledge finds the form for two apparently self-excluding truths which contains the unifying word of solution. And to retain this hope is morally possible to faith so long as the impossibility of the compatibility of what is apparently contradictory is not proved, and so long as it possesses the powerful impulse to remove in honest and robust labour the difficulties which press. From this self-dependence of faith, which makes it sure of its facts, even with a knowledge which is still imperfect, there follows the duty which is not always sufficiently recognized, to reject by ecclesiastical authority only such Christological doctrines as make the origination of faith impossible, because they exclude by their image of Christ the fundamental fact of redemption by Christ, and all are to be considered as fellow-workers and not antagonists whose doctrine acknowledges this fundamental fact.

## FIRST SUBDIVISION.

### THE PRE-EXISTENCE OF CHRIST.

§ 100.

The incarnation of God in Christ, the necessity of which the first part of the System of Doctrine has proved, must be evident on a new side, because of the doctrine of sin in its necessity and significance. On the one hand, the incarnation is a miracle, *i.e.* an original and immediate Divine act; but on the other hand, instead of dismembering the system of the universe, it produces and serves its establishment and final consummation. This result happens because the Divine principle which perfects revelation even to incarnation, is the same which is already working in the pre-Christian time in the history of religion especially, and indeed even in the creation, the Logos, who also communicates the eternal self-revelation of God, in God, for God. Only by this knowledge of the pre-existence of the Divine principle working in Christ is the incarnation of God in Him known according to its central meaning, reaching to the depths of God and the world. The *possibility* and *necessity* of the incarnation generally has its final basis in God as holy love; for its *realization* and its necessary form, the pre-Christian history of humanity and revelation comes into regard as the presupposition. When the time was fulfilled, God sent His Son.[1]

*Observation.*—Comp. §§ 31-33. The doctrine of the pre-existence of the higher nature of Christ is now especially a frequent object of assault,[2] whilst rightly handled it is the doctrine of the living, real possibility and necessity of the incarnation, and at the same time is that whereby the second creation can livingly attach itself to the first. The dignity of the God-man also first comes into its full light, when He appears on the one hand the goal of the first dispensation, and when on the other hand the whole race is destined to be appropriated by Him. He is the centre of the history of the world, who sends His rays backwards and forwards to enlighten, because by relation to Him everything is organically combined into the unity of a universal plan.[3] He *appears* in the fulness of time, *i.e.* when the possibility of His manifestation existed because of the receptiveness for Him historically prepared on the ground of creation and government, whilst the living potentiality, the productive ground of the possibility of the incarnation, was eternally in God. But He appears, in order by His historical realization to be the permanent determining principle of a new epoch. We consider in detail first the eternal pre-existence of the higher side of Christ in God, or the connection between Christology and the Trinity; secondly, the pre-existence of the Logos at the creation of the world; and thirdly, in the history of religion and revelation.

1. The connection between Christology and the doctrine of the Immanent Trinity.

The Christian consciousness, having itself attained to clearness as to its own contents, needs to conjoin the doctrine of the Person of Christ with the Christian idea of God, that is, the Trinitarian. For Christian faith knows God to be dwelling and living in Christ truly, perfectly, and in unique

[1] Gal. iv. 4.
[2] And the views thereupon are not without influence upon the treatment of the Johannine question.
[3] Col. i. 18; Eph. i. 20, etc.

manner, and humanity in Him as united with the Deity eternally, as the Deity is in Him. But this knowledge only harmonizes with the idea of the eternal God, if there is given in God Himself a real and eternal ground of the possibility of becoming man in the special mode of being (Hypostasis) which He has eternally in Himself, and which is perfectly revealed in Christ. If, namely, the incarnation of God in time had not its eternal, real ground of possibility in God as the Word, and if God had not an eternal self-disposition for incarnation in Himself, incarnation would be an absolutely new thing for God Himself (even for His thought and volition); God Himself would be mutable, and the incarnation simply something contingent to Him, and coming from without; mutability would not only affect the action of God, but even His being, because the Scriptures as well as Christian faith do not see in Christ a Divine act merely, nor do they even see in Him a power working upon Him, after the manner of prophecy or inspired men, but a unique being of God of eternal duration produced by a Divine act. Christian faith bears in itself the necessity of thinking the being of God in Christ as essentially different from the presence of God in the world generally, as varying even from the being and dwelling of God in believers. For as the word speaks of faith *in* Christ, Christ has for the Christian religious significance, because, bound to Him, he knows himself bound to God and God present in Him, and that as redeeming and perfecting, and in Him exclusively. Ebionitism, that mode of thought which sees in Christ only a creaturely nature, be it never so high, contradicts the Christian consciousness; for a creature could not be our Redeemer and Perfecter, a creature would be a dividing mediator, a *contradictio in adjecto*. Against such a Christology everything would avail which the Evangelical Church urges against the worship of saints. A mere creature cannot be the object of religious adoration or invocation, and the Christendom of all ages has repudiated the adoration of a man, but has yet known and practised an invocation of Christ, or of God in Christ, and in Christ's name, and is in this matter at one with primitive Christianity. That there is in Jesus a special indwelling of God, and not an influence merely of a Divine power upon Him, even Sabellianism acknowledged in the form again assumed by Schleiermacher, and thus stands upon a ground which does not simply maintain the appearance of what is Christian, but certainly bears a Christian character in itself, inasmuch as Schleiermacher at any rate confesses to an economical doctrine of the Trinity, although he also thinks himself compelled to maintain a simplicity of God in Himself which knows no distinctions, and therefore repudiates an immanent Trinity.[1] We must also so much the more acknowledge Sabellianism as a Christian mode of thought, that the knowledge of the immanent Trinity must always issue from the economical Trinity, from history. He who maintains the latter, has therefore won the basis or the starting-point, which logically leads to the immanent doctrine. And the breadth thus given is to be the more maintained to be the rule of the Church, that on the one hand the treatment of the idea of the simplicity of God is defective and incomplete in almost the entire ancient Dogmatics, does not coincide with the Ecclesiastical doctrine of the Trinity, and yet enjoys a wide diffusion in the common mode of thought; and on the other hand, since Evangelical piety starts with the world of revelation, and therefore with the revealed Trinity, with historical redemption and justification, first laying hold upon this point of Christianity with precision, and does not start with the doctrine of the immanent Trinity. For it is only from Anthropology and Soteriology that Evangelical religion rises to the true knowledge of the Trinity.—On the other hand, it is to be as definitely said, that although a Christian character must not be always refused to the Sabellian mode of thought, Theology cannot halt there. It has been shown in the ancient Church, and also after Schleiermacher, that either advance is to be made therefrom with the ancient Church to immanent distinctions in the internal Divine essence, and specially to the belief, that there corresponds to the peculiar and permanent being of God in Christ an eternal determination of the Divine essence; or else the peculiar being of God in Christ is allowed to fall, and recourse is had to a mere Divine influence upon the man Jesus, or to a being of God, like that which is found in other believers, especially in the perfectly righteous, recourse being made therefore to Ebionitism. If, namely, the dignity of Christ

[1] Comp. vol. i. pp. 400, 401.

which distinguishes him is actually found by the Sabellian mode of thought in a peculiar being of God in the Redeemer, only at the price of recurrence to eternal distinctions in God could it be avoided, that this special peculiar being of God, because not based in the essence of God, should be derived from the world only, *i.e.* from the peculiar receptiveness of the humanity of Jesus for the Divine nature, which is everywhere absolutely identical, therefore that it should be put upon him, so to speak, from without;[1] whilst nevertheless that special individuality of the human receptiveness is rather referred to God, or to the Divine counsel to dwell in the individual activity of humanity in Christ. If, on the contrary, it is recognized that this varying receptiveness of the world has its ground itself in God, indeed that a receptiveness for a special and eternally lasting mode of being of God in Christ must be willed, it will follow that this mode of Divine being must be before this receptiveness, because such receptiveness is prepared in humanity for it and through it, so that this special mode of Divine subsistence not merely exists according to a subjective conception, but is objectively and eternally in God, different from the being of God, which did not become man, distinct also from every other being of God in the world. And we are thus relegated to the internal essence of God as the foundation of the perfected revelation of God in Christ.— Just as little can halt be made at the mode of thought which came into vogue after Schleiermacher, assuming that God was originally in Himself without distinction as Father, and that He has only made Himself triune in reference to the world, or, having become so both for the world and through it, He has only willed His essence to be triune out of love to the world.[2] This would lead back to a mutation in the essence of God itself; add to which, that what is constituted by the will of God, falls into the circle of the creature. But inasmuch as there accrued to the Divine in Christ a personality from the world because of its circumscription, a capability of suffering

[1] Compare vol. i. p. 370.
[2] Thus Christlieb, *Moderne Zweifel*, 1870, pp. 266, etc., and similarly von Hofmann; Weiss in his six *Vorträgen über die Person Christi*, p. 158, thinks, after the manner of Beryllus, that His hypostatic distinction only pertains to the Divine, as it is in Christ, from the Person of Christ, which circumscribes the Divine in Him and lends Him human personality, so to speak.

would be supposed in God. Although in these views the endeavour to demonstrate a special mode of Divine being in Christ is to be recognized, they do not assume that what is definitive or formative for the same has its ground in the eternal essence of God, but derive it from the idea of the world, or from the real world which circumscribed the Divine essence, and thus violate the immutable perfection of the Divine essence; God is thought to be a material which He shapes according to the need of the world, or allows to be shaped or personified from the world. Such personality borrowed from the world by God in Christ, or increasing by such means, is only the anthropological antithesis to the ancient doctrine of a personality of the humanity of Christ borrowed by the Logos from, and having a suspicious relationship with, the pantheistic modes of thought which make God to attain personality in men. If it is once conceded that the idea of God permits distinctions in the Divine essence, what shall hinder the supposing them eternally in God, instead of making them arise first for the sake of the world, or through the world in any way and its finitude,—a view which must lead back to God, unless a Pelagianizing self-dependence and freedom be attributed to humanity, which effects its apotheosis? The Divine immutability as well as the special mode of being of God in Christ remains secured, if we say, in harmony with Christian faith, that the pre-Christian Heathen and Jewish idea of God has been especially transcended by means of Christianity at the impulse of Christology, because in the one Divine Being, the personal archetypal Spirit, eternal distinctions are known to be assumed as equally necessary, although their more intimate constitution may always be concealed from us,—distinctions which are also presented in the world of revelation, seeing that God, not something else, has willed to reveal Himself therein. What is characteristic of the God-man is therefore not merely a special receptiveness for a being of God in itself eternally without distinctions, whether this receptiveness be produced by creaturely freedom, or by a constitution of the world otherwise independent of God; but this receptiveness is produced by God for the mode of the being of God as the Logos present eternally in Him and willing to reveal itself, the eternal Divine image, which becomes the fulfilment of the receptiveness in question, which is of course also unique.[1] There answers to the Divine in Christ a distinction of God Himself in His eternal being, and consequently the centre of the Christian religion is established in the eternal essence of God Himself, as it corresponds with its absolute character, which simple faith already perceives in its fashion. The absolute God-man is not a transient Divine manifestation, as the old Sabellianism taught, which has no simultaneous Trinity; nor does he introduce a change in God Himself which has first entered in time, but what is supposed to accrue to the Deity only in time apparently, is really an eternal predisposition of Himself, to reveal which belonged to His purpose of love from the beginning.

*Observation.*—The doctrine of the eternal possibility of the incarnation is overstrained by the supposition of an eternal actuality of the same, of an eternal God-humanity in God, to which Beyschlag's theory has an inclination, and which Goodwin, and also the Quakers and others, teach in their manner. And the necessity of eternal distinctions in God is overstrained by Arianism and Subordinationism, and generally by the supposition that personality pertains to every one of these distinctions in the same sense, as to the one absolute personality which is first constituted through them, or as to an individual human personality. Little intuitive knowledge as we possess of the mystery of the internal essence of God as distinct in itself, still we know that God is one, and that this unity is not an impersonal essence, as the idea of a genus is in itself impersonal, and only becomes personal in the single individuals which present it. For this would be Tritheism. To apply the idea of genus to God would be polytheistic, and is repudiated by the Athanasian Creed. Accordingly we may say with John of Damascus:—The one Divine personality has three τρόπους ὑπάρξεως, and is in these in threefold manner—it is a threefoldness. Definitely as we must connect our doctrine with the Trinity, and that in such a way that a special mode of Divine being may be permanently complete and indeed proper to humanity only in Christ, we must as definitely, unless we would create insuperable difficulties for Christology and the unity of the Divine Person, hold ourselves aloof from the Tritheism which makes of the Trinitarian distinctions three individuals, to whom God is the mere generic idea, and which

[1] Col. ii. 9.

therefore deprives the one God of personality, or passes over into Tetradism.[1]

2. If, as has been shown, the Christian consciousness is internally necessitated to rise for the grounding of the Person of Christ to the internal Divine essence, the question must be asked in the second place, how the Divine Essence is compatible with the fundamental Christian fact, *the incarnation of God*, how this fundamental fact is *possible*, as well as whether it is permissible to speak of a necessity for the same originating in God. The same question is then to be considered from the side of the humanity.

The *possibility* of the incarnation of God would have to be denied, if God were simply the abstractly simple Monad, for in that case He could not be master of Himself, and therefore could not complete the act, by means of which, without losing or changing Himself, in accordance with an eternal purpose, He gives Himself a being in unity with humanity, a being which He did not previously possess. Further, in close connection therewith, incarnation would not be possible, if its sense were that the one absolute personality in its three modes of existence, and thus in its totality, has become man even transitorily. But this has never been the opinion of the Church, as was already shown in the struggle with the so-called Patripassian tendencies. It is not God in His absolute totality who has become incarnate; here also the doctrine of the immanent Trinity enters and elucidates, disclosing the possibility Monarchianism lacks. For by virtue of the fact that God is distinct in Himself, He can preserve Himself

[1] See vol. i. p. 385. Even Philippi says with justice (ii. pp. 142, etc.): The Divine Essence is God Himself as the absolute Holy Love, so that, inasmuch as we suppose only one Divine Essence, we consequently suppose only one Holy Love, only one Eternal, Almighty, Omniscient, we do not at all acknowledge and reverence three Eternals, Almighties, etc. (similarly Frank, *System der christlichen Wahrheit*, pp. 392, etc.). If, then, the one Divine Essence is for us identical with the one self-conscious Holy Love, we shall only be able according to this reasoning to speak of one understanding and one will, only of one self-consciousness and one self-determination or freedom in the Godhead. He appeals on this point to the Athanasian Creed as well as to Carpov. Three self-consciousnesses and three freedoms one would not wish to teach, he says, in the Deity; it is only needful to make the attempt to immediately acknowledge that it cannot be said. If, moreover, the Church speaks of three persons in the Godhead, it does not associate with the word person the same idea as we are wont to associate with the word to-day.

in self-communication without self-detriment, in Himself permanently being and working even without Himself; according to one side of His essence, He can even communicate and reveal Himself, whilst He is and remains at the same time in Himself (namely, as that to be revealed). In fact, the Christian Church also teaches that the incarnation is indeed the will and act of the triune God, but that the incarnation does not extend to the one and entire absolute personality of God. The self-communication can notwithstanding remain an absolute self-communication, since the absolute God Himself is in each of the hypostases or modes of being only in different manner. It is more accurate to say: Not the Father, not the Holy Ghost, but God the Son, God as Logos becomes man. The Father is the primary basis and absolute commencement of the Trinity, He becomes manifest by means of the Son, His absolute, objectified image. The Father represents in the Trinity, which has no mere physical and logical but also an ethical necessity, the primary basis, the original truth and the holy nature or the ethically necessary. On the other hand, the Son is the principle of the Divine movement, in logical, ideal relation the principle of revelation, objectivation, in ethical relation the principle of freedom, whilst the Holy Spirit as the third principle re-conducts the circle of movement from the opposite to its commencement, and thus becomes in relation to the world the principle of immanent, proper living spirit, intellectually and religiously the principle of internal certainty, ethically the principle of the proper internal sanctification in free conscious loving impulse.[1] Thus the will of incarnation can be immediately carried out as little by the Holy Spirit as by the Father. It is not an incarnation of the Holy Spirit as well as not of the Father. The Holy Spirit is in God as well as in the world the potence which re-conducts the distinctions to unity; consequently His work can everywhere only begin, when the distinctions, which would be united, are already supposed; and the distinctions will be supposed by the objectifying Son or by God as the Logos, both in the world and God. The former is the creative Word, places the eternal internal world-thought of God in objective realization as a relatively independent thing distinct from

[1] Comp. § 31 b., vol. i. pp. 420–447.

God, but also an infinitely manifold thing, and distinct in itself by means of a characteristic individuality. The Holy Spirit, on the contrary, perfects indeed ever deeper unions with God, but always solely on the ground of the activity of God as the Logos which constitutes its distinctiveness and independence, and therefore which objectifies the thought of God.

This His objectifying work only reaches its goal, inasmuch as He attains the organ for His full realization in the world, for His central revelation. In the Son of man, the Son of God can become the image of God realized in the world, the world has attained the acme of its objective realization as opposite to God. In Him the creation is first consummated, the world as an objective, absolute value by absolute receptiveness, is given as capable of God, but in such a way that with this highest point the beginning is made of the personal union of the world with God, of the re-conducting of humanity to God, by the incarnation of the Logos. In this the Divine Principle of union, the Holy Spirit, must of course be also regarded as effective, but not in such a way that the Holy Spirit represents the Logos, but that the effect of the central self-revelation, *i.e.* of the incarnation of the Logos, is in Jesus, that the Holy Spirit Himself passes from the Logos to the humanity of Christ Himself, and by the execution of the union of freedom with the ethically necessary up to the point of the perfect interpenetration of both, Christ becomes the historical punctual source of the Holy Spirit (see § 105. 3).

The Son is the eternal principle of freedom, progress, history, but of freedom which is required by the ethically necessary of itself. Therefore God as the Logos, or as the universal principle of revelation, first reveals the presupposition of all freedom of the creature, or reveals the necessary, and therein the Father. So it is in the creation, and its dependence upon immutable laws of nature; so it is in the moral *law* of conscience and the Old Testament, to which then the physical and moral dependence of man on God corresponds. This that is ethically necessary, Christ also everywhere presupposes; He always looks back to the Father's will as to the ethically necessary. But His task is, like His will, to transform law into freedom, under which He is made (Gal. iv. 4) in the joyous obedience of a son. In Jesus, God as Logos attains the position in which He can reveal Himself as He Himself is, as Divine Freedom in a human life.

The incarnation of God as the Logos is certainly not to be in any way represented as physically necessary for God. God does not need in Himself incarnation in order to His self-realization. Whilst in His internal being potence and act are given as eternally alike, the incarnation is a work of the will of love. But love is not caprice. According to its nature, love cannot be satisfied with the mere opposition of the world to it as a second thing. It would appropriate the second thing, and would give itself perfectly to be appropriated. Thus God is not satisfied with the blessedness and majesty He has in Himself. From the beginning He has willed the second to himself, the world, in order to communicate Himself thereto, to be manifest for it and in it, and to dwell in it for its glorification and blessedness. The almighty power of the Divine Love makes the world a mirror of the Triune, and would unreservedly communicate the fulness of Deity to humanity, without any other limitation than that of the logically and ethically impossible. The self-existence of God, in which God as Logos also participates, cannot of course be immediately transmitted to humanity, but can only be reflected by the latter on the basis of what is constituted, in so far as the power of self-reproduction has been bestowed thereupon. For everything else, on the contrary, the communication of which is not prohibited by the idea of God, humanity forms no limitation. The will of perfect self-communication also has the power to create for itself an adequate organ (comp. § 62).

*Observation.*—Perfect, and therefore also personal, humanity could certainly not become one person with an individual personality like to it, and just as little with the one absolute personality of God; but this is by no means required even by the idea of incarnation, since the Logos of Himself is neither a person in the same sense as the absolute Divine personality, nor as an individual man. So it has been shown that God does not become man in all His three modes of being, *i.e.* as the absolute Divine Ego, as the absolute Divine Personality. But it is only the Deity as Logos that becomes incarnate, although God as the Father and Holy Spirit dwells in Christ. Thus, therefore, a double Ego cannot arise in Him.

3. Even in the creation and in the history of religion, the efficiency of God as Logos has its relation to the incarnation (comp. §§ 62, 65).

This consideration aids the verification of the incarnation as possible and necessary, even starting with the *world*. In creation the first concern indeed is with positing a different, relative, self-dependent being opposite to God; but, on the other hand, creation from the beginning reckons upon a consummation. Humanity was not to remain a fragment, but God created man in His image, and holiness, love, wisdom, and therefore Divine life, are especially supposed to be therein, the perfect expression of which the God-man alone is. The New Testament shows the Divine likeness to have become real through the Son, the Divine image.[1] The first Adam is a type of the future Adam.[2] He points, by what he lacks as well as by what he already possesses, namely, receptiveness for a higher something, to this future Adam, in whom the higher something will be given. He can only become pneumatic by means of the Lord from heaven.[3] Thus every individual already points to the perfect Divine revelation by shortcoming and receptive capacity. And even on the side of the community it is the same. Destined to become a perfect organism, humanity needs and expects for its consummation the head; indeed, according to the apostle, Christ is the centre for all spheres of creation and all rational beings.[4] If in him and in him alone God is wholly manifest in the world, He is manifest in him for all spirits, and is their unifying centre. It has been shown previously, that the world with its lability could only have been created, with its sin could only have been preserved, with reference to the God-man. The eternal idea of Him destined to realization it alone was, which could be surety for God as the creator of a free world, that, although fallen, it should be still worthy of conservation and be redeemable. Tertullian rightly says that, in creating Adam, God already looked to the *Imago Christi futuri*. Indeed, the creation of nature already has a relation, though mediate, to

---

[1] Col. i. 15; 2 Cor. iv. 1, etc.     [2] Rom. v. 14.
[3] 1 Cor. xv. 45, etc.; Eph. i. 9, 10.     [4] Col. i. 30; Eph. i. 9, 10.

him who would be the point of unity in the universe. In opposition to hatred to nature, to hatred to art, science, and state, it is important for the healthiness of Christian piety to be assured of this, that the first creation, if sin be left out of view, is not with its vital laws alien, but friendly, to the Christian principle, is a type or symbol of its manifestation. Even prior to Christ, God as Logos is efficient in the world, and (with Christ) does not come into the world from without or abruptly. " In Him was life, and the life was the light of men." In Christ, a relation already begun comes to consummation. But it is not every human individual who is able or destined to become God-man by the Divine self-communication, but only the humanity of Jesus is by its signal organization, endowment, and preservation, the consecrated place where the God-humanity can come to realization. The creative power of the Divine love was able to prepare in the sphere of human nature, and in a selected place in the same, a universal or central receptiveness, such as the Divine love and wisdom desired, which only thus attains a central unique revelation in the world.

Finally, a glance must be taken at the connection of the efficiency of the pre-existent Logos with the history of humanity, especially with the history of religion.

Conscience and freedom form the starting-point. The Logos creates even the historical preparation for His manifestation by the implanting and education of the consciousness of the good and holy will of God, and by constituting the corresponding form for the ethically necessary, freedom. By the two together the need for His manifestation and full revelation is aroused historically.[1] The Logos, the universal Word of God in men, calls them, so to speak, to the Logos in Christ, to the God-man.[2] In reference to this point of view, law and prophecy move together, however different they otherwise are. Even the law points to a future which shall be absolutely in accord with the holy will of God,[3] and in the prophetic promises the same Divine will continues which was directed in the giving of the law to the realization of the Divine will. But in neither is there any realization of the incarnation of the Logos, but only an ideal being of the Divine in humanity. The Divinely Good

[1] Gal. iii. 24.   [2] Comp. John v. 38.   [3] Rom. iii. 21.

revealed in both has begun to unite itself with the *knowledge* of men, but still stands opposed to the will and the being of the same. The Logos Himself, the Divine Principle of Freedom, still remains without incarnation, although He advances from the shadowy outlines and symbols He presents to knowledge to ever more precise disclosures of His approaching manifestation in the world.[1] Thus the doctrine of the ancient Fathers of the Logos σπερματικός, who made Christians even prior to Christ, lacked authorization, as did the no less premature and unhistorical view of many teachers of the Church, that the pious of the Old Testament already possessed by prophetic anticipation the same as Christians.[2] The sacrifices of the Old Testament brought no atonement as yet to what was innermost in man (to the συνείδησις); therefore also no permanent atonement;[3] they merely had reference to single offences, and guaranteed the certainty that there was no expulsion as yet from the theocratic community, but a share still in its blessings, and especially its promises. The forgiveness of sins is to be understood in a similar way, of which the pious speak in the Psalms especially. The possession of the pre-Christian time could not therefore satisfy or weaken the desire for the manifestation of Christ, but necessarily enhanced it. The totality of men was not yet changed in the inward parts. The spirit of the new birth and kinship issues from Christ, and although Israel as a unity, or the king as the representative of this unity, is called son, still the individual is not yet called a son or child of God in the New Testament sense;[4] it is Christianity only which is the religion of freedom through the Son who makes free.[5]

On the contrary, it is a suitable task for Christian science to know the universal power of the pre-existent Christian

[1] Matt. xi. 11–13; John viii. 56.

[2] This is opposed to John viii. 56, vii. 39, and the doctrine of the Hebrews of the τελείωσις through Christ. Rom. iv. does not say that Abraham has the same as the Christian, but he was well-pleasing to God in his faith, because on the way to the N. T. he was receptive also for the future acts of God. He enjoyed peace, so far as he needed it, in the undeveloped consciousness of sin prior to the Law.

[3] Heb. vii. 11, 19, οὐδὲν ἐτελείωσεν ὁ νόμος, ix. 9, xi. 40.

[4] Delitzsch on Ps. lxxiii.

[5] John viii. 32; 2 Cor. iii. 17; Rom. viii. 21; Gal. iv. 22, etc., v. 1, 13; 1 Pet. ii. 16; Jas. i. 25, ii. 12.

principle and His efficiency, even in the heathen world, and thus to bring to light the truth in that thought of the Fathers respecting the labour of the Logos even in pre-Christian humanity.[1] Especially in reference to heathen philosophy may it be mentioned that the ideals of the highest good, of virtue and duty, it presented, and which were concentrated in the Stoa most livingly to form the image of the wise man who is the king, contained a kind of substitute for what was given to the Hebrew people in the Law, and especially in the Messianic ideal. But it is not casual that we hear nothing of a priestly ideal on the part of this philosophy. Hellenic morals would not base upon atonement, penitence, and conversion, so much as in trust in the proper noble nature and freedom. The religious residue, which might possibly have withdrawn from the superficial conception, was volatilized later on at the same time with the belief in the mythology, and sought a morbid satisfaction in a mixture of religions, and in a mysticism which lost itself in the empty infinity of the ″$Oν$ and its own apparent sublimity, but was almost deprived of the ethical impulse. Israel therefore remains the centre of all preparation for the God-man.

4. However important it is to divest the manifestation of the God-man on the earth of the appearance of a mutation in God or in His purpose, and of the abrupt in relation to creation and pre-Christian history, the novelty and originality of the manifestation of Christ ought to be just as little removed.

The Divine purpose is related, indeed, not merely to an action or influence, but to a unique mode of Divine being in the world, for which an eternal self-disposition, corresponding to that mode of being, exists in God by means of the self-determination of His love. In such eternal self-determination to incarnation is preserved the true element in the ancient doctrines of a heavenly humanity, or the Adam Cadmon. But the false element therein is the assumption of an already real humanity in the eternal sphere, by which the earthly humanity of Christ would be made semblance, and only something eternally fact would be shown, not anything new to be realized. Christ would in that case be an alien in our race, universal pre-existence would then be assumed.

---

[1] This point has been already generally treated in the First Part, § 65, etc.

In the *creation*, further, the working of the pre-existent Logos might be so thought, that in Adam the germ of the God-humanity already was, the will of the incarnation attempted to be realized already in him, but was frustrated by sin, whilst in a normal development the psychical Adam would have become the God-man by immanent progress.[1] But the apostle insists, in opposition to such an immanent development, that[2] the creation of Adam and the manifestation of the Lord from heaven are two different Divine acts, which are successive only. The opinion is also exceptionable, that the God-humanity has been so implanted from the beginning in the human race, that Christ was only the product of the productive power of empirical humanity. Rather is a new Divine act requisite for his production, and indeed such an act, as is more than the bare " release "[3] of a germ already existent from the beginning, but still hindered in its emergence. To the latter view the Traducian doctrine is related: *Christum naturaliter exstitisse in lumbis Adami.* As in Adam all human germs were already from the beginning, so also was the soul of Jesus; and in spite of the Fall, through all generations the pure *massa adamitica* has been miraculously preserved and transmitted, until the time came when a man pure of soul and body might issue from Mary.

The ground of such views lies in the Augustinian requirement that the whole creation should have taken place in a moment on God's part, and the motive is a false conception of the Divine immutability and its relation to the world. Like the unity of the world, the latter is secured for us by the unity of the all-embracing Divine purpose, without our having to change on its account the efficiency of the secondary causalities into appearance in an acosmistic manner, or obliterating on the other hand the qualitative difference of the Divine productions by contracting the same into one act.

Finally, as far as the efficiency of the Logos in *history* is concerned, the incarnation is here again anticipated, if with Tertullian and others, even some recent writers,[4] incarnations

---

[1] Thus Thomasius thinks Adam has been destined to be the historical head of humanity.
[2] 1 Cor. xv. 45.  [3] Comp. K. Schmid, *Darwinismus*, 1876.
[4] *E.g.* Steinwender, Hengstenberg.

or "exercises" in incarnation in various forms are seen in the Old Testament theophanies. If the Logos entered into other incorporations, *e.g.* in angels, this would lead to a very external relation to humanity. Each of these revelations would become a mere theophany in changing dress. Others allow that by the sacred history the elements of the pure humanity of Christ were gradually won in Israel, or assume even in Abraham the sinking of the germ of the God-humanity into the Israelitish people, which was then efficient in its history, and made symbols or types of its real manifestation which were ever more definite.[1] Lange thinks that by the Divine cultivation of Israel its natural basis was so sanctified and consecrated, that in the series of continuous births, birth and new birth coincided more and more by virtue of a hereditary blessing.[2] The God-human elements which have been formed by a series of consecrations have then been gathered in Mary. Even Olshausen speaks of a holy line, in which the incarnation was prepared, as Michael Baumgarten speaks of the fleshly pre-existence of Christ in Israel.[3]

All views of this kind tend to prejudice the novelty of Christianity, lead to a redemption and sanctification of men by the Logos instead of by Christ, and indeed prior to the manifestation of Christ, and for the purpose of aiding the production of Christ by the productive power of humanity before Him. Such a series of thought culminates in the Romish dogma of Mary's immaculate conception free from inherited sin. As opposed to all, we must maintain that pre-Christian humanity is not so productive as to generate Christ; it is still impure, unredeemed, non-united to God; it does not transcend the category of susceptibility for God. But the preparation of humanity for Christ is to be ethically thought, consists in the consciousness of sin and the longing for salvation, and may not be transposed into a physical process, which can only lead to fruitless speculations.

[1] M. Baumgarten, *Comment. z. Pentateuch*, i. 63. 2, 9.
[2] *Pos. Dogmatik*, pp. 325, 453, 467.
[3] *Comment. z. Ev. Matth.*

## SECOND SUBDIVISION.

### THE INCARNATION OF GOD, OR THE TEMPORAL PRESENCE OF CHRIST ON EARTH.

§ 101.—*Relation of the Ideas of Conservation and Creation to that of Incarnation.*

The God-man is neither the mere product of the conserving nor of the creating activity of God, nor finally does He come by virtue of the self-positing of God as man; but He is a *new creation* which presupposes and conjoins itself with the first creation, and in such a way that conservation and new creation become elements of a higher something into which they enter. This higher something is the *Incarnation* of God in Christ, and Christ is constituted the infinite commencement of a new development, namely, of the perfected participation of humanity in the Divine life and spirit.

1. The Scriptures have three kinds of designation for the Divine act affecting humanity in the person of Christ.

*In the first place,* God has appropriated humanity, or has assumed flesh and blood therefrom, by participation,[1] in order to dwell in it.[2] The assumptive act of God was then described by dogmatics as *assumptio humanæ naturæ*. In this case the human nature of Christ is thought as already given for the Divine act, namely, by the race, in Mary, and it is included in this view that the Divine act attaches itself to the *conservation* of the world.—But the prophets are also momentarily, and Christians as children of God are permanently, adopted by God. In them also God desires to dwell and walk.[3] God is also on His side personally everywhere present and efficient. If halt is therefore made at the mere

---

[1] Heb. ii. 14: μετίσχιν αἵματος καὶ σαρκός.   [2] 2 Cor. v. 19; Col. ii. 9.
[3] John xiv. 17, 23.

category of *assumptio* and indwelling, and the two words merely express a relation of God to the world *given* to Him, what is peculiar in the manifestation of Christ does not find expression; we do not come to anything specifically new, and incarnation would only be a figurative mode of speech. In this case the Logos only has or bears a man; He has not become man. God would not then have so appropriated humanity to His being, that this man was the manifestation of the Divine image actually in the world. This conception would not have decisively vanquished the Ebionitic tendency as yet, and therefore the Epistle to the Hebrews has still other designations.

Of a higher type, therefore, is a *second* mode of expression, which does not see in Christ a nature out of the Adamitic world merely, upon which God exerts an influence in *assumptio* and indwelling, but the product of a new creative act of God. According to this mode, Christ owes His existence itself to a supernatural Divine act. It belongs to this class, when Paul calls Him the second Adam, or when he calls Him begotten of the Holy Ghost by the power of the Highest.[1] —But no single man even comes to exist, because only the species, the world of conservation, is productive. Side by side with the Traducian factor, or the co-operation of the world of conservation, Creationism and Pre-existentianism also has its place in the origin of every man; for every man is so highly esteemed, that God co-operates creatively in the origin of his soul, that he is a special and eternal creative thought of God.[2]

It might then be said that there is in Christ a *new*, higher *creation* than in Adam. But even Christians are called a new creation.[3] By the formula that Christ is a new creation, we should indeed have secured His miraculous origin, but not for a moment His permanent purity and freedom from sin. If He were a new creation simply, He would manifestly be no more than a creature, and this statement would again incline to Ebionitism, although to a higher form of the same. Were then, nevertheless, the idea of the Divine indwelling

---

[1] Rom. v. 14; 1 Cor. xv. 22, 44, etc.; Luke i. 35; Matt. i. 20.
[2] Comp. vol. ii. pp. 93, etc.
[3] 2 Cor. v. 17; Jas. i. 18; John i. 13; 1 Pet. i. 23.

superadded, and were it said that in Christ the creature, who is a new and higher creation, dwells the fulness of Divine gifts, faith could never hold to a mere creature without idolatry: a creature would be no suitable mediator. If God is only dynamically and not essentially in Christ, however inseparably associated, we could not know ourselves as united with God when united with Him, and the self-communication of God in Him would not be perfect.

A *third* formula runs: "God is revealed in the flesh,"[1] or Christ has come from heaven in the flesh;[2] "the Word became flesh."[3] But if this is understood to mean that God as Logos has assumed human flesh as a garment, or has transformed Himself into a man, at least into a human soul, and is in this sense fashioned as a man, He would only play the drama of a man without having become man. Or if the Logos is supposed to have narrowed or contracted Himself in order to dwell in Christ, side by side with a perfect human nature to which a soul also belongs, such violence would certainly bring us an unthinkable mutation of the Divine essence, and we should have in such an expression no bond between the two natures, and therefore again no incarnation. All these meanings stand also opposed to a true, permanent humanity of Christ, which is so definitely maintained by the two first formulas. So, lastly, the opinion that a Divine personality came and placed itself upon this man, binding the human and keeping it down in its place, would not involve incarnation; this would be a species of Cerinthianism. The Divine act of incarnation cannot be the humiliation or mutilation of humanity, but only its elevation.

2. IDEA OF INCARNATION.—The Christology which teaches a mere constitution of Himself in the person of Christ by God as man or in human form, would steer clear of the Ebionitic, but would founder on the Doketic. The Christology of the *assumptio*, and that of new creation, maintains the anti-Doketic tendency, but does not yet adequately express the Divine in Christ and its association with the man, does not overcome the Ebionitic tendency fully. Thus the right path is pointed out to us. We must attain to such an inter-

---

[1] 1 Tim. iii. 16; comp. 1 John iv. 6.   [2] John vi. 41, 51; 2 John 7.
[3] John i. 14.

weaving of the Divine conservation, creation, and manifestation, that whilst excluding the Doketic and Ebionitic views, all three co-operate to produce the complete idea of the incarnation of God. If we go the right way to work, the first glance already shows that the difficulty has its centre of gravity not in the problem of the union of the two first elements, but in their union with the third. For it can make no difficulty to suppose a new creative Divine act in addition to the old creation, and with the application of its elements. The creative activity of God is not exhausted by one act and product; but, without detriment to the unity of the Divine plan of the universe, it successively calls the elements of that plan into existence, in such a way that the later do not deny their connection with the earlier, and the latter does not deny its receptiveness for the former. On the contrary, the question has more difficulty, how the *assumptio* and the new creation agree with the third element. This third says that God is not merely in Jesus as He is everywhere, that He does not merely work upon this man in the way of power, but that God as Logos, as that special eternal mode of being of the Deity, unites Himself perfectly and indissolubly with Jesus, and thus may be said to have become man in Him, because as Logos He has His being, His perfect revelation in this man, and has become a living unity with this man. Thus we shall now understand the Johannine formula in i. 14 correctly. "The Word became flesh" can neither mean that the Logos ceased to be what He was, and began to be *man* only, nor can it aim at describing a mere theophany in human form. On the contrary, in the ὁ λόγος σὰρξ ἐγένετο the strongest possible expression is given for the actuality of the humanity of Jesus, but in such a way that this realization is a revelation, indeed a realization in the world of the Logos Himself.

3. This, then, being the idea of incarnation, the main objections against this idea may be removed. Since the sense is not that God as the Logos has to cease being what He was, but that He became what He was not, nor is a mutation of His essence meant by this becoming, the main difficulty can only lie in the following point. Jesus is a creaturely being, such as lies in the idea both of the *assumptio* of a man

and in the idea of the new creation. Now if He has creative activity in Himself, the creaturely has to be placed in relatively independent objectivity as a second thing opposite to the creating God. Thus the question arises, how the matter shall be harmonized, that the Logos, who as such is opposed to the creature, shall at the same time become and be what apparently can only be an object of His action and influence? In this the cause must apparently be at the same time its own effect.

The solution follows a closer analysis of creaturely being and correct distinction between the idea of the first and second creation, by which the latter turns out to be an intermediate idea between incarnation and the first creation, together with conservation, seeing that it holds both distinct, but is also destined to unite them. If the idea of creation generally issued in its product always being a pure creation,[1] the incarnation of God would certainly be impossible in such a creature. In the first creation, the difference between the world and God *must* enter.[2] God as Logos constitutes man in an existence independent of Himself, and distinguishes Himself from him. But the second creation also falls under the idea of creation. Is then the world nothing but real separateness from God? does its difference from God describe its whole idea? It would certainly in such a case be extra-Divine, as Deism would have it, if not un-Divine; rather is that distinctiveness willed as the presupposition only for the self-communication of God and living community with Him, and this latter is from the beginning destined by God for it, although not produced by God, and to the full idea of the rational creature is so very pertinent, that its consummation depends on the appropriation of the Divine communication. The idea of man is so constituted with God, that a Divine element, the Spirit of God, pertains to its realization, and the empirical man only attains his own truth by appropriating the latter. The New Testament ascribes to Christians in general, that by the self-communication of the Holy Spirit, which may and should become in them inseparably permanent, they become partakers of the Divine

---

[1] Thus Gunther, and after him Delitzsch.
[2] ὁ πρῶτος ἀδὰμ χοϊκὸς, ψυχικός, 1 Cor. xv.

nature;[1] it speaks of their being born not from beneath, of earth or the flesh, not of the will or blood of a man, but of holy seed, of God, of course only by means of Christ, the corn of wheat which must die in order to rise again in rich fruit.[2] The Christological problem, then, does not require the abrogation of the distinction between the human and Divine; it leaves its rights to the first creation. But Christ is also the second Adam, the second creation, and the idea of this suffices to form a bridge between creation, by means of which man is placed outside of God in an independent existence, and incarnation, inasmuch as in Christ, as in Christians a union of the two is found without detriment to the permanent distinction between the Divine and creaturely. And the incarnation of God is distinguished on the one side from the marriage of the human and Divine in faith, as far as the humanity of Jesus is concerned, just as on the other side the universal is distinguished from the simply individual charismatic receptiveness as far as the Divine side is concerned, like the communication of the Divine without measure (οὐκ ἐκ μέτρου), which is an entrance of an eternal mode of Divine being into the Person of Christ, is related to the communication ἐκ μέτρου.[3] And finally also by the fact that in Jesus the unifying of the Divine and human was never preceded by a time of their mere separation, since Christ is a God-human living unity, the Son of God by nature, whilst we are only children of God by adoption, by implanting into the principle of filiation, which rests or lies in Him as having become man. The eternal image of God is also imprinted by His God-humanity upon the actuality of the world, and has become apprehensible as the humanly actual archetype by the faith through which we become His copies. Thus the Divine purpose of love is fulfilled, which is at the same time *self-communicating* and *participant* (or appropriative). The Divine *communication*, by means of which a new higher humanity than the Adamitic arises in Christ, and by which He effects His own, indeed gives Himself to humanity as a property, that even humanity may in a special sense

---

[1] 2 Pet. i. 4; John i. 13.
[2] John i. 13, xii. 24.
[3] John iii. 34; 1 Cor. xii. 11; Rom. xii. 3-5.

become a property of the Logos, so that it pertains to Him Himself, namely, as manifest and realized in the world by humanity or living a historical life in it. That especially not only God as Logos belongs to the humanity in Christ, but that the latter is even appropriated by Him, this He wills by virtue of the *participation* of His love in humanity, which is only the other side of the communicating love of God. But this participation effects that the humanity of this Person is now also inseparable from the Logos as a property, who finds therein the self-revelation he desires. Through the two together Christ is absolutely the God-man, in whom the eternal Divine predisposition to incarnation has come to realization, and humanity is raised to unity with God. But all this depends on the fundamental truth, that the Divine and human, little as their difference may be ignored, must not be thought as foreign and self-exclusive. And these two requisites are manifestly fulfilled at the same time, when the distinctions are so thought that the very thing which distinguishes the Divine nature and the human from one another, becomes at the same time that which unites the two. The last and inextinguishable distinction between God and man is then,[1] that to God alone pertains self-existence or aseity, which interpenetrates all attributes and lends them their Divine impress. He alone has of Himself absolute fulness of life, spirit, and love; man, on the contrary, made by God, is absolutely dependent on God, is therefore without aseity, but is at the same time, according to the Divine love, destined to godlike participation in the Divine attributes. His difference from God shapes itself therefore into need of God, into receptiveness for God, which longs for His self-communication. On the other hand, the self-sufficiency and blessedness of God, which are absolutely grounded in Himself, because His majesty is in its inmost essence majesty of love, frames itself into the actual volition of community with the world, which is receptive of Him, in communication and participation. Thus that which forms the inextinguishable difference between the two, forms straightway their union. The abyss of the Divine riches and the abyss of the creaturely poverty and man's infinite need, so to speak, call to one another,[2] and attract each other, until they over-

[1] As the Wurtember Reformer Brenz recognized.     [2] Ps. xlii. 8.

flow and unite in Him, in whom the fulness of the Godhead dwells bodily. The two-sided attraction is of an ethical kind, but the Divine love has first loved.[1]

4. Thus then it is also possible, in opposition to all pantheistic and magical theories of intermingling, to apprehend how in the idea of incarnation not an identity of the Divine and human, but unity is posited in difference, inasmuch as the idea of creation is not destroyed in that of incarnation, but is preserved. The creaturely element of the humanity of Christ, however high it be, remains secured by the fact that it has not eternally to reckon the Divine its original being, but only through receiving it. Its course is not, as Pantheism would have it, immediately Divine, but is only filled with God by the free love of the Logos, and the latter makes it a property in participation, in order to give it a share in itself, and thus to receive it into His Trinitarian life. There thus also remains straightway assured as an eternal element in the humanity of the God-man the same distinction from God, which forms the ultimate difference between God in Himself and the creature. For it does not acquire the aseity of God. Only by receiving on its side does it eternally acquire the fulness of the Godhead, and may reckon this possession its own being, its realized complete idea, whilst the triune God has His fulness in eternal aseity, but by His free love as Logos accomplishes this highest act. The eternal disposition or self-determination of the Logos to incarnation is consequently realized in such a way that it conjoins with the previous world of *conservation,* in order to bring the creation of man commenced in Adam to *perfection,* by God as Logos not merely dispensing power of His own upon a man, but by accomplishing the absolute self-communication, by having His own full self-revelation in this man as His own, as He gives Himself to this man to be his own, and in both together realize the God-humanity.

*Observation.*—Many think that the principal hindrance to a satisfactory Christology is contained in the doctrine of the two natures. They would therefore have but one nature, a view which then necessarily becomes Monophysitic or Ebionitic, unless there is a relapse to a confusion of the

[1] 1 John iv. 10.

Divine and human. But Schleiermacher, to whom reference is especially made, has (in spite of his denial of the immanent Trinity) by no means annulled the difference of the Divine and human in Christ generally, but considers the former to be that which assumes, and the latter that which is assumed, and indeed considers the God-human life of Christ to be the common act of the Divine and human. According to our exposition, the Divine and human do not stand dualistically apart in Christ. By means of the above positions, and especially the mediating idea of the new second creation as not merely like the first distinguishing from God but also uniting with God and yet not transcending the idea of humanity, the same truth is again accepted, which Luther held, when for a satisfactory Christology he demanded a new higher idea of humanity, of which we are to speak " in new tongues." He means thereby a higher idea of human *nature*, transcending empirical, Adamitic humanity, which should not merely not oppose the unifying Divine act, but should attain its realization thereby.

§ 102.—*The Unity of the God-Human Personality.*

The attempts to apprehend the God-man as a personal living unity, are necessarily wrecked, when start is made from the idea of the personal Ego, be it human or Divine, in order to find therein the foundation for the God-human living unity and the bond of the unity of the natures, instead conversely of attaining the unity of the God-human Ego as a result of the union of the Divine and human side in him. If a double personality is to be avoided, we should arrive by that method either at the denial of the personality of the human nature (*i.e.* essentially as in Apollinarianism) or at an anthropocentric Christology. If, therefore, the road is closed beginning with a personal Ego, we must start by preference from the unifying of the two natures; and to this end it is the less requisite to diminish the truth and perfection, whether of the humanity or the Deity, in the interests of the unity of the personality of Christ, that more narrowly regarded the basis of the personal living unity of the God-man is straightway latent in the perfection of the two sides.

1. As the Christological history of the pre-Chalcedon period started from the natures, and not from the idea of the person, the Chalcedon Synod still held the formula that the two natures coalesce to form a hypostasis, according to which the one person of the God-man would become the end or result of the union of the two natures. The later theology certainly held a different view. It took the Ego without the nature for the basis, in order to attain the unity of the natures. To it the unity of the natures consisted in this Ego, whether thought as Divine or human, being supposed to form the one centre, the real substantial point of unity or germ for the future living unity, and to embrace the two sides with all their contents, *i.e.* the natures. But this might be attempted in a double way, either starting from the Divine side, as was done in the Middle Ages especially, or from the human side, as frequently happened in more recent times. According as this Ego was thought Divine or human, the Divine or human side came into decisive and immoveable preponderance. If, then, the Ego were further defined—which would certainly be an empty abstraction without the nature—as a spiritual independent being, a whole in itself, repelling any different thing from which it is distinguished and incommunicable to what is different to itself, a view accepted not only by Romanist Dogmatists,[1] but even by Strauss for instance, then the Ego (the person), whether thought to be Divine or human, is neither capable nor in need of an intimate union with a thing different to itself, and a communication to a different thing than itself becomes an impossibility. If in such a conception the Ego is thought to be Divine, and this definition of it is applied to the hypostasis of the Logos, it follows that self-consciousness and self-determination, *i.e.* that personality, is to be denied to the human nature, in order that it may not necessarily repel the Divine Ego and be necessarily repelled by it, but that

[1] Thus Liebermann, iii. 416, *persona* is *totum aliquid et completum, quod sui juris est et alteri non potest communicari.*

rather a union with the Divine may enter.¹ But such mutilation of the humanity would itself be contrary to the Chalcedon formula, that the humanity as well as the Divinity is to be thought τελεία in Christ. Self-consciousness and self-determination are not something unessential to the idea of man; the immanent tendency of every truly human nature to self-conception and self-determination ought not to be interrupted or arrested by the *Unio*. A Divine Ego, which substituted itself for the self-apprehension of the human nature or its tendency to personality, would absorb an element which belongs essentially to complete humanity. The Lutheran Christology, perceiving this, as it does not accept that definition of *persona*, teaches a *communicatio personæ*, and will not think the humanity of Christ to be ἀνυπόστατος. It is rather ἐνυπόστατος in the Logos, *personata* by its Ego. In this case that definition of the Ego is abandoned. But apart from the fact, that in this instance the hypostasis of the Logos must be wholly thought after the manner of a human Ego (for otherwise it could not be at the same time a human person), the Ego of the Logos could only be called a human Ego, if God and man were, in reference to personality, an identical thing or identity, if God were in Himself eternally a human Ego, or God and man were only distinguished gradually, and not by the Divine self-existence. But such identification of the two in the ultimate resort has a Pantheistic tang. The Lutheran dogmatic theologians have therefore a sense indeed of the mistake in thinking the *persona* as repelled, indeed they regard the *persona* as communicable, as a *natura* so to speak, but still they do not break with the method of taking the *persona* instead of the *natura* as the starting-point for the unity of the personality of Christ; they rather start from a Divine Ego as the fundamental constitutive factor in this personality. But it as little suffices to start from a *human Ego* for the solution of the problem of the God-human living unity, and to describe this Ego to be a *completum totum* of itself, which must repel that from which it is distinguished and form the immoveable, firm, as well as incommunicable nucleus in the Person of Christ. In this case the Divine would have only a

[1] Therefore the Lutheran theologians do not accept this definition, but teach a *communicatio* also of the *persona* of the Logos.

contingent, supplementary, and precarious position, to which also without the same there would remain a personality complete in itself and purely human. This would be the so-called *anthropocentric* Christology, which reserves for humanity the nucleus of this person, and leaves for the Deity only a peripheric position, vainly seeking to distinguish itself clearly from Ebionitism.[1]

*Observation.*—The two possible forms of abstracting the interests of the God-human living unity from the two natures, and of starting from the idea of the Ego, in order that the Ego may be the principle of unity for the personality of Christ, lead therefore, because of the indivisibility of the Ego and its nature, to a permanent preponderance either of the Divine or human side, and therefore diminish either the one or the other of the two natures. Instead of an equal regard to the factors in the perfect idea of the eternal God-man, we only hold in this case a Divine or a human unity, together with accidents of the other nature. The idea of God-humanity is consequently abandoned. To avoid this result, in the interests of the perfection of the two natures the expedient may be adopted, which considers Christ in a Nestorian manner merely as a combined nature, but a God-human living unity is not attained.—In the modern Kenotic theories there is a vague sentiment that to begin with the *persona* does not lead to the desired goal, and they therefore think themselves compelled above all to depotentiate the Logos, *i.e.* they allow the Logos to become a mere Divine *natura*, and then permit Him to elevate Himself to actuality in unity with the human. And in a similar manner, Philippi desires to recur from the personality (*i.e.* self-consciousness and self-determination) to a deeper something, that there may be room for the self-consciousness and self-determination of the humanity in union with the Divine.—But, to afford a perfect help, the idea of *persona* generally and especially in its application to the Logos will have to be revised. Generally speaking, this means it cannot possibly be thought as repelling or repelled; it must be thought as the product of the *natura*, in God as well as in man. In relation to the humanity, the definition of Boethius, which long enjoyed a large regard, is far better than that modern definition: *persona est animœ rationalis individua substantia, i.e.* a special mode of being of the rational nature, and in reference to the Trini-

[1] The opposite to this view is formed by Schleiermacher's dictum, that the Divine is the innermost self of this person.

tarian *persona* of the Logos the definition of the *Conf. Augustana I.*: *persona* is *quod proprie subsistit*, for in this definition neither *incommunicabilitas* nor the *ens totum et completum* is reckoned in its idea. Seeing that reference is rather made therein to the *substantia* or *subsistentia*, this already teaches us not to begin with the Ego in order to gain a knowledge of the personal living unity of the God-man. On this matter, as has been shown, Luther had a very definite presentiment, and the Lutheran dogmatics has at least pre-eminently busied itself with the *communicatio naturarum* and their *idiomata*.

2. It is the more necessary to abandon the road to the personal living unity of the God-man, and the attainment of the Divine or human as the bond of union, through the *persona*, since on grounds of logic and of fact the Ego cannot be placed at the head as the bond of union; rather *can* the personality of Christ be the result alone of the process of the *Unio*. The Ego in Christ cannot possibly be thought as a simple peculiar substantial point, incommunicable side by side with the Divine or human nature, forming an exclusive totality and repelling everything not itself. In this case we should never escape from that magic circle of the exclusivity of the Divine essence in relation to the human, or of the human in relation to the Divine, from which Christology so long suffered. And it would also be in contradiction to what has already been said, according to which the human is not self-sufficing, but longs for the Divine, just as conversely the Divine communicates and participates. And add to this especially, that it may be rightly asked, whether the Ego, either in God or in man, is a substance *per se* and abstracted from the nature or essence. If the three Divine hypostases in God were only three special Egos by the side of and extra to the Divine Essence, they would stand in a merely contingent and external relation to the one Divine Essence, and we should have Tritheism. But the one God is rather eternally the one personal archetypal Spirit in and through this triality itself.[1] And similarly in relation to man we must abandon the superstition that the Ego is a substance *per se*, separate from the spiritual nature of the man, from the soul and its functions. The Ego in man is only the spirit or the spiritual nature itself in the function, to which it essentially tends as rational, to apprehend itself in thought and

[1] §§ 31*b*, 32.

volition. The Ego is always present as an act merely. It only has its existence in the act of self-diremption and return to self, the reflection of the spirit from itself and into itself, which thus produces itself as Ego, *i.e.* as a self-conscious *natura*. The Ego is the product of the rational nature, is its act, and arises through its perpetual actual self-constitution. Human nature is in itself the faculty and tendency to know oneself and to determine oneself, and the Ego is nothing else than the spiritual nature of man himself engaged in this self-reflection. By this self-volition and self-knowledge the human spiritual nature is able to assert itself against what is inimical, to repel it, but to no less combine with what is friendly without self-detriment, as well with the race as with God. With the self-volition and self-knowledge there is demanded a self-distinction from God and the race, and therefore a preservation of the distinction, such as § 101 requires, but not a repelling and self-exclusion. For the human nature would be straightway negatived in volition and knowledge, if open receptiveness for God and the human race did not belong essentially to its nature, to its self-knowledge and self-volition. Thus on a new side we are interdicted from pursuing the road which must lead to the denial of the human personality, and therefore to Apollinarianism and a theophanic Christology, or else to anthropocentric doctrines. Everything by preference points us *to begin with the union of the natures instead of with the Ego, Divine or human,* as to some extent the ancient time up to the Creed of Chalcedon, and then again Luther, desired *in order from the* Unio *of the natures* to attain the personal *living unity of the God-man.* Nothing can be therefore more remote from the solution of the problem, than the attempts to turn from the supernatural origin of Christ, *i.e.* from the fundamental unifying of the natures, and the desire to transform them into a natural product of the race.

3. Starting, accordingly, from the natures, it is certain to us *in the first place,*[1] that their union contains no contradiction, that rather have they a direct reference to one another, even by virtue of that which is distinctive in them, and an internal relation to one another, the human because of its receptiveness and need, the Divine because of the Divine love. If, then,

---
[1] According to § 101.

there is such a union of Divine and human nature, its result is a God-human living unity, in which distinction and unity must and may be preserved very equal. *Secondly.* It is certainly insufficient to stop at this God-human living unity; it must also become actual, personal, living unity, and therefore self-conscious and self-determining. And then the question arises: Can its God-human character remain fast in this respect,—do not the human and Divine separate again in the sphere of self-consciousness and self-determination, so that the actual living unity is severed? This might issue, if the human Ego was thought of as a special substance by the side of the human nature, for then this human Ego as purely human would stand over against the Divine nature, without the *Unio* itself extending into the purely human Ego and making it itself God-human. But the case is otherwise, if the Ego, even the human, is no separate substance *per se* side by side with its nature and distinct therefrom, but if the Ego is only the nature itself in its actuality as conscious and willing. *Thirdly.* When therefore that God-human living unity, to which the two natures are united, arrives at self-consciousness, the *self*, which is the contents of the self-consciousness, is necessarily nothing else than the existent God-human living unity. Everywhere, indeed, the self-consciousness of a being, if it is to correspond with truth, can simply be just the ideal image of that being. But the being which has resulted from the union of the natures is God-human being. Therefore the self-consciousness of the God-man, to be true, must also be God-human; He will necessarily know Himself as God-man, and that in reference to volition and self-determination. For it must be the God-human living unity, its self, which determines itself, otherwise we should not have self-determination in this living unity. Consequently the Divine *Unio* also extends into the sphere of consciousness and volition, instead of suffering lesion or interruption at this point.

4. If we would now, in the first place, fix the *humanity* in Christ, it may be shown how the *Unio* of the natures is confirmed and established by the perfection of the humanity, namely by the self-consciousness and self-determination of the same, instead of being abolished. The self-consciousness of this man only being true and perfect inasmuch as he knows

and thinks his own being as it is, and this being happening to be of the kind that it does not merely have the Divine outside of itself but received into its own property, the self-consciousness of the humanity of Jesus images this its union with the Divine, and in the humanity of Jesus as developed and perfect there is no self-knowledge without a knowledge of Himself as originally united with God. Similarly there is no self-volition without a willing of Himself as also actually united with God, as the humanity already is in itself. And this also means, that the knowledge and volition of this man will be God-human, and therefore a new bond of the *Unio* will be added to the original bond of the natures in themselves. There is to be seen therein only in reference to the Divine-human being the no less God-human self-actualization. This man, the more he knows and wills himself as becoming, the more he knows and wills himself as the perfect receptiveness of humanity for God, which has become partaker of the completion of its fulness by means of the $\pi\lambda\acute{\eta}\rho\omega\mu\alpha$ $\theta\epsilon\acute{o}\tau\eta\tau\sigma\varsigma$. This unity with God as Logos it knows as its own state, as the *complementum* of its full idea, in such a way indeed that it knows and wills, what it has and is, in dependence upon the Divine principle in it, such as Christ also everywhere expresses this. But the formal side of this human knowledge and volition is certainly never Divine, but is and remains distinct from the Divine principle in itself. For otherwise an *exæquatio*, an annulling of the difference between the human and Divine, and therefore a dissolution of the incarnation, would be the result. But the solving of the problem of the God-human, personal unity cannot have as its task the dissolution of the God-*human* person.

5. And if we turn, in the second place, to the *Deity*, after the *Unio* the humanity also includes the knowledge and volition of God, and, inasmuch as He knows and wills both His perfect self-communication to this humanity and also His participation in and His perfect appropriation of the humanity, He also knows and wills Himself as God-human, namely in the Logos. It is true that it is not God generally who has become man in Christ, but God as the Logos, and even here it ought not to be required that the formal side of the Divine knowledge and volition cease, rather does it remain distinct

from the human. This is the truth of the Dyotheletism maintained in the struggle with Monophysitism and Monotheletism in the Eastern and Western Churches. But, in the first place, the contents of the Divine and human knowledge is the same, namely God-human. Further, God indeed has His absolute self-consciousness and His self-determination only as the Triune, and not in the Logos *per se*, just as in the three hypostases even there are not three separate self-consciousnesses and three self-determinations. But notwithstanding God knows and wills Himself after the *Unio* as united with humanity, namely in the Logos. But the union itself exists every moment, on the Divine side under the type of continuous communication and appropriation, on the human side under the type of appropriating, having, and being by receiving. And as the Divine side is for the human the *complementum* of receptiveness, the human in relation to the Divine is the *complementum* or fulfilling for its love. A Divine self-knowing and willing exists in this man. For even the Father and the Holy Ghost have made a dwelling in him, but, as man or incarnate, God only knows and wills Himself inasmuch as He has as Logos become man.[1] On the other hand, were the knowledge and volition of the Divine and human side also one in a formal respect, we should have identification, as opposed to which the Church maintains, that, if the Divine and human natures in Christ are indeed united, but not identified, they must also be distinct in their manifestation. According to the idea of both, the initiative must issue from the Divine side, from the Triune God, by the mediation of the Logos who wills to become man, and the human side must maintain itself in a receptive attitude, not being passive, but appropriating what is shown and willed by the Divine. Thus, then, God as the Logos or as the revealing principle thinks the Divine thoughts, which are to be revealed to the God-man, on the ground and by virtue of the original *Unio*, so to speak, in Him. And

---

[1] It is not the Logos *per se* who knows Himself in Christ, for the Logos has no proper self-consciousness apart from the Father and Spirit. Also, it is not (the personal) God generally, but only God as Logos who has become man. But in Christ the Father and Spirit also dwell, so that God certainly personally knows Himself and is in Christ, but has only carried out the incarnation in His mode of being as Logos.

the God-man sees or perceives what God shows him.[1] Similarly God as Logos produces the Divine contents, the Divine ends to be realized as the definite impulse in the God-man, and He accepts them livingly and realizes them. To these ends belong pre-eminently the perfect actual being of God in Christ. The personality of Christ is therefore nothing else than the God-humanity, reflected, conceived, and willed in itself, which by virtue of the *Unio* is already initially the real God-human totality, but which must now also become in knowledge and will God-human. An analogy to this united self-knowledge and willing of the Divine and human in the God-man is given in *conscience* (with its relation to the will), in which a Divine knowledge becomes at the same time human, affording knowledge in which we have a knowledge of the Divine and of the holy law as the thought and will of God, in which nevertheless this Divine thought and will becomes at the same time our own knowledge, and in which we receive into ourselves a Divine volition as an impulse, which can and ought to become our own volition at the same time. An analogy of a higher grade lies in the witness of the Holy Spirit,[2] which likewise becomes our own consciousness, the witness of our own spirit, associated with the knowledge of the objectivity of this witness to our acceptance into the Divine kinship, and with the Divine impulse to the manifestation of this kinship.

Accordingly a double personality is excluded in Jesus, and it is at the same time shown, how Jesus in spite of His union with the Logos attributes to the "Father" that He gives Him His works and His $\delta \acute{o} \xi a$, and shows Him His will. For by the Logos the Father speaks to the developing, and not yet perfect, God-man. The Logos is the substantial living ground of the same; by Him the will of the Father, the ethically necessary, is revealed. He is originally united with this man, He determines His will. He is to be thought originally and from the beginning the living Divine substratum of this person, and this substratum forms itself

---

[1] John v. 18, etc. Thus Christ can say that He does nothing except what the Father shows Him; that He does at all times what is well-pleasing to the Father, viii. 29.

[2] Rom. viii. 16.

increasingly in Jesus into actually conscious and volitional humanity, in order to bring the God-humanity to full actuality.

*Observation.*—By what has been said, despite the acknowledgment of a perfect humanity even on the side of the personality, an anthropocentric Christology is excluded. The latter might have a good sense, if the meaning were, that in this man God prepared Himself the central place of His dwelling in the world. But this is not intended; an anthropocentric is opposed to a theocentric Christology. The latter would, it is true, be thought incorrectly, if the absolute Divine personality, *i.e.* the Triune God, were represented as incarnated in Christ, for God has only become man as Logos, not as absolute personality; this person is formed and determined by the creative Logos. He constitutes the human nature in Him a person, and is therefore the principle who forms the person in Jesus, although, as has been said, God as Logos only, and not as the absolute personal Deity, constitutes this person together with the human nature. Nor does the humanity make the Logos personal, a view which would again conduct to limitation or suffering in the Divine. Generally, humanity adds nothing to the perfection of the Logos, but the latter is the central spiritual principle in the person of Christ; and although the Logos is not *per se* an individual personality, nor yet the one Divine personality, but one of the factors (Ego-points) by which this is eternally constituted, still the human side with its self-consciousness and its self-determination so little receives a preponderance therefrom, that it rather acquiesces in the statement that this person only has its existence in God as the Logos. He forms the permanent basis of this person; He is its centre, not first made so by the human will; but He must also be called the principle which forms this person from the beginning, seeing that He called it into being creatively, but in such a way that He forms the one and fundamental factor in the Divine person itself. In the Logos God knows Himself to be the principle of the second creation as well as the first, but in such a way that He knows and wills Himself in the latter by means of absolute self-communication (§ 101).

## § 103.—*The Uniqueness of the God-Man or Christ as the Second Adam.*

The Logos could only become perfect man in Christ, because Christ was not an individual merely like others, but the Son of man, and destined as such to be the creaturely centre of the world. Again, He could only be the Son of man or the Second Adam, who is at the same time the last, by the incarnation of the Divine world-centre or the Logos.

Rothe, *Theol. Ethik*, § 555, etc.

1. The Logos has not merely assumed human nature generally, but, in order to become man, He was only able to assume human nature in the man who should be at once the second and the last Adam. Human nature generally, indeed, is receptive of God, and no single man can attain the realization of his idea, unless a Divine element becomes human in him by the agency of the Holy Spirit (§ 101). But this is not yet God-humanity. For the living unity of God with human nature, which is God-humanity, the universal *capacitas humanæ naturæ* for the Divine is insufficient; only the measure of that receptiveness attained by human nature in the second Adam suffices, which Paul calls the pneumatic. This is the justifiable element in the positions of the *F. C.*, which suppose the *capacitas* for incarnation not to be universally equal in humanity, but think them prepared first by God in Christ.[1] And in this view it is also given, that the *homousia* of the humanity of Christ with ours, however perfect it be supposed, cannot possibly exclude the uniqueness of the position of the humanity of Christ in the organism of the race. In general, the Church of all times has acknowledged the importance of this side of Christology. All great ecclesiastical parties, and most small ones, acknowledge Christ to be the second Adam and the head of humanity. Nevertheless, this truth has

[1] *F. C., loco cit. Sol. Decl.* viii. §§ 50, etc., 62, 64, 68–71.

remained hitherto a treasure but little realized, whilst it is adapted to form an important mediating idea, by means of which a series of Christological difficulties is resolved, and a welcome light is cast upon several other dogmas. It is to be no less hoped, that the more this truth becomes a conscious and actual common possession of Christendom, the more will the unity of the churches be necessarily furthered. Were this doctrine of Christ as the second Adam appropriately united with the doctrine of the humanity of Christ, and developed, neither the impersonality of the human nature nor the modern Kenotic theories would be found necessary, nor, finally, could the older Reformed Dogmatists possibly have been so scandalized that humanity should be receptive of the fulness of the Divine Essence of the Logos. But this doctrine of the second Adam may itself again be conceived in very various ways.

2. We have seen before,[1] that it was a physical conception of the first Adam which supposed all men to have been (*locati*) in Adam, which supposed him to be them, their totality, their real collectivity, in which case either individuals must become a mere accident to him, or his person must be volatilized into a mere idea. A similar view has also prevailed concerning Christ as the second Adam. Inasmuch as he is the archetypal man, he is, it is said, archetypal humanity, the totality of empirical men is included in him, he is properly them,—a view supposed to aid his substitutionary significance. This view may partly attach itself to the Divine side, namely, to the circumstance that the Logos is the real principle and prototype of all, which has no reference here; for the Logos is not like Adam the human real principle of our race, but the Divine, and on this statement that God as Logos is the creative real-principle there is no controversy. This conception has partly attached itself to the doctrine of so many Dogmatic theologians of the impersonality of the humanity of Christ. Because he is not a human person, he has assumed human nature in general, therefore the whole human race. But if the humanity of Christ has come from the elements of the Adamitic humanity in Mary, and Christ was an actual man, He is also an individual man, distinguished from all other

[1] See vol. ii. p. 43, and pp. 341, 350.

men by a definite individuality pertaining to him;[1] otherwise the necessary *homousia* with us would be wanting. If it be said that Christ is the *Homo generalis* or universal man in a physical sense, that He is them all exactly as they are and live, the plurality of men would be changed into semblance, and such opposition to Nominalism, which only knows a conceptual and not a real federation of the race, would be a no less exceptionable Realism, essentially of a Pantheistic kind; under words of a Christian sound we should have Panchristism. It is customary with those who do not even acknowledge the idea of Christ as the head of humanity, to make it appear, whether from design or from lack of discrimination, as if what the paragraph expresses were identical with this exceptionable and monstrous view of Christ.[2] Moreover, the newer Pantheism is certainly itself often guilty of the fault it blames in the physical conception of Christ as the *Homo generalis;* when, for example, like Strauss, it calls God the omnipersonality, resolving Christ into the ideal Christ, who is supposed to signify the same as God.

3. The true conception of Christ as the head or representative of humanity bears an ethico-religious character. Christ is indeed an individual, but every individual does not necessarily present a one-sided individuality of humanity, and indeed even in his inner being. In Christ, God as Logos has so united Himself with His humanity, that He is the seat of His absolute revelation. Since the world must serve this purpose, He has been able to prepare for Himself in humanity the receptiveness adequate to Him, *i.e.* universal receptiveness; and inasmuch as this receptiveness is a realized one, and this humanity answers to its idea, it not merely has a value for the whole, for every human individuality also has that, but it has a universal significance in the sense that this individual is constituted for becoming the determining power over all,[3]

---

[1] Just as He calls Himself a man in John viii. 40.

[2] Thus Schwarz in his *Geschichte der neusten Theologie*, who also in the later edition leaves the protests long ago laid against his views unregarded. Even Röthe might have taught him something better, *Theol. Ethik*, ed. 1, II. § 555, p. 289, and ed. 2, I. § 52, p. 192.

[3] Compare hereupon Schleiermacher, *Ueber den Begriff des höchsten Gutes*, collected works on Philosophy, vol. ii. 1838, pp. 491, etc.: "The duration (of the central individual whose educative power affected the mass in an original

inasmuch as He is supposed, as the prototype realized in the world, so to determine all, that although in infinite variety they are supposed to reflect Him again according to their individuality.[1] Thus with Him the principal or central beginning is given of a new humanity, which, born of the heart of God, is in a position to be the power of union for dissevered humanity. He is in this sense the central individual for humanity, because He exhibits humanity, not merely as free from imperfection, but also from one-sidedness, its intensive full idea. We are wont in other cases so to frame the idea of the races that we excise from empirical individuals what distinguishes them, and to retain as the generic idea what is common to all individuals. The true idea of man cannot be attained in this way, because of his ethical character. Starting from the totality of empirical humanity only, what is faintest is alone left as what is common to this totality; indeed, it might be doubted whether the moral and religious still belong to the idea of man. Christianity does not proceed thus. It ventures the claim, that the true idea of man is to be formed, not after the totality of empirical men, but after Christ alone. It opposes Him to all others as *the* man; and therefore, because in Him the complete idea of humanity appeared archetypically in a determining power which extends to all, and thus there lives in Him the power of the whole, of true humanity, He is called the Son of man; He is not the product of empirical humanity, but of the idea of humanity destined to perfect every one else. If it is said, therefore, that every individual man, and Christ also by consequence, must have a distinguishing individuality or characteristicalness, His universal position in itself and with respect to others is His individuality or uniqueness. The first Adam is the father of the natural humanity, which divides itself endlessly. Christ is more than Adam. " He who loves

way) is extended to the measure of its power. But not in the sphere of expression and representation,—but only in reference to the inner side of the problem, of penetrating all states of the individual life with the absolutely highest consciousness, is it allowable to think—presupposing that the reason may live as absolute in an individual being—that such an one may evoke a living type which should even dominate in the end the whole race, and remove by this affinitative connection all separation in regard to this (the religious) sphere, so that through its means every one is mediated by every one."

[1] Compare § 70. 1 Cor. xv. 45, etc.; Rom. viii. 29; Phil. iii. 21.

father or mother more than Me, is not worthy of Me,"[1] for He is destined to be the stock of pneumatic humanity. Thus He is the second Adam, inasmuch as He is at the same time the last Adam, the perfecter of the creation which was only begun in the first Adam. The goal of creation is first reached in Him, and since He alone is the absolutely universal person, He has His individuality in the fact. He can only be the redeemer of all by being equally related to all individualities, inasmuch as all are equally in great need of Him, and are made for communion with Him, as He has reference to them. He can only unite humanity, which has parted into profound oppositions through sin, because the national, generic, and all other natural differences of humanity are incidental to what is innermost in this person. Though He must enter into these historical forms of life, He has simply utilized them as the organ or medium of presentation of His universal contents, and thus sanctified and consecrated them. He is therefore not the physical archetype of man: Adam is this; but as the archetype He is the pneumatic archetypal man, the heart and head of humanity in the spiritual sphere. To be so, the Divine life, particularly the life of religion, must be in Him in archetypal and productive form. For indeed in each of the moral spheres—in art, science, politics, etc.—there is a ray of the Divine, but in the life of religion there is the focus of them all. In it as the focus all potencies rest, which in those moral spheres pertain to relative independence. Though, therefore, it may happen that the historic personality of Christ does not show itself productive in all these single spheres of themselves, universal spiritual endowment is still to be accorded Him, because in Him full receptiveness, as well as the receiving or the appropriation of the Divine life, or the life of religion, is in absolutely perfect manner, and is therefore also presented and communicated in perfect manner. And this central life which lies in Him, and issues from Him, has also the power of conducting all the potencies and special gifts of humanity to development and consummation. Agreeably, therefore, to the *Unio* with the Logos, the universal principle of light and life, He is in historical human form the fountainhead of all the pneumatic life of humanity, for which

[1] Matt. x. 37 and Luke xiv. 26.

the highest and finest moral relations, such as prince, father, mother, eldest brother, friend, bridegroom, are used as emblems.[1]

4. But this central position in regard to humanity, indeed to the world of rational beings, Christ only assumes by the uniqueness of His association with God, or by the fact that there is not simply in Him a Divine effect, a transient being of God or one of the Divine powers, but that in Him the essential Deity, the Logos Himself, became flesh. Only by the incarnation of the Logos in His totality as the Divine image and world-centre is He possible, who is destined to be the historical universal middle-point of the world without one-sidedness. No single man can assume or give himself this central position, indeed none of the one-sided human individualities can have it. Even the bare central *receptiveness* for God could not aid apart from a special Divine act. But love, that central fact in God, will reveal itself in realization in the world, not by teaching merely or by self-exhibition, for this does not satisfy love, but by the participating and self-communicating act of love, central receptiveness for which was lacking in humanity. Now this cannot be found in the expanse of the dead starry vaults, nor in the breadth of vast nature, but in the sphere of personality alone. For human personality is a Microcosm, although in individually various manner. Moreover, in the compass of natural humanity, which has parted asunder into an infinity of individualities of a one-sided kind, nay, has been corrupted and distracted by sin, cannot be the place where God attains central indwelling, and can erect the personal sanctuary of humanity. Therefore God first *creates* for Himself within humanity the adequate place for His self-revelation and communication in Him, in whom the pure central receptiveness of human nature has been constituted by the creative efficiency of God. Therefore He could not arise in the way of mere natural generation. But just by the fact that God, namely as Logos, as the Divine centre of the world, finds in the humanity of Jesus the place for His central self-revelation, and appropriates the receptiveness of this man, this man becomes the creaturely centre, primarily of humanity as the source of redeeming, per-

---

[1] Luke xix. 12; Rom. v. 12, viii. 29; John iii. 29; Matt. ix. 15, xxiii. 37; John xv. 14, etc.

fecting life, and according to the indications of Scripture even beyond humanity. Our planet certainly, a vanishing point of the universe, is nevertheless deemed worthy of the great deed of the perfect revelation of the Divine love. And for this reason, because His love does not depend on the magnitude and bulk of the place of its revelation, but on the satisfaction of the need and the receptiveness, which are found together on this earth the more, the more deeply the noble human creature has fallen by sin; further, because love, according to its nature, straightway seeks what is humble condescendingly and compassionatingly, and finds in condescension to the world of sin a more radiating revelation of its majesty than it could find *anywhere else* in the world of pure spirits.[1] But nevertheless it is impossible that such a Divine act and the person, in whom the Logos Himself lives as a Divine image which has become realized in the world, should have a redemptive significance for the earth alone, and not rather for the whole world of spirits, although not universal. The incarnation of God is also a cosmical and metaphysical fact, as good as, nay better than, the creation of men and rational beings generally. It has a cosmical significance answering thereto, just as love is one in heaven and on earth, and associated thereby all pure spirits must desire to form one Divine community. Therefore the Holy Scriptures say that into this mystery of the Person of Christ even the angels delight to look, and that Christ has also become the bond of union between men and the higher spirit-world.[2] This was the Divine satisfaction and joy to regard the misery of our race, and straightway to make it the scene of the most majestic revelation of His love and grace, from an insignificant point of the universe, "a Bethlehem of the universe," to cause the most far-reaching blessed effects to emanate. But such gift is first made to the dwellers on the earth. Unto us, unto us is the Saviour first born. Why should we therefore detain ourselves upon cavilling thoughts instead of opening our hearts wide with the prophets and apostles, or with a Luther, in joy, thanks, and praise for the Son who was born unto us, who was given to us? By such thanks shall we also cause more joy to the spirits outside of humanity than

[1] Heb. ii. 14.   [2] Col. i. 20, etc.; Eph. i. 10, 22; 1 Pet. i. 12.

by the question in reference to them, whether they are not possibly depreciated in comparison with us by the fact that humanity has been made in His person the centre of the spirit-world, and thus of the universe.

*Observation.*—Moreover, since the principal thing in man is spiritual, rational nature, as in the higher spirits, and since there are not different species of reason (reason has no plural), in the consummation there is no specific distinction between the higher spirits and the world of man.[1] That Christ is also the head of the higher spirit-world, and therefore has a significance for beings without sin, proves his absolute necessity on a new side.

5. If the humanity of Christ is destined to be the centre of the creaturely world, because the Divine centre of the world has absolutely united Himself with him, it is evident anew, that in spite of the doctrine of the human personality of Christ, an anthropocentric Christology is to be still repudiated; rather would this man himself not be at all apart from the person-forming Divine act. Indeed, since in Christ the essential Deity Himself has His central place in the world, and since God is eternally and inseparably one with Him; since, consequently, he who sees Him sees the Father, *i.e.* His perfect image, in Him is the sanctuary of humanity, the God-man is deserving of adoration.[2] We worship no man; but in this man is the presence of the Deity realized in the world by the Logos, in whom is the Personal God, and God as Logos has united Himself with this man, that we may comprehend Him, and desires to be apprehended and adored in this man. Allied with Him, we are allied with the Deity Himself, not with a creature merely, and by this humanity as mediatorial we are at the same time united with the Deity. Further, because the Divine fulness of love fills His human receptiveness, humanity absolutely returns in Him the Divine love. Thus He is at the same time the prototype for us. Similarly His knowledge is absolutely free from error; standing in the Divine centre, He sees everything in its truth, for in that centre all truth rests, the ideal and real. To Him, therefore, the world is not dis-

---

[1] Compare Doctrine of Angels, § 45, and Luke xx. 36.
[2] John xiv. 9; Phil. ii. 10; Rom. x. 9, etc.; 1 Cor. i. 2.

sipated into an endless multiplicity or chaotic entanglement. His knowledge, penetrating the depths, knows the essence and law of the world in their relation to the kingdom of God in the simplest way. And because, as the true knowledge of God shows, true reality also lies in love, therefore the power over omnipotence, as over everything physical, over space and time with their contents, and truth also, stand in inseparable association with this love; where the love of God has really entered into the world, there must power and freedom dwell. To the perfect Son of man nothing finite can be of itself a limitation restricting Him; the perfect God-man must have Divine power potentially, and in exercise, too, according as wisdom prescribes to His love, which will not of course seek to gain humanity by force, but by ministering patience, until the time come, in which love contemned becomes love judicial, in which by the revelation of Christ everything is brought to decision, and in which all the kingdoms of this world are become the kingdoms of God and His Christ.[1]

*Observation.*—In what precedes we have considered the full idea of the God-humanity according to its fundamental features, the personal living unity as well as the uniqueness of the God-man, therefore the God-humanity as realized, and it was then possible to elaborate both definitions. The union of the principal Christological definitions resulted as quite possible, where the fulfilment of the universal receptiveness of humanity has made the latter the adequate personal organ of the Deity. But at this point the last main difficulty opens : How is the historical Christ to be thought of in the state of humiliation ? The true humanity of Jesus requires quite elementary beginnings, which form the strongest contrast to the Logos. Is Jesus, then, even in this state to be called God-man ? And if so, if He is to be called a developing personality, how does His growth consist with the immutability of the Logos ?

[1] Compare § 32. 4.

## § 104.—*Growth as the Essential Form of the Realization of the God-Man.*

Growth having been ordained for humanity, and Christ presenting true humanity in an actual human life (§ 103), a truly human growth pertains to Him. Since, on the other hand, God can only be perfectly manifest in Christ, when the whole fulness of the Divine Logos has also become the proper fulness of this man in knowledge and volition, and therefore has become God-human, with the growth of the human side there is also necessarily given in Him a growth of the God-humanity, and the incarnation is not to be thought as at once completed, but as continuous, nay augmentative, seeing that God as Logos ever seizes and appropriates those of the new sides which are generated by the true human development, just as, conversely, the growing actual receptiveness of the humanity combines consciously and voluntarily with ever new sides of the Logos. But in spite of this growth within the *Unio*, the Logos is from the beginning united with Jesus in the deepest bases of being, and the life of Jesus was always God-human, inasmuch as a receptiveness never existed for the Deity without its fulfilment. Human growth and Divine immutability harmonize, inasmuch as God as Logos can enter without self-detriment into history, for the end of a progressive self-revelation in humanity, and this humanity is capable of being increasingly incorporated with the immutability, again without the alteration of its nature.

1. With the question as to the relation of the eternal Logos, and of the eternal thought and volition of the God-humanity given in Him, to the temporal God-human life of Christ, we come in the first place to the point of transition

to the life of Christ on earth, which again presents its difficulties. It might indeed be thought that the temporal life of the God-man is something secondary, transient; for the Christian community adheres to the exalted Christ, as He is yesterday, and to-day, and the same to all eternity, to the glorified Head, not to Jesus in the state of His mere humiliation. But Christ's earthly life is not incidental; the knowledge of it is the only right way leading to the knowledge of the exalted Christ.[1] There lies a profound wisdom as well as an internal necessity in the fact that the Church in its annual cycle of feasts lives through the life of Christ again, from the manger to the ascension, and only by this method of accompanying Christ in spirit even to the cross is the exaltation of the Lord comprehensible in its internal meaning. Only so does His love to us become actually and historically manifest and cognizable, as it has itself been only thus manifested in its whole force. If we would solely know a glorified Lord, without including His earthly life, suffering, and action in the image of His glorified person, the knowledge of the exalted Lord, detached from historical fact, would float in the air and be mere matter of speculation. In this case it would also be denied to the historical work of Christ that it had effected or procured anything; there would remain in connection with that work only the exhibition of what was eternally existent. Indeed, the consequence would be that even the glorified person of the God-man would be volatilized into "the ideal Christ," or the spirit of Christ. And were it so, there would even apart from His growth arise a difficulty. On the one hand, the *revelation* of God in Christ must at least in its beginnings have come to a conclusion upon earth, although Christian faith certainly also knows of a Second Advent of Christ. On the other hand, Jesus existed in external humiliation, and this is necessarily a *veiling* not merely of what He would be, but also of the Logos, who will have in His perfected person His adequate organ, His existence and extension realized in the world. Both these points, however, the veiling in humiliation and the initial absolute revelation, go well together. Humiliation and dignity do not absolutely exclude each other, if the veiling

---

[1] To this belongs His whole self-presentation, and not His work merely.

is in itself somehow in its turn a revealing. The Gospel of John here gives us a hint, when it sees in the elevation on the cross a revelation of the glory (δόξα) of the Son of man. That which is the veiling of His majesty by humiliation, is straightway a revealing of His Divine love. And there nevertheless breaks forth from the veiled inner majesty and sublimity of this person in the very midst of His humble life so much glory, that this humiliation of His stands contrasted therewith, and even by the contrast becomes a means of the revelation of His ethical sublimity, together with which, according to the measure of approximation to its perfection, the majesty of power also increases. For the physical is dependent on the ethical.

2. Still it is not merely a question in Christ's earthly state of that humiliation, which by self-abasement, because of God-human love, became a mere foil of His inner dignity, but it is also a question of the *growth* and increase of His actual humanity in body and soul, which could not be without influence upon the form of his God-human living unity at the time. Even this growth begins with humiliation and imperfection, although at every moment it works what it will; on the other hand, it is in itself increasing exaltation. How then consists with such growth the *Unio* itself from the first beginnings of this human life, as well as the Divine self-sameness of this person? The latter seems to be most completely secured in the old Lutheran doctrine, according to which the humanity of Jesus attained from the first moment the full possession and use of the predicates of the Divine majesty, and remained in their enjoyment. But since that theology could not possibly deny the growth of the humanity, it was compelled to assume in all consistency a developing humanity side by side with a humanity absolutely perfect from the beginning, and fixedly identical, and therefore a double human life. Further, even the full possession of the Divine attributes, omniscience or holiness for example, as proper to the humanity from the beginning, must necessarily destroy the possibility of a true growth of the humanity. The more recent Kenotic theories, therefore, in the opinion that the Divine fulness is a hindrance to the *Unio*, seek how to create this fulness out of the means, in order that the

natures may coincide from the beginning and correspond, and thus a true growth, certainly not of the human merely, but also of the Divine, may result. But thus, instead of an ever more perfect unity of both sides, we should simply have two lines of a parallel movement of both; a unity of person would be as little seen as a progressive growth. We can only attain to a living reciprocity of both sides, the result of which alone is the perfected God-humanity, if the Divine side, from which the initiative must issue, is not reduced to the measure of the human, but has in itself a wealth which far transcends the beginnings of humanity, and the ever fuller communication of which to the self-disclosing receptiveness is the basis of the growth of the God-human unity, so that thus the fulness of the Logos would be eliminated, and at the same time the efficient principle of growth is set aside.—As little certainly would it, on the contrary, suffice to suppose the God-human unity as in no wise existent from the beginning, but to introduce it only in the course of the earthly life of Christ, whether in the middle or at the end.[1] This would mean that at the beginning Jesus was only a man, but by His development He has been enabled to be exalted to God-humanity. He owed to His virtue elevation to God-like dignity. But this view, which inclines to Ebionitism, makes the manifestation of Christ more dependent on the revelation of human power than on its receptiveness, and would therefore be contrary to the fundamental Christian view, according to which the Deity is that which is self-communicating, and the humanity is essentially and originally receptive. Did Christ receive God-humanity as a reward for His righteousness, the former would be an appendage. Rather is even His sinlessness to be apprehended as not without a peculiar endowment, distinguishing Him from the beginning.

If, then, we must exclude both views, a *Unio* complete from the beginning, which admits no further development of the same, as well as a beginning which is no *Unio* at all, the problem must be to describe a being of the *Unio*, which yet includes the possibility of, nay, the necessity and tendency

[1] Rougemont does the former, in this point like Cerinthus, considering Jesus until His baptism as a mere Adamitic man, and from that point as the second Adam. The second is done by Socinianism in a certain manner.

for, a growth. That not the humanity of Jesus merely, but also His God-human living unity, was at first incomplete and in need of increase, is clear already beyond all contradiction, when we regard the corporeality of Jesus, which was still mortal on the earth, and the Apthartodoketes are rightly rejected, according to whom, by virtue of the *Unio*, Jesus was immortal from the beginning, and was only supposed to have given Himself mortality by a negative miracle. It is undoubtedly the teaching of the Church, that the corporeality of Jesus is in the exaltation associated more firmly than before, inseparably indeed, with His total personality, but that on earth it was only separably associated therewith. Therefore the unity of the God-human total personality was not perfect at the beginning. But generally also there belongs to growth, side by side with a continuity and self-sameness of the one who grows, a relative separability and a separateness of the different factors, which must assert their independence, in order to unite again in a higher manner. Man, that unity of body and soul, has a development generally only because the factors of his being do not remain and advance, so to speak, in motionless coalescence. Rather does the body, without prejudice to its association with the soul, follow in relative independence its own laws of life, and a higher union of the body and soul than the natural is solely the fruit of a moral process, which applies the plasticity of the body to generating a higher unity of the human personality, in which the body is the willing and capable organ of the spirit. The soul, again, as far as it alone is concerned, is a moral growth, impossible without a temporary precedence of knowledge before will, that the latter may apprehend and affirm what is known and rational, and even thus present a higher and firmer unity of the soul with what is rational and with itself in knowledge and volition. And the same thing will necessarily also be true of the unity of the Logos with the humanity. As in the case instanced, the body, as contrasted with the soul, has a certain independence, acting according to its own law of life, and has notwithstanding a receptiveness for the determining power of the soul, and it is only the result of process that the body becomes the voluntary organ of the soul, nay, the mere organic side and manifestation of the personality, so at the higher stage is our soul or the rational being related to the Divine pneuma. The soul has a distinct and relatively independent being, not as contrasted with the body merely, but also with the Divine, and moves in relative separation therefrom according to its own law of life. But as there pertains to the law of life of the body its receptiveness also, nay, its need, for the determining power of the soul, so there pertains to the law of life of the human soul the receptiveness and the need for God. Indeed, that which, looked at from beneath, is the determining power of the soul, regarded from above is in itself receptiveness for the Divine pneuma.[1] Now in Christ, by virtue of the Logos, there is present the *Fons Spiritus Sancti* itself, not merely pneuma. Since, then, the Divine side or God as Logos cannot of itself enter into a state of potentiality, whilst the human side has nevertheless to first subject itself to development, the actuality of the former side at the beginning extends beyond the human. There cannot generally be at once actual knowledge and volition in the latter, consequently the human side cannot be made immediately participant in the knowledge and will of God as Logos, who ever conserves and rules the world. So far at first the actuality of the Divine Logos-life necessarily extends beyond the humanity; but this relative externality of the Divine and human sides, this relative independent assertion of both sides (of the human in increase, learning, temptation, and opposition), does not divide the two, does not destroy the unity of this person,[2] but renders it possible that both the Logos should exercise an influence on the growth of the God-human person, and that the humanity should carry out the unity existing in it with the Logos also with consciousness

---

[1] The νοῦς is in itself receptive of the pneuma.

[2] As the newer Kenotic theories think, which on this ground allow themselves to be urged on to their positions as to the depotentiating of the Logos, and which still only apparently avoid the initial relative externality or preponderance of the Divine side. For the Logos who has emptied Himself does not nevertheless unite the Logos in every respect with man from the beginning; if the emptying is not partly an annihilation of the life of the Logos, that life is still present somehow without being united with the humanity, and therefore still towers above the humanity in this respect. This is the *Logos über der Linie* in the later teaching of Thomasius.

and volition. Thus the *Unio* itself is not to be regarded as a rigid and motionless whole, but as a whole which is in process of realization, as a whole which is perfected in ever higher form.—The necessity of this growth not simply for the human side generally, but of its growth through ever richer extension of the *Unio* over the sides of the humanity which were not at first developed at all, and therefore of the growth of the humanity, which is at the same time a growth of the God-humanity, becomes the clearer if we reflect upon the following consideration. The *Unio* cannot merely depend upon *God's* knowing and willing Himself united with humanity in the Logos. For this would only be a one-sided *Unio*,[1] namely, one which lays hold upon this man and makes Him its own, and would not be the full idea of the incarnation, although many stop at this assertion, and therefore make no progress in the uniting of the two sides. That *Unio* is manifestly higher and more complete, which does not simply present a uniting of God with human nature, but which is *reciprocal*, inasmuch as the humanity on its side knows, wills, and realizes this *Unio*, and therefore itself also appropriates the Divine side. Only in this way does the *Unio* become a double-sided, and therefore increasing, union; and only thus are the distinctions of the natures themselves preserved therein adopted into the service of the *Unio*. And in this way only also is the doctrine of a perfect humanity, with self-consciousness and self-determination, instead of being a danger to the unity of the person, made fruitful for it and for the complete idea of the God-humanity. For even the humanity knows and wills itself to be God-human. But the necessary presupposition for all this is, that the God-human living unity is one which is self-motive, and not a complete unity unchangeably settled from the beginning. It is accomplished through the efficient and enduring distinctiveness of the factors, of the Divine and human, indeed even the distinctions within the human itself. The human side is not merely passively assumed, but it is also on its side livingly determined within its own vital law, and determined to co-operation in order to produce the perfect realization of the God-humanity, because by receiving it attains to the appropriation of the

[1] According to the language of the Lutheran theologians, a μονόπλευρον.

Divine. It is not mechanically overpowered and selflessly compelled by the power of the indwelling Logos, but the Deity limits, not indeed His working in the world generally, and still less His own life, but nevertheless His influence in and His real communication to the humanity to this extent, that the humanity may remain true to its own law of life, which indeed also originates in the creative Logos, and which predetermines and attracts it to progressive and actual union with Him. This is the ἡσυχάζειν of the Deity, which Irenæus, Melanchthon, and Chemnitz still teach, and by means of which the interests are more pertinently regarded, which sought their satisfaction in the self-kenosis of the Logos.

3. But how then is the God-human unity to be thought, which must not be absent even from the beginning, but which *is*, that it may *become*, *i.e.* that it may equalize the realization and the absolute idea of the God-humanity, which is initially a mere potential beginning? If we are unsuccessful in laying down adequate positive propositions upon this point,— seeing that we do not know for a moment the beginnings of the process by which, in our own case, spirits and body marry, —still we may attain to negative or limiting statements. The two-sided *Unio* cannot at the outset exist in the sphere of knowledge and volition proper, which presuppose self-consciousness, neither in relation to nor by the agency of the same; for neither human will nor consciousness can be actually existent at the outset. Therefore, at the outset only, the conscious will of *God* can be present in the *Unio*, without God-humanity of the actual will and consciousness being already the result. And the other limit lies in the fact, that it cannot possibly be said, that by the self-positing of the man as Ego, and by self-determination, man generally first becomes man, and capable of God-human *Unio* of some kind. For the self-positing and self-determination of the man is somehow preceded by a potency, human essence or human nature, which strives after self-actualization in knowledge and volition, and is not a nonentity, and which distinguishes him from other beings, and makes him already man. The human soul must be from the commencement of its existence of another kind to the soul of animals, namely, endowed with impulse and power toward that self-positing in the form of conscious-

ness and volition. Accordingly, maintaining the mean between these two limits, we say that if the *Unio* cannot begin in the sphere of the actual human consciousness and volition, it may yet begin in the sphere of the human nature existent from the beginning; God may wed His essence and life, His nature, with the nature of this man in unique fashion, different from the being of God in the world generally. The Divine Essence may move and rule in the very beginnings of this child of man, indeed may mysteriously unite Himself with his soul, that it may become the sacred place in which God as Logos, the Divine world-centre, will find His adequate realization in the world. As, then, no moment is conceivable in which the humanity was nothing but an empty form, the loving will of the God who is about to become man keeps back no communication for which there is receptiveness. And if even plants long for the light, why should not the humanity of Jesus in unconscious drawing and impulse already gravitate according to its innate basis of life, and be not merely passively appropriated by Him, but somehow already a participant of the Logos life? Were this the case, then at no moment would there be in Christ a human element, which the Deity had not assumed, in order to fully satisfy the receptiveness according to its existing measure, and there would similarly be no moment in the life of Christ in which he did not bear a God-human character. And so, conversely, since the *Unio* of the Logos with the humanity, God never knew Himself without the man assumed, but God knew Himself to have become man, although neither in such a way that the relative solubility of the factors of this person, and thus a true development by a process which makes the mutable immutable, was excluded, nor in such a way that the one absolute Divine personality became man, but God knew and willed Himself as having become man only in the Logos.

*Observation.*—The ancient Christian analogy, which compares the union of the Divine nature and the human with the union of body and soul, permits of being still further applied to the increasing realization of the God-humanity. Every human individual, the idea of every one pre-existing in the Divine counsel, can only be so conceived in his realization, that the creative will of God begins to wed, so to speak, this idea with an earthly reality. And this Divine idea, with which the individual is put into relation by his creation, forms the background of the empirical life, its depth and its height. It places itself before the eyes in the awakening self-consciousness as the ideal, with the realization of which is born into the world the eternal ideal nucleus, so to speak, of the personality. In Christ there is the eternal nucleus, which is to enter into realization in the world, not merely a Divine idea, but a reality, God Himself as the eternal Logos who wills to become man. And the development of Christ proceeds purely and with Divine security, because God, bearing in Himself the purpose of the perfect incarnation, has so allied Himself from the beginning with this human nature, that He essentially determines its development from within, and brings the real Divine archetype, which He is Himself as the Logos, to presentation in a creaturely life.

4. It is therefore of importance not simply to maintain, but to further elaborate, the distinction of the *two states*, the state of humiliation and that of exaltation, which was first definitely laid down by the Reformation with its more enlightened interest in the true humanity of Christ. It is neither to be permitted that the state of humiliation should become a semblance by the premature dating backwards of the state of exaltation, nor that it should be eternalized, so to speak, by the God-human development not attaining the goal of absolute humanity, in which the appropriation of the Deity and the humanity had become perfect and reciprocal, in which God knows Himself as having become human, and the humanity knows itself as assumed into the Deity and perfect, and God as the Logos knows Himself to be appropriating. The development of the doctrine of the first temporal state is first laid upon the Christian Church at its evangelical stage, because of the high importance which pertains to the high-priesthood of Christ in relation to the doctrine of justification by faith. To the state of humiliation the *being man* itself is not indeed to be attributed; for otherwise either that state must be made eternal, or humanity must be again laid aside. In both cases a state of the exaltation of the humanity would be permanently excluded, which would leave for it no humiliation any longer

remaining. Nor are individual elements or circumstances merely of the earthly life to be attributed to the humiliation into which Jesus entered, but everything in which the God-man still stood in a state of development, in disproportion to His idea. Nevertheless, accurate dogmatic expression will have to distinguish between humbleness and humiliation. This entrance into a condition of development, which was certainly a state of humbleness, because it means a distinction between idea and reality, is still not to be called in itself a state of *humiliation*, neither in such a way that God, nor that the God-man, was Himself the one humiliated, for He was not man before He entered into the earthly life; the assumption of a really pre-existent humanity, which was to be humiliated to earthly beginnings, would bring something of a Doketic nature into the earthly humanity and its growth, for instance an eternal incarnation instead of a temporal, or at least an element of human existence, which would not be humbleness as yet. Before He was, the God-man could neither be humiliated, nor could He humiliate Himself. Nor, moreover, could the Deity, unless we would pass over to the Kenosis of the Logos. On the other hand, to the time of humbleness, to which His earthly state lowered Him, there belongs of course a voluntary *self-humiliation*, which was not as yet given in God-human development *per se*.[1] This self-humiliation belongs, strictly speaking, to the time of the conscious God-human life. But what was outwardly humiliation regarded inwardly by the eye of faith, because voluntary self-humiliation, in its augmentation is at the same time an augmenting revelation of the Divine $\delta\acute{o}\xi a$ of His love, although that augmenting self-humiliation was not merely present to the worldly glance, but also included in relation to the consciousness and volition of Christ an augmenting self-transposition and condescension in and to us in self-forgetful love which is full of sacrifice, through which self-sacrifice His God-human development, the ever-augmenting inner transfiguration and self-realization of the God-man, was not interrupted, but constantly perfected. And as defined by the previous amplification, the opinion is excluded, that the God-*human* existence was already in itself and in general

[1] Phil. ii. 6, etc.; 2 Cor. viii. 9.

a state of the humbleness or even the self-humiliation of the Logos or the God-man, although it may of course be said in the wider sense that the incarnation and what it included is a self-humiliation of God, just as Hamann calls creation a work of the Divine lowliness. There is signified thereby the condescension of the Divine love, which does not despise the humble, a disregard, so to speak, of His majesty and glory, which allows Him to see a greater good in condescending to poor sinful humanity, indeed in desiring to live in an actual man. There is a Divine self-forgetfulness of love, which loses itself in its objects, and shuns nothing to save them, nay, surrenders itself to them in unreserved self-communication. Only there is never in this condescension the love which loses or abandons itself, neither its power nor its conscious vitality, but it is its perfect self-activity. In this συγκατάβασις of the Divine love the religious motive of the Kenotic theory obtains its rights, without adopting the false consequences of the thought. The converse of all loving self-humiliation is rather the spiritual δόξα of love, which is not lost, but active therein.

*Observation.*—After the fundamental positions won, we can now advance to the single particulars.

FIRST HEAD: *The act of the incarnation of God in Christ, i.e. His natural God-humanity, or the doctrine of His holy nature.*

SECOND HEAD: *The ethical God-humanity, or the doctrine of His holy personality.*

THIRD HEAD: *The official God-humanity, or Christ's God-human functions on earth.*

# FIRST HEAD.

## CHRIST'S NATURAL GOD-HUMANITY, OR HIS HOLY NATURE AND ITS INNATE PREROGATIVES.

### § 105.

The act of the incarnation cannot be a common act of the Divine and human nature, but proceeds from the former alone. It allies itself with the first creation or conservation (§ 101), but is notwithstanding supernatural, because by a creative Divine act the second Adam is called forth as the perfect, universal, and central receptiveness of human nature, the elements of the first creation being appropriated, in order to become by the reception of the fulness of the Divine self-communication the absolutely realized God-man, in whom God as Logos has become man, and the Son of man by this very means knows Himself to be the Son of God. This supernaturalness of the second Adam (§ 102) has for its more exact definition His *birth of a virgin*, and is, positively regarded, a *unique indwelling and working* of God Himself, the product of which is a holy, God-united human nature (§ 104), by virtue of which Jesus was from the beginning God-human, and capable of presenting at every stage an archetypal human life.

Comp. Schleiermacher, *Der christl. Glaube*, ii. §§ 96, 97, 98.

1. The incarnation is indeed not complete from the beginning, but rather gradually developing. It is still to

be so thought that the existence of Christ is never a merely human existence; there is from the beginning implanted in Him a God-human life. Its development must be preceded by a corresponding basis, innate, not first made by a human act. As regards the Divine act which takes the initiative, we must then start from what was the ancient Christian view, that the human *soul* constituted the medium for the Deity who would become man, and that through its mediation the sensuous organism was appropriated and formed from the elements of the human race given in Mary. And the soul itself is not given by Mary nor by the race, but by a Divine creative act. Indeed, as regards every human soul, it is not the race, the generic process, which is the sufficient cause of its origin, since Creationism represents an essential element of truth; the race can only modify what is given creatively. But here the question relates to the creative constituting of the soul of the second Adam, who, although He can assume the imperfections and frailty of human nature, can by no means assume pollution from the race. Every created human soul shows itself then, next, as the plastic force for the formation of the body from the elements presented by the race. But the human spirit of Jesus made by the Logos stands from the beginning infinitely above all other human souls. Not merely is He, like Adam, $\psi υ χ \grave{η}$ $ζ \hat{ω} σ α$, but He is characterized by a central receptiveness for God, and is thus potentially the second Adam or the pneumatic man,[1] creatively called forth it is true, and so far creaturely, but adapted for the manifestation in Him of the Divine image as a fact in the world. Therefore the human soul of Jesus, constituted by the Logos and at the same time united with Him, therefore a pneumatic soul, evokes at the moment of its origin from the elements of the mother, which are not of themselves as yet a human being, and by uniting itself with these elements, a human structure, on the one side like to us in nature, and on the other side so organized as to correspond with the pneumatic man who is to be realized. Thus two points present themselves for consideration: first, the connection with the world of conservation; secondly, the supernaturalness of the origin of this man.

[1] 1 Cor. xv. 45, etc.

2. CONNECTION WITH THE FIRST CREATION.—So certainly as this man was not a product of the circle of life in which He appears, and indeed generally cannot be regarded as the act of empirical humanity, but the act of the Divine idea of humanity resting in the Divine counsel and destined to realization, an idea with which the efficient will is united when the time is fulfilled;[1] so certainly also the new man, who is God-man, cannot be associated with the ancient world merely, inasmuch as, after He has become in a supernatural manner, He adds Himself thereto as a member, but, in order to become such, He must also stand from His commencement in a living and internal connection with humanity, and with its history prior to His days, not ideally merely, or because as the idea of the God-man, or more immediately as the idea of God, He is the prototype of humanity and defines its history, but really also from the side of God and of man, although the real incarnation did not begin before Christ, neither in Israel nor elsewhere. The Logos has not entered abruptly, or from without, into humanity; but He was ever in the world; indeed the Divine centre of the world, which after all had been made by it in order to reveal Himself therein progressively, brings forth in Christ Him to whom He may communicate His innermost essence, and in whom He may Himself appear. And as far as humanity before Christ is concerned, although it has not productively participated in this new act, it has done so efficiently. The receptiveness of human nature for the appearance of Christ has a history especially in the Old Testament. The growing longing for Him in the ever more definite shaping of His image, has drawn as it were into humanity the Logos who desired to become man. The living desire for Him pertaining to the historical conditions of His appearing is fitted to exclude an abrupt magical miracle even from the real historical side. In this mediating, not effective, activity of the race the Spirit of God also works. But this Divine activity belongs to the world of the first creation, or to conservation, and the efficiency of the Holy Spirit in Mary

[1] Even the apparently contradictory statements of Schleiermacher upon this point may be harmonized, in the sense that to him Christ is the act or effect of the ideal humanity eternally given in the Divine counsel.

does not transcend its limits, and does not therefore forestall the incarnation. Rather does everything return to this point: the Holy Spirit prepares for Himself in humanity, especially in the people of hope and longing, receptiveness for the Messiah as a living desire. This ripened receptiveness of the old humanity for the new humanity or the God-man is the *faith* wrought in Mary by the Spirit of God.[1] This faith is the spiritual bond between Adamitic humanity and Christ. Of a further preparation of humanity for the conception of the God-man than what lies in faith, and therefore in the psychical sphere, there was no need. True, the depravation by sin also extends to the corporeal side. But no purification of the corporeal element of Mary by the Holy Ghost preceding the act of the *Unio* is necessary, that Mary should not communicate impurity. She had not to communicate purity to Him; deficient in holiness, she, like all, needed the redemption and new birth through Christ, and not through the mere Logos. Rather let us say it is God as Logos who makes the pure soul of this man, and imparts to it by His own *assumptio* or appropriation the power at the same time to reject all that is impure, and only to adopt from Mary the essentially good substance of the elements in a harmonious manner. The power of self-protection lies with perfect sufficiency in the soul united with the Logos, which gives itself its corporization from Mary, and not in Mary. We therefore teach that the same pneumatic soul, the creation of which is at the same time incipient incarnation, provides itself with a body, seeing that as a plastic force it evokes a human form from the elements of the mother, and in the act of appropriating these elements purifies and harmonizes them, as far as is pertinent to the beginning of a God-human life still subject to growth and human weakness (§§ 104. 4, 105. 1).

*Observation.*—The passage of the Apostles' Creed: "Conceived of the Holy Ghost" (*de Spiritu Sancto*), refers back to Matt. i. 20, and need not therefore be understood of the Spirit in the Trinitarian sense (see above, pp. 162, 163), as if an incarnation of the Holy Ghost were meant to be taught. Rather is the πνεῦμα ἅγιον (Matt. i. 20 and in the Creed) the less precise ancient Christian designation of the Divine Essence generally,

---
[1] Luke i. 38, etc.

out of which (*de quo*) Christ has come. To the Holy Spirit in the Trinitarian sense is only to be ascribed, according to the Scriptures, first, the internal preparation of humanity for the Divine incarnation, and secondly, after the *Unio* the animation of the humanity of Christ by the Divine power issuing from the Logos. Christ is anointed with the Holy Spirit, and thus becomes *Fons Spiritus Sancti*. Everything Divine, so far as it becomes the subjective inner power of the man, is wont to be ascribed in the Scriptures to the Holy Ghost, but not the incarnation of God, in which rather the Divine principle of *objective* revelation or the Logos finds His manifestation.

3. The essential completion of the first stage, that of association with the sphere of conservation, is the new creation, which here passes over into incarnation (§ 101). The human soul of Jesus is creaturely, but being at no moment without the Logos, is from the beginning a pneumatic humanity. What in us is new birth, is in Him Divine incarnation. He is God-man, and that from birth.—To His supernatural origin is attributed by the Holy Scriptures and the Church His *birth of a virgin*, *i.e.* the origin of Jesus without the co-operation of a man. But it appears sufficient to assume for Christ an origin not explicable by the race-connection, and therefore a supernatural or miraculous Divine act, and no dogmatic interest seems to require the exclusion of the participation of a male. Certainly, if we might suppose that the sinlessness of Jesus is only secured by the birth of a virgin, this exclusion would readily follow. But even by the agency of Mary inherited sin might communicate itself, unless with the Romanist doctrine we would absolve Mary from inherited sin, or we would absolve humanity generally therefrom.[1] The guarantee for the natural holiness of the child Jesus cannot in fact lie outside of Him in Mary, but only in the Divine power of the pneumatic man united with the Logos, which effects a correct, and not a perverted coalescence of the elements from Mary, in order that all the stages of life may be normally run through by Jesus. And if the guarantee for the natural sinlessness of Jesus lies in His inner being solely, in like manner in the origin of Jesus from wedlock the Divine power of the Logos in the soul of

[1] With Pelagius and a few moderns.

Jesus might, it would seem, ensure the rejection of everything impure. And in this case the conception of a virgin would only be of importance for Mary and her course of life, but not for the Person of Christ, which can only owe its exaltation and purity to itself. Indeed, it appears possible to bring the latter to view as having its support in itself without the supposition of a birth of a virgin. Schleiermacher adds to this, that the Evangelical conception of marriage, as distinguished from the Romish conception, does not permit origin from marriage to be regarded as less honourable than the origin of Adam, and conjectures that a false disregard of marriage as a holy state pleasing to God, together with the elevation of the adoration of Mary to dogmatic significance, may have contributed to the early promulgation of the doctrine of the birth of a virgin. Seeing, therefore, that the birth of a virgin does not secure what it is meant to do, its acceptance is, he says, that of a superfluous miracle. The miracle is, he thinks, rather to be seen in that Divine act, by which Christ became the new creation, inexplicable from the time previous, but endued with the power of purifying everything arising from the parents. This would assert, he adds, far more than the removal of the male factor, and the question is destitute of importance in reference to the dignity of the Person of Christ. There is no mistake that it makes a very great difference, whether or not with the denial of the birth of a virgin it is wished to deny the supernaturalness of the origin of Christ. As far as Schleiermacher is concerned, he maintains a miracle in the origin of Christ. Nor does he refer to what appears to be the leading motive in the more recent denials of the birth of a virgin, that it especially contradicts all analogies and natural law. And he rightly does not lay stress upon this. The more recent investigation of nature knows manifold modes of propagation,[1] and in one and the same kind of being too. If men did not always exist, and if the essence of man lies in reason, in any case the supposition remains necessary, that the first men did not arise from the community of the race. Finally, he also does not seek, and rightly, to show from the New Testament itself,[2]

---

[1] Comp. Oscar Schmidt, *Descendenzlehre*, 1873.
[2] As, *e.g.*, Keim essayed, *Leben Jesu von Nazara*.

that Joseph was the natural father of Jesus, but he opposes the relative portions of the early history as having been derived from tradition, and not attested by Christ.

But criticism, which is unfettered in the Evangelical theology, must also hold itself free from dogmatic prepossessions. If no attention be paid to the dogmatic reasons against the credibility of the relative Scripture passages, the *critical* reasons can scarcely be called important. The history of Christology shows, that the birth of a virgin must have belonged to the primitive Christian type of the Evangelical tradition; for even all Ebionites do not deny it, and the section which did deny it was regarded by the Church as heretical, as the Ignatian letters already show. This type of doctrine is common to Matthew and Luke, and the latter had copious information upon the holy family, indeed had had a special record thereupon, which he incorporated in his Gospel. Schleiermacher's *dogmatic* reasons, moreover, show nothing in favour of the necessity of the origin of Jesus from wedlock. The *purity* and goodness of marriage itself is not denied by the birth of a virgin, although it is affected with sin in the sinful. Its holiness and Divine institution are taught by the same Holy Scriptures which have this narrative of the birth of a virgin. Nor does *the identity of nature* of Jesus with us contradict this birth. For if origin from the community of the human race constituted humanity, Adam would not be a man. The identity of nature of Jesus with us remains fully assured, if His soul was a human soul, if He was born of Mary, if He received His organism from elements in her, and if she nourished Him with her life-blood. But if then the birth of a virgin is possible without a diminution of His identity of nature with us, supposing Christian doctrine could only attain to the construction of a double possibility of His mode of origin, the decision might fairly have to depend upon the historical testimonies which bear witness to the birth of a virgin as the form of His origin which has actually occurred, especially if no special historico-critical suspicions exist against the relative sections. And we may go a step further. It is true the verification of the birth of a virgin by means of the sinlessness necessary is insufficient. For if it is said that the sexual instinct has a sensuously egoistic side essentially, and therefore that the products of generation essentially have sinfulness, this may be conceded; but it does not follow that Mary could not of herself have propagated sin, and the main fact will still depend even thus upon that Divine rejection of all impurity, which Schleiermacher maintains. But there are other grounds which commend the supposition of a birth of a virgin. To suppose the highest element of pre-Christian piety as the originating element of this person is not a question of decorum merely, but a dogmatic necessity, if the supernaturalness of His person, which even Schleiermacher maintains, is not to lack the point of spiritual alliance in the receptiveness of Mary, and if the miracle is not to be supernatural in a false sense, that is to say, abrupt. And to this requirement origin from marriage is not suited. Instead of this, the moment of the origin of Christ or the incarnation must coincide with the moment of highest attachment and devotedness to God, or of faith in its Old Testament blossoming. If this psychical link of connection in Mary's act of faith had been wanting (Luke i.), the exchange with a physical medium, the co-operation of the male, could form no compensation for the absence of the more important spiritual link. Without this point of connection, the miracle would immediately become a magical one. And further, the birth of a virgin was by no means indifferent with regard to the mind of the mother, but of incalculable influence. It was of importance for the whole education and development of the child, that she should know from the first that there was something extraordinary in this child. But the necessity for the birth of a virgin follows most decidedly from the peculiar being of Jesus, and this leads to the positive manner of His origin. The generation of Jesus in a marriage of two descendants of Adam with limited and particular individuality does not harmonize with the new creation, which is accomplished in the second Adam, and with the incarnation in Him (§ 101). Not with the latter, because therein God as Logos transposes Himself into a human life, and creation here passes over into the incarnation, which can with difficulty be combined in thought with natural generation. And, next, origin from marriage would of necessity conflict with His uniqueness (§ 103). In Jesus the man is supposed to appear, who does not present a one-sided, limited individuality, but who is of universal significance. But He could not issue from the procreation of a single human pair without inheriting any of the one-sidednesses, blameless though they be, of human nature, just as indeed undeniably the individuality and natural one-sidedness or limitation of individuals coincide with their descent. From marriage an individual like others, a talent or a genius might have arisen; but He who is unique of His kind, the Son of man, could only have originated in generation without detriment to His uniqueness and dignity, if the parents did not effect what they must effect, if they were for a moment concerned, the communication to their offspring of a one-sided individuality imparted by them. If it is said that they brought forth Jesus, but they did not bring an individuality limited like their own, but in this respect their causality was sisted or suspended by a Divine act, this would mean the postulating of a new negative miracle, it would be the supposition of natural causality, and the removal of it again by a miracle in a respect not separable from it, and the non-allowance of its working according to its natural manner. But this would immediately be to heap up aimless miracles. How much more simple the fact appears, if the creative act of God, which even Schleiermacher requires notwithstanding, and which must in any case be supposed in still more original fashion in the first Adam, is thought to be so powerful that in attachment to the believing receptiveness of the virgin the pneumatic man is produced, who thus belongs on one side to humanity, and is incorporate, because from the elements, the blood and life of the mother, He becomes a historic man and a member of the race, but is not therefore a mere product of the same, but is destined as the second Adam to become its prototype and head.

The birth of a virgin is not therefore a new miracle, which is added to the new creation in this man, which is at the same time incarnation; it is only the negative determination necessary for the realization of this new creation and incarnation, whereas Schleiermacher's denial of the birth of a virgin, whilst he maintains the new creation and incarnation, must add new miracles on two sides, in the first place a miraculous substitute for the point of connection which Mary has to supply, and, next, a miraculous suspension, not merely of the sinful influence of the parents, but also of that influence which is not to be separated from the working of their causality, if more than a mere semblance thereof is to remain. The participation of the mother cannot of itself have produced the cosmopolitan character of the Person of Jesus, the peculiarity of which just consists in its universality and centrality (§ 102). For what she gave, was only the virgin receptiveness,—faith on the one side, and on the other side the *stamina* of human nature which were capable of appropriation. But the two of themselves were incapable of the generation of a man, whether with a one-sided individuality, or an individuality which was not one-sided. The productive cause, as in the case of Adam, is purely the Divine agency, only that, as distinguished from Adam, the being of Jesus does not consist merely in the material taken from the earth together with a rational soul, but is of a God-human, holy nature,—a difference which it owes not to its lack of a human father, but to the Divine act, which by the intervention of Mary constituted the God-human totality of the Person of Jesus. This leads us to the consideration of the innate prerogatives of the God-man.

*Observation.*—With what has been said, Rothe, among modern theologians, agrees. Rothe (*Theol. Ethik*, ed. 1, vol. ii. p. 279, etc.) requires the birth of a virgin, because all procreation has in it the autonomic working of the sensuous nature. In his *Stillen Stunden* he shows how the uniqueness of Jesus as the central individual of humanity requires the absence of the co-operation of the male. Comp. his *Dogmatik*, vol. ii. pp. 120, etc., on the idea of the central individual. Lange (in his *Positive Dogmatik*) and Sack have expressed themselves in a similar manner.

## § 106.—*The Essential God-manhood.*

By His supernatural birth Christ has essential God-manhood, with peculiar prerogatives of a corporeal and spiritual kind.

*Observation.*—Certainly even in Christ the physical (the

innate) and the ethical are to be accurately distinguished. But the first having in Him its proper relation to the second, it cannot be represented without a glance at that for which it affords the possibility. The moral process, however, is reserved as the object of special consideration.

1. What is now required is, on the one hand, not to diminish the prerogatives given in the God-human nature of Jesus, and on the other hand to think as perfectly as possible of His identity of nature with us. Dogmatics has, at times, attributed to Jesus the prerogatives of Adam in Paradise, or else, for the sake of the *Unio personalis*, has straightway ascribed the Divine prerogatives of the Logos to His psychical and corporeal nature (*e.g.* a natural incapability of death). On the other hand, in order to think Him quite like ourselves, some have allowed Him to assume a sinful organism, which He has been supposed to transform in a holy manner by virtue of His holy personal life.[1] The Ecclesiastical doctrine has to seek the mean between the two exaggerations. Accordingly it does not deny that Jesus, like ourselves, besides the imperfection which is given in the first stages of growth, was also affected with those weaknesses which are called $\pi\acute{a}\theta\eta$ $\dot{a}\delta\iota\acute{a}\beta\lambda\eta\tau a$, such as susceptibility to hunger, frost, fatigue, etc. In fortunate inconsistency, despite the doctrine of the *communicatio idiomatum* we have discussed, the Church permitted itself to be led in this case by the interests of the belief that He has necessarily assumed full identity of nature with us, and therefore even our fallen nature, with the evils and weaknesses which are to be regarded as the consequences of sin, only not sinfulness itself, which He came to cure. By virtue of His Divine power the Logos might have, it was said, communicated a majestic form to the humanity of Jesus, but instead of this He desired humiliation in likeness to us. Thomasius nevertheless rightly requires, that Christ has not so entered into our natural mortality, which is a penal state for us, and into the state of the common guilt, inasmuch as that state is an evil, a burden to be borne, as if He had

---

[1] The former appeared in Monophysitic manner, *e.g.* on the part of the Apthartodoketes; the other appeared in Edward Irving, Menken, and others. Several exegetes, like Holsten, also incorrectly attribute the latter doctrine to the Apostle Paul.

Himself personal guilt, but only in such a way that He did not enter into our guilt-laden common life as a stranger, but actually belonging thereto, has performed the law according to His Father's and His own loving will concerning it.

2. Amongst the *prerogatives* pertaining to Him, by virtue of the *Unio*, Dogmatics reckoned, besides the *anhypostasia* which has already been spoken of, the *singularis corporis et animæ excellentia*, to which is to be attributed *summa formæ venustas et elegantia*, the *equalis temperies* and *naturalis immortalitas*, and on the side of the soul the *impeccabilitas* or *anamartesia*, to which was yet to be added a special intellectual endowment. Christ must not be lifted above those imperfections of human nature which were to be first set aside by ethical means. And, on the other hand, the *Unio* with the Logos could not be without effect from the beginning, but has rather communicated to Jesus peculiar prerogatives of body and soul.

The *Venustas* cannot be an end in itself; it is moral beauty only which is of imperishable worth. And this virtuous beauty, although according to its full idea related to the body, is not innate, but is an ethical good, namely, that which appears of free will, by means of the ever more victorious illuminating and animating power of the Spirit. We have certainly no right to think, with the ancient Church, *e.g.* Clement of Alexandria, the form of Christ unbeautiful and ugly, in order that the beauty of His soul may shine the more gloriously for this foil; and a Doketic contempt for the body can find here no point of support, for this would mean that what is innermost in Jesus has not entered in an animating manner at all into His corporeality, and become manifest therein. Rather, wherever anything ideal or spiritual is revealed in matter or corporeality, it is of necessity beautiful. But if, conversely, Greek and also many modern representations would portray in Christ the archetype of human beauty, this is as little to be praised. It is not the beauty of His body, enchanting like Apollo, which can work to redeem, but ethical beauty; it is the sacred head once wounded which has conquered the world, and it is moral beauty which has led beyond heathenism into the realm of peace and sanctification. It is therefore only permitted us to say that His body was a corresponsive, worthy temple of the spirit, free from all natural disfigurements or special defects. The power of this pneumatic man evoked a certain good natural form, which had notwithstanding for its purpose that moral influencing which makes the outward the expression of the inward nobility, and only after the faultless completion of this task, is the full glory of the eternal beauty and majesty of the Son of man to be expressed.[1]

Still more important is the *æquabilis temperies*. The natural one-sidedness of the temperaments has become an abnormity in us. For whether the careless and easy alone, or the quiet and unmoved, whether the fiery and restless or the profound and earnest sentiment rules, sin is there.[2] Every individuality, Christ's excepted, starts from a one-sidedness of a psychical kind, which even shows itself in the bodily constitution, in which indeed sin, taking it into its service, makes itself specific, although every individuality should bring about by its means the appropriation, from the basis, of the good of the other. In Christ now there is by nature no such one-sidedness of temperament. He could not fall into sins of temperament, but He was not released from the task of making the *æquabile temperamentum* consciously and volitionally into the God-human *character*, of confirming the bond of the harmony of the natural powers, and of subduing by a real process of will their manifest and necessary initial looseness of connection. Though He was full of natural goodness, still the all-round virtue His life displays is no mere bloom of a holy nature, but is at the same time a moral work; He is adapted to be the example and prototype for men of all temperaments. But His natural God-humanity, as it did not anticipate such a result of His self-culture, has made the same, on the other hand, perfectly *possible*.—It agrees herewith that no such dependence upon a national type can be attributed to Him as a one-sidedness of temperament would have brought, an inadmissible limit to the inner universality of His person and its presentation. Every

---

[1] 1 Cor. xv. 47; Phil. iii. 21; Tit. ii. 13. A beginning is found in Luke ix. 29; Matt. xvii. 2.

[2] Comp. Martensen's Sermon on *Ein Jeglicher sei gesinnt wie Jesus Christus auch war*.

one of the nationalities, as they are, is associated with sin, and is possibly to be originally explained from the crystallization of one-sidednesses of temperament. Therefore nationalities are not eternal. Christ, on the contrary, was certainly to start with a member of Israel, but in such a way as not to be an alien to the heathen world, or that His typical character ceased in relation thereto. He is a true Israelite, and presents in His person the truth of Israel, because it is the true being of Israel to be Jehovah's servant, the world-historical organ for the revelation to the world. He is the centre of Israel in such a way as not to cease to be the true centre of humanity, the Son of man and the second Adam, thus realizing Israel's destiny. He is a blessing for all races in the innermost sphere immediately, for other spheres mediately. Further, in order that His body might be capable of being the perfectly corresponding organ of His will, adapted to the presentation of the God-human life, He must be free from natural weakliness or sickliness, and must be in possession of natural soundness and force, which was also equal to the greatest strains and privations,[1] and again steeled itself morally. In natural endowment he had the pliant basis for the perfect mastery of His body, for the animating subjection of the same to the will of the spirit.[2] Indeed, nature and spirit were so united by His power of will (a fact which also broke forth in His transfiguration), the Spirit was so far already naturalized in Him by the ethical process, that this unity of the natural and spiritual already attained shows itself in His *miraculous power*. This is not described in the Gospels as innate, nor is it to be resolved into a mere work of God; it is described to be God-human, to pertain to His ripened personality, not a gift lent to Him from without for a time, but an ethical product of His own peculiar power, which as God-man He possessed by virtue of the continuous coalescence of the Divine and human. And generally, the ever more perfect naturalizing of the spirit in Him must even upon earth influence His body in a spiritualizing manner.

On the other hand, a *naturalis immortalitas* must not be

[1] Luke vi. 12, 13, comp. with v. 20, etc., iv. 2; Matt. iv. 2 also calls to mind His passion.
[2] Matt. iv. 2; Luke ix. 28, 29; Matt. xiv. 25; John vi. 19.

ascribed to His body. If the *Unio* had effected this, it could only have died, and participated in His death, by a negative miracle. As certainly as the *Unio* of the Divine nature with His soul remained without interruption, so was His body at first only associated loosely with His soul. It is therefore not to be said of Him that He by nature *non potuit mori;* but still it does not follow that we may say of Him that *non potuit non mori*, and therefore that we may assert a natural necessity of death unchangeable and external, to which He, like us, must have succumbed. This would be to injure the dignity of His person, if not the voluntariness of His death. Rather as regards His will the mortality of His body, which was inherent therein, would have been superable, much more than in the case of Adam; but He had entered into the state of guilt-laden humanity, and He would not abandon that state, although He could. If, therefore, neither a naturally necessary immortality, nor a naturally necessary mortality, is to be asserted of Him, the formula is valid with respect to Him, *potuit mori et potuit non mori*.[1] His body indeed had not this double power, but His person. The latter, moreover, could not propose to itself the problem of the removal of the dissolution of His soul and His body, but only this, to make His body the perfect and ready organ of His soul. This resemblance to us, by which His body considered in itself was subject to death, unless the energy of His will opposed itself to what it did not want, became at the same time a ladder for Him, to feel the misery of His brethren, and to be able to transfer Himself with His sympathy into the penal state consequent on sin. Since, on the other hand, even before His resurrection, the ethical union of body and spirit in Him was already so perfect, indeed no merely physical necessity of dying lay upon His person, —death was a thing inappropriate for Him. He must have felt quite otherwise than we do the unnaturalness of death, death finding in the holy Son of man no real handle.[2] Nevertheless, the perfecting of His person is only given with the vanquishing of the possibility of death by His resurrection, so that even in relation to this perfecting death was the last enemy to be conquered.[3]

[1] John x. 18.   [2] John xi. 33, x. 18.   [3] Rom. i. 3, 4; 1 Cor. xv. 26.

3. THE INNATE SPIRITUAL PREROGATIVES OF THE GOD-MAN.—In a spiritual respect also the second Adam had a share in human development from elementary beginnings. He did not therefore enter straight into freedom and knowledge as an actualized spirit, but He was of necessity spiritually also a real child, boy, youth, man. He therefore increased spiritually also, as Luke has informed us, that He might sanctify all the stages of human life by passing through them all in a normal manner.

On the other hand, notwithstanding, He could not at any moment (as has been already shown) be a mere empty form of receptiveness, be it a central form even, for otherwise humanity would have been an idle time in Him, without also being potentially incarnation, which would be a Cerinthian view. It cannot even be said of us sons of men, that we are spiritually at the beginning merely a *tabula rasa* in reference to knowledge, as Materialism and Empiricism would have it; a mere empty *liberum arbitrium,* as the Romish doctrine loves to think man on the side of volition, apart from the *dona superaddita* of Adam. To find the right mean between these two extremes of an initial perfection and an initial void, the latter of which would logically lead to Rothe's doctrine of the initial non-existence as yet of the rational soul, is of course difficult. The beginnings themselves of an ordinary human life being shrouded in mystery, we can only in this case argue backwards from actual later life, building upon the fundamental proposition, that what follows in normal development is nothing else than the realization of the commencement, perfected by means of the *form of freedom and consciousness,* and containing in itself *potentially* what follows. On this matter Lange and Martensen have made the best statements. There could be no question of a certainty of truth in us, of a self-evidencing of truth to us, if our spirit were an empty table, if our nature were not so framed by the hand of God that what is true appeals to our nature in a wholly different manner from the untrue, and if we, because empty, were also created indifferent to truth and error, it simply depending on what took possession of our soul first, for example by authority. And it is quite the same on the side of morals and volition. This potency to be presupposed of all actual knowledge we might call the *natural knowledge*, which rests in the ground of the soul, in such a way indeed that the soul is not yet actually master thereof, but that it is destined for the soul, and the soul for it. In an ethical and religious respect we may call this human beginning *natural freedom* and *natural conscience*. This is the spiritual immediateness of the life of feeling in an intellectual and practical respect. But whilst *we* are sinful, and full of inclination to error, it is otherwise in Christ. Spiritually He also begins as a child like us, but with a normally pure life of feeling and perception. There is already a holiness, a holy nature, poured out upon this child; in Him the noble scion, pure as the lily, which has become the symbol of His origin, is grafted on the tree of humanity; He is a bud, which will burst as a majestic blossom, and in the child in Mary's womb, in this bud, there is a soul which already includes the profoundest mysteries. The art of a Raphael has given us a clear conception, how even from the child's eye may beam forth an infinite depth; as He lay in Mary's womb, the angels desired to look in the spirit upon the portentous mystery, which the nature of this child already embraced, and to see therein the miracle of Divine love and wisdom.[1] For here is the man who is not merely encompassed by Him in whom we all live and move and are, but with whom the Son of God, the Divine centre of the world, has entered into a union of an unique kind; and the relation of God as the Logos to Him, and the converse relation, is from the beginning so close, that in Him lives the breath of the Creator of the worlds, who here desires to found the living centre of the world, nay, the birthplace of a new world, and so close therefore that this Divine and human child cannot come to self-consciousness, without at the same time knowing God to be in Himself, without knowing Himself to be the Son of God, and God to be His Father. Even before self-consciousness and freedom are actually there in this Son of God and humanity, His holy nature cannot but have the most intensive and pure impulse towards the Divine, and, as by a natural tact or an antipathy to everything impure and egoistic, this child is secured against evil even in the life of feeling, perception, and intuition, and that before it has,

---
[1] 1 Pet. i. 12.

knows, and wills itself. A holy natural security guides it, to use Martensen's beautiful expression, which does not permit it to turn from its road, and which appropriates nothing which would contradict a pure harmonious development. Thus not merely guarded by the eye of His mother, but from within by His nature, He might have a sinless development. But in order to make visible to us how the union of the Logos with pneumatic humanity might be even in the beginning of its existence much more significant than what might be supposed according to the visible efforts of the child which appear without, the following consideration may be borne in mind. Already when we look at the genesis of thoughts, how they arise in us originally and independently, whether they be the suggestion of love or knowledge, we notice that there is in our souls a mysterious world, not made by us, with a wealth compared with which our actual productions are poverty; and although we are not masters of that wealth, still such happy moments show us what we should and could be. But, separated from God, we always close the doors again, we erect barriers in false freedom, indolence, and unrest, which divide us from our wealth, and ourselves from ourselves; and thus we remain unfruitful, until we are again brought to the right posture in our true centre, until we open and commit ourselves to the power of the Spirit of Christ, who makes one from two in us, causes our empirical man to surrender itself to our ideal man, that the ideal may step forth from its night into realization in us, and may ever more win power in us. Now in the second Adam that mysterious living basis was the Logos Himself. He was the $\hupokeimenon$, the substratum of this Person.[1] He existed behind the external and actual life as the infinitely rich fulness and goodness. But He was never separated (as is the case with us) from the reality by a chasm, or even by an abnormal realization, but it also pertains to Christ's holy nature that this Divine fulness can freely stream in and play, so far as every stage permits. And when the free self-conscious development began, in order to allow the elements to enter by turns, which are united in the totality of the pneumatic man, then each of His acts of freedom opened, so to speak, new doors to this inward pleroma,

[1] Schöberlein, *Jahrb. f. d. deutsche Theol.* 1851.

until there ripened from the blossom of the Divine child the fruit of the God-human character, until the God-human potency was wholly actualized, ethically and officially, and He could say, " It is finished." However, this leads us to the second head. For, as far as the remainder of His innate characteristics are concerned, the *anamartesia*, this has been already verified on one side, that of the essential original sinlessness; and as far as regards the relation of this to freedom, this has to be treated under Christ's ethical God-humanity.

# SECOND HEAD.

## THE ETHICAL GOD-HUMANITY OF CHRIST.

### § 107.

Christ's holy nature or natural God-humanity (§ 106, 2, 3) became a perfect God-human character by means of a real and productive process, genuinely human and moral as well as pure. The natural God-humanity remains the necessary *presupposition* of the purity of this process; the necessary *form* of its purely human course is the passage of Christ through the decision between opposite possibilities on the side of knowledge and volition. The pure *result* of this process is the inner transfiguration of the natural God-humanity into God-human *character*, or the ethical God-humanity.

1. The contents of our paragraph are most definitely expressed in the N. T. Already, generally, an ethical development is attributed to Jesus: "He increased in age, wisdom, and grace with God and man," of and in Himself.[1] This is specially seen in the temptation of Jesus in the wilderness, in His struggle in Gethsemane, and in the contests which Luke especially narrates.[2] Not the reality merely of all this, but its necessity is made prominent, especially in the Epistle to the Hebrews, in the interests of the typical character and high-priestly purpose of Jesus. The teaching of the Church has not elaborated this side hitherto as definitely. Not Monophysitism and Monotheletism only, but Dyotheletism also, emphasizing in a one-sided manner the activity of the Divine nature, curtailed the true humanity and its development, whilst

---

[1] Luke ii. 52.     [2] Matt. iv. 1; Luke iv. 13, xxii. 28.

in the 18th century only the action of the humanity was regarded, and consequently a God-human development was not described. It is requisite to see, upon the human side, not passivity merely, nor mere activity, and upon the Divine side not merely a quiescent being or inactivity, and not to permit the human will to be influenced by omnipotence, but to think a self-conditioning working of the *Divine* according to the laws of ethical development of a human life, and therefore a self-limitation of the Logos in reference to His working and the introduction of Himself into the actual life of Jesus. The truth of the *human* will and its being determined by the Deity, such as the *Unio* requires, blend in the fact that the willing of the humanity is a willing determined and animated by God. Every impulse from the Divine side has only then become *God-human*, when the human will is not merely impelled and passively urged by the Divine, but when the Divine will has at the same time become the actual human will. Approximations to this knowledge are found in Luther in the *Kirchen und Hauspostille*, as well as in the Reformed Christology. But although the necessity of an ethical process in Christ has been almost as good as universally acknowledged in more recent times, there is by no means an agreement upon the manner in which that process is to be thought. We have to consider the true humanity of Jesus upon the side of will, of feeling and cognition.

2. In reference to the *Sinlessness* and *Prototypical character* of the ethical life of Jesus, Schleiermacher on the one hand,[1] who would concede no proper temptation, and would take the history of the temptation therefore to be a parable, and Edward Irving, Menken, Collenbusch, and others, on the other,[2] stand farthest apart.

Schleiermacher says, indeed, that the formula *non potuit peccare* is insufficient, because this might be also understood of a mere power over and without Him, which kept Him from sin, whereas in Him, in His Person itself, there must have necessarily been the principle of sinlessness by virtue of His

[1] *Christl. Glaube*, § 98.
[2] To these approximate those who, like Schultz, *Jahrb. f. deutsche Theol.* 1875, suppose in Christ (after Holsten) not merely a likeness to sinful flesh, but a σὰρξ ἁμαρτίας, although without actual sin.

essential unsinfulness. But this latter is, he thinks, to be supposed in Christ as absolutely perfect from the beginning, and a real process to be excluded, which worked an actual moral growth in him. If even a minimum only of struggle or temptation were ascribed to Christ, there would have been a minimum of sin in Him. The struggle against an inner attraction would, he teaches, presuppose an evil germ in Him, against which He had to fight. Inclination and disinclination were certainly present in Him as states of feeling, but without leading to temptation or struggle with Himself; rather because of His essential unsinfulness were they mere indications for Him, by which His activity was solicited.—Thus Schleiermacher thinks of the spiritual life of Christ simply as an eternally clear mirror-surface, as a stream which flows still and even. But in this case there is no actual development of the God-human potency in and out of itself, but merely a revelation, a display of the ever perfect unsinfulness. Essential Unsinfulness is consequently so thought by Him that it excludes a really acquisitive moral process.

Irving and Menken,[1] on the contrary, say that Christ must have necessarily become most like us in that particular in which we most needed change; and since here we suffer assaults from the flesh, in the Lord, in His flesh, there must also have been a contradiction to the Spirit; He must have assumed our corrupt nature, in order, in the most earnest struggle of His soul, to first give it a new birth in His Person; He did not assume a humanity such as Adam had before the fall, but a body of sin.[2] There existed in His natural will, according to Irving, a rebellion against the will of God; His human nature had the principle of sin and error in itself, was not merely capable of error and falling, but inclined to all evil. In the way of faith, he says, without any other helps than those which every pious man may have from God, He was compelled to bear this nature anew, and this task He completed, and thereupon His resurrection became to Him the reward of His holiness. The Logos was not able, he thinks, to impart any prerogatives to Him. Nevertheless this share in sinful nature did not make Christ sinful,

---

[1] Compare also Mansi's *Councils*, xi. 597.
[2] They appeal to Rom. viii. 3; Col. i. 22.

for His Person never entered into actual sin. — According to this teaching, involuntary evil inclinations are not sinful, an ethical estimate simply attaches to the acts of freedom. Further, the relation between the Logos and Jesus is in this case thought in a manner so loose and external, that the *Unio* would be degraded to something essentially inoperative and idle. And this is a Nestorian characteristic. On the other hand, sinful human nature would certainly have a merely external relation to the human Person of Christ. The latter is supposed, indeed, to have had the task of giving new birth to something by which the Person did not become sinful. But if in Jesus the sinfulness of nature does not belong to the Person, this must also be true of us, and innate sinfulness does not pertain to our person, which would be a Pelagian characteristic, also showing itself in our not being supposed to need for our redemption Christ as the Atoner. And with this superficial consideration of evil state there is something Manichæan interwoven, inasmuch as in the mere nature, apart from the relation to the person, an evil is supposed to be given which makes a new birth necessary. But it has been previously shown that there is in nature, and especially in the body as such, no sin, unless it is associated with a subject or a person, who is affected thereby. That a sinful nature was also to be assumed as necessary to perfect incarnation is not proven, and would only be provable if sin were essential to human nature. — Finally, Christ's work is supposed to have been the new birth of the sinful nature, by the annihilation of the same in the death of His body. But it is a physical conception of sin to view the necessity for redemption as grounded in the body only. And if it is said, How can Christ remain our example if He was not affected with natural sinfulness? the answer is to be returned, that the self-communication of the Logos to Jesus was not such that it spared Him earnest labour, although this labour was not a restoration of His Person from sinful contradiction to holy unity, but (see below) the labour of our redemption as well as of His moral self-perfecting.

In order to avoid both extremes, the point of importance is whether it is possible to show an actually ethical and yet sinless development, in which a place is also left for wrestling and struggle. We saw earlier, that at the beginning the humanity of Jesus still comes short of the goal of the full realization of the Divine life in human personality. Then it is to be shown that this divergence of the human and Divine does not necessarily bring sin. The converse of this is, that the actual life of God as the Logos still transcends the beginnings of the God-human life. This makes the solution possible. For supposing, in order to actually perfect itself, the *Unio* to be an increasing one, the relation of communication and reception must continue. All development, indeed, presupposes on the one side a totality as a potency, which bears the power of the whole in itself; but, on the other hand, self-evolution cannot take place without a distinction of the moments (§ 104, 3), which actually form themselves in a normal evolution one after another, and therefore relatively diverge or part asunder. Especially on this does the possibility of an ethical development or process depend. In what, then, does the natural separability of the factors in Christ consist, which without detriment to a natural harmony of the same needs not be excluded, if the God-human character is supposed to be its work? We have here to consider two points: the one the separability of His *knowledge* and *volition* in relation to each other; the other the relation between the *body* and the *soul* of Christ.

His knowledge cannot remain immediately one with His will. If in Him also actual knowledge did not precede the will, to impart aim and direction to the latter, He could not possibly have had any problem which was first to be solved. There was therefore even in Christ, and for His personal consciousness, a difference between what was to be and what was.[1] Nor can His knowledge immediately or forcibly determine His will, but it was requisite that, instead of being hurried along as by a foreign power, the will should decide freely, and by means of a twofold possibility conceived, for the Divine as such, as it was given in the basis of His nature. Thus there was in Christ a human interchange of different functions. From actions and teaching, from functions therefore of predominant volition and thought, He turned back into Himself and into God, so that the holy har-

[1] Gal. iv. 4; Luke ii. 49.

mony and collectedness of His nature was not merely a matter of nature, but also His ethical work.[1] His will had a double possibility, not merely in that He could will or not the end proposed by His knowledge, but also, in the second place, in that by virtue of the union of *body* and *spirit* in Him, and by virtue of the originally distinct, although sinless, laws of life of both these in themselves, He had the possibility of allowing a place for the tendency of the sensuous life as well as that of the spirit. The flesh of itself would, for example, preserve and maintain His life,—a fact in itself fully innocent, and indeed necessary; nor is the flesh already of itself by nature, or immediately by itself, really in correspondence with the will of the spirit, but is to be first determined by the latter, for which it has receptiveness, and has, in the next place, its relative independence. It is not the will of the flesh to be sacrificed; otherwise, Christ's death would be a sacrifice no longer, but a physical event. And thus the tendency of the flesh to self-preservation, innocent in itself, His natural fear of death, might come into conflict with the plan of Christ, if for the sake of our redemption that plan imposed what was unnatural to Him. In such a case, then, it pertained to His spirit to make His will the deciding power in opposition to the flesh, and instead of being determined by the flesh, to produce a higher and established unity by His will. Without such a twofold possibility, and the labour of increasing real excision of the false, there would not be in Christ a free and moral, but only a natural process. But such a struggle, which is not merely epideictic, and is a real moral process, we shall not have first to assume in His office. If the latter is to be considered under the point of view of love, His pre-official life has to preserve, in relation to Him and by His means, the analogue of that which is in us living faith, or the consciousness of Divine Sonship. He could not have the knowledge of His Divine Sonship as an infant; He could only gradually participate therein with the growth of His human self-consciousness, which was also self-apprehension in His individuality and uniqueness. And when at the first visit to the Temple, apparently for the first time, it flashed up in Him in the holy city, in the midst of types of Him, He knew it also to be His

[1] Luke iii. 21, vi. 12; Matt. xxvi. (Gethsemane).

mission (δεῖ με), to be about what was His Father's. God is to Him Father in a special sense, therefore He also knew Himself in a special sense to be His Son.¹ And to assert and carry through this consciousness He knew to be His mission. He, this man, must remain in the Divine home. Nothing is said of His already being conscious of Himself as the Redeemer of the world. On the contrary, He labours first at His personal mission: "I must be in that which is my Father's," whilst He said later on, "I am in the Father, and the Father in me." He must first possess Himself wholly, before He lovingly communicates Himself, and have His home in the Divine element. Thus He is still occupied with the carrying out of a personal, and not an official, purpose. He *can* carry it out, for the unity of the Divine and human is already existent in Him as such, and so far actual that He has in the Divine His pleasure and vital air. But He *must* also carry it out; for this living atmosphere, in which He has commenced consciously to move as in His highest good and the truth of His personality, will be more and more constantly appropriated by Him. He is embraced by the Deity, which on its side has unchangeably united itself with Him, and assumed Him; and thus God is already in the boy in unique manner. But *He* also must be in God, must grasp the Divine with His will, and make it His own (p. 335). Only by this means can God be perfectly in Him, and when He has inwardly glorified the Father in Him, then will the Father glorify Him in Himself.² And since His official life must already have for its basis the fullest and most secure consciousness of His Divine Sonship, we shall have to regard the fact that the consciousness of His Divine Sonship was not a merely periodical effulgence, but, with much character, developed itself to full clearness and permanence as the centre of His official mission until His thirtieth year. And this was certainly not possible without great contests. For His humility must straightway, before the perfecting of His God-humanity, form the point of connection for struggles, which would be evoked by the glaring contrast between the Divine Sonship and His lowly reality, as well as by the Messianic representations, even of those dearest to Him.

[1] Luke ii. 49.     [2] John xiii. 32.

It was requisite that the tempting question which was still possible, "Art Thou also really the Son of God?" should be excluded, and every doubt thereon definitively vanquished; but this was only possible by the union of the highest humility and patient surrender, with the highest, heroic, believing courage, which was at the same time silent, and which awaited with self-possession the time of its revelation.[1] Accordingly it should be asserted that there was in Christ no physical necessity not to sin, and still less to sin; there was not in Him the potency or real possibility of the sin, which is in us inherited sin. But as the original *Unio* still included the separability of the elements of His Person, the progressive realization of the God-humanity in Him was also not of the kind that it anticipated His free decision, and determined His will in relation to good, in the manner of a natural necessity, but, conversely, that realization progressed, mediated by the continuous real labour of the suppression and excision of false possibilities by His will. In this respect the *potuit non peccare* is to be said of Him. But if the question is further asked whether also *potuit peccare*, or whether rather *non potuit peccare*, the answer to this question indeed appears to require a *scientia media* denied us. Still the following may be said. The thought of a possibility opposed to the good was certainly possible to Him, nay, must even be conceded in Him; but this thought is still not evil thought, the possibility thought is not yet realization, it is not even real possibility as yet, or evil potency; rather by the instrumentality of conscious and deliberate conquest of the false possibility thought, have the good will and true knowledge to become realized as an exclusive apprehension of the good as such. But this possibility is merely a necessary element or point of transition, a fact which need not and must not be made to occupy a single moment of life. The essence in Christ's Person is His God-human nature, and not a *liberum arbitrium* indifferent to good and evil. This holy nature is also present and efficient in the acts of the decision upon and excision of false possibilities. Thus there is no necessity in Him to lack pure love; on the contrary, it is certainly not physically, but ethically impossible to disclaim pure love, since He wills and carries it through as

[1] Heb. xii. 2.

the dominant power freely in Himself. He is, so to speak, the man new-born by nature, or born of God. Freedom of choice between opposites has never in Him, by virtue of His love, been actually separated from His holy nature. Rather, however great was, and must have been, the inner movement and tension of opposites in Him, however profoundly this His God-human unity may have been affected or bent, so to speak, by contest, through which it had to confirm itself, nevertheless it was impossible that the bond of the *Unio* should be severed, because this man maintained a holy opposition, an abhorrence to evil, as soon as it was placed as such before His eyes, just as on His part the Logos had the immutable will to be united with this man. If, therefore, freedom is regarded as the necessary form of volition, as the element, without the use of which, if only transitional, no real moral acquisition was to be accomplished, there is a truth in saying that He was not compelled involuntarily to avoid sin; but if regard is had to that by which the moral acquisition of Jesus was encompassed, to the inherence of His holy nature and the final end of the Divine will in Him, as well as to His own good free will (John viii. 29), then of course it is not to be called a happy chance merely, but a fact well motived, that Christ did not sin. There was a higher than a physical necessity for Him to both fight and conquer. The conflict was earnest. The *Unio* was no lifeless *Unio*, but must always be renewed and maintained by struggle and temptation. The victory did not take place of itself, or by an isolated Divine act; the false possibilities were to be excluded by the developing human will of Christ also, as they were by the Divine will in eternal manner. The height is to be actually scaled, and it was actually scaled by the second Adam.

This moral process may also be considered as the *growth of His God-manhood*. The mission still to be accomplished confronts him, it is true, as the will of the Father, as the necessary; but He has to transform it into free delight, to recompose it into freedom. And in doing so, He realizes at the same time His own God-human nature.

But despite a moral progress, can Christ be always regarded as God-man? Doubtless. His human development certainly requires that knowledge and will should relatively diverge in

Him. The former must, so to speak, afford to the will the aim or ideal, that the will may grasp and realize it. Christ has such a task before His eyes when He speaks so often of the will, of a teaching, of the Father,[1] of a hearing or seeing of heavenly things. And the radical attitude and direction of His will towards this is obedience.[2] That which is still wanting to Him, to the growing God-man, personally or to His work, He knows to be the will of the Father, which is still objective to Him and to be fulfilled. But, at the same time, he knows it to be the realization of His nature as the Son of God.

But it might then be asked: Why is not the Logos described as this objective something which He still lacks? Seeing, that is to say, that during the growth of Jesus, the Divine, which still belongs to the full idea of the God-humanity, cannot yet be actually in Jesus, the compatibility of a being of the Logos in Him with a God-human development is indeed very clear, but why is it not the communication of the Logos which is described as not yet realized in Jesus, but the will of the Father? But the Logos was indeed not external to Him, but already within Him as the basis, the living substratum of His Person. The answer therefore is: that which is ethically necessary for Christ is represented in the will of the Father. This the Son of God has to transform into freedom and love. And this is, in addition to being the realization of the paternal will, also His own personal mission, the realization indeed of the God-human nature. Therefore also Christ calls the same thing which He describes as the will of the Father which He must accomplish, His personal transfiguration by suffering and His glory.[3] And the development of His God-human nature into actuality is on the Divine side a ceaseless renewal and confirmation of the *Unio*, and that in such a way that the Divine life actuates the unfolding human life more and more. God as Logos does not withdraw Himself from the increasing desire and receptiveness of this man; He first grasps and fills the knowledge of this man with the contents

---

[1] John viii. 28, 38, iii. 11, 32, iv. 34.
[2] John viii. 39; Rom. v. 19; Phil. ii. 7, etc.
[3] John xiii. 31, etc.; xvii. 5, comp. 4.

of his will, and then His will as well. But in the will of the Father, to which He is obedient, the Son of God no less knows His own freedom and transfiguration to be willed, and is therefore in obedience, not δοῦλος, but the free Son of the house.

3. This leads us to the God-human EMOTIONAL LIFE. Jesus shows the traces of the most delicate perceptive life, of the most living mobility by spiritual joy as by mourning and sorrow. But the ethical perfectness and purity herein is especially proved by the fact that the opposite dispositions, however powerfully they enter, always remain in harmonious union, inasmuch as, where one has given the key, the other is always in concord, or immediately makes itself felt in reaction. This is only possible by a single power, which stands above both, and always keeps them in equilibrium. This is the Divine life, the ζωὴ αἰώνιος in Him.[1] The life of Jesus in God is its own blessedness exalted above contradictions, and it is allied with the purest love and readiness for sympathy and sacrifice. This blessedness of His could never be beclouded in its innermost circle.—And the perfectness of His life of feeling is shown in the *relation to God as well as to man*. By the knowledge of His unity with God, Jesus has the same form of faith, which already approximates to sight. Undoubting certainty of truth arises from the presence of the same in Him, and is most intimately allied to His self-consciousness.[2] Especially do the believing power and intensity of His prayer belong to this place.[3] There is of course expressed therein His human need, His distinction from God, and therefore also from the absolute actual Logos-life. The Divine indwelling does not exempt Him from creatureliness; His Divine-human life does not exempt Him from the necessity for prayer and supplication.[4] But His dependence upon God is at the same time unity with God. Therefore His prayer is a familiar conference, and absolutely at home in the goods of the house of God, He knows that God always hears Him, and can say: "All thine is mine." Therefore His prayers give thanks for what He asks before it comes to pass. As

---

[1] John xiv. 6.   [2] John xiv. 1, 6, 9.
[3] John xi. 41, 43; Matt. xi. 27; Luke vii. 34; John xvii.
[4] Heb. v. 7.

His prayer welled forth from His unity of being with the Father,[1] that unity is ever renewed by this communion with God. In His praying life He follows, on the one hand, the inner drawing, the delight in the Divine, and always gains the ever fuller union with God, with the Father's will, which is at the same time the truth of His existence. His prayer is the middle point of His activity, the holy altar upon which He ever consecrates and offers anew His humanity to God, and this is always in turn penetrated and illumined by the Divine.[2] This is especially shown in His transfiguration, which took place whilst He was praying.[3] We see therein that the δόξα of the Logos is evermore communicated to Him through prayer. His humanity, evermore fully opening itself to prayerful intercourse with God, and surrendering itself to God, was straightway as a praying humanity the receptiveness in which the actuality of the Logos could always more fully introduce itself. And thus prayer was the innermost seat of the advancing incarnation.[4] In prayer the soul of Jesus evermore draws into itself its vital element, the Logos, willingly allowing itself to be determined by Him; through prayer the Logos evermore perfectly communicates Himself to the humanity, although, as has been said, the God-human unity also already co-operated in His prayer.

But to the perfectness of His emotional life also belongs the purity and power of His sympathy[5] *towards men.* Although born amongst a particular people, He still remained at heart the true man, or man absolutely; therefore His sympathy was related to humanity generally as well as to His own people. And His sympathy was as absolutely pure as all-comprehensive. It had relations with the spiritual and corporeal ills of men, but in their order; and it was not the physical, but the spiritual ills, the sin and guilt of men, which caused Him the profoundest pain. Further, His sympathy was so heartfelt and perfect, that He was prepared to share with men actually all evils without exception which are the consequences of sin, except sin. This is the self-

---

[1] John x. 30, xiv. 9.
[2] Luke iii. 21, etc., vi. 12, comp. 13.   [3] Luke ix. 28, 29; Matt. xvii. 2.
[4] Luke iii. 21, etc.; John xvii. 1, 22, 24.
[5] John xi. 33-35, xiii. 34, iii. 16; Luke xix. 41; Matt. ix. 36.

oblivion of His sympathy, which does not spare or consider itself, but which certainly shows thereby its superior invincible power of conquest over everything inimical. This is the majesty of His God-human character, and this inward sublimity has also mirrored itself in His outward manifestation. His Person must have exerted a wonderful power of riveting those who were receptive, and His image indelibly imprinted itself upon His disciples.[1] Judas Iscariot himself bears witness after his own manner to the power of His personality, powerful in its still purity, and putting what was deepest in man in motion. But before John He stands as the Son of man full of grace and truth, as the eternal manifested Divine life itself.[2]

4. The PERFECTNESS of His KNOWLEDGE, or His freedom from error and His wisdom. This perfectness certainly, as regards its extent, relates at first to His knowledge of God and of Himself; this is central knowledge.[3] Still it follows thence, that it did not embrace everything concrete;[4] it does not follow that He was subject or accessible to error, and therefore that He erred. In no case could any error be produced by Him, nor could anything false even be affirmed as true. It is true His most immediate mission could not have been to correct every error as it came to Him from without; this was not His office. On the contrary, false Messianic representations, for example, such as were current amongst the religious of His people, might be deposited in Him in His youth, without appropriating affirmation, and without instant rejection, before the time for Him to reject had come. But He could never appropriate anything erroneous as true, for in such a case there would be a co-operation in the production of what was false, though occasioned from without, and the affirmation of the false is always a desire to know more, or a thinking to know more, than one does know, is thus a violation of humility, the virtue of "docta ignorantia." The false Messianic ideals of the religious of His people must have been capable of being deposited in His consciousness, although they were a kind of temptation.

[1] John i. 14, xiii. 1, etc., xvii. 1, passages full of intuitive contents.
[2] 1 John i. 1, etc.   [3] Matt. xi. 25–27.
[4] Matt. xxiv. 36; Luke xiii. 32, xi. 13; Matt. xxi. 19.

It must have been His most peculiar moral work to reject at the right time these false possibilities, which especially consisted in the perverted position of the predicates of exceptional power and holiness in relation to the Messiah and His kingdom, and which were adapted to tempt, so long as they were still morally possible. And His freedom from error rests upon a positive perfectness of His knowledge. His knowledge did not arise from human instruction, from invention or speculation; but also not from inspiration, for He was more than a prophet. Rather does it follow from His nature, that He is an autodidact in the highest sense, namely θεοδίδακτος, because of the progressive constant working of the Logos in Him. "I do not speak of myself,"—as a mere man, for which you take me; but the Father shows Him all. His nature being one with God, God-human, He lives in heavenly things with conscious will. Although He only knows Himself to be perfect, He knows Himself also to be the Son of God, as God knows Himself as Logos in Him. And thus He has the knowledge of the truth, or wisdom, because He is Himself the truth, the truth of what is human, to whom also pertains the Divine as a property, and the truth of the Divine, which has become man in Him.[1] His knowledge is acquired knowledge and to be morally restrained, but only acquired on the ground of His nature by means of the self-consciousness of His nature. Whilst therefore with us thinking and being part from each other in a twofold manner,—(for there is for us a thinking which is not being, but thinks it is such, whilst it is imagination and error, and further, there is for us a being which is not yet knowledge),—the former has no place in Christ; on the other hand, the knowledge of Jesus was indubitably progressive. But although, accordingly, omniscience cannot be attributed to Him on earth, there still pertained to Him in Divine things the perfectness of knowledge which belonged to His office.[2] In us certainly that which is not yet knowledge has error for its positive converse; but simply because we have the tendency to take, in premature conclusion, the limited circle of our present knowledge for the whole, and thus to operate in indolence, impatience, or self-conceit, as if it actually

[1] John xiv. 6.     [2] Matt. xi. 25, etc.

were the whole. But Christ is also an example of humble veracity, of restful and yet unintermittent progress. Whence could the thought come to Him that the beginning is the end? Rather did He stand notwithstanding in the Divine centre, from which He also contemplated the world. In principle He bore in Himself the truth as a single totality, which must have immediately reacted against everything false desirous of occupying its place.[1]

[1] Comp. Rothe, *Stille Stunden*, 1872, p. 160.

# TRANSITION TO THE DOCTRINE OF THE OFFICE OF CHRIST.

## § 108.

From the time of His Baptism, Christ's matured divine-human personality passes over into His *official Godmanhood*. Thenceforward, He knows and wills His personal perfection as the absolute revelation of God to the world, making it His obligatory life-work[1] or office by self-revelation and self-communication to be the perfect organ of God's redeeming and perfecting revelation.

1. An attempt may be made in two ways to efface the limits between Christ's pre-official and official life. First, it may be said that Jesus did divine-human works—such as miracles—before His public appearance, as He did afterwards. This is the account given in the Apocryphal Gospels, against which the sober spirit of the Church early and rightly rebelled in its formation of the Canon, because such a view would have been inconsistent with the reality of the divine-human development as well as with the continuity of moral life in the God-man. Or, conversely, it may be said that only during His public life had Christ a certain and clear consciousness respecting His Person and mission, as well as a clear perception of the character of the world, the consequence of which view would be that He must at first have made experiments with Himself and on the world. But He must have first possessed Himself before He could give Himself and appear officially. Uncertainty respecting His mission, its aims and methods, would be a proof of immaturity, while a

[1] Ἔργον, John xvii. 4.

public appearance without maturity would not be obligatory, but presumptuous and indicative of sin, as a subsequent vacillation and change in His aims or plans would indicate error respecting Himself and the world. It is therefore of importance to hold fast the distinction between Christ's pre-official and official life, although the two are not to be placed side by side in an abrupt way. For of course His work brought Him experience, as well as personal assaults and moral conflicts,[1] and the execution of His work brought about the glorification of His person. In general, the ethical Godmanhood had to approve itself also in His public life, nay, to unfold itself under new aspects, so that His official action and passion may be regarded as another exercise of His holy moral character, and therefore of His personality, namely, an exercise related to the world. The distinction, however, between His pre-official and His official life must also be regarded as a distinction in His person. This is partly grounded in the nature of the case, partly attested by the representation of the New Testament. We cannot suppose that His inner personal life was quite the same before His office as during its course, and therefore that He lived a secret Messiah-life before His office, only then revealing it to others, for this would mean that the beginning of His Messianic office did not coincide with His ripeness for office, but that this ripeness previously existed in a quiescent state. And just as little can He have lacked maturity on His public appearance, so that He was subject to uncertainty or deficiency in His official work, *i.e.* when He stands forth and has to act in the consciousness of $\dot{\epsilon}\xi o\nu\sigma i a$. In point of fact, the N. T. by no means depicts the *Baptism* of Jesus, which was His introduction into office, merely as an event for the people or the Baptist, but as an occurrence having an inner personal significance even for Jesus Himself, and fully equipping Him for His office, and therefore forming an epoch also in His personal life.[2] This epoch-making aspect of Christ's Baptism was more fully maintained by the ancient Church in its Feast of the Baptism than by later days, with

[1] Heb. v. 8.
[2] Cf. my treatise on the Baptism of Jesus in Piper's *Zeugen der Wahrheit*, 1874, i. 172-187.

the exception of the Reformed Church, which gives higher significance to the anointing (*Unctio*) with the Holy Spirit, the importance of which is rightly acknowledged by Nitzsch among moderns. On the other hand, of course, the epoch-making aspect of Christ's Baptism ought not to be enhanced with Cerinthus to such a degree that the Incarnation of the higher principle would have to be dated from it, nor yet with Rougemont [1] to such a degree that before the Baptism Jesus must be regarded merely as a sinless physical man, and only from the Baptism as pneumatic. This would be to sever Birth and Baptism, whereas Luke [2] informs us that Christ was anointed to His office on the ground of His possession of the Spirit. We must not keep all thought of vocation and office away from Christ before the Baptism. It would be an abrupt and abstract view not to allow the thought of vocation to exert its influence also on Jesus in His volition and thinking, as is the case normally in every man. If, for all these reasons, the two epochs—the life of Jesus before and that after His Baptism—must neither be identified nor severed from each other, it becomes necessary to delineate an inwardly prepared, but still really new, progress from the calm life of Jesus in Nazareth to His public life; and also conversely His official life, certainly as it presupposes ethical maturity, is still a continuation, attestation—and in so far a growth—of His ethical Godmanhood.

2. In what, then, does the sameness, and in what does the progress, of the two epochs consist? Both may be set in the clearest light by considering the relation of the personal to the generic consciousness. At first the person must apprehend and possess himself in his relation to God and in his distinction from the genus.[3] At this point his personal life of faith forms the centre. But the generic consciousness must also be received in a living way into the personal. Thus only is the personal consciousness perfected; and this must be done indeed by the obligatory love, which places the person at the service of the genus, and by which everything individual is subordinated to a single conscious aim, to which the personality then sacrifices himself. Although, therefore, the pre-

---

[1] *Christus und seine Zeugen*, trans. by Fabarius, 1859.    [2] Luke iv. 18.
[3] § 107, 2. Cf. vol. ii. §§ 40, 62, p. 219.

official period is devoted to the work of self-culture, if it is to be a preparation for the vocation, it must needs have already an intrinsic, ideal relation to the latter. Let us consider this point more closely. Already before His Baptism, Christ had the Divine-human self-consciousness, although the task of ratifying and attesting it was still incumbent on Him.[1] On one side this self-consciousness must have been a blessed one; He knew Himself pure, and in the undisturbed relation of Son to Father. But the more He came to know the world and humanity, the more He must have perceived the unhappiness, the sin and guilt, burdening men, and found Himself in sharp contrast with their aims and pursuits. Now, from the very contact of His blessedness and riches with the wretchedness and poverty of the world, there must have sprung up in Him, on one hand, abhorrence of sin, and on the other, loving thoughts, not of judgment, but of mercy, which had relation to His life-mission to humanity. At the distinction of His person from the genus, at a merely *negative* tendency of His generic consciousness, He could not stop. There was added loving sympathy not merely towards His more immediate circle, but towards humanity. We see this from the very act of His coming to John's baptism, which was as little a bare ceremony to Him as it was a baptism of repentance.[2] What led Him to this act, Scripture declares in the words: "Thus it behoves us to fulfil all righteousness."[3] What, then, is the *service* which Jesus wishes to present in John's presence, since it cannot have been repentance? The Johannine baptism was not only a baptism of repentance, but had an essential relation to the approaching kingdom of God. Nay, the kernel in true repentance is fervent longing for God's holy kingdom, and readiness to devote oneself to it in denial and forgetfulness of self. Thus then Jesus, in whose heart lived sorrow for the sin of the world, and longing to save it, along with desire to surrender Himself for its sake, recognizes in the baptism of John the divine challenge to Him to make the confession of readiness, in perfect denial and forgetfulness of self, to devote Himself to the kingdom of God. Further, His pure consciousness of God's holy righteousness, as well as the whole theocratic institution with its

[1] Luke ii. 49; § 107, 1.   [2] Cf. Piper's *Zeugen*, p. 179 ff.   [3] Matt. iii. 15.

sacrificial cultus in Jerusalem, at which He had been present according to law, testified to Him the way in which salvation can come and God's kingdom be founded, namely, by atonement and redemption. Thus that confession of willingness to fulfil all righteousness included in its meaning readiness to sacrifice Himself, even to the point of death. Even the outward symbolism of John's baptism—the submersion of the outward man in order to rise again to new life—was preeminently adapted to express the readiness to give Himself up entirely for the good of God's kingdom. Afterwards, Jesus Himself called His passion a cup, which He must drink, and His death a baptism with which He must be baptized.[1] This may be a hint to us respecting the way in which Christ regarded His baptism, so far as it was a service. It is to Him a symbol of the baptism which is to plunge Him into the bitterest sufferings. He makes His baptism an expression of the most perfect readiness for self-sacrifice in behalf of the Messianic kingdom. This sacrifice He presents to God, even as Luke speaks of a prayer of Jesus at His baptism. God accepts it; and this service of Christ's had for its divine converse a divine *gift*. His prayer opens heaven, and there sounds over Him from heaven the divine answer: "Thou art my beloved Son, in whom I am well pleased," upon which the endowment for the Messianic office followed. God Himself here performs the first baptism with the Holy Spirit—the foundation of all subsequent baptisms. By divine word and act the Son of man receives the absolutely satisfactory answer to His question, to His declared readiness to surrender Himself to and for the world. He receives the divine assurance, no longer merely of His personal, but also of His official Divine Sonship, and therefore that He has not merely the inner or subjective, but also the divine, objectively sealed, vocation to devote Himself to the redemption of humanity. To seek such objective assurance, and that within the O. T. ordinances, was part of the righteousness which He had to fulfil. Thus, in Jesus' baptism, the confession of His readiness to sacrifice Himself for God's cause, the lowly humility that commits itself to God, and the desire to be inducted into His office by the Father, are united with the fulfilment of that wish. He is

[1] Luke xii. 50; Mark x. 38.

inaugurated by the O. T. for the founding of the new covenant. Henceforward, by Divine gift His personal perfection is ripened into redeeming strength in reference to His wisdom, His knowledge of heavenly things, His holiness, His might and miraculous power.[1] The kingdom of heaven has already come down, and is present in Him, for He is in heaven, and heaven in Him.[2] His person is the personal revelation of God, the world's centre. "The angels of God ascend and descend upon the Son of man." And this consciousness, including in it withal His mediatorial mission between God and the world, is a new thing even to His personal consciousness. Such a person has now for His aim and object nothing less than entire humanity. Jesus is led towards humanity by His love as well as by the consciousness of Himself as the true Son of humanity pertaining thereto. His central position in relation to the race is shown first in His love which embraces entire humanity without exception, and with perfect cordiality, and again in this, that His chief concern is with that which is central in every man, with the founding of new Divine life.

Nevertheless, His ethical, personal Godmanhood was not so concluded in His baptism that the absolute consummation of His ethical Godmanhood was already given prior to His office. Rather, as the office is the fruit of the ethical maturity culminating in His baptism, so it imposes new problems on the Person, the solution of which forms the transition to the absolute consummation of His Person, and therefore raises it to a new stage. Thus, office and person intertwine in Him. If before His baptism the process was personally ethical (self-culture), now it is officially ethical, which also initiates a higher stage of His ethical Godmanhood. Hence even during His official life, assaults have to be repelled, which have withal a personal side.[3] But then again He interweaves both His personal consummation and that of humanity in the closest way with that central position of His. If He wills the redemption and consummation of humanity, He must also will Himself as the centre, outside which is no salvation; and in willing His central position and personal consumma-

---

[1] John iii. 11-13, cf. ii. 24; Matt. iv. 17; John i. 51, 52.
[2] John iii. 13.   [3] Luke xx. 28.

tion, He wills the redemption and consummation of humanity. There is no centre without a circle, no circle without a centre. Thus, in virtue of the love by which He wills Himself as the Head of humanity,[1] and makes Himself such, He reckons the consummation of His people part of His personal consummation, often calling it His own glorification.[2] And by the two together He glorifies His Father.[3]

[1] John xviii. 36, 37 f.
[2] John viii. 54, xi. 4, xii. 16, 23, 28, xiii. 31, 32, xiv. 13, xv. 8, xvi. 14, xvii. 1, 5, 10.
[3] John xvii.

# THIRD HEAD.

## THE GODMANHOOD OF CHRIST AS OFFICIAL.

### § 109.

The usual division of Christ's official activity into a threefold office, rightly understood, is justifiable both historically and in itself.

LITERATURE.—Cf. Ernesti, *Opusc. Theol. de Officio Christi Triplici*, 1773, 411 ff. Ritschl, *ut supra*, i. 2. 503. iii. 360 ff. Frank, *Syst. d. chr. Wahrh.*, ii. 194 ff. A. Krauss, *Das Mittlerwerk nach dem Schema des Munus triplex*, *Jahrb. f. d. Theol.* 1872, xvii. 595–655. Ebrard, *Chr. Dogm.* ed. 2, ii. 398.

1. It has long been usual in the Evangelical Church to represent the work of salvation in the form of the diverse function or office of Christ, either twofold or, still more completely, threefold.[1] The division into prophetic, high-priestly, kingly, in the Reformation age was especially worked out by Calvin.[2] In the Lutheran Church, J. Gerhard was its first successful advocate.[3] Still the mode of treatment varies very much, even where a triplicity is accepted, and not merely, as often happens, the priestly and kingly offices. Some find all three offices already in Christ's earthly life.

[1] Beginnings are found, in addition to the Epistle to the Hebrews (see below), in the Testament of the Twelve Patriarchs, where the distinction and the interdependence of the kingly and priestly offices are worked out. Eusebius has already the threefold division. Respecting other traces of the same in Lactantius, Gregory of Nyssa, etc., cf. Krauss.

[2] *Instit.* L. ii. 15. 1.

[3] J. Gerhardi *Loci Theol.*, Loc. iv. *de Persona et Officio Christi*. Still the Brentzian Catechism current in Würtemberg also has already the threefold division. The other Lutheran dogmatists in the 16th century, and even L. Hutter, usually have a twofold division, the prophetic office being joined to the priestly.

Others transfer the kingly office to the state of exaltation (so Keckermann, among moderns Thomasius, v. Hofmann, and A. Schweizer), whereas the Socinians do not acknowledge the priestly office also on earth, but only the prophetic. In this case, therefore, the doctrine of the offices is divided according to the doctrine of the states. Further, the offices are made so independent by some, and represented with such a want of inner continuity, that the unity of Christ's work and mission is lost. This is the case not merely when no connection is conceded to the prophetic and priestly offices with the kingly upon earth, but also, conversely, when the kingly alone is supposed to retain a place in the state of exaltation, the priestly and prophetic not continuing.[1] Moreover, the particular offices are very differently defined, and do not by any means always attain a clear and sharp conception. The *prophetic* office is often placed in the background, and even attached to the priestly, because the latter in the O. T. is in part a teaching office. Where it emerges independently, it is viewed now as an office of *legislatio* (so especially on the Romish side), now as a teaching office in general, embracing law and gospel; finally, even Christ's holy walk and example, as well as His miraculous deeds, are reckoned part of the prophetic office.[2] The *high-priestly* office is discovered partly on earth in Christ's vicarious obedience, active and passive, partly also in heaven in His intercession, which presents His merits or wounds to the Father (so Calov and some of the Bengel school). The benediction also is connected therewith. The intercession and benediction are occasionally defined in such a way that the kingly office suffers loss from them. Finally, not merely is the *kingly* office to some extent resolved into the prophetic and confounded therewith (knowledge being treated in an intellectualistic spirit as the all-ruling factor and

---

[1] Frank, on the other hand (*ut supra*, ii. 195), will have no juxtaposition of the three offices in any form, and hence rejects the doctrine altogether, because the work of atonement embraces everything, the prophetic office as a pre-supposition, the kingly as a consequence.

[2] Hollaz (*Examen Theologicum acroamat.* P. iii. sect. 1, cap. 3, qu. 101) ascribes to the prophetic office the institution and conservation of the preaching office and the Sacraments, nay, even the gift of the Holy Spirit, vocation, illumination, conversion, regeneration, renovation—briefly, everything pertaining, *e.g.*, to the kingly office.

the kingdom of Christ vanishing into a mere ideal kingdom of truth or virtue, *e.g.* in Rationalism), or in a spiritualistic way resolved into mere spiritual operations, but conversely also it is employed to serve as the basis of clerical or hierarchical authority. Where it is framed on the pure N. T. type, and fixed independently and definitely, it is explained now merely as the exercise of redeeming power within the individual soul in order to its assurance of salvation or sanctification, now as the founding and conserving of the Church, now—with reference to the doctrine of the two states—as the dominion of the exalted God-man in and over the world. The Lutherans are fond of speaking of that *regnum potentiæ* over the universe, which Christ indeed always had essentially in virtue of His Deity, but which He concealed if He did not lay down in the state of exinanition, completely resuming it in the exaltation; the Reformed, on the other hand, rather emphasize the *regnum gratiæ*, which issues according to both Confessions in the *regnum gloriæ*.

2. In this way the inequality and uncertainty in the representation of the redemptive work on the scheme of the doctrine of offices supplied to criticism sufficient points of attack; and thus it is not to be wondered at that Ernesti's attack on the whole doctrine found response, modern writers also following in his wake and redoubling his assaults.[1]

Ritschl attacks even the word "office" as unsuitable, because office is a special calling with a view to realizing a legal or moral community upon conditions of law.[2] He prefers "calling." But a law is not merely established by "positive" human enactment; there is also a Divine law; nay, the latter is the basis of all actual law. For this reason also law is by no means in contradiction to the moral, although not identical therewith; and just as little ought law to be ignored or negatived by the moral. Office denotes a unity of law and duty, and more definitely than the word calling implies an antithesis to mere private life, however

---

[1] So especially Ritschl, *ut supra*, Frank (ii. 195 ff., 222), whilst Schenkel, Beck, and others at least do not follow the present division. On the other hand, Schleiermacher uses it, and it is followed by Marheinecke, Lange, Martensen, Reiff, and others.

[2] III. 376 f.

well ordered, and therefore implies a relation to a common life, and the public interests of such a life which have a claim upon official activity. The allusion to a "legally privileged office" and its clerical abuse, moreover, is here irrelevant, and the expression "calling" is just as exposed to the possibility of abuse as "office;" for one may speak of subjective in opposition to objective calling, but not of subjective office. More to the point seems the objection common since Ernesti's days, to the effect that the expressions prophet, priest, king, are figurative, therefore indefinite, lacking in clear precise distinctiveness, and overlapping in their meaning; or if a definite idea be attached to each of the offices, they fall apart into an independence which dissolves the unity of the work of salvation. But as concerns the first point, or the allegation that the three titles affirm nothing definite and distinctive, but the one is rather already involved in the correct idea of the other, this objection applies indeed to such a doctrine of the offices as is often met with in the history of Dogmatics, but not to the doctrine rightly treated. The demand underlying this objection is just; but we shall see presently that the offices may be definitely distinguished in idea notwithstanding their interconnection. Further, it must indeed be conceded that these three offices had a different signification in the theocracy of the O. T., a signification transcended in Christianity. In the old covenant the priest slew the sacrificial victims, and watched over the purity and holiness of the ceremonial law in behalf of himself and others; the king stood at the head of a particular commonwealth, and by means of power and authority had to watch over the outward existence of the political community; the most usual work of the prophets was to guard the welfare and progress of the community by means of the Word. All this is transcended in the new covenant, where the ends and means of the three offices are partially different. But despite these differences, which indeed are conceded beforehand in the typical application of the O. T., a common element is left, which is pre-eminently adapted for use in the language of the N. T. And that definite ideas may be attached to the expressions without prejudice to their figurativeness, is suggested by the fact that in the O. T. kingship and priesthood were kept separate by law. Prophecy again rose in opposition to both, according to need. From this it follows that what characterizes the essence of each of the offices constitutes something well capable of distinction from the rest, and that they do not merge into each other, although a prophet like Moses had also the kingly, or a king like David the prophetic character, nay, although prophecy sees the consummation of the theocracy in the union of the three offices in One.[1] Also the objection that the three offices ought not to be co-ordinated with each other, or treated as of equal worth, because on the contrary the work of atonement alone is the central work, to which all Christ's functions are related, is not convincing; for the atonement, which the high-priestly office specifically subserves as means, is not an exhaustive description of the saving good which we owe to Christ, although the fundamental and central one. For the knowledge of the truth or of God also is an essentially precious good, and its communication is no mere presupposition and means in reference to the atonement; and just so the kingly office also is no mere consequence of the high-priestly office. The founding of the new personality and of a new common life is the final aim, to which even Christ's high-priesthood is subservient.[2] But, to speak generally, a relation of mutual conditionality or dependence obtains, without prejudice to the independent significance of each one of the three offices or functions of Christ. To each one its special significance must be assigned, but in such a way that they are all to be closely combined with the entire personality and treated as its self-manifestation. By this means the unity of the work of salvation is discerned, which unity is preserved in detail by the fact, that no one of the offices fills up a moment of time alone, but the others are always co-operative, although one exists in preponderance according to the historical relations and functions. Herewith at once the further position is established, that the earthly life ought not to be assigned to the prophetic and priestly offices only, and the state of exaltation only to the kingly, as if the kingship were not yet active in the state of humiliation, nor the prophetic or high-priestly in the

---

[1] Cf. vol. ii. p. 273.

[2] Frank himself must again concede that Christ must be thought as King before the completion of the work of redemption on earth.

state of exaltation. Just as little ought the high-priestly to be conceived without the kingly, which first confers its full force and significance on the former, as the Epistle to the Hebrews shows. This also implies that the different offices ought not to be divided between the two natures, as if one belonged only to the Divine nature, the other to the human.[1] But this view does not, as we shall see afterwards, preclude the state of exaltation adding something new to the threefold office; nor, again, can any contradiction to the inner unbroken interconnection of the offices be found in the circumstance, that Christ's mediatorial work puts now this, now that side in the foreground.[2]

*Observation.*—The exposition given shows from a new side, that the ordinary division of Christology into the doctrine of the Person, States, and Office of Christ is untenable. On the other hand, our method commends itself, because it embraces all three under the doctrine of Christ's Person. For if the former division be adhered to, there must necessarily be conflict about the doctrine of the States between the doctrine of the Person, which is incomplete without the doctrine of the States, and the doctrine of the Offices, which yet again are merely the Person in His actuality or self-revelation. At the same time, in our way provision is made most naturally for unity and continuity, despite the plurality of states and offices. It also follows that no separation of the natures is possible in reference to the work of Christ, when the offices are thus referred to the Person; for if the acting Person in the work is the God-man, His activities are Divine-human.[3]

3. In point of fact, the excellency of the doctrine of Offices

---

[1] As *e.g.* Ritschl would have the prophetic activity conceived as Divine revelation, the representation of God to men, the priestly action merely as the representation of men to God,—a distinction which is of course precarious if all Christ's action is regarded, really and objectively, not merely in subjective conception, as Divine-human, because the act of the God-man.

[2] Krauss aptly says (p. 648): "The three offices are the different relations of collective mediatorial acts to the requirements and conditions of mediatorial activity." P. 600: "The *tria munera*, according to Calvin, are not three actions or classes of actions to be distributed between different historical periods, but three sides presented by the mediatorial work to speculative research." Although Schleiermacher raises objections against the threefold division of the offices in old Evangelical doctrine, yet the advantage of its use preponderates with him on historic and dogmatic grounds, and he himself follows this division in his exposition of the work of Christ.

[3] Among moderns, Frank also acknowledges this, *ut supra*, p. 231.

is not merely the plastic character of the expression, easily yielding a clear sense, but also its *historic* and *intrinsic* worth. The former lies in this, that the beginnings of this division are found already in the ancient Church, and that the word Χριστός, Anointed, is early referred to the fact of His being King, Prophet, Priest. Just so the division has New Testament support.¹ This triple division is of special value, because it sets in vivid light the continuity between the O. T. theocracy and Christianity; for it is these three offices through which the former was founded and preserved. The fact of the consummation of the O. T. being given in Christ may be made specially clear by this, that in Him is demonstrably given the consummation of the offices, through which the O. T. became what it was. Now the three offices of the old covenant had the following meaning. The office of the kings and judges had to control the relation of the citizens to the theocracy, to keep them together as a community, and guard them against foes external and internal. The priests presided over the relation of the Church to God as mediators of reciprocal intercourse ; for as they presented prayers and sacrifices as from the Church, so again they distributed blessing as from God. They were the nation's mouth to God in prayer and sacrifice, and God's mouth to the nation in dispensing blessing and theocratic forgiveness. The separation of these first two offices was acknowledged to be necessary from the days of Moses and Aaron, and was specially indispensable under the kings. But, on the other hand, this separation of authorities was often the occasion of jealousy and discord. Hence a *third* office, bound to no order, not permanent or hereditary, but only arising in time of need—the *prophetic*—had to play the part of mediator, to kindle new love and enthusiasm for the theocracy, and by this love not merely to establish peace between the authorities, but also to lead the developing revelation onward.² Now, that this severance of the powers, although at first necessary on account of sin, as a bulwark against their abuse, is still an evil, is acknowledged even by O. T. prophecy, and the innermost pulse, so to speak, of the history of prophecy is to be found in

[1] Acts ii. 22 ; Rev. i. 5, iii. 14 ; John xviii. 36 (βασιλεύς); cf. Eph. i. 7, 20 ; Col. i. 12-20 ; Phil. ii. 5-11 ; ἀρχιερεύς ; cf. Heb. vii.-ix.
[2] Cf. Schleiermacher, *Chr. Gl.* ii. 112 ff., § 102 ff.

the effort to interweave these three offices together, and to contemplate them in the Messianic image, instead of in their distribution among several persons. For not one of the three could exist in its full force and purity, if the rest were wanting to it, and if the capacity for all three was not found in one person. Now in Christ—this is the meaning of the triple division—the threefold office was united, not merely in the way of addition, externally, as in a triple crown, but inwardly, or in such a way that they mutually interpenetrate, and each one of the three, rightly understood, carries the two others in itself, but in its own fashion. Thus Christ's entire official action forms a unity as a true mirror of His person; but observation is directed to this one collective activity, or vitality of His Messianic person, which forms a finished whole, under three definitely distinguishable points of view.

4. But how the three offices mutually interpenetrate in His action, how each of them requires the force residing in the others for its own completion, will be rendered evident by considering the *intrinsic value of this division*. If we look first at the *humanity* to be redeemed by Christ, the character of the force necessary for healing and for imparting full health to the individual and the whole follows from the character of the need and the malady to be removed. Now sin, as we saw, leads to darkening of the consciousness of God, the world, and self, so that henceforth sin and error by a sad reciprocal influence evoke a state of spiritual darkness. Over against this state, Christ is the $\phi\hat{\omega}\varsigma$ $\tau o\hat{\upsilon}$ $\kappa \acute{o}\sigma\mu o\upsilon$ by teaching and example—the *prophetic* office. Again, sin works guilt, and the consciousness of guilt is not incidental, but necessary to the consciousness of deserved punishment. To abolish guilt and punishment, to bring atonement, is the proper *high-priestly* function. But since, finally, sin advances to inherent and generic evil, becoming evil propensity and evil strength, which bring with them decay and death to the world, the Redeemer must also have the *power* to impart to the world the principles of regeneration, sanctification, and the new life, and thus to vanquish sin itself along with its effects, even death. But all this takes place in such a way that the perfecting of the individual is also the perfecting of humanity or of the kingdom of God. Thus He is also the *King*.—But the same

truth may also be seen from the standpoint of *God*, whose perfect revelation is to appear through Christ's official activity. Over against the three foes—error, guilt and sin, death [1]—stand *Wisdom*, holy *Love*, and holy *Power* animated by both as a healing power and a revelation of God. In these three fundamental definitions God's revelation of Himself is completed, and thus the threefold office of Christ is also the pure mirror of the perfect idea of God. For in His living personal activity or office Christ is also the Divine-human, historically-realized image of God, and restores that image in us through illumination, justification, and sanctification. Hence there must always be essential defects in the fundamental apprehension of Christianity, where this union of the three offices in Christ is not acknowledged, where His individual words, acts, sufferings, are not considered from the view-point of this unity, where they are rather severed from each other, or even one only is neglected. Hence a touchstone for the integrity of Christianity, or the completeness of a system, is to be seen in the attitude taken to Christ's threefold office. The Socinians and Rationalists stop in reference to Christ's office on earth at the *prophetic*, discovering its mediatorial element in teaching and example only, whereas they transfer the priesthood and kingship to the state of exaltation. This presupposes either that sin has its ground in error, regeneration therefore being a consequence of a better, more powerful knowledge of the truth (Intellectualism), or that the natural strength of the will, stimulated perhaps by example, is a match for sin. The reflex effect of this view on the conception of Christ's Person is the notion, that there is no need of such arrangements as the incarnation in order to the improvement of the world; nor would the incarnation be possible, if the fundamental relation between God and the world is conceived deistically; and therefore living communion would not be the aim either of God or man. The sole emphasizing of the *high-priestly* office would give countenance to a quietistic Mysticism or Antinomianism; nor, without enlightenment respecting Christ's holiness and our unholiness and guilt, would a wholesome consciousness of guilt arise, and therefore it would not be

---

[1] Cf. Leydecker, *De Veritate Religionis Reformatæ s. Evangelicæ*, l. iv. c. 9, 3; Krauss, p. 606.

remedied. Such a reconciliation would be magical. Rather sincere repentance is necessary in order to appropriation of the merit of Christ. When, finally, the *kingly office* is taken into view in a one-sided way, a false tendency to the Christian commonwealth, to the outer side of God's kingdom, will insinuate itself, a Practicalism or Hierarchism, either in absolutistic, or aristocratic, or democratic form, where the chief stress is laid on the visible side, instead of on the inner religious process. But even if merely one office is left out of account, important perversions must needs creep in. For without the prophetic office the preparation of man for the work of salvation would be wanting; without the high-priestly only so much remains of the prophetic and kingly as is congruous with a humanistic form of the general life. But if the basis were thus withdrawn of a real second birth of humanity through Christ, the other two offices also could no longer be known in their entire force and significance. Finally, were the kingly office placed permanently at least in the background, the redemption of the individual would be severed from the founding of a new general life, and an unchristian Separatism and Individualism would enter instead of the Christian common spirit. The advance from faith to love would come to a standstill. The grace of forgiveness itself would be made subservient to a spiritualistic Egoism. On these grounds all three are necessary to the completeness and perfect efficiency of Christ's office.

5. This is perhaps now conceded without further remark. But it is harder and yet not less important to recognize that these three offices are not merely united in Christ co-ordinately, so to speak *cumulative*, but are so mutually interpenetrative, and that as well in the state of humiliation as of exaltation, that all His speaking and acting, doing and suffering, are to be regarded as a manifestation of His entire office, and are consequently to be considered under a threefold aspect. Some, for example, are inclined to put Christ's *kingly* office during the state of humiliation far in the shade, and to let it really only take rank after the resurrection and ascension. But if Christ did not already enter on His office as the king, which He is in Himself, and for which He was born, the ethical value of His humiliation will be very seriously diminished. The

greatness of His condescension even to death, and its inner value, are only rightly perceived against the background of the royalty pertaining to Him properly and by divine gift, the background of His inner regal majesty. Hence in what follows we shall begin with the *kingly office*, which pertains to Him actually as the result of His ethical Godmanhood.[1] Just so it is common to find His *high-priestly* office in His last days only. But He not merely bore in Himself the priestly mind, which certainly shone most brightly in His last days, from the beginning, but exercised it in labour, prayer, and blessing. Even in the demonstrations of his power He was partly determined by His high-priestly love.[2] Nor did He exercise His *teaching* office without the consciousness of His kingly office, nor without the high-priestly gentleness and patience which adapts itself condescendingly to the understanding of backward souls. He would have free spirits, won through their own conviction and the might of His love. Although, therefore, regarded from the standpoint of His person, the *kingly* office and consciousness is the first thing— the basis—in His official life (for in it lies the consciousness of His authority and right in humanity, of His vocation or duty and its force), yet this king travels the toilsome way of prophetic and priestly action, of teaching and suffering, in order to win spirits and His kingdom in them, and to implant the free, conscious obedience which they owe to Him as the Revealer of the perfect law, nay, as already the personal law in Himself. Finally, it is usual to find the place of the prophetic office more in the beginning merely of Christ's historic work. But it pertains to Him also at the end, nay, in the exaltation.[3]

---

[1] The Socinians consider Christ before His resurrection merely as a holy individual man; He became the Head of humanity first through His resurrection. Apart from the hiatus thus arising in His person, his high-priestly action loses its substitutionary meaning, unless He performs it as Head. His action is thus absolutely that of a virtuous private man. Even His moral action, *e.g.* towards His mother, is only perfectly intelligible on the supposition that He acts even towards her as King of the Divine kingdom.

[2] Matt. viii. 17, ix. 36.

[3] *Thomasius* departs so far from the triple division of the offices that he would put the two states in their place. The offices are said to coincide with the states, —the high-priestly office, to which the prophetic is merely introductory, coincides with the state of humiliation, the kingly is to be reserved for the state of

## FIRST SUBDIVISION.

THE OFFICE OF CHRIST IN THE STATE OF HUMILIATION

FIRST POINT.

### § 110.

Christ has the full power of the true Messianic King, as even His name affirms (*i.e.* of King in the Divine kingdom), although in His state of humiliation He exercises it in great measure only in veiled form. He is a King, who must first acquire His kingdom; and this cannot be done by *mere* demonstration of power. Still less are glory and dominion His absolute end; but He places the regal *power* which He possesses at the service of the spiritual redemption, the result of which will be the kingdom of glory or the consummation.

*Observation.*—Although, according to what has been said (§ 98, 3. § 104), we cannot accept a self-emptying of the

exaltation. Similarly Frank. But the prophetic office is not merely introductory, preparatory; it has for its contents not merely the reconciliation, but also the consummation of the world. Wisdom and true knowledge of God also are independent blessings, as error is an independent evil (see p. 385). It is true that the doctrine of the States stands in intimate relation to the doctrine of the Offices of Christ, but not so as that the state of humiliation represents only the one office, the exaltation the other; but the well-founded *three* offices extend over the two states in such a way that each of them is revealed in each of the two states, but in each after its own fashion. Were not the three, even the kingly, revealed already on earth, our knowledge, *e.g.* of Christ as King, would have no historic basis. Whether in the state of exaltation we find no place for the prophetic office, as Frank along with Thomasius fears in opposition to the old Lutheran Dogmatists, we shall see afterwards. Accordingly, the matter divides itself for us in the order of the two states in such a way, that in the first Subdivision we consider Christ's office in the state of humiliation, in the second the same in the state of exaltation. The former is His *historically temporal*, the latter His *eternal* office. The unity of the two will consist in the fact, that in the former, rightly understood, something eternal is revealed, while the latter retains its vital relation to time and history. Still less than Thomasius is Von Hofmann right, when in reference to the state of humiliation he puts into the foreground only the prophetic office, the teaching and example of self-attesting righteousness.

## THE KINGLY OFFICE.

Logos in the sense of the modern Kenosis, and ought not to regard the origination of the God-man Himself, which was a manifestation in humiliation, as a self-humiliating act of the God-man (for He must have existed already, and that without humiliation, if He was to have the possibility of humbling Himself, but He was not before He appeared in humiliation), yet we have a right to speak of a state of humiliation, nay, even of self-humiliation of the God-man. We do not indeed speak of the former, because the being man in itself would involve or be humiliation (§ 104, 4), but because it pertains to the reality of humanity to reach the dignity designed for it through a course of development, an ethical process, and compared with this dignity of the goal the beginnings must be humble. Again, we may speak of humiliation, nay self-humiliation, not indeed of the Logos, but of the God-man, inasmuch as He not merely spontaneously renounced the outward glory and dominion, to which His personal greatness implied a just claim, but, what is far more important, so plunged Himself into our wretchedness and sinful fellowship, that it became to Him the deepest suffering. That the Logos also, dwelling in Him and forming one person with Him, participated herein in the way befitting Him, is not excluded by what has been said (§ 104, 4).

1. The usual method of beginning with the prophetic office and ending with the kingly is right, if we do not contemplate Christ's work under the view-point of His official Divine Sonship, and therefore do not connect Christ's Person and work as closely together as we have considered it fitting to do (§§ 99, 108). But on that ordinary method the inner official endowment and the official consciousness found no adequate statement. In this way the kingly office of Christ on earth especially was abridged; for when it was treated last, it was natural for the heavenly form of His kingship to receive altogether preponderating notice. It is true, the earthly life of Christ's Person, with which our entire second Division from § 105 on is occupied, as a state of humiliation is in every way a limitation in the revelation of His fulness of *power*, and in every way an unlimited revelation of His *love*. But still not merely the consciousness, but also the revelation of His kingly position, must find place on earth, because otherwise history would not supply the fitting attestation, that He is Head of God's kingdom, nay King of kings. His

394   THE DOCTRINE OF THE OFFICE OF CHRIST.

very love itself must needs reveal the *power* of His person, so far as this was compatible with the ethical character of the process, into which He desires to draw men, and with the suffering which this free process must bring to Him. It is beyond doubt, that the official name " Christ," as the translation of מָשִׁיחַ (Messiah), alludes most directly and primarily to kingship, and that therefore the interpretation of what the word Christ means must start from king. It is not accidental that the Messianic prophecy of the Old Testament begins with kingship, and that the greeting of the angels to the earth proclaims the new-born one as King; that the word from heaven at the baptism of Jesus, "Thou art my beloved Son," again takes up the word of the second Psalm respecting the Messianic king, and also that before His suffering Christ enters into Jerusalem as King. As certainly as in His suffering He outwardly divests Himself of His power and chooses to stand defenceless, so certainly also His suffering first receives its full meaning from the fact that the King suffers for His people. Plainly, the spontaneity and greatness of His love are only set in their true light when the exposition has shown how, although already a King on earth, although He not merely might have been rich, but inwardly was rich, Divine might standing every moment at His service, He yet for our sakes became poor.[1] It is of great, even ethical importance, that His official life has a place not merely in the state of humiliation, but of self-humiliation (§ 104, 4), a fact which seems to be neglected by the modern Kenosis—Frank excepted. Hence, in considering the kingly office first, we satisfy a Christian interest. His entire redeeming action is elevated above caprice, because in Himself He is King of men, having a right in them as well as a mission of fundamental import for them. In saying this, we still remain true to the weighty principle, that from attested personal moral perfection, which we must conceive as already matured at the baptism of Jesus, power also flows, because perfect morality must be the true power even over nature. The ethical character of His kingly office is already assured to us by our having started from the ethical Divine Sonship of the Second Head, while the ethical continues in the official Sonship (§ 108). The very first fruit of His inner

[1] John xviii. 37; 2 Cor. viii. 9; Phil. ii. 6 ff.

ethical maturity is the Messianic ἐξουσία, just as the heavenly kingship is the first fruit of His suffering.

2. The *Messianic* ἐξουσία. He begins His official life in the possession of a kingly consciousness, in order to impart His riches, to gain, to conquer that to which He has a right, to take possession of His kingdom. It is true they are individual personalities whom He seeks at first, but in them He seeks the kingdom of God, the community of redeemed, sanctified, and blessed spirits. But He is not experimenting whether He is destined to be king, whether He will succeed in *becoming* king, but He knows that He is the One endowed with Divine fulness of power, to whom, if His dominion is despised, judgment remains.[1] He does not owe His kingly position to the choice or submission of others. He is King and Lord, whether they acknowledge Him or not. He knows that He has a *right* in men, even as it is their *duty* to be His subjects; for He knows Himself united with the creative Logos, through whom they have an essential relation to Him, even as since His baptism His Divine official calling binds Him to them. The consciousness of His kingly power and authority animates His entire conduct, appearing in kingly acts and words. The full Messianic ἐξουσία resides in Him, and He makes use thereof.[2] He is not a teacher like others, who expose their theories to the danger of being surpassed by successors,[3] but He speaks ὡς ἐξουσίαν ἔχων, as one who is Lord in the realm of religious truth.[4] His words are decrees and laws, which will outlast heaven and earth. In the kingdom of God He has absolute power of legislation and forgiveness, power over the keys of the heavenly kingdom![5] Not merely after His passion, but even before,[6] He is conscious to Himself that He has all ἐξουσία in heaven and on earth, that the Father has given Him ἐξουσία over all flesh. Hence He lays claim to the most unqualified, although free, obedience, to a love that sacrifices all to Him, placing Him higher than

[1] Luke xix. 14; John v. 21 ff., 27.
[2] Matt. vii. 29, ix. 6, 8, x. 1, xxi. 23, 24, 27, xxviii. 18; Mark i. 22, 27, ii. 10, iii. 15, vi. 7, xi. 28, 29, 33; Luke iv. 32, 36, v. 24, ix. 1, x. 19; John x. 18, xvii. 2.
[3] Matt. v. 17, 18, xxiv. 35.          [4] John xviii. 37.
[5] Matt. ix. 6, xvi. 19.
[6] Matt. xi. 27; John xvii. 2; cf. Matt. xxviii. 18.

the tenderest natural moral relations.[1] He gathers a circle of disciples, whom He equips with full authority—a narrow and a wider circle—and establishes ordinances for them, the office of the Word, Baptism, the Holy Supper, and Church discipline.[2] He has and exercises the power of *miracles*, and the faculty of imparting that power.[3] As His miraculous energy issues from His ethical Godmanhood, so it has ethical effects for its end. But this end is reached only through miracles being something of themselves, not mere moral acts, not mere teaching (although they are this also), namely, demonstrations of His *power*, inspiring confidence in His words and acts. His power over nature is no disturbance of its order, but a victorious resistance to intrusive unnature, and in this way a pledge and type of that consummation of the world in general, which will be His work.[4] Finally, His high-priestly action and passion also are encompassed by His free power.[5]

3. But as His entire conduct bears an ethical impress through its ἐξουσία and freedom of will, so also He will carry out His work only in the way of freedom on the part of men. Hence He will not and cannot at once exhibit the kingdom of heaven as a kingdom of power and glory. The motives for adhering to Him must not be corrupt, which would be inevitable, if He had based it at once on sight, instead of on faith in His person.[6] He unveiled His power so far, in order to draw to Him the attention of those filled with the Jewish Messianic ideal; but this being accomplished, He imposes on them the duty, under the attraction of His teaching and His person, of learning their need of redemption and seeking the Redeemer in Him. Those bound to Him by spiritual ties then became more and more willing to submit to the remodelling of their Messianic ideal, and to spiritualize the idea of the Messianic kingdom into a kingdom of atonement and holiness. It then becomes increasingly manifest that He does not use His ἐξουσία that He may have at His command a slavish obedience, and secondly, that He requires obedience in the

---

[1] Matt. x. 32–39.  [2] Matt. xviii. 15–19, xxvi., xxviii. 19.
[3] Matt. x. 1; Mark iii. 15, vi. 7; Luke iv. 36, ix. 1, x. 19.
[4] John v., vii. 23, ix. 39, xiv. 12.  [5] John x. 18; Matt. xxvi. 53, 54.
[6] Luke xi. 16; John xx. 29.

form of receptiveness for His gift. The soul of His kingly office is *Love*. It demands and initiates a process, the end of which will be the glory and visible triumph of the kingdom of God. Hence it conducts Him, who is King in Himself, to the Prophetic and High-priestly office, save that even there Christian knowledge regards Him as κύριος ; He is King in the kingdom of truth, He is also the King who dies for His people.

SECOND POINT : THE PROPHETIC OFFICE.

§ 111.

Christ is the *Prophet* as Revealer of Divine *truth*. He has perfectly revealed as well as fulfilled the Divine Law, and is the consummation as well as the end of prophecy. He is all this because the Divine knowledge is His knowledge, or His Divine-human wisdom, nay, His testimony to the Divine is a testimony to and setting forth of Himself.

Schleiermacher, § 103, ii. 115 ff.

1. In relation to Christ's prophetic office, we are not to think of the communication of particular rules and wise doctrines, but of a self-revealing or self-declarative totality, which presents itself to the spiritual contemplation and lays hold of man in a living way. His knowledge, despite its limitation (§ 107, 3), was perfect, because He stood in the centre of truth. What He says of the kingdom of God, of the world and its historic course, is infallible, because He is the personal centre of the new real world of the heavenly kingdom, ruling all the courses of time, both presiding over them judicially until the final judgment, and also leading on the world's consummation. Because He is consciously in the whole, nay, because the living totality of truth—Deity and humanity—is united in Him, even His individual words and acts spring from that whole, the whole is exhibited therein under a special aspect, individual truth being thus blended with the whole. Because He has a mysterious inner relation

to all the souls of men, He knows what is in the men who approach Him; and conversely, because all men have an essential relation to Him, His words have so piercing and familiar a tone. This is the wondrous charm of His words, their unfathomable mysterious depth despite all their simplicity, that they are ever uttered, so to speak, from the heart of the question; for the harmony which binds together and comprehends in one view the opposite ends of things, is livingly and consciously present to Him, since everything is related to His kingdom. Other words of men this or that man might have spoken; nay, most that is spoken or done by us is merely a continuation of others through us, we are simply therein points of transmission for tradition. But the words which He drew from within—those precious gems, which attest the presence of the Son of man, who is the Son of God—have an originality of a unique order; they are His, because taken from that which is present in Him. In this sense His prophetic activity is simply self-manifestation. Certainly, where in the accommodation of love He condescends to men in figurative speech or in simple talk intelligible even to children, or avails Himself of ordinary, especially O. T. ideas, He there suppresses the rays of His originality. But when He does this (*e.g.* in the sayings respecting γάμος, δεῖπνον, ἀμπελών), He does it in order to fill the O. T. husk or the types and forms taken from nature with the highest truth, the true contents. As the manifested personal truth and the true life, He is indeed the *goal* to which men must be led. But by His prophetic activity He makes Himself also the "*Way*"[1] in His character of Teacher and Example; and He leads the man who confides in Him, even if at first merely as the Master of wisdom and the Model of life, by the acknowledgment of Him as Pattern to the acknowledgment of Him as the Archetype and Incarnate Wisdom, in a word, to the acknowledgment of His absolute dignity, no longer raised above us by a simple difference of degree. But this leads from the form of His prophetic activity to its *contents*.

2. The proper and ultimate object or content of His teaching and exposition in His prophetic activity is necessarily *Himself*, and that as regards the totality of His being, in which is con-

[1] John xiv. 6.

tained the very truth of the Divine and the human, the highest good for men. The teaching of Christ in the last resort is always teaching about Christ. From this it follows that His prophetic office, with His Person, embraces also His whole office. But of course the wisdom of His teaching love adopted a *progressiveness* of development for the sake of men, to whom He gave what they were able to bear at the time.[1] Thus at first especially He spoke much of God's law, of God and the love of God, of the kingdom of God, His righteousness and its treasures, without at once saying that all these were personally present in Him. Rather, at first He leaves His person out of view, kindles love for righteousness and sorrow for its loss, and then with greater confidence and freedom commits Himself to His people as He in whom righteousness has appeared. *The history of His entire life* has in it a side, by which it belongs to the prophetic office, to His self-presentation. This is true of His words, His acts, His miracles and sufferings, His death and resurrection. They all teach somewhat of His Person. In all He is the true Witness,[2] who goes triumphantly to death as a martyr for truth and goodness. At the same time, all this teaches us that His work is more than teaching, *i.e.* Christ's teaching office itself points spontaneously to the other offices. The teaching as such does not communicate life; but in teaching that He can and will communicate life, and in offering Himself vividly to contemplation, He exerts a kindling influence, by His *witness* to Himself He draws men into a higher region, into the process of spiritual generation or the New Birth, by which He proves Himself to be their Mediator and King. Because His testimony has the power to draw the receptive into the fellowship of His entire Person, He ascribes emancipating power, spirit and life, to His word.[3] Again, His words would not have had this overwhelming power, unless they sprang from His kingly, confidence-commanding spirit, unless they had suggested that He "has authority." Finally, it pertains to His teaching office that it is *sufficient* for all men and all times. For His prophetic activity is a setting forth of His Person, and His Person carries in it the truth which

---

[1] John xvi. 12.   [2] $\mu\acute{\alpha}\rho\tau\upsilon\varsigma\ \pi\iota\sigma\tau\acute{o}\varsigma$, Rev. i. 5, iii. 14; 1 Tim. vi. 13.
[3] John viii. 31, 32, vi. 63, 68.

forms the hinge of the world, and is infinitely fertile and inexhaustible for all generations and nations of mankind. Every new, precious development within the Church is always demonstrably the unfolding of what is given by Him in the various spheres of life of which His Spirit lays hold. Nothing higher can be conceived in the religious sphere than the personal unity of God and man, and no higher, more comprehensive description can be given of the aim of the world's history than that it reflects that unity given perfectly in Him. Hence there can be no objective perfectibility of Christianity; but the perfecting of Christian humanity is subject to the law, that every true advance is also a profounder understanding of what existed and is given us in Him.

3. These considerations also define the *relation of Christ to O. T. prophecy.* He is the perfect Prophet and consummation of prophecy even in a *formal* respect. For what He teaches and announces is His own certain knowledge, springing from the presence of the truth in Him. It is not merely revelation by Him through isolated workings of the Spirit, but the natural outflow of His wisdom, which has its roots in His divine-human essence. And as regards *contents*, the prophecy of the O. T. was partly legal teaching, partly prediction and promise. Christ even developed the *law*, but differently from the prophets. He reduces the multiplicity of laws to unity,[1] conducts from the outward work to inwardness of disposition,[2] and especially exhibits the rightness, the ideality of the law in the reality.[3] Thus is Christ the realized law, which passes into the Gospel; in setting forth Himself, He sets forth the law as *lex viva præsensque.* Hence Christian ethics has no longer an abstract, cold command and prohibition incapable of giving life, the only motives of which are fear and hope, and which so often leaves us helpless and dumb in the conflict of life. But the Christian law of morality is He who as the personal Love has at once perfectly "revealed and fulfilled" the law, and is thus the consummating end of the law.[4] And in the same way also Christ is the end of predictive prophecy and its consummation,—the former, inasmuch as all pre-Christian prediction is fulfilled in Him and we need no

[1] Matt. xxii. 37 ff.
[2] Matt. v. 20, 28.
[3] Matt. v. 17; John viii. 29.
[4] Rom. x. 4.

longer look for Another; the latter, inasmuch as He is already the crown of the revelation of the divine mysteries. True, even He still gives prediction in reference to His kingdom and His Person, the disciples again receiving of that which is His. But N. T. prediction is distinguished from O. T. by the circumstance, that to it the highest thing is already present in Christ, and from the wealth of what is present follows the prophecy of the supply of what is still lacking. Christ's prediction is thus an act of His self-consciousness, of the consciousness of the power present in Him. O. T. prediction, on the other hand, arises from the poverty of the present, from need still unsatisfied by momentary workings of the Spirit. In Christendom there is no prophecy which is not received from His Spirit, and is not simply a development of His prophecy.[1] This prophecy refers not to the history of the kingdom of this world, like that of the O. T. which was closely interwoven with the nationality, but to the history of the conflict between the world and the Spirit of God; and He announces neither a cyclical movement nor a *progressus in infinitum* in relation to the history of humanity, but an advance through penal and life-giving visitations to the secure goal of the consummation, which is simply the revelation of the wealth enclosed in His Person.

THIRD POINT: THE HIGH-PRIESTLY OFFICE OF CHRIST.

A.—*Biblical Doctrine.*

1. *The Old Testament.*

§ 112.

The O. T. does not profess to be the perfected religion of atonement, but to predict it. It predicts that religion in such a way that at the same time it prepares for it by revealing on the one hand the Divine holiness and justice, and on the other the grace, which seek their

[1] Cf. Rom. xi., 2 Thess. ii., and the Apocalypse with Matt. xxiv., xxv.

interpenetration typically in sacrifice, prophetically in the Messianic idea.

LITERATURE.—Scholl, *Das Opfer im A. T., Studien der Württ. Geistlichkeit*, iv. 1, v. 2. Hengstenberg, *Christologie des A. T.*, ed. 2, 1854–57, *und die Opfer der H. Schrift*, 1852. Bähr, *Symbolik des mosaischen Cultus*, 1837, 1839. Kurtz, *Das mosaische Opfer*, 1842. Delitzsch, *Comm. on Hebrews*. De Wette, *De Morte Jesu Christi expiatoria*, 1813. Steudel, *Bibl. Beleuchtung der Versöhnungslehre, Tüb. Zeitschr.* 1831, iv. H. Schultz, *Theol. des A. T.* ed. 2. Ritschl, *ut ante*, ii. 167 ff. Oehler, *Theol. des. A. T.* 1873–74. Riehm, *Begriff der Sühne im A. T.* 1877.

1. All civilised nations, in their hours of self-reflection, have the consciousness that they are in sin and depravity, under a ban of guilt, and seek reconciliation with the Deity in the most sacred acts of worship, especially in sacrifices. But in Israel the consciousness of the need of reconciliation takes a more earnest and energetic tone, acquiring a persistency which makes itself felt in the entire system and government of life. This normal tendency of piety is here reached by the consciousness of dependence being kept pure and by the economy of the law. In this way the perversion is excluded, which, while it acknowledges something *evil*, refers it to a primary evil power, thus making it absolute and regarding it as unavoidable suffering, either directly as in Dualism proper, or indirectly in the theories which identify evil with finitude or corporeity, and therefore with creation. On the contrary, Hebraism, instead of stopping at physical evil, goes back to the root, to sin, which the law forbids. Where, as in the case of the Patriarchs, the consciousness of absolute dependence is preserved pure in virtue of the perception that the One Almighty God is Creator of the universe, and that a good harmonious world issued from the hand of One who is at one with Himself, there a pure advance to the stage of the law is possible, through which the consciousness of dependence on God's power becomes the definite consciousness of dependence on God's will, and thus obtains a moral, teleological character, by which further man's freedom is appealed to and made responsible. Through the economy of the law the universal law of conscience attains concrete

shape, and at the same time the consciousness of sin and the need of atonement, which are developed partly by the law itself, partly by prophecy. *What, then, is the relation of law and prophecy to atonement?*

2. First, the law, concentrated in the Decalogue, demands holiness, and that under threat of punishment; again, it ordains sacrifice for certain sins. As relates to the former, it says: This do and thou shalt live;[1] and by unbelieving Judaism this might be understood to mean, that man is called upon to obtain righteousness before God purely by his own means, nay, supposing he is a sinner, to redeem himself. But this view would at most be possible, if the law considered man as unpolluted and standing in unbroken strength, or if it were satisfied with the mere legality of the outward work. But the law also forbids inner evil lust, it requires humility before God and faith. Even in the O. T. men are not presumed to be good and morally strong, as if all that is necessary were knowledge of the good to determine the will. Little indeed is said in the age of the law of inherent sin. Impotence to good is not proclaimed along with the requirement of the good. This would be to cripple the effort to fulfil the law; whereas the experimental certainty of moral impotence could and should only be the result of right moral effort, which of course may partially succeed in the sphere of works. But sin is looked for in the O. T. in the case of all men,[2] and when it exists, abolition or expiation is required. Nor does the law say that contracted guilt is expiated by *amendment*. To be holy is simple matter of obligation, so that past guilt cannot be expiated thereby.[3] The O. T. does not admonish the sinner, who remembers his past sins, merely to strive after amendment in the future, but enjoins on him to seek forgiveness, to be concerned about expiation for the past. Although conversion is required, the thought still remains: God must cover sin (directly or

---

[1] Lev. xviii. 5.     [2] Vol. ii. p. 303.

[3] When in Prov. xvi. 6 love shown to a neighbour and fidelity are described covering former guilt, this does not put human merit in the place of Divine ce. Quite similarly, in Ezek. xviii. 21 the conversion of the sinner, and in . xxviii. 13 and Ps. xxxii. 2 the confession and remission of offences, are bed as a means, not of making expiation, but of obtaining mercy from

indirectly through the priestly order established by Him), man cannot cover it; he must rather uncover it before God by confession, that God may then hide it from His face by a mediation, through which God beholds man.[1] Conversion itself includes the acknowledgment of a pollution contracted, which is still present, of a guilt still to be removed even after the sinful act is past. This guilt, which may extend also to the commonwealth, nay the country, needs forgiveness, and the law demands expiation, in order that man may be certain of forgiveness. Nor does the demanding law give amendment, but even increases the knowledge of sin by demanding expiation.

3. *Sacrifice*, then, was instituted by God as an expiation. The law does not require the rendering of an expiation by our own means, just as also it does not stop at the demand for holiness. In that case the Israelitish people would be the most wretched of peoples, at conscious variance with themselves and God, in a state absolutely devoid of peace. But, on the contrary, there is also in the O. T. a *manifestation of Divine grace*. The Holy and Just One is known already by Moses as the True, Patient, Merciful One.[2] Indeed, manifestations of Divine grace toward sinners form a part of the law, are arranged in definite order and attached to definite conditions in the *sacrificial service*, especially in the expiatory offerings. God gives man a legal means for making atonement, that he may again know himself at peace with God. Through the regular sacrifices for the people the entire national life in its usual course is environed by a grace, which on the basis of expiation maintains a state of peace even in reference to the sinful man, provided only he does not sever himself from the religious community of his nation. Certainly only a portion of the sins of individuals could seek expiation by sacrifice; the more grievous ones were simply to be atoned for by punishment, and thus there was a strict limitation to what admitted of expiation. Again, it is asked: What is the meaning of this manifestation of Divine grace annexed to the sacrifices? *What does sacrifice effect in rela-*

---

[1] Cf. Riehm, *Begriff der Sühne im A. T.* 1877, p. 12 ff.

[2] Ex. xxxiv. 6, 7; Num. xiv. 18, cf. Jonah iv. 2; Joel ii. 13; Ps. lxxv. 5, 15, ciii. 8; Jer. xxxii. 18; Mic. vii. 18, 19.

[1] Cf. Riehm, *Begriff der Sühne im A. T.* 1877, p. 12 ff.
[2] Ex. xxxiv. 6, 7; Num. xiv. 18, cf. Jonah iv. 2; Joel ii. 13; Ps. lxxxvi. 5, 15, ciii. 8; Jer. xxxii. 18; Mic. vii. 18, 19.

*tion to peace with God?* Had the sacrificial scheme, as divinely instituted, at least some real effect, namely forgiveness of sins? That the blood of beasts of itself, or the mechanical offering of the same, has expiatory force for men, is not merely expressly repudiated by the Psalms and Prophets,[1] but contradicts the institution of the sacrificial service; for it is only through God that the sacrifices avail for the reconciliation of man.[2] Hence the notion[3] is baseless, that the law regarded the expiatory sacrifice as a real, self-efficient substitution for man. Nor is the view[4] correct, that כִּפֶּר means "to cover," *i.e.* give an equivalent, and thus *pay* the debt by *mulcta*. This would make the rite of expiatory sacrifice a riddle, nay superfluous, for in this case forgiveness could scarcely longer be spoken of; if the point at issue is merely parting with property, the distinction between expiatory and other offerings would collapse. At all events, grace also is involved in the substitution of the beast by the law. It is better to apply the meaning "to hide," and by this means to guard.[5] But Ritschl thinks that, according to the O. T., the sacrifice is a defensive covering (כִּפֶּר) over against Jehovah, necessary to those desirous of approaching God on account of His majesty and holiness. "Jehovah's presence," it is supposed, "is fatal to the creature approaching Him, not merely to the sinner. For the holiness of Jehovah is His unapproachable majesty.[6] Now the Israelite, although a finite creature, has in the sacrifice a means of defence against Jehovah. But the sacrifice, even the expiatory sacrifice, has no special relation to expiation and guilt. For only the sin of rebellion against the covenant-relation is penal and excites the wrath of God; but for this there is no sacrifice, there the execution of the punishment takes place. A sacrifice for sins, not committed 'with a high hand,' is not ordained according

---

[1] Ps. l.; Isa. i.; Amos v. 22; Jer. vi. 20, xiv. 12.

[2] God has given man the sacrificial blood as a means of returning to a state of peace: Lev. xvii. 11.

[3] De Wette, *De Morte Christi expiatoria*, 1813.

[4] V. Hofmann, *Weissagung und Erfüllung*, i., *Schriftbeweis*.

[5] So Ritschl, *ut ante*.

[6] A view refuted by Wolf Baudissin in his *Studien*, 3 Heft, 1878. Cf. also Riehm's notice of this treatise of Baudissin in *Stud. und Krit.* 1880, and his treatise *Begriff der Sühne im A. T.*

to the O. T., or necessary on account of the Divine justice. For God's justice, according to the O. T., is not by any means punitive justice, but is merely the consistency with which God conducts to its destination, to salvation, the covenant-keeping nation."[1] But the idea of God, which makes Him a consuming God to finite men as such, would be more like Moloch than Jehovah. Such ignoring of objective sin and guilt in the matter of sacrifice would harmonize only with a negative physical idea of God, not with the ethical idea of God in the Old Testament. According to its teaching, God's will is not merely to show love to all, provided only they do not stand in open rebellion against the covenant, but His justice wills the salvation and well-being of the nation only in such a way that it is directed to the realization of the good Divine law and against all evil with fiery wrath.[2] One consequence of the conception of sacrifice in the O. T. as a hiding of the finite creature from a consuming God, quite apart from sin and guilt, is that all sacrifices must have essentially the same meaning, the expiatory offering in its manifold shapes the same significance as the peace-offering. But this is not merely to overlook the ethical character of the O. T.; in this way the great, carefully-elaborated variety of the sacrificial ritual, especially of the expiatory sacrifices, is not really explained.

For these reasons *Riehm* rightly gives to the defensive covering by sacrifice a reference to sin and guilt, nay, even to symbolic substitution for punishment.[3] Nevertheless a doubt may be justifiable as to the way in which he reaches this interpretation. "The sacrificial animal," he thinks, "is not a symbol of the soul of guilty man," and he would not even regard the slaying, with Oehler, Delitzsch, and others, as a symbol of punishment. It is simply the complete, irrevocable

---

[1] Ritschl, ii. 110–117, 172.

[2] Cf. Riehm, *ut ante*. Ritschl's resolution of the idea of justice into that of consistency in the carrying out of God's purposes of *love* in reference to the well-being of the nation transforms the ethical world-aim of God in the O. T. into an eudæmonistic one, but is also in Ritschl a preparation for his exposition of the Christian doctrine of sin, guilt, and atonement, the main fault of which lies just in the deficiency in accurate knowledge of the Divine justice and of its importance for love.

[3] Riehm, *ut ante*, p. 64.

surrender of the animal's life. The blood has defensive significance,[1] but not because it is the blood of a slain animal, but because it is life springing from the divine breath of life. This life, because springing from God, is a noble, holy gift to God for the purpose of appeasing the divine wrath. But then certainly it is the destructive power of this wrath, the reaction of the divine justice against the impurity of sin, which is exhibited in the rite; this takes place through the fire, which destroys the sacrificial portions, as well as through the consumption of the portions by sacred persons in a sacred place.[2] Here the anger of the holy Jehovah against the impurity of sin is viewed as transferred to the sacrificial animal, but only after the slaying. Thus certainly a symbolic exhibition of the *poena vicaria* takes place, the sacrificial portions being hence called "most holy." Nevertheless the symbolism acquires a somewhat irregular look, if this anger is supposed to be shown only against the already dead body of the animal, whereas it is so obvious to include in this reference the slaying of the animal, especially according to the fundamental O. T. view of the connection between sin and death. Further, the surrender of the animal to Jehovah takes place definitively before the slaying. The confession of sin on the part of the offerer with imposition of hands on the animal[3] irresistibly invites us not merely to consider the slaying of the animal as a means of obtaining the blood, but to give it also a symbolic reference to the fundamental thought of the O. T. of the significance of death. On these grounds the following answer may be given to the question, why the sacrifice, particularly the blood of the slain beast, is defined as a means of defence against Jehovah. The blood is certainly to be regarded as the life, and thus as a precious gift to Jehovah. But this gift, at least in the expiatory offering, has a reference to the sinner and to the wrath of the holy God against sin; as pure life it represents the God-pleasing character, which the sinner ought to have. But further, the life presented in sacrifice to God is also a life surrendered to death, after confession of sin over the animal

---

[1] According to Lev. xvii. 11.   [2] Riehm, pp. 18, 27, 68.
[3] Lev. xvi.: סָמַךְ. Thus also Hase (*Chr. Dogmatik*, ed. 3, p. 226) apprehends the expiatory offering.

with laying on of hands. This life, as atoning and made expiatory through death, although brought into relation to sin, is nevertheless a life well-pleasing to God, as the application of the blood shows, whereas the exhibition of the anger of Jehovah against sin is continued in what is further purposed with respect to the body. Since now the life separated from the body draws the gaze of God upon itself in the blood, God sees the sinner, so to speak, through it, the sinner's guilt and sin being hidden from Him, so that He overlooks it and exercises forbearance. In the expiatory sacrifice, therefore, there is a gracious arrangement, which gives the sinner a means of redeeming himself from the wrath of a holy God through a life given up to death, in which not indeed a real, but a *symbolic* substitution is involved; but at the same time the life of the sacrifice that has passed through death is a *symbolic* means of cleansing and consecration. If the substitution is not real, neither is the effect of the sacrifice real *in itself*. Nevertheless it ought not to be said, that the *result* of the sacrifice was merely symbolic. The sacrifices are exhibitive and convey a real blessing to man, without however being the real efficient cause of the blessing. As a divinely-established institution they have in them somewhat of a sacramental character, for they renew participation in the theocracy and its promises; the reconciled man is warranted in again regarding himself as in a state of peace and in presenting the peace-offerings. But, on the other hand, they still only have the power to establish man in the outward community of the theocracy. Since expiation is necessary according to the law, and yet the blood of beasts cannot actually expiate, the symbolic sacrificial institute is still not an abolition of guilt. The guilt is simply overlooked. Further, while it is a manifestation of grace, it is merely a manifestation of Divine *long-suffering*, and has not the power to purify the conscience.[1] The deeper reason of this fact lies in the circumstance that the atonement was for the individual offences, to which the sacrifices apply, not an atonement for *the sin*, for the guilt-burdened state. For this reason the full and proper forgiveness of sins, the atonement for the entire man, is reckoned in the Old Testament itself

---

[1] Rom. iii. 25, 26; Heb. vii. ix.

among the blessings of the new covenant which was to be looked for.[1] Hence the Cocceian school taught that the O. T. contained merely a πάρεσις, an overlooking of sin and guilt in long-suffering, not an ἄφεσις.[2] The usual but indemonstrable supposition, on the other hand, was: the pious of the O. T. enjoyed through Christ's eternal *sponsio* the same as we do.[3] The sacrifice is rather merely a God-given sign or pledge of merciful forbearance still continued. But the more the sacrifice was abused by mechanism and superstition, the clearer it became to the more enlightened, that the animal sacrifice is disproportionate to the greatness of sin and the Divine holiness, to whom the whole earth belongs,[4] that the sacrifices pleasing to God are a contrite spirit and a broken heart.[5] And the deeper the knowledge of sin became through the operation of the law, the clearer became the perception that only a new covenant could save, a covenant creating new hearts and bringing a perfect expiation, which man cannot originate and for which he cannot find a substitute.[6]

4. THE MESSIANIC IDEA.—The true sacrifice must be, not an animal sacrifice, but the sacrifice of man himself, not merely as the subject, but also as the object—self-sacrifice. The human sacrifice interdicted in the law sacrifices others, not the guilty man, and is thus a caricature of the sacrificial idea. In it the only surviving truth is, that sin and guilt forfeit life, or are worthy of death. But where is the true sacrifice, where is the man, who could be or offer a sacrifice acceptable to God? The nation has no such man to produce out of itself. Thus hope is directed to God, that He who founded the Mosaic sacrifice, will also complete it in the true atonement. He alone can give the Just One, who is the true sacrifice as well as the true priest. But the legal standpoint seems to stand in opposition to the Messianic idea; for even

---

[1] Jer. xxxi. 34; Zech. iii. 9; cf. Heb. viii. 12.   [2] Rom. iii. 25 ff.

[3] This is not contained in Rom. iv., but only that they received what they needed. Deeper knowledge of inherent sin was still wanting in the O. T.; hence the consciousness of the need of atonement referred at first, and before the stage of prophecy, primarily to individual offences, while their forgiveness was not removed from the provisory state of the ἀνοχὴ θιοῦ.

[4] Amos v. 21; Hos. vi. 6; Isa. lxvi. 2; Ps. l. 10 f.

[5] Ps. li. 17, xxxiv. 18.

[6] Ps. xlix. 7, 8; Mic. vi. 6, 7; Isa. xliii. 24 f., xliv. 22; Jer. xxxi. 34.

if the Righteous One were present, the law seems to forbid Him to cover the sin of the nation and stand security for the nation. For the law discovers the responsibility of the individual personality before God, and aims at summoning it to independence in relation to the race (§ 73b, 1. 83, B.).[1] But this is only one side of the question. After the law has worked deeper knowledge of sin,[2] it discloses in the age of prophecy both the connection of individual evil acts with the inherent state and that of personal guilt with the community, and represents the isolating of the personal consciousness from the common guilt as sin. Moreover, a preparation for the Messianic idea lies in the overcoming of the one-sided legal standpoint.[3] Instead of the subjectively limited standpoint, which desires to see well-being and suffering distributed every moment to every individual merely according to the degree of personal worth, the truth begins to be perceived, as formerly shown, that suffering, nay disproportionate suffering, may even be a distinction and honour to the glory of goodness (Job). Such suffering, which serves for proof that goodness (or God) is able to gain its true, unselfish friends, who sincerely love God for His own sake, not for the sake of reward, has in it already somewhat of a substitutionary nature. It is for the good of the world, because it reveals the glory of pure love to righteousness, and strengthens faith in virtue. But still more significantly than in the Book of Job appears the God-given, suffering Righteous One in prophecy, where His willing, sacrificial surrender becomes the source of salvation to the nation.[4] The expiatory security for the nation cannot be given by the O. T. priesthood or kingship, but by the *Righteous Servant* of God.[5] He is the nation's centre, the personal covenant, *i.e.* the personally manifested unity of God and the nation. And since the divine thought of the nation is thus realized in Him, in Him also lies the power to call forth a holy race, acceptable to God. He is the security of its consummation, and Jehovah beholds His people in Him. But He is the security by being the absolutely Righteous One, and therefore answers to and satisfies the righteousness of

[1] Ezek. xviii. 4, 22; Hab. ii. 4.    [2] Vol. ii. p. 271.
[3] Vol. ii. p. 328.    [4] Isa. liii.; Zech. xii. 10.
[5] Jer. xxxiii. 8, 15 f.; cf. vol. ii. pp. 271–275.

God. This is shown in the fact that He innocently but willingly suffers for the misdeeds of the people. And here the Messianic idea weds directly with the sacrificial idea. The Messiah is outwardly laden with the deepest sufferings, which should fall on us as punishment, while inwardly chastening His spirit in intercession and spiritual anguish. But if He thus answered for guilt, righteousness also may now be planted by Him. He makes many righteous by bearing their sins, He takes the strong captive, and through humiliation advances to victory, to royal dignity. In this way, through the priestly action of the Messiah, the idea of kingship is re-born to spiritual strength.

## 2. *New Testament Doctrine.*

### § 113.

It is the unanimous doctrine of the New Testament, that in Christ the atonement is found, and with it the basis for perfect redemption. The means thereto described is the God-pleasing self-sacrifice, offered by Christ for the world in accordance with God's loving will, who desires to see the world reconciled with Himself through the sacrifice. Christ's self-sacrifice is not considered as a mere attestation of His righteousness and holiness, or as an instructive indication of the fact of God's eternal reconciliation with sinners, or of His eternal readiness to forgive, but rather as the effective cause of our salvation, especially of the forgiveness of sins, so that, without prejudice to the pragmatic-historical necessity of His death, a Divine necessity of an official nature also resides in it.

LITERATURE.—Gess, *Der geschichtliche Entwickelungsgang der N. T. Versöhnungslehre, Jahrb. f. deutsche Theol.* 1857, p. 679 f., 1858, p. 713 ff., 1859, p. 467 ff., 522; Ritschl, *Rechtfertigung und Versöhnung,* ii. p. 208 ff.; Weiss, *Theol. N. T.,* ed. 3, pp. 72, 164, 304, 520, 637.

1. It is true that *Jesus,* like the Baptist, above all demands repentance or change of mind in order to entrance into the kingdom of God, from which some have wished to infer, that

according to the N. T. the fulfilment of the moral law procures salvation, just as the Sermon on the Mount also is a sermon on morality. But the right change of mind includes above all the acknowledgment of guilt and culpability,[1] and the forgiveness of sins is treated as the first Divine gift necessary to us. Whoever feels himself poor in righteousness, and hungers and thirsts after it, to him it shall be imparted as God's gift.[2] Even John's baptism is a symbol not merely of cleansing, but also of readiness to rise into the death of true repentance that seeks atonement. It demands the self-denial of confession of sin, but with reference to forgiveness.[3] And Jesus does not cause forgiveness to be imparted for the sake of moral observances. To the paralytic He promises forgiveness of sins, without previously requiring holiness.[4] Only the debtor, to whom much is forgiven, loves much.[5] The sacred act, by which entrance into the Church is marked, is Baptism; and from the beginning the gift of forgiveness has been regarded in the Church as the first and certain fruit of this entrance.[6] The keys of the kingdom of heaven open admission into it by opening the treasure of forgiveness.[7] At the institution of the Holy Supper the new covenant is described as a covenant of forgiveness.[8]

But then it is said further: "Jesus so often spoke of forgiveness, without asserting that His work must needs mediate or procure it. According to undoubtedly genuine passages," or as others say, "in the period previous to the approaching catastrophe, His Gospel consists in this, that He makes known God as a Father full of grace and goodness, instead of as a wrathful Judge. Such is the case in the parables of the lost son, sheep, coin.[9] Jesus seems not so much to have procured as announced forgiveness, by teaching men to adore God as Father. His death, however, retains the meaning of an attestation of His moral greatness and of martyrdom for His doctrine, to which also the doctrine of free forgiveness belongs." It is true indeed that Jesus often leaves His Person unmentioned when speaking of forgiveness,[10] and on the other hand names

---
[1] Luke xiii. 5, vii. 47, xv. 21; Matt. vi. 12.    [2] Matt. v. 3, 6.
[3] Mark i. 4; Luke iii. 3.    [4] Matt. ix. 2 ff.    [5] Luke vii. 44 ff.
[6] Luke xxiv. 47; Acts ii. 38, v. 31, x. 43, xxvi. 18; 1 Pet. iii. 19 ff.
[7] Matt. xvi. 18 ff., xviii. 18; John xx. 23.
[8] Matt. xxvi. 28 (Luke xxii. 20).    [9] Luke xv. So Keim.
[10] *E.g.* Matt. vi. 12, ix. 2, xviii. 27; Job xx. 23.

His Father,—the reason of which has been already mentioned in the section on the Prophetic Office. But it is no contradiction to this fact, that other passages emphasize the close connection of His person with the reconciliation of men. To the undoubtedly genuine sayings of Jesus belong the words of institution of the Holy Supper. A contradiction between His earlier and later doctrine is unproveable. From the mention of the Father it only follows, that any conception of Christ's work of atonement, which refused to see the ultimate source of that work in God's fatherly love, or to see in Christ's Person and work a revelation also of the Father to the world, would be one repudiated by Christ Himself. The parable of the lost son implies no setting aside of the merit of Christ. Rather the father's going to meet the son has been itself historically realized in Christ. Christ nowhere teaches that there is an atonement apart from and outside Him. Many other passages directly and indirectly contain the opposite.[1] It lies on the surface, that Jesus could not from the first beginnings, and before His disciples had come near to Him in heart, give them, with their far different expectations, distinct information respecting the sufferings and death awaiting Him, however long before He Himself knew of them.[2] But still He frequently at fitting times even describes His course of suffering and death as a task imposed on Him by God.[3] His suffering and death are to Him not merely an occurrence or misfortune, and have in His eyes not merely the empirical necessity, that by the pragmatic continuity of His history He cannot avoid death without unfaithfulness to Himself, after the knot had become inextricably twisted. Rather this purely empirical necessity, coming from without, to succumb outwardly to the superior power of His foes, unless He were willing to give way to them, would not have been decisive to Him and His freedom,[4] unless above it there had stood a quite different, Divine necessity, which has reference to His calling as Redeemer, and into which even the sin of the world against Him is taken up

---

[1] Matt. xi. 25–27 ; Mark x. 45 ; Matt. xx. 28, xxvi. 28 ; John xiv. 6, xv. 4.
[2] John ii. 19, iii. 14 ; Luke iv. 23, cf. Matt. v. 10.
[3] Luke ix. 22, 31, xii. 49, xviii. 32 ; Matt. xx. 22 ; John iii. 14, vi. 51, 62, vii. 33, viii. 21, xii. 24, 27, 32, x. 11, 17, 18, xiii. 11, 33, xiv. 31, xv. 13, xvi. 7.
[4] John x. 17, 18 ; Matt. xxvi. 53, 54.

as an instrumental means for the realization of the Divine counsel, which to Him is the ἐντολή of the Father, which He desires to obey.¹ The dialogue between Moses and Elijah, the representatives of the law, and Christ,² is a dialogue between law and Gospel. They talk with Him of His exodus, i.e. His death. This implies an inner connection between the demand of the law and the death of Christ, that all the righteousness of the law may be fulfilled, and the revelation of grace and truth may follow. And this point of view emerges expressly in the words of the Lord, not merely in John. Such is the case when he says: He gives His soul a ransom for many.³ The fruit of His substitutionary suffering and death is forgiveness. The Holy Supper is so ordained in remembrance of His person, that it is at the same time meant to be a remembrance of the shedding of His blood for the forgiveness of sins.⁴ Christ's death and the redemption of men from guilt are here combined, the latter as effected by the former, and therewith the O. T. feast of redemption—the Passover—is completed and superseded. The objection ought not to be made, that Christ's sacrifice is indeed compared in several respects with the Passover, but the Passover was a peace-offering, not an expiatory sacrifice. For it was no pure peace-offering, since it was associated with purifying by the blood. Certainly, too, it was no atoning sacrifice, but the yearly renewing of the O. T. covenant-sacrifice, and therefore had in it the character of the O. T. covenant. But this covenant did not rest on a perfect or real expiation, but on the overlooking of sin by forbearance (מִכְסֶה): But even this overlooking had at least a symbolic expiation by a pure life for its presupposition, as the sprinkling or hiding of the doors

---

¹ Matt. xvi. 21.; Mark ix. 12; Luke xviii. 31, ff., xxii. 37, xxiv. 26 ; Matt. xxvi. 24.

² Luke ix. 31.

³ Matt. xx. 28. λύτρον ἀντὶ πολλῶν contains the thought of a substitution. Whereas according to Mark viii. 36, 37, the whole world is not equal in worth to the soul, and could not serve as an equivalent for its ransom, the effect of Christ's death is so valuable to God that it may serve as a ransom, Mark xiv. 24.

⁴ According to Luke xxii. 20 ; Matt. xxvi. 28. But neither ὑπέρ nor λύτρον implies that Christ suffered temporal or eternal death as a Divine punishment in their stead. For they were not rescued from temporal death by His death, but from the curse of guilt ; they are indeed delivered from eternal death, from destruction, but not by His enduring it vicariously.

shows. How much more, therefore, could the new, the perfect covenant only be perfect on the ground of the perfect expiatory sacrifice, the perfect, real expiation. Therefore the words of institution say, that the *new* covenant is now founded by the shedding of His blood for the forgiveness of sins. The new covenant has its essence in the fact, that in it that is given which was wanting to the old.—Further, the *lamb* certainly was not usual in expiatory offerings. But the name ἀμνός (in the Apocalypse ἀρνίον) frequently given to Christ must not on this account be stripped of expiatory meaning. The sacrifice of a lamb occurred in expiatory offerings.[1] Moreover, it was the most frequent, because forming part of the daily sacrifice. Finally, it was the specific sacrifice in the Passover or the yearly covenant-feast of the O. T., so that when Christ by His sacrifice of Himself founded the true covenant, He was most suitably designated the true Paschal Lamb, with which also the time of His death agreed.[2] If we linger in particular at the Gospel of *John*, the Baptist's saying, ἴδε ὁ ἀμνὸς τοῦ θεοῦ αἴρων τὴν ἁμαρτίαν τοῦ κόσμου, comes into view. Αἴρειν does not indeed signify "to bear" in the sense of enduring or suffering, but of taking away. But that this taking away does not take place by mere teaching or example, is shown by ἀμνός, and indeed ἀμνὸς θεοῦ, which points to the sacrificial idea. Hence also not merely the taking away of sin, but primarily of guilt, must be thought of, and therefore expiation. The lamb here may not of course be the Paschal lamb, but Isaiah's figure of silent, patient innocence. But in what sense One suffering like a pure lamb can deliver from an immoral nature, and by this means take away sin, is undiscoverable. Thus, it is not sanctification, but atonement which is thought of. Although it is not expressly said that the Lamb takes the ἁμαρτία upon Himself, still the thought must lie at the basis, that the Lamb removes the ἁμαρτία of the world by bearing it away, *i.e.* still therefore, innocently taking the guilt and its curse upon Himself. John refers the account of the Brazen Serpent to Jesus Himself.[3] Undoubtedly the lifting up of

---

[1] In the sacrifice for lepers, Lev. xiv. 12 f.
[2] In the Revelation Jesus is called Lamb 29 times, in allusion to Isa. liii. Cf. John xix. 36; 1 Pet. i. 19, cf. ii. 24; 1 Cor. v. 7.
[3] John iii. 14–16.

Christ, typified by the lifting up of the Brazen Serpent, refers to Christ's lifting up on the cross. The Crucified is described as the sign of salvation to those looking in faith, as the serpent lifted up was a σύμβολον σωτηρίας.[1] But it is an enigma how Christ can apply the horrid image of the serpent, which slays and curses, to Himself. That the elevated, transfixed serpent might become the symbol of deliverance, is easily intelligible; its transfixing is the slaying of the hostile animal which is punishing Israel, and thus a sign of deliverance from its deadly poison and the divine penal judgment. That Christ did not bring ruin, and is not a means of punishment, like the serpent, as little comes into account in the image as that the serpent is not punished, but made harmless. On the other hand, as *the serpent* represents the divine penal judgment or the curse, which however is terminated or nullified by the transfixing of the serpent, so Christ represents on one hand the curse hovering over us, which He takes on Himself, entering into our curse, and this curse withal is abrogated by His lifting up on the cross, or by lighting upon Him. Thus the serpent is a sign of God's penal judgment, and also by its lifting up a monument of judgment sisted, like Christ. In other places, especially in the parable of the Good Shepherd, the Redeemer speaks more distinctly of His substitutionary love, which sacrifices even life for men.[2] By His death He gives a proof of love, which saves us from spiritual death. But why must the Good Shepherd prove His life by dying, instead of preserving His life for His people? By His physical death He has not guarded His people in a physical respect. Is the meaning perhaps: He prefers to die rather than leave His task unfinished and renounce it? Was His death merely the incidentally unavoidable consequence of the circumstance, that having come into the *status confessionis*, He could not flee away? No, He describes it, as remarked before, not as a mere occurrence befalling Him, having no necessity in itself, but as belonging to His spontaneously undertaken calling. Hence He says also, ἁγιάζω ἐμαυτὸν ὑπὲρ αὐτῶν,[3] which does not mean: I make myself holy, *i.e.* I complete my moral probation. With this the adjunct is incompatible: ὑπὲρ αὐτῶν. Rather the meaning is: I consecrate myself to death

---

[1] Wisd. xvi. 6.    [2] John x. 15, cf. xv. 13 f.    [3] John x. 18, xvii. 19.

for them, as the sacrifice is consecrated. This consecration to death was already assumed at His baptism;[1] it is now accomplished. By sacrificing Himself, He surrenders Himself as a holy gift for them, that they may be holy, *i.e.* consecrated to God and God's property. Ὑπέρ may indeed also mean for the good of; but at all events the substitutionary disposition lies in the passage.[2] Finally, by the fulfilling of Christ's calling (to which also His death essentially belonged) Satan is stripped of the power which He has over sinful humanity.[3]

2. THE APOSTOLIC DOCTRINE.—*James* speaks of forgiveness of sins in the name of the Lord, *i.e.* of Jesus, but does not further explain the relation of forgiveness to Jesus thus implied. He mentions Christ's death as an example of patience and endurance.[4]

What is said in the discourses of *Peter* in the Acts,[5] of baptism in the name of Jesus for the forgiveness of sins, to which the gift of the Holy Ghost is annexed, is developed dogmatically with greater precision in the First Epistle of Peter, with an allusion to Isa. liii.[6] Christ's suffering, although an example to us, has still a quite unique, unrepeatable character.[7] We are not bought with gold or silver, but by the precious blood of Christ, as of a lamb without spot or blemish. He has borne up our sins (*i.e.* the guilt of sin) on the cross (not: sacrificed, for they are not suitable for a sacrificial gift).[8] They are thus laid upon Him, or He has taken them on Himself and borne them; He has suffered death (which was the specific consequence of guilt for us), namely, that guilt might be blotted out, and the effect is our ransoming from the burden of guilt, which would have brought destruction to us. Herein lies without doubt the idea of the substi-

[1] Mark x. 38, 39.

[2] Other significations of the death of Jesus are found in John. It subserves Christ's glorification in itself as the supreme, most glorious revelation of love, and because it conducts Him to glory, xii. 27, 28, xiii. 31 f., xvii. 2; again, because it is the means of Christ's exaltation, makes possible the sending of the Holy Ghost and brings life to the world, vi. 51, vii. 39, xvi. 7. Finally, by His cross, as by a banner, God's scattered children are gathered together, xi. 52.

[3] Luke xi. 21, 22; Matt. xii. 29; John xii. 31.
[4] Jas. v. 14, 15. [5] ii. 23, iii. 13, 21, 26.
[6] i. 2, 11, 18 f., ii. 24, iii. 18, iv. 1. [7] 1 Pet. iii. 17, 18.
[8] Nor can ἀνήνεγκε signify: He endured the sin of men, but He bore it up on the cross in order to annihilation. Cf. Col. ii. 14.

tution of His love for us,[1] although not that His death was also a penal suffering to Him. In the words καθαρισμός, ῥαντισμός, by themselves, indeed, expiation and sanctification are not definitely distinguished, as also in ἁμαρτία sin and guilt are combined. But that in ῥαντισμός the forgiveness of sin, *i.e.* of guilt, is principally thought of, is favoured, apart from the O. T., by the circumstance that Peter makes the imparting of the Holy Spirit, and therefore sanctification also, follow first on the forgiveness of sins. True, by the death of Christ, the Just One, the guilty pollution of the unjust, which excludes from the divine fellowship, is effaced. But still sanctification is not viewed as an immediate effect of His death, but merely as the restoration of the right to draw near to God, and to enter into fellowship with God, which on its side brings power for that sanctification of the life, which is of course the end.[2] As the people of the O. T. became, by the blood of the covenant-sacrifice with which they were sprinkled, a divinely-consecrated people of God, so believers are sprinkled with Christ's blood (ῥαντισμός), and by this consecration to God become partakers of eternal blessing.

The *Epistle to the Hebrews* places Christianity under the view-point of the *perfecting* of religion and revelation, or of the covenant between God and man begun in the Old Testament. Now, the nature of every religion depends on the idea of the priesthood, *i.e.* of the way in which it conceives that the relation between God and man is mediated.[3] Consequently the perfecting of religion depends on the perfecting of the priesthood. This, it is true, was instituted in the O. T. by God, and had already to do with expiation. But the priests of the O. T. were not pure and acceptable to God in themselves. Further, they were mortal, the priesthood passing from one to another according to the law of physical inheritance merely, but in no case finding its permanent holder. Again, because these priests were sinful, mortal men, who themselves in turn always needed atonement, they could not occupy a really mediatorial position between God and sinners. The priesthood of the O. T. was not therefore efficacious. If it is to be perfect, it must be united with *kingship*, and that a perfect

[1] iv. 1, i. 18 f., ii. 24.     [2] Acts ii. 38 ; 1 Pet. ii. 24, cf. i. 22 ff.
[3] Heb. vii. 12.

one, whereas the two were separate in the O. T. This union, already prefigured in Melchizedek and announced in Ps. cx., is realized by the Person of the *Son*, in whom the Divine power and dignity are united with the sympathizing love of the brother.[1] In virtue of His majesty and purity, He is *able* to realize the idea of the Priest. He is able to introduce into immediate fellowship with God, into the Holy of Holies in heaven, into which He entered by death. But how has Christ realized the idea of the priesthood? Every priest has to sacrifice. Hence the perfect priesthood first exists when the perfect priest offers the perfect sacrifice, and thus realizes the idea of sacrifice. Now, in the O. T. the sacrifice and the priest were separate from each other. The priest offered something else than himself—beasts or things. But God desires man himself, not his gift. Man must make himself, his will, nay, his person, a sacrifice. It is God's right and will to demand this. Christ, then, has realized the idea of sacrifice by this, that He offered Himself as a sacrifice to God through the eternal Spirit in Him. As He is King and Priest at once, so is He also at once Priest and Sacrifice. He presents Himself—the pure, most precious good—in His spirit of substitutionary love for us, and God is well pleased in Him, nay, causes His good pleasure for Christ's sake to rest upon us.[2] But in what does the sacrificial act well-pleasing to God or the sacrifice of Christ more precisely consist? Certainly His whole life, as a life of most devoted obedience, is a continuous self-sacrifice; but He shows His absolutely selfless surrender to God and to us by spontaneously giving His life or blood in high-priestly sympathy with us.[3] In this way His sacrifice has a connection with the ordinance of the O. T., which knew no remission without shedding of blood.[4] In that ordinance the author sees a Divine law expressed in acts, namely, that forgiveness and release from unhappy arrest under guilt cannot follow offhand without a means of propitiation ordained and accepted by God. As according to the

---

[1] This lies already at the basis of the introduction, i. 1-4; cf. ii. 11, 17. The same thought is expressed in the Apocalypse by saying that Christ is a Lion as well as a Lamb, v. 5, 6.
[2] Heb. v. 7-9, ix. 12-15, x. 9, 10, vii. 25.    [3] ix. 12-14.
[4] ix. 22, cf. vers. 7-9, vii. 27, ix. 26.

whole of Holy Scripture, so also according to this epistle, death is the just punishment of sin. Nevertheless Christ's death is not brought into immediate connection with the divine justice, but into mediate connection in two ways. *First*, it is the devil, who, of course, according to God's just ordination, has through sin acquired authority over men, and received power to execute the punishment of death.[1] Of this authority and its use he must be deprived, if man is to be set free from the fear of death, under the ban of which he is held by the devil. But, according to the author, this depriving of the devil was only possible by Christ submitting to the bodily death ordained to men as a punishment, which Satan received power to execute. For what reason in this way only he does not specify. But in the view, that deliverance from the just death was possible at the cost of a death, lies the idea of substitution, and in the view that only at this cost, and not by violence, did the devil lose his power conferred by God, lies an allusion to the fixed, just, moral world-order. *Secondly*, according to the Epistle to the Hebrews, it was necessary that even the heavenly temple should be purified, because without expiation Christ could not have entered into it as our Advocate, *i.e.* have opened it to us and brought us fellowship with God.[2] The meaning of this obscure passage is not: the heavenly temple is impure in itself; even its destination for such as are still sinners cannot defile it. Rather the course of thought is as follows. *Sin* defiles the land and Israel's earthly temple. Hence it had to be purified yearly by sacrificial blood, that God might not depart from Israel, but the nation might through its priests draw nigh to God. But the earthly is a shadow and parable of the heavenly temple, which is likewise touched by sin and needs purifying. That is, the effect of sin and guilt reaches into heaven; it cannot be indifferent to God, His honour is affected thereby. Sin, whether unpunished or unatoned, is a stain as it were, touching the honour of God and of His temple. It still leaves a place for just blame or accusation, unless punished, until it is at least expiated. As, then, the sacrifice of atonement in the O. T. purifies the temple, so that God neither departs from it nor is inaccessible to the people, a place of meeting with God

[1] ii. 14. [2] ix. 23-26.

on the contrary remaining to them, so through Christ's blood, whose effect reaches to heaven, because the Exalted One renders it prevalent before God, the heavenly temple is purified from pollution by sin (*i.e.* guilt), and the interrupted communion is restored. Why the blood is necessary is not investigated more precisely; allusion only is made to the principle already expressed in facts in the O. T., that without shedding of blood is no remission; but apparently there is at least indirect reference to the justice which made Christ's sacrifice necessary. At the same time, this passage proves that purifying by the blood of Christ cannot mean that His death or blood sets us free from sin, making us holy in this sense. Rather, like the sacrifice in the O. T., it has reference to expiation, to the effacing of the stain of guilt.[1] On the other hand, through His blood entrance into the heavenly temple is opened to Him, and through Him to us,[2] and in this lies the necessity of His death.[3] He can now in the heavenly temple present Himself to God as the pure and lofty Mediator, able to make powerful intercession for us with the Father on the ground of His once-offered, but eternally-prevalent sacrifice on earth.[4] He is perpetually our heavenly High Priest,[5] not as if He first became the perfect sacrifice and priest in heaven, and was not both upon earth. Rather by what He suffered on earth He proved His absolutely perfect self-renunciation and surrender, His sacrifice being therefore a sacrifice once for all; but when it is accomplished and accepted by God, it conducts Him into the heavenly temple, and His earthly sacrifice, as it was offered by His eternal Spirit, is eternalized by His immortal love comprehensive of us, and neither needs nor is capable of repetition.[6] But, again, by the idea of *Surety* (ἔγγυος) the Epistle to the Hebrews knew how to exhibit clearly the transference to us of the salvation procured by Christ, even as it applies the similarity of

---

[1] So, too, in the expression, purifying of the συνείδησις, ix. 14, 22, x. 2, 22. Purity from sin is of course the goal, still it is only possible in communion with God, and communion is only possible when the expiation has been *previously* made, just as in the O. T. the priest could only come into the temple after the slaying of the animal and the pouring out of its blood.
[2] ix. 26. Cf. xii. 24, διὰ τοῦ ἰδίου αἵματος εἰσῆλθε into the heavenly σκηνή.
[3] ix. 14, 22, x. 2, ii. 17, 9, cf. i. 3.   [4] vii. 25, ix. 25 f.
[5] vii. 24.   [6] ix. 14, x. 10.

Christ to us and His high-priestly συμπάθεια to show how He could make our ruin His own. He is Surety[1] in a double respect. On one hand *to God*, namely, for this, that the re-opening of divine communion (the temple) will not tend to the disparagement of guilt or of the divine justice, not to the abuse of grace; for, on the contrary, they who again count the blood of the N. T. unholy, and pervert the propitiation of the N. T. to wantonness, must be exposed to condemnation with full definiteness.[2] To this end Christ is security to God for this, that, by His doing complete homage to the divine will and sacrificing Himself fully to it, God's will shall obtain perfect sway in the world in the case of His people, whereas they who remain in unbelief will fall under condemnation. Therefore God accepts this security of Christ for mankind, and sanctions the covenant established by the Surety—a covenant of forgiveness.[3] But Christ also offers Himself as Surety to *men*, even as the covenant established by Christ's expiatory sacrifice, which was accepted by God as an expiatory covenant-sacrifice, has two sides. He desires to be their Advocate with God, nay, so surrenders Himself to them that by way of testament He assigns Himself to them, and that they are able to repose confidence in Him, because He seals His fidelity by death.[4] He makes their cause His own, that they may make His cause theirs, and by faith espouse the contents of Christianity.[5]

According to *John*, Christ has come that He may take away sins, *i.e.* the guilt of sin, and consequently the punishments incurred thereby.[6] This was done by Christ being the personal propitiation (ἱλασμός) for our sins,[7] and indeed mainly by His death, for "the blood of Jesus Christ cleanses us from all sin."[8] Here, too, the meaning cannot be that Christ's death or blood cleanses us from *evil*, or that Christ abolishes our enmity to God, but Christ is thought as an expiatory sacrifice for *guilt*, which exposes to punishment. According to John, also, the just consequence of sin is death, the destruction of the soul.[9] But as a means of propitiation for the sin of the

---

[1] vii. 22.    [2] vi. 4 ff., x. 26.    [3] viii. 12, x. 17, cf. x. 26 ff.
[4] vii. 22, viii. 6, ix. 15–17.    [5] iv. 2.
[6] 1 John iii. 5, ἄρῃ; cf. John i. 29.    [7] 1 John ii. 2, iv. 10.
[8] 1 John i. 7    [9] 1 John iii. 14 : cf. John v. 14, iii. 16, viii. 24.

whole world, Christ's death delivers from destruction.¹ This fact involves His substitution,² not indeed in the sense that He took on Himself eternal death for us, nor so that He became the object of Divine wrath and punishment. But still for our sakes He took the physical death which is punishment to us. Add to this, that by intercession He is our advocate with the Father.³ Although it may be true that God is not described as the object of the ἱλάσκεσθαι or ἱλασμός, but man, it does not follow from this that the thought of God's reconciliation to the world is strange to the N. T., or still less, that it knows only of a reconciliation of the world to God in the sense of the world giving up *its* enmity to God. This view is condemned by the passages of the λύτρον, sacrificial lamb, etc. Rather it must be said: in the N. T. ἱλάσκεσθαι is to *expiate* (not to reconcile); but the expiation of man is a reconciling of God.—That the sacrifice of Christ is an essential part of God's eternal counsel of salvation, the *Apocalypse* expresses by designating Christ the Lamb slain from the beginning of the world.⁴ And when it is said of the blessed, that they made their garments white in the blood of the Lamb, their dress, therefore, or their appearance in God's eyes being acceptable to God and pure, because God beholds them, so to speak, through Christ, namely, through Him as sacrificing Himself for them as their propitiation, this figurative language without doubt implies both Christ's substitutionary disposition towards us, and the imputation to us of the sacrificial death of Him who bought us.⁵ This sacrificial death is viewed both as a means of redemption from destruction and as a deliverance of believers from the dominion which Satan has over them, and from Satan's accusation before God.⁶ Christ is not merely a priest, but in consequence of His priestly service is raised to God's throne, and thus, as in the Epistle to the Hebrews, the union of priesthood and kingship is realized in Him.⁷

But most of all *Paul* speaks of forgiveness and atonement or restoration of peace with God, and his main idea—the

---

[1] 1 John ii. 2, iv. 10, iii. 16.
[2] Cf. John xi. 51, 52.
[3] 1 John ii. 1.
[4] Rev. v. 6, 9, 12.
[5] vii. 14, xii. 11, xiv. 4; cf. 1 John i. 7.
[6] v. 9, xii. 10.
[7] i. 13 f., 5, xi. 15, xii. 10, xvii. 14, xix. 12 ff.

justification of the sinner before God—has atonement for its postulate. But he brings forgiveness into the closest connection with Christ's Person, who is our peace, more precisely with Christ's death. From that death, indeed, he derives various other consequences. On its ground Christ is exalted above every name,[1] has thereby procured His people as a possession,[2] redeemed them from sin and the devil,[3] established peace between the divided nations, nay, between heaven and earth, angels and men, and thus restored the universe to its integrity.[4] But the first and fundamental thought with him is ever that by His blood, by suffering and death, Christ has brought forgiveness of sins, ἄφεσις ἁμαρτιῶν, not merely πάρεσις, brought δικαιοσύνη before God or peace with God.[5] To describe this he uses the figures of cancelling an indictment, or a ransom and purchase, as well as a sacrifice, especially propitiatory sacrifice.[6] But in his more dialectic, sharply conceptual style, Paul strips the figurative expressions of their veil in order to describe the thing itself more precisely. He does this by exhibiting more definitely than any other N. T. author both the distinction and the independent rights of the law and the Gospel, of justice and grace, and also their inner connection and mutual relations. By the law he does not understand the mere ceremonial law; on the contrary, the idea of the moral law preponderates in him,[7] although he does not expressly distinguish the two. Hence his doctrine respecting release from the law by the Gospel by no means refers merely to the abrogation of the ceremonial law, but also to release from the legal standpoint generally, where the law, as an alien, binding authority, fettering man's freedom and threatening punishment, as a γράμμα, stands hard and

[1] Phil. ii. 8 ff. ; Rom. xiv. 9.
[2] Rom. viii. 2 ; 2 Cor. vi. 16 ; Tit. ii. 14.   [3] Col. i. 13 ff.
[4] Eph. ii. 14, i. 7-10 ; Col. i. 20.
[5] Rom. iii. 25, v. 1-9 ; Col. ii. 14 ; Eph. i. 7.
[6] Gal. iii. 13 ; 1 Cor. i. 30 ; Col. ii. 14. It is true neither in Rom. viii. 3, nor in 2 Cor. v. 21, is Christ designated by ἁμαρτία as a sin-offering ; but still, in 1 Cor. v. 7, He is described as the Passover, which was a covenant-sacrifice, further, as sacrifice in general, Eph. v. 2 ; 1 Tim. ii. 5, 6. Also in Rom. iii. 25, by ἱλαστήριον ἐν τῷ αἵματι, "means of propitiation through His blood," a transition is made to conceiving Christ as a propitiatory sacrifice. Cf. 1 Cor. xi. 25.

[7] This is specially evident from Rom. ii. 12 ff., 17-27, vii. From the ceremonial law, περιτομή is mentioned by him with special frequency.

immoveable simply outside man, *i.e.* outside his will and inclination. According to the apostle, the law itself is holy, just, and good, and not merely is its demand to be obeyed inviolable, but also its statement that transgressors are worthy of death, which is the wages (*i.e.* just reward) as well as fruit (*i.e.* natural consequence) of sin.[1] The connection between guilt-laden sin and death, which in the pregnant sense (analogously with the idea of life), along with physical death, signifies also the destruction of the soul, misery, and combines in itself all evil, is established by the ὀργὴ Θεοῦ, His holy *justice which punishes moral evil*. This justice is not merely directed against the sin of definitive unbelief (the sin against the Holy Ghost), as Ritschl thinks, as if all antecedent guilt and sin needed no expiation, and in so far were forgiven in advance, if amendment follows, *i.e.* if sin ceases. God's wrath is directed against πᾶσα ἀνομία.[2] The law, which is God's holy, energetic will, therefore binds the transgressor under a κατάκριμα, or κατάρα.[3] This curse is thought as God's curse, not as a mere subjective mistaken notion of the guilt-laden man, still less as a threat of the law given ostensibly only by angels, not by God. For this very reason, to the apostle the enmity of God is by no means primarily man's enmity to God, which may be abolished by amendment and changed into love, but God's enmity against sinners as such, by which they are excluded from Divine fellowship and blessedness, and without the abolition of which deliverance from death is impossible. But this abolition, according to Paul, cannot take place offhand by simple pardon; for the justice, in which the sinner's desert of death is rooted, is to him by no means simply the "consistent working of God for the salvation of believers," for this would be merely wise goodness, but only by a means of propitiation, which is demanded by His justice, and which, when it has been given or established, has value not merely for man and his consciousness, but objectively for God—value of such a kind that now, after God's justice is

---

[1] Rom. i. 32, vi. 23, v. 12 f.

[2] Rom. i. 18, ii. 5–11, iii. 18, 19, v. 19; Eph. ii. 3. Similarly John iii. 36, where the μένει affirms that the wrath of God abides on sinners even before they despise the Gospel.

[3] Rom. v. 18; Gal. iii. 13.

pacified, His wrath is appeased. This means of propitiation is given by God not merely to "the Church," but to humanity in Christ, who is therefore called in the Epistle to the Ephesians our personal peace, more precisely in Christ's official but free obedience and death for our sakes. Now it has been thought that "Paul involves himself in a contradiction, when on one side he builds his theory of the atonement by Christ, and its necessity, on the validity of the holy law, whereas this foundation is again destroyed by the end of his doctrine—release from the law. For when he speaks of the legal ceremony as transitory, and of the abolition of the law, the law only retains significance for non-believers; but then it has no eternal validity in itself, but must be regarded as abolished in respect to true knowledge—the knowledge of faith, and there merely belongs to it in subjective representation the right to require punishment for the sinner, or expiation by Christ. Rather on this contradiction there ensues as the final result, that God may remit punishment and forgive sin freely, and without a mediating cause rendering it possible. The interpolation of the sacrificial death of Christ is thus to be considered merely as a stepping-stone, by which Paul reached the pure knowledge of God's free love and forgiveness without a propitiation being first necessary. And this is the Gospel." But Paul nowhere says, that the law, whether that demanding obedience or that demanding punishment, is destroyed.[1] The economy of faith so little abolishes the law, that, on the contrary, the law is ratified and established thereby.[2] This he says in the very face of the passage which has spoken at length of the atonement. On this account he can also teach that the justice of God, now revealed without the law ($\chi\omega\rho\grave{\iota}\varsigma$ $\nu\acute{o}\mu o\upsilon$), i.e. not on the basis of works of the law, is testified not merely by the prophets, but also by the law,[3] inasmuch as the law by this means receives its fulfilment and ratification in every respect. How then do the two agree— the $\kappa\alpha\tau\acute{\alpha}\rho\alpha$ $\tau o\hat{\upsilon}$ $\nu\acute{o}\mu o\upsilon$, or the earnestness of the law both

---

[1] Rom. vii. 2, 4, is significant in this respect. The apostle says not, as the parallelism might lead to expect, that the law is slain or dead, but Christians are dead to the law, freed from its claims, which are death to the sinner. The indictment, indeed, written as it were on the basis of the law (Col. ii. 14), is destroyed, but not the law.

[2] Rom. iii. 31.         [3] Rom. iii. 21.

demanding and judging, and release from it? The first may be easily seen. For if by the Gospel the law is actually written in the heart, it is abolished as a limiting and alien γράμμα standing outside man, and on the other hand preserved as to its contents and aim. But certainly love to goodness and God—the source of strength—is impossible, so long as the spirit of fear rules by reason of the burden of guilt. Hence the second part of the question is here more important. The ground-thought of the apostle is: Christ does not lead to the Gospel by a breach with the law, but by acknowledging and ratifying its right He leads beyond the κατάκριμα into the *kingdom* of grace.[1] The way in which reconciliation or release from the condemnation of the law is gained is not by our obtaining at least initial sanctification through Christ's example or Spirit. Not once does he say, that the law sanctions the forgiveness mediated by Christ for the sake of the following sanctification,[2] but we were reconciled to God by the death of His Son by grace or gratuitously when we were yet enemies.[3] The apostle's course of thought is as follows. We stood under the just curse of the law. We are redeemed from it by the fact that Christ subjected Himself for our sakes to the effect of the curse applying to us. He is made sin for us, *i.e.* treated as a sinner, that sin may not be imputed to us, but that we may be righteousness before God, Christ's righteousness, which is the content of our faith, being imputed to us.[4] That the thought of a real substitution of Christ rules here, ought never to be denied. Only even here the meaning of the substitution is neither that we are to be set free from bodily death by the bodily death which Christ suffered for us, nor that Christ stood personally under God's

---

[1] Gal. ii. 19 ; Rom. viii. 3, 4.

[2] Still less does the apostle think of sin dualistically, in the sense that sin is identical with the body or the flesh, and the slaying of the body or flesh of Christ denotes the slaying of sin, after the destruction of which even the Divine wrath has lost its object. For apart from such an anti-Pauline, Manichæan conception of sin, this physical theory of redemption is opposed by the fact that it must clearly require physical death also from us, whereas the apostle requires spiritual death. Rom. viii. 3, 4, cannot be understood as Holsten wishes. Paul does not think of Christ as a sinner. 2 Cor. v. 21 says : Although sinless, He is treated as a sinner. By the very fact of sin slaying the Just One, it is judged and condemned.

[3] Rom. v. 10, iii. 24.      [4] 2 Cor. v. 21 ; Gal. iii. 13.

curse and suffered spiritual death; but for our sakes He was
treated as if He were sin, He suffered the same curse as
according to the law was due to the transgressors. In this
way, then, the second paradox is intelligible: "By the law I
am dead to the law,"[1] *i.e.* in relation to the law I am like one
dead to or judged by the law, and am thus free from the
accusation or claim of the condemning law against me, namely,
because through faith I am implanted in Christ's death. But
this took place not in opposition to the law, but through the
law, and thus according to the law, inasmuch as Christ has
satisfied the claim of the law (δικαίωμα), and therewith set
aside the κατάκριμα of the law. Hence, finally, it is said,[2]
God set forth Christ openly as a means of propitiation by His
death, and that εἰς ἔνδειξιν τῆς δικαιοσύνης αὐτοῦ, *i.e.* not, as
a sign of His gentleness and goodness, still less of His creative
self-communicating holiness; for not Christ's death, but His
life begets the new life. Rather, the meaning of these words
is clearly apparent from the immediately following contrast
between the past period and the present. In the former, God
merely bore with sin in long-suffering, therefore did not really
and thoroughly expiate it, although also He did not reveal
His punitive δικαιοσύνη as merited; now, the latter is
revealed in Christ's death. The time of long-suffering is not
an expiation, an atonement of the world's sin, and therefore
not forgiveness, but also not judgment, but a postponing of
punishment, and for this very reason not a revealing, but a
veiling of justice. With this period of overlooking or im-
munity from punishment, which yet is no true atonement or
forgiveness, and which, if it were the final stage, would imply
indifference to guilt and the distinction of good and evil, the
present period is set in contrast: εἰς ἔνδειξιν τῆς δικαιοσύνης
ἐν τῷ νῦν καιρῷ, and everything is thus summed up: This is
done, first that He may be just, therefore assert Himself just and
prove His justice, which would not be the case with mere
long-suffering or with forgiveness without means of expiation,
and secondly, that He may make just, *i.e.* justify or declare
just all who believe in Christ Jesus. By the revelation in
Christ of the justice that condemns evil, or of sin and guilt in
their desert of death, on one side the guilt of sin and the justice
of God have received their due, and on the other by this very

---

[1] Gal. ii. 19; Rom. vii. 4, cf. vi. 6, xv. 18.   [2] Rom. iii. 25 ff

means mere πάρεσις passes over into ἄφεσις. For this reason indeed the reconciliation of the world is ascribed to God, it is the work of the Father,[1] but this καταλλαγή took place through Christ as ἱλαστήριον. Now, the imputation of sin to man ceases; on the other hand, faith is imputed to him, *i.e.* the contents of faith, the righteousness of Christ.[2] The result of this to believers is freedom from the decrees of the law, and now the peace of God, the Holy Spirit of adoption, who also gives the law of God being and force in us, can be imparted to the reconciled man, on whom the Risen Intercessor confers forgiveness.[3] With the cancelling of guilt, with atonement, is given the objective basis for *justification*. The curse and ban of sin, laid on us by guilt, is abolished; with it the wall of partition, separating God from sinners, falls down, and the communication and sway of the Holy Spirit can now begin. If, then, we ask in conclusion, how, according to the apostle, the curse of the law could be transferred to Christ, and conversely how His δικαιοσύνη could be transferred to us, he also gives hints on this point. The former was the work of Christ's love, which is substitutionary disposition, having just the same meaning to Paul as the συμπάθεια of the High Priest in the Epistle to the Hebrews.[4] But here the Pauline doctrine of Christ as the Second Adam and the Head of humanity specially applies.[5] And the transference of Christ's righteousness to man is mediated on one hand by the intercession of the exalted Lord, which applies the Divine grace to them,[6] and on the other hand by faith, which is a becoming one, a marriage, with Christ, who died for our sins, and rose again and is exalted for our justification.[7] Thus it is the living communion between the Head and us, by which Christ's work of atonement is taken out of the circle of outward and mechanical sacrificial service, as well as out of erroneous notions of an arbitrary clemency and forgiveness which are indifferent to justice, and enters the region of a higher ethically organic system of things, in which the law of substitution vitally rules through love on the one side and faith on the other.

---

[1] Col. i. 20 ; 2 Cor. v. 21.   [2] 2 Cor. v. 18-21.
[3] Rom. iv. 25, viii. 34.   [4] Eph. v. 25-29.
[5] Rom. v. 15 ; 1 Cor. xv. 22 ; Col. i. 18, ii. 10, 19 ; Eph. i. 22, iv. 15.
[6] Rom. viii. 34, iv. 25.
[7] Rom. vi. 1 ff., vii. 4, viii. 3, 4 ; 2 Cor. v. 14 ; Col. ii. 12.